WX ?
224
PEC

Organisational Development in Healthcare

FHSW

Approaches, innovations, achievements

Edited by

Edward Peck

Director
Health Services Management Centre
School of Public Policy
The University of Birmingham

Forewords by

Nigel Edwards
and
David Fillingham

RADCLIFFE PUBLISHING

OXFORD • SAN FRANCISCO

Radcliffe Publishing Ltd
18 Marcham Road
Abingdon
Oxon OX14 1AA
United Kingdom

www.radcliffe-oxford.com
Electronic catalogue and worldwide online ordering facility.

© 2005 Edward Peck

All rights reserved. No part of this publication may be reproduced, stored in a
retrieval system or transmitted, in any form or by any means, electronic, mechanical,
photocopying, recording or otherwise without the prior permission of the copyright
owner.

British Library Cataloguing in Publication Data

A catalogue record for this book is available from the British Library.

ISBN 1 85775 896 X

Typeset by Advance Typesetting Ltd, Oxford
Printed and bound by TJ International Ltd, Padstow, Cornwall

Contents

Foreword

The interest in organisational development reflects a growing realisation that many of our previous managerial methods are inappropriate and that a new set of techniques and approaches are required.

For much of the history of the NHS there has been a tacit understanding that the writ of policy makers and managers was circumscribed and the actual business of delivering care was largely outside the scope of management or politics.

Politicians have long believed that left to its own devices the NHS pursues the interests of providers, and from the early 1990s onwards the aim of reform has increasingly been to try and directly affect the way that clinical services respond to the needs of patients. Most reforms have been top down and the way they have been implemented has often meant that many clinical staff have been left untouched by them. In some cases managers protected clinicians from some of the harsher aspects of the changes, in others reform was simply an activity carried out by managers with only limited clinical involvement.

Although the NHS is a ready market for management fashions, albeit some time after they have been tried and abandoned elsewhere, the current interest in organisational development is more than this. It is recognition that the imperative for reform, from society, politicians, changes in medicine itself, legal changes (such as the Working Time Directive) and a range of other legal, technical and cultural pressures is now irresistible. It represents a realisation that the traditional methods of policy and management practice are no longer adequate for the task and that a new repertoire is required, one that involves moving into areas where management has not usually been accepted or welcome. However, this change exposes some serious weaknesses in existing models of management.

Firstly, as Henry Mintzberg has pointed out, the hierarchy that conventional organisations use to transmit strategy and commands to the front line is considerably less effective in healthcare and may even be disconnected. Attempts to reconnect it by more rigorous command and control techniques have not proved to be very effective and organisational development offers the opportunity to engage front line staff in a new way that is not manipulative or directive but which tries to align the objectives of users, government, organisations and clinical staff.

The second weakness is that much NHS management is atheoretical – instead it is pragmatic and experience based. This is quite effective for managing organisations in a steady state but it is a less secure basis for embarking on a major change programme in which past techniques and certainties may no longer operate. This bias for action over reflection, strategy and planning is reinforced by the short-term focus of performance management and the political cycle.

These weaknesses would matter less if there was not a further significant problem with the current change programme. The approach of policy makers has been to develop a series of initiatives in silos. In many cases these policies have emerged from different sources and in response to different contingencies and as a result have objectives that may not be consistent with each other. This leads to much of the change management agenda being a long list of separate projects with their own objectives, timescales and delivery mechanisms. It can become almost impossible to see how they fit together – there is an absence of a convincing meta-narrative that could help those responsible make sense of the changes, see the connections between them and understand how they do or do not fit together.

Organisational development can help to provide a solution to a number of these problems. It can help make sense of what is happening, create narrative and provide a vehicle to engage front line staff. But, there are also hazards. There is already a tendency for reformers to talk about issues in abstract, highly conceptual and managerial or specialist language. I asked a group of organisational development practitioners to role play explaining their work to a newly appointed consultant orthopaedic surgeon – a group known for their direct and no-nonsense approach. When they finished I ask them to say what they thought the surgeon might say. They did this with breathtaking honesty and the results were too indelicate to report here but they were devastatingly critical and accurate, reflecting the inaccessible and self-referential nature of the accounts they had produced. As this book points out, creating a new set of jargon, techniques and alchemy will surely mean that organisational development is as divorced from what clinicians do, what patients experience and what the public expects as previous reform programmes. Change ideas, such as case management for long-term conditions that should directly appeal to what clinicians want to achieve, could become yet another project carried out by management that will pass when the enthusiasm wanes and which totally alienates those it should most appeal to.

This book provides a key guide to leaders trying to engage their staff in changing their organisations by bringing together theory and experience. This is important as too often theory is neglected and there is inadequate reflection on experience.

Nigel Edwards
Policy Director
NHS Confederation
September 2004

Foreword

Picture, if you will, a large district general hospital in an old industrial town in the West Midlands of England. Let's call it Anytown NHS Trust. Two of its directorate managers, William and Mary, are asked by the trust to implement quality improvement programmes in the outpatient departments for the specialties they manage. The trust needs to cut its outpatient waiting times or else it will be in hot water with its local primary care trust (PCT), the strategic health authority (SHA) and goodness knows who else.

William is in his mid-twenties, a bright and articulate former NHS management graduate entrant trainee. He has been on a number of courses in continuous quality improvement (CQI) and knows all about plan–do–study–act cycles and matching capacity and demand. William picks off some of the more ambitious nurses and sends them away to be trained by the Modernisation Agency. Immediately upon their return, he initiates a number of quality projects. The doctors and many of the clerical staff don't like the changes at first, but William persuades them that some short-term inconvenience is worth putting up with in order to hit the year-end targets. When it comes to presenting to the board in April, William can claim some impressive achievements.

Mary takes a different approach. She has worked at the trust for 15 years and knows that it can be a very conservative place. She starts by talking to a wide cross-section of staff about their day-to-day frustrations. She also gets them to interview some patients and to produce a vision of how the service could be better. She runs local training sessions herself using Modernisation Agency materials and also sends staff off to a neighbouring hospital to see what they have done. She spends a lot of time with the senior doctors and the clerical staff, working through their problems and concerns. At the board presentation in April, Mary takes a back seat and some of her colleagues themselves present what they have done. Their results are not as good as William's and they feel discouraged.

Twelve months later, William has been promoted to a board position in a PCT in the nearby big city. The changes he made at Anytown have been dismantled and waiting times are on the increase again. Mary's team, however, is going from strength to strength. Their results are outstripping the best of what William ever achieved, and what's more, staff in other parts of the hospital, knowing that Mary had a 'difficult' department, want to learn how they have done it.

What has the simple tale of the tortoise and the hare got to do with organisational development (OD), the subject of this book? In short, Mary was an effective organisational developer, while William was simply a peddler of the latest management fad.

Learning from Kaiser Permanente, the US healthcare provider, is currently much in vogue in England. Feacham *et al.* (2002) argued in the *British Medical Journal* that Kaiser produced much better care, more cost-effectively, than the NHS. Dixon and Light (2004) have suggested, also in the *BMJ*, that the NHS should adopt the vertical integration favoured by Kaiser. Other kinds of technique that many think should be transplanted into the NHS from the USA include evidence-based clinical guidelines and better chronic care management. All are worthwhile approaches that can add value for patients, but all too often such US-derived healthcare techniques don't survive the trip across the Atlantic. That's because they work in the context of the culture where they have been developed. Kaiser is successful because it balances the following.

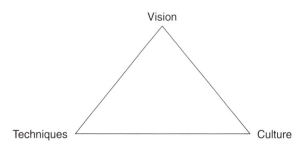

Kaiser's short lengths of hospital stay are neither simply about the way in which primary and secondary care interrelate nor just about generous levels of medical staffing. Kaiser has a powerful vision which is widely promulgated by management and owned by staff at every level. This can be summed up in the widely shared and often-quoted belief that 'hospitalisation is a system failure'. The reason this vision holds such power is the remarkably strong web of social networks, mostly clinically dominated, that underpin the Kaiser organisation. Its approach is that at any one time a third of all doctors are in a formal leadership position, a third are in informal leadership positions and the remaining third are being prepared for leadership positions. It is the cultural embedding of effective techniques aligned with a powerful vision that has led to Kaiser's success. Attempting simply to transplant the techniques without reference to the cultural context simply won't work.

All of this suggests that organisational development should be a core competence for anyone wanting to bring about improvement in healthcare. However, since joining the Modernisation Agency in 2001, my eyes have been opened to the arcane rivalries and strongly held feelings that often exist among those working in the fields of OD and CQI. Indeed, at times, these seem to take on the tenor of an almost religious schism! Normally mild-mannered and self-effacing professionals can become quite strident when excoriating the failings of a wishy-washy developmental approach or of a painting-by-numbers style of quality improvement.

As a consequence, this book by Edward Peck and his colleagues is an invaluable addition to every practising health service manager's bookshelf. To echo the words of a popular country song, this volume makes it clear that 'the secret of life is there ain't no secret' (Peters, 1996). In OD terms, the answer is that there is no single right answer. Any approach to quality improvement must take account of people processes if it is to succeed in practice and not simply be an abstract theory. To be effective, any OD intervention should be founded on a rigorous and systematic evidence base. The particular blend of theories and approaches that are chosen as a help and a guide should depend on circumstances and cultural receptivity at a particular point in time.

The Modernisation Agency has worked hard to reconcile the many potentially competing approaches to organisational development and quality improvement by embracing them within its discipline of health and social care improvement. This is a wide-ranging body of knowledge drawing on many fields of academic endeavour and linking it to practical experience. The Modernisation Agency is working to make this available to a much wider range of health service leaders through its improvement partnerships. These aim to take Mary's approach to quality improvement rather than William's! The objective is to combine the tools and techniques of quality improvement with effective organisational and leadership development. In this way, impressive results are not only delivered in the short term but are sustained over time and pave the way to ever greater successes.

My own practical experience in this field over the past three years would lead me to leave the following messages with you to ponder as you turn the pages ahead.

- **Use theory to serve your purpose but don't be a slave to it.** Concepts and frameworks can help but they can also be deceptively attractive. Never forget, for every complex problem there's a simple solution, and it's usually wrong.
- **Beware the professional cynics and nay sayers.** Evaluation is vital; it's important to understand what works and what doesn't, and to measure benefit gained as a return for taxpayers' hard-earned money. But beware evaluating too early. Sustainable results often take years not months to deliver. Beware also those evaluators who seek failure simply to prove an ideological point.
- **Apply the wet Tuesday afternoon test.** A GP colleague of mine used to say, 'Show me what this will do for me and my patients on a wet Tuesday afternoon in November in Stoke on Trent' – a good challenge! Never forget that the ultimate test for any OD intervention in healthcare is how far it improves the quality of the patients' experience. Does it help in our mission to relieve pain and suffering, to care for the sick, to protect and to heal?

I hope you gain a great deal from reading this book and I hope it helps in the efforts that are underway to transform our National Health Service.

David Fillingham
Director
NHS Modernisation Agency
September 2004

References

Dixon J and Light D (2004) Making the NHS more like Kaiser Permanente. *British Medical Journal*. **328**: 763–5.

Feacham R, Sekhri N and White K (2002) Getting more for their dollars: comparison of the NHS with California's Kaiser Permanente. *British Medical Journal*. **324**: 135–43.

Peters G (1996) The secret of life. From *Independence Day: the best new women of country*. Sony Music Publishing.

About the editor

Edward Peck is Professor of Healthcare Partnerships and Director of the Health Services Management Centre at the University of Birmingham. He has spent the past 15 years undertaking, and thinking and writing about service and organisational development, at one time as Director of the Centre for Mental Health Services Development.

He lives in Gloucestershire with his family and too many ponies.

About the contributors

Perri 6 is a senior research fellow in the Health Services Management Centre at the University of Birmingham, having previously worked at King's College London, the Universities of Strathclyde and Bath, and at the think tank Demos. A political scientist specialising in public policy and public management, his recent books include *E-governance: styles of political judgment in the information age polity* and *Towards Holistic Governance: the new reform agenda*. He has also published recent articles and chapters on 'joined-up government' internationally, New Labour's 'modernisation' programme, individual consumer choice in public services, data sharing and privacy, global syndication of regulation, public policy and personal social networks, and developments in neo-Durkheimian institutional theory. He is currently working on data sharing and privacy, personal responsibility for health, managing across networks of organisations and a book with Edward Peck on the organisational dynamics of policy implementation.

Murray Anderson-Wallace and **Chris Blantern** are the joint managing directors of Inter-logics Ltd, a specialist consultancy that has for several years been researching, developing and applying relational approaches in a range of organisational and community contexts across the public, commercial and not-for-profit sectors in the UK, Europe, the Middle East and North America.

Deborah Davidson has worked as an organisational consultant with a wide range of organisations in the fields of health and social care and supported housing, and joined the Health Services Management Centre at the University of Birmingham as a senior fellow in August 2003 having previously worked at King's College London. At HSMC, Deborah is involved in delivering a number of national leadership development programmes and co-runs educational modules on leadership and organisational development. She is a graduate of the Tavistock Institute's Advanced Organisational Consultation programme and took her Masters in 'Consultation and the organisation' with the University of East London.

Jeanne Hardacre has a background in general management in the NHS, in acute care, learning disability, mental health services and community care. While working in the NHS as a senior manager, she specialised in people development, management development and supporting the 'human dimension' of organisational change. As a senior fellow at the Health Services Management Centre at the University of Birmingham, Jeanne leads the centre's programme on leadership, designing and delivering development initiatives for senior managers, clinicians and practitioners in primary care, acute, mental health and integrated health and social care organisations. She is currently researching how NHS organisations interpret and use organisational development to bring about change and modernisation in services.

Alys Harwood runs *Source – people energy management*, an independent development consultancy specialising in adult learning, team building, change leadership and organisational development. She has used storytelling as a development tool throughout her career, starting as an occupational therapist in mental health, and thereafter in managerial and training and development posts in NHS trusts, the Institute for Health Services Management and the King's Fund. She is one of the creators of the Lifeforce Energy Profiling process discussed in Chapter 12. Alys is a master practitioner in neuro-linguistic programming and is currently studying for an MA in creative and transactional writing. Her website is at www.sourcelife.co.uk

Jane Keep is a leading practitioner on the processes of strategic change in the NHS and the wider public sector. She has studied, researched, taught and practised human resources and organisational development for over 14 years at a senior level in the NHS. Jane has also worked at national policy level and undertaken a number of research and action research projects, writing some key HR papers and OD research evaluation papers for the NHS. She has a MPhil in critical management, where she studied ethics and values in the NHS, and her work in this area has extended over 13 years, predominantly on participatory cultures and values-based change/leadership in NHS workplaces. She also has a Masters degree in organisational development.

Hugh McLeod PhD is a research fellow within the Health Services Management Centre at the University of Birmingham. Hugh's main research interest is the development and application of process-oriented approaches to service improvement in healthcare settings. His work has included the assessment of outcomes associated with the pioneer redesign programmes led by the NHS Modernisation Agency. Hugh's research activity has also focused on the impact of changes in governance arrangements and financial incentives on patterns of emergency hospital admissions and length of stay, prescribing and dental treatment.

Lynne Maher is a trained nurse who specialised in critical care and also held a variety of senior operational management posts across acute care. Lynne has successfully led a number of improvement initiatives, both locally and nationally, and has contributed significantly to developing improvement capability and understanding within the NHS. Currently, she is the National Head of Innovation with the NHS Modernisation Agency, exploring the potential of using creativity and innovation tools and techniques for the NHS. Lynne is studying for a doctorate, with a major emphasis on sustainability of change for improvement. Lynne is an honorary senior fellow at the University of Birmingham Health Services Management Centre and also acts in an advisory capacity to the fire service, which has recently launched a national improvement programme.

Christine Oliver is an independent consultant and systemic psychotherapist working to facilitate individual and organisational change. She is senior lecturer on the MSc in systemic psychotherapy and the MSc in systemic organisation and leadership at Kensington Consultation Centre, London. She provides training and consultancy in systemic organisational development for a number of organisations in the UK, as well as working in Finland and Sweden. In her work, both as a practitioner and an academic, she is committed to developing practical theory. She has a primary interest in consultancy methodologies for structuring dialogue to engender reflexive consciousness and practice in the workplace.

Jean Penny is a diagnostic radiographer who has worked in the NHS for over 30 years. Currently, she is the National Head of Improvement Development with the NHS Modernisation Agency in England. She has worked across a wide variety of national improvement programmes and she leads the development of the popular *Improvement Leaders' Guides*. Currently, Jean is leading work on developing capacity and capability in improvement skills throughout the NHS and with the NHSU by building the discipline of improvement in health and social care. The aim is that 'every person is capable, enabled and encouraged to work with others to improve the service they provide'. She was awarded the OBE in the Queen's Birthday Honours list in June 2003.

Vega Zagier Roberts trained originally as a psychiatrist and psychotherapist in the United States. She came to the UK in 1984 as a Fellow of the Action Research Training Programme at the Tavistock Institute of Human Relations and since then has worked as an organisational consultant to teams and organisations. She is Director of the Management and Leadership Programme in the West London Mental Health Trust, a senior associate of the Health Service Management Centre at the University of Birmingham, a visiting tutor on the Tavistock University of East London MA course 'Consultation and the organisation', and supervises consultants and researchers in both the private and public sectors. Her special interests include working across organisational boundaries, for example post-merger culture building and developing effective interdisciplinary and interdepartmental relations. She is also an accredited coach working with individuals at middle and senior levels to develop their leadership potential. Her approach in all these activities involves balancing attention to systems and structures with attention to group and organisational dynamics, with the aim of enhancing emotional intelligence and organisational and personal effectiveness. She has lectured and run workshops on leadership and change in the USA, France, Switzerland and Italy.

Kieran Sweeney holds arts and medical degrees from Glasgow, a research Masters from Exeter, and honorary fellowships of the Royal College of General Practitioners and the Royal Society of Arts. After completing his medical undergraduate training he completed an extended general practice training programme in the southwest of England, Paris and Brittany. He works as a general practitioner, lecturer in health services research at the Peninsula Medical School and as a policy manager for primary care at the Commission for Healthcare Audit and Inspection. He is part of the Health Complexity Group, a collection of healthcare researchers looking at how the insights from the complexity sciences might help to explain the process of change in healthcare organisations.

To Ingrid, Imogen and Caitlin

Introduction

Edward Peck

Organisational development (OD) has never been so in vogue in the NHS. Most primary care trusts (PCTs), and many acute trusts, have director-level posts with an explicit OD responsibility and nearly all have middle managers responsible for commissioning and/or providing OD. One overarching approach to OD – service improvement – is the guiding principle of the Modernisation Agency (MA) in England and is contributing significantly to the unprecedented interest in the topic. OD is coming to be seen as central to the achievement of the ambitions for modernisation and the aspirations for transformation of healthcare in the UK held by policy makers, managers and clinicians. Activities described as OD range from process mapping by clinicians through team-building for clinical and corporate teams to organisational reconfiguration; it will be an unusual healthcare organisation that is not engaged in at least one such activity at any point in time.

Despite this interest, not to say enthusiasm, it became apparent to my colleagues at the Health Services Management Centre (HSMC) and myself that there is no published introduction to OD that sets all of the potential approaches in an NHS context, let alone one that examines them critically. This book fills the gap, providing managers and clinicians in healthcare with an introductory text which will explore the ways in which the theory and techniques of a variety of 'schools' of OD can help them in embedding reflexivity, learning and change into their organisations or departments. It will also be of interest to students of leadership, management and change whatever their background, and to those already involved, or contemplating a future, in organisational development in the public services.

Crucially, this book argues that OD is the business of every healthcare manager and clinical leader, and should not just be seen as something brought to organisations by external experts. While it would be foolish to suggest that everything these managers and leaders do in their roles could legitimately be called OD, much of their work could serve to further enhance the reflexivity and learning of their organisations if informed by the ideas in this book. In this respect, therefore, careful reading and application of these ideas will improve the quality of management and leadership of health and social care.

However, it is much more than a simple cookbook of tools and techniques. Although it contains most of the available wisdom about ways to improve healthcare, it does not attempt to reduce this knowledge to a series of checklists and platitudes. It is not apologetic about bringing in theory when theory is called for in order to improve understanding, yet it is hopefully also much more accessible than some of the epic generic overviews currently available. In some respects this

The final chapter – the Conclusion – contains a broader reflection of the popularity, claims and limitations of OD. It is perhaps the most theoretical of the chapters, and one that critiques some of the assumptions that underpin the earlier parts of the book. This chapter is very much an optional read, and those who prefer certainties to challenges should perhaps give it a wide berth, but others may find that it addresses some of the doubts and misgivings they have experienced while perusing the rest of the book, or indeed, while being practitioners of, or participants in, OD processes. It seems to me that just because this is an introductory text, edited by someone who spends much of their working life 'doing' OD, there is no reason why it should pretend that there are not ambiguities and paradoxes within this particular field of human endeavour, just as there are in most others.

It is important to record that I am not suggesting that the eight 'schools' introduced here cover the entire range of OD interventions that are either in the literature or currently being practised. I look forward to discovering new ones, and hopefully always being open to the acceptance of new ideas and the recasting of old ones. Not all of the eight will be to your personal taste, and my view of any theory (and practice) is that it is only worth adopting if it opens up new and illuminating perspectives on your life in organisations. In approaching the interventions explored in this book, I would merely suggest that you suspend disbelief until you have explored the individual 'schools' and their interventions and found them either winning or wanting. On only one occasion have I ever found myself rejecting an OD intervention out of hand, a session which began with the group facilitator inviting us to focus on the crystal placed in the middle of the room in order to partake of its spiritual energy; but maybe that says more about me than about the intervention!

I tried very hard to exclude from explicit discussion in this book two theoretical strands that managers and clinicians from healthcare backgrounds often find very difficult to grasp (frequently because of the way that they are expressed). The first is social constructionism and the second is post-modernism. However, as these two strands provide the intellectual underpinning of so many of the ideas explored in this book, I have reluctantly relented and references to both appear in many of the chapters. I thought that it might be helpful if I gave a brief introduction to both ideas here. They have some similar characteristics which tend to point OD practitioners in the same broad direction.

The former theory asserts that the world is constantly being formed and reformed by our interactions with it. Given the wide variety of our emotions, experience and expertise, the world within which each of us lives is therefore unique. Thus, social constructionism argues that all of our social institutions – including our organisations – are phenomena that come about as a consequence of the local conversations (in talk or in text) that take place between participants in these institutions. The meanings that we attribute to organisations are thus multiple (because each of us has our own), negotiated (because we seek to find common ground with others), contested (because finding such common ground can be difficult) and transient (because we are frequently discovering new meanings in these conversations and discarding old ones). Social constructionism holds that such conversations have the power to shape the culture of the organisation, and thus the attitudes of its members to change. As a consequence, the attention of many organisational development practitioners is drawn to the potential for the manipulation of these conversations, in particular conversations between individuals. A fuller account is provided in Chapter 11.

Post-modernism is a many-sided and slippery concept. For the moment, it is perhaps most useful to focus on two aspects. First, it heralds the death of the grand narrative of society and history and celebrates the growth of multiple and often competing accounts of who we are, where we have come from and where we are going (in healthcare as well as in life). The search for one definitive account of 'reality', which is presented as central to modernism, is rejected. Second, it argues, the latter half of the twentieth century – and, indeed, the early years of the current one – have shown us that the world is both more complex and less controllable than modernism would have had us believe. Post-modernism, then, when applied to organisations, suggests that we have to recognise the legitimacy and influence of a number of disparate voices, to respect the divergent interests and perspectives that they represent, and acknowledge the uncertainty and unpredictability of the environment within which these voices interact. It leads organisational development practitioners to focus on the identification of stakeholders and their contrasting perspectives and the potential for these perspectives to spark unexpected yet fruitful outputs when brought together. Further discussion of post-modernism can be found in, for instance, Chapters 8 and 9.

I am not asking you to accept lock, stock and barrel either of these theories as plausible descriptions of either the world or organisations. Indeed, when applied to OD, I think there are problems with both and these are explored in the Conclusion to this book. For the moment, I am merely suggesting that you do not glaze over when the terms 'social constructionism' and 'post-modernism' appear in the chapters that follow.

Finally, I want to make a few acknowledgements. I would like to thank all the contributors both for their insights and for having the patience to write them down for a pittance. Thanks are also due to David and Nigel for taking the time to contribute their forewords. The publishers deserve praise for having the good sense to commission the book and for being supportive without being intrusive. Anne vanderSalm has enabled me to complete this task in more ways than I have space to enumerate. I would like to apologise to my family – Ingrid, Imogen and Caitlin – for spending too many mornings over Christmas 2003 and Easter 2004 in my study, but I hope that the dedication of this book to you is some small compensation. Lastly, thank you to all of the health and social care managers who have allowed me to intervene in their organisations over the past 15 years; I hope it was as enjoyable and fruitful for you as it was for me – long may it continue!

Professor Edward Peck
September 2004

Part 1

Organisational Development in Healthcare: mapping the territory

CHAPTER 1

What is organisational development?

Jeanne Hardacre and Edward Peck

Introduction

There can be no doubt that organisational development (OD) is currently in vogue within healthcare. Several crude but credible measures are indications of this. Perhaps the most obvious is the recent growth in job titles which include the term 'organisational development'. Over the past five years, there has been a remarkable trend for human resources (HR) directors to become directors of HR and OD, for training departments to be renamed organisational development teams, and for roles such as OD facilitators, heads of OD and even OD specialists to become mainstream within the functions and structures of NHS organisations. Many NHS organisations now also have directors of modernisation or service improvement where the key responsibilities of the postholder seem to call for the application of techniques derived from OD. The term 'organisational development' has thus become common parlance in NHS boardrooms, in managers' offices and to some extent, where links to service quality, clinical governance or professional development have perhaps been made, among clinical practitioners.

So what does OD mean in the NHS? With so many people talking about it, creating jobs with responsibility for it, writing strategies about it and insisting on the importance of it, one might assume that they would broadly agree what it is. And yet when the simple question is posed to many of these individuals, 'What is organisational development?', the responses are fascinatingly diverse. The reply often involves a wry smile, a knowing look or an expression of faint exasperation. There then follows an explanation that reshapes the question from a simple 'what is OD?' to a more pointed 'what do I personally understand to be OD?' or 'what does OD mean in this organisation?'.

Thus, while the question may seem straightforward, the answer is very unlikely to be. Replies typically confuse rather than clarify. They are often characterised by a reluctance to commit to a universal definition, coupled with an uneasy search for just such a unifying explanation. In part, this lack of confidence in producing a definition within the NHS reflects the disparate origins of the range of interventions and approaches that have come to be known as OD within both public and private organisations. Tracing these origins is rather like unpicking different-coloured threads, which, over time, have become meshed together into a multicoloured weaving. Each thread has its own distinct colour and texture, which adds to the overall appearance of the fabric, but each one has blended with others, and has perhaps faded or softened with time, and may have lost its own original distinctive characteristics.

This chapter attempts to tease apart the threads of organisational development, separating out the different strands of thinking and practice that lie behind each. The chapter then briefly examines definitions of OD, and goes on to discuss what distinguishes OD from other approaches to change, and how this can help us to recognise its distinctive contribution. Some of the central approaches to OD are outlined, and finally some of the current issues pertaining to OD in the NHS are introduced. Crucially, by the end of this chapter, we will have established a working definition of OD that will be adopted throughout the rest of the book.

The origins of organisational development

Appreciating the number and range of threads that have shaped OD can help to build an overall understanding of what contemporary OD encompasses and why it is apparently open to so many interpretations. The main strands that have shaped its development are described in the following sections.

Human process thread

One of the central threads of OD lies in work carried out by Kurt Lewin and colleagues in 1946 (Marrow, 1969). They ran workshops exploring interactions between members of groups, which involved an observer making notes on the behaviour of group members towards each other. At the end of each day, the workshop leaders and the observers met to discuss the behaviour and interactions they had seen in the groups. While it had not been planned for group members to participate in these discussions, some of the group members asked to sit in and listen to the debrief sessions. This led to the participants contributing their own perceptions of what had happened in the groups and why, with challenging debates ensuing about how behaviours were intended and interpreted. By the end of the series of workshops, these feedback sessions had become more important learning experiences than the group work itself. The experience led to the development of the National Training Laboratory (NTL) and an approach known as T-group training.

T-group training focused on the way in which people in groups understand how their own behaviour impacts on other individuals and thus affects group processes. This focus on processes between individuals within groups remains a core feature of some OD interventions and informs some of the discussion in Chapter 6, albeit that the emphasis there is more on processes both within and between groups (and, indeed, organisations); the chapter argues that this focus on individuals is not by itself likely to impact significantly on organisational functioning.

At an individual level, OD interventions in this category would typically include activities related to personal development, including building self-awareness, enhancing personal skills and effectiveness, and ensuring coaching and mentoring. Such individually oriented interventions are underpinned by the assumption that each individual is a key player in determining the broader dynamics of human processes within a system (although they may underestimate the extent that systems determine the experience and behaviour of individuals, again as argued in Chapter 6). As a consequence, it is important that the way each person influences social processes is altered (and hopefully improved) by intervening in the way that they behave as an individual member of the system.

The tendency for activities in this category to be linked to individual development explains the trend in some organisations of associating OD with the training and development function. The relationship between leadership development and organisational development is explored further in Chapter 3, but it is sufficient to note here that the growth of the importance of 'leadership' (in terms of both emphasis in policy documents and proliferation of leadership development programmes) has to be viewed as a major intervention in the healthcare system. It is this strand of OD – focused on the actions of individuals – that is the source of the idea that organisational development is integral to the everyday behaviour of organisational members. This could be termed the 'pantheistic' view of OD; it is potentially always and everywhere.

At a team level, human process interventions are commonly evident in team building and team development activities that attempt to improve the understanding, relationship and communication between members of teams. This sort of OD intervention may extend beyond merely focusing on the human dynamics within work groups to also encompass exploration of the accountability and procedures of the team and the outputs and outcomes that they achieve together. Interventions may include process analysis to consider retrospectively what happened, why and how people feel about it (as discussed in Chapter 5), and also activities such as storyboarding (*see* Chapter 12) in order to surface difficult issues and make it possible to 'discuss the undiscussable'.

The principles of human process interventions are also apparent at a wider system level, where the focus of attention is on the human processes between different groups of staff in a department, different departments of an organisation or different organisations within a whole system (*see* Chapter 7). Large group events (such as the 'open space' events described in Chapter 4) often draw on human process approaches to OD in achieving their desired outcomes.

Survey feedback thread

A key player in the emergence of a second thread of organisational development was Rensis Likert (Baumgartel, 1959). In 1947, his work in developing attitude surveys led to his undertaking an employee survey in the Detroit Edison Company. He and his team were asked to advise on how the company could use the data gathered from the staff about their perceptions and attitudes to improve the management and overall performance of the company.

They discovered that if the survey results were reported back just to the managers, and not shared more widely with employees, then little change occurred. However, if a manager discussed the findings of the survey with the staff and involved them in deciding what to do about the findings, then positive change came about. This approach became known as 'survey feedback' and part of its effectiveness has been attributed to the fact that it 'deals with the system of human relationships as a whole and it deals with each manager, supervisor, and employee in the context of his own job, his own problems, and his own work relationships' (Baumgartel, 1959, p.2).

The survey feedback thread is evident in many contemporary OD activities and particularly those associated with the HR function where the emphasis lies in integrating the aspirations of staff with organisational success as coherently as possible. It could be argued that *Improving Working Lives* (DoH, 2000a) is an example of an initiative that attempts to respond to such staff aspirations while seeking to enhance recruitment and retention in support of the *The NHS Plan* (DoH, 2000b). Similarly, the annual staff survey in the NHS involves establishing staff attitudes as a way of diagnosing the state of the organisation, and interventions emerging from such a diagnosis would typically include work–life balance initiatives, competency frameworks, appraisal processes, career planning and capacity-building activities. It is in interventions such as these that the strong link between OD and HR is created and maintained, to the extent that in many organisational hierarchies the former is subsumed within the latter. From this perspective, OD can look as though it is part of the warp and weft of the organisational procedures that seek to govern the life of its members.

Action research thread

The T-group and the survey feedback approaches described above share a common feature. In both, information about people in an organisation (whether about their behaviour or their attitudes) is discussed and analysed together with those people themselves, rather than outsiders trying to make sense of the data or observations without their input. This collaborative approach to understanding situations and solving problems is acknowledged as a powerful way of engaging people in changing things about themselves and the processes they are involved in. These approaches based on making clear links between researching an issue and taking action to address the issue have been developed further and become known as 'action research'.

Action research is still the backbone of many OD interventions (*see* Cummings and Worley, 2001) and often characterises OD as an approach to achieving specific change. The application of action research in undertaking OD is explored in more detail in Chapter 4. Here it is important to note that the involvement of organisation members in understanding their organisation and deciding how to improve it is central to action research. This key thread of OD continues to shape many contemporary OD interventions, such as appreciative inquiry (*see* Chapter 11) and critical incident analysis, as well as NHS modernisation techniques like the plan–do–study–act 'collaborative' approach to improvement (*see* Chapters 5 and 13). There is also an obvious link to action learning – which is currently very popular in healthcare settings – where the proposition is that there should be no action without reflection/ research and no reflection/research without action.

Socio-technical thread

While many of the threads of organisational development originated in the US, significant contributions also came from the UK. An example is the thinking and practice that emerged from the work of Eric Trist (e.g. Trist and Sashkin, 1980) at the Tavistock Institute in London during the 1950s, and which ran in parallel to some of the developments described above. A focus of family therapy at the Tavistock Clinic was working with the whole family group (e.g. parents and children simultaneously) within an action research model. Trist made insightful links between group dynamics in a therapeutic setting and those in an organisational context.

Some of Trist's workplace research observed self-managing mining teams and led to the development of new work designs where skilled workers were provided with autonomy and discretion to use information to solve problems, make decisions, vary tasks and manage their own performance. Embedded in the approach was a concern that has become central to OD, that is, the connection between structure and culture in the life of effective organisations.

The term 'socio-technical' refers to a system (e.g. an organisation) comprising of a human part (the people and their relationships) and a technical part (the tools, procedures and accountabilities that guide and measure task performance; *see* Cummings and Worley, 2001). Socio-technical approaches to OD therefore emphasise the inter-dependency of the social and the structural/technical elements of organisations and ways in which these can work more effectively together. This interaction between cultural and structural approaches to OD is examined in more detail in Chapters 9 and 10 as well as in the Conclusion. Undertaking structural reconfiguration (e.g. mergers), enhancing employee involvement and job design, and pursuing initiatives to enhance productivity and job satisfaction (e.g. total quality management initiatives) can all be traced back to this thread of OD. It also contributes another important component to the confusion about OD within healthcare, where OD is often presented as synonymous with the frequent structural changes that occur in the NHS.

Strategic thread

The original ideas that shaped organisational development are important anchors in appreciating the way OD has developed as a set of theories and practices aimed at improving organisations. However, while observations of contemporary OD analysis and intervention in 21st century organisations sometimes reflect the threads discussed above, they also appear to encompass activities and processes that do not resonate particularly closely with them. Why is this? What else is going on?

During the 1980s and 1990s, the environment in which organisations were operating appeared to experience a pace of change that accelerated at an unprecedented rate.

Technological, economic, political and social factors have created a world where organisational survival largely depends on the ability to anticipate and adapt to the future, and to deal with uncertainty and ambiguity in a manner that it is claimed has not happened before (although this may be a claim of every generation and might appear somewhat odd, for instance, to the entrepreneurs of the industrial revolution). An outward-looking, strategic and dynamic perspective has become an essential component of organisational life, coupled with a flexible and adaptive approach to managing organisations (as frequently opposed to a planned and deterministic one). As one of the pre-eminent management gurus of the past 20 years, Mintzberg (1994) has argued: 'the whole nature of strategy making – dynamic, irregular, discontinuous, calling for groping, interactive processes with an emphasis on learning and synthesis – compels managers to favor intuition. This is probably why all those analytical techniques of planning felt so wrong ... Ultimately, the term "strategic planning" has proved to be an oxymoron' (pp.318–21).

For OD, the challenge has been to remain relevant in this new context. While the original threads of OD have traditionally been seen by managers to add value, the principles behind them were based on altogether less turbulent and more predictable organisational variables. For OD to continue its appeal, it has had to make a clear contribution to supporting organisations in the midst of uncertainty. Responding to this new view of the challenges facing organisations, Chapter 8 of this book explores the implications of complexity theory for OD in healthcare.

The strategic thread of OD that has emerged from these changes is multifaceted, but has become conceptualised in overall terms as supporting organisational transformation. Defined as, 'a multi-dimensional, multi-level, qualitative, discontinuous, radical organizational change involving a paradigmatic shift' (Levy and Merry, 1986, p.5), organisational transformation is viewed as revolutionary and rapid change as opposed to the more evolutionary and gradual change involved in traditional organisation improvement. The Conclusion of this book returns to the potential contribution of OD to the desire for so-called transformational change in the NHS.

Organisational development's potential contribution to organisation transformation has spawned the growth of the strategic thread of OD, adding new and wide-ranging dimensions to the field. The overall purpose of strategic OD is to improve the alignment between an organisation, its strategy and its environment. Practically speaking, in healthcare, this thread would typically encompass both inward-focused and outward-focused initiatives. Under the former, interventions might include clarifying values and missions, developing governance and performance management arrangements, enhancing knowledge management and visioning possible futures. Within the latter, activities could include managing the process of mergers and acquisitions, developing strategic partnerships and other networks with external organisations, and engaging communities and the public.

In summary so far

Tracing the threads of the OD tapestry reinforces several key messages and raises some significant challenges. In many ways, the early strands complement each other, with their approaches clearly grounded in participation, reflection, feedback and empowerment. The more strategic dimensions, which have been woven in at a later stage, have undoubtedly changed the picture of OD in both the private and public sectors. In some ways, these more recent trends in OD thought and practice have tended to dominate the overall scene.

Understanding organisational development is, therefore, no mean feat. It is a huge leap – in both conceptual and pragmatic terms – to join up some of the early OD initiatives with some of today's transformational change programmes. For example, how can OD be about intensive individual or group development work as well as being about policy-driven, multi-organisational strategic mergers? What can these approaches possibly have in common to warrant their both belonging to the same field of human endeavour? Or is it the very elasticity and imprecision of the term 'OD' that has resulted in its popularity and longevity?

French *et al.* (2000) attempt to explain this paradox with an overarching interpretation of OD, which straddles the decades and their various approaches: 'The field of organization development offers a prescription for improving the "goodness of fit" between individuals and organizations and between organizations and environments' (p.v). As the next section will show, this is just one of many suggestions as to how we can define the essence of organisational development, but it does serve to demonstrate that any definition will need to be both specific and inclusive if it is to prove robust.

Defining organisational development

Organisational development is often referred to as being based on the applied behavioural sciences (e.g. Cummings and Worley, 2001). This is such a broad field, encompassing disciplines ranging from psychology, sociology and ethnography to organisation behaviour and human resource management, that the description could be viewed as less than helpful in trying to understand how OD differs from any other way of managing organisations. The attempt to articulate the essence of OD has exercised the minds of theorists and practitioners for decades, and has led to many attempts to create a comprehensive definition. Box 1.1 presents a typical sample, showing how definitions have altered over the past 35 years.

Box 1.1: Definitions of OD over the decades

'Organization development is an effort (1) planned, (2) organizationwide, and (3) managed from the top, to (4) increase organization effectiveness and health through (5) planned interventions in the organization's "processes", using behavioral-science knowledge' (Beckhard, 1969, p.9).

'Organization development (OD) is a response to change, a complex educational strategy intended to change the beliefs, attitudes, values and structure of organizations so that they can better adapt to new technologies, markets, and challenges, and the dizzying rate of change itself' (Bennis, 1969, p.2).

'... change of an organization's culture from one which avoids an examination of social processes (especially decision-making, planning and communication) to one which institutionalizes and legitimizes this examination' (Warner Burke and Hornstein, 1972, p.72).

'... enhancing the congruency between organisational structures, processes, strategy, people and culture, developing new and creative organisational solutions and developing organisational self renewing capacity' (Beer, 1980, p.10).

'... a process of planned system change that attempts to make organizations better able to attain their short- and long-term objectives. This is achieved by teaching the organization members to manage their organizational processes, structures and culture more effectively. Facts, concepts and theory from the behavioural sciences are utilized to fashion both the process and the content of the interventions. A basic belief of OD theorists and practitioners is that for effective, lasting change to take place, the system members must grow in competence to master their own fates' (French *et al.*, 2000, p.3).

'A system-wide application of behavioural science knowledge to the planned development and reinforcement of organisational strategies, structures and processes for improving an organisation's effectiveness' (Cummings and Worley, 2001, p.1).

'Ultimately, OD is a social technology that helps human systems remain competitive in an era where organizational operating domains are turbulent and all labor systems are wide open to the forces of change. Development means change and it requires learning' (Carnevale, 2003, p.2).

The various threads of OD that we identified earlier in this chapter are all apparent within these definitions, and the difference in emphasis from one definition to another is largely shaped by the various theoretical orientations of the respective authors. Earlier definitions acknowledge the external environment, but emphasise internal organisational processes and their effectiveness, highlighting the need for OD to enable organisations to become conscious and critical of these. The focus on OD as a means of achieving organisational objectives emerges strongly in later definitions, with particular reference to the need for adaptability, congruence, review and innovation in delivering these. Despite mentions of dizzying rates of change and turbulence, it is worth noting that most of the definitions are rooted in the modernist (as opposed to post-modernist) tradition, with their emphasis on the centrality of rational planning using facts and knowledge that are apparently consensual.

While it may be academically accurate to link OD with the behavioural sciences, it offers little practical insight into the meaning of OD in a setting such as the NHS. It suggests that OD is about using what we know about how people behave in the ways in which we manage and improve organisations. But this simple interpretation risks being all things to all people; it almost implies that anything done to improve an organisation is OD. As noted above, it leads to the 'pantheistic' version of OD. If this is true, how does OD differ from management? More constructively, it does suggest that knowledge of the theory and practice of OD is vital to effective management and provides protection against the danger of seeing OD as only being something done to an organisation and its members by an outsider. However, we do need to do better than this if we are to provide a working definition for this book.

Recognising organisational development

French *et al.* (2000) have attempted to make sense of the various OD definitions by analysing the common features between them. Their conclusion is firmly that, 'organization development is not just "anything done to better an organization"; it is a particular kind of change process designed to bring about a particular kind of end result' (p.2). They outline a set of characteristics which they believe distinguish organisational development from other approaches to organisational change. Their list of features, while not perfect, can help us to characterise OD in healthcare and includes the following.

1 The nature of the change effort is long range, planned and sustained, based on an overall strategy.
2 Organisational development activities are educative, reflexive, self-examining, based on building self-sufficiency and often underpinned by action research.
3 Organisational development interventions focus on work-related groups of people, their beliefs, attitudes and values, and the human processes between them.
4 The overall goal of organisational development is not just enhanced organisational effectiveness and organisational health but, in addition, it aims for an organisation's culture and processes to change in order that it is continually reflexive and self-examining.

French *et al.*'s analysis makes a very significant contribution to the debate about how OD differs from other approaches to managing organisational change. However, it is the last feature on the list above, related to organisational self-renewal, that is potentially the most helpful in distinguishing OD processes from other change management initiatives. This aspect of OD illustrates the difference between creating a 'changed organisation' – one that used to be 'x' and is now 'y' – and creating a 'changing organisation', that is, one that accepts that change is continual and that the key to ongoing success is learning to constantly anticipate and adapt. Such a 'changing organisation' has built into its structures and processes ways of gaining and reflecting on multidimensional views of itself, making sense of these perspectives and translating them into interventions in support of transformation. This is the perhaps the most appropriate ambition for OD: to create changing organisations.

More specifically, in considering the role and contribution of OD in healthcare, this ability and willingness of agencies to be continually reflexive and self-examining about their own culture and processes provides a very useful benchmark. It helps us recognise OD when we see it, understand the extent to which it is central to an organisation's strategy, and assess the importance of OD in achieving organisational objectives. Crucially, it also helps us to decide which OD activities are appropriate and relevant in different circumstances.

In short, understanding this central tenet of OD helps to make sense of the whole concept, both theoretically and practically. It clears some of the fog, allows us to focus our view and to some extent provides a shared point of reference. What it cannot do is provide a blueprint for undertaking organisational development; that is, it cannot prescribe the most effective interventions in all circumstances. This is perhaps where much of the confusion around OD remains; achieving such conceptual clarity neither reconciles the often competing schools of OD nor the need for managers and practitioners to make choices between them (although it may help in making those choices).

So, understanding the essence of OD and even being able to suggest a working definition is obviously important for clarity of purpose and meaning. But it does not in itself hold the key to organisational solutions. A single such key does not exist. Many different keys may be needed to unlock the stubbornly jammed door to an improved organisational future (or, indeed, something a little stronger, such as the crowbar of structural change). Our appreciation of organisational development – both conceptually and in relation to local organisational needs – may enable us to discard straight away some of the options on the large key ring that we hold in the knowledge that they simply will not fit. We then have to work out which of our keys we should use, and how, to ease open the doors we wish to move through. This is where we move from understanding OD to applying what we know in practical terms.

The next section considers some of the main overarching approaches to organisational development that have proved to be important in enabling managers to select appropriate keys to unlock doors to the future. They are not interventions in themselves. Rather, they suggest further refinements to the criterion of reflexivity and self-examination that has emerged as central to the definition of OD that has been developed in this chapter.

Central characteristics of organisational development

Any potential interventions available to managers or practitioners – such as those outlined in Chapters 5 to 12 – need be judged against the criterion of the extent to which they will enhance the creation of a 'changing organisation'. Many aspects of this selection will relate to local context. However, the approaches identified and summarised below give more food for thought around the ways in which OD interventions have the potential to help an organisation become continually reflexive and self-examining. The ways in which these disparate interventions will assist any organisation can be partially judged against the extent to which, in the local context, they will enable them to reap the benefits of action research, organisational learning, sensemaking, images of organisations and systems thinking. Summaries of these ideas bring into this chapter many of the most influential writers and texts on organisations and OD of the past 25 years. Many of these ideas are connected and sometimes mutually reinforcing (e.g. the work of Weick on sensemaking and Morgan on metaphors).

Action research

As highlighted above, research has shown that there are certain common characteristics associated with the theory and practice of organisational development. One of these is basing OD on action research. As we have seen, the action research process has its roots in the survey feedback thread of OD and comprises a cycle of activities starting with data gathering for diagnosis. As summarised by Golembiewski *et al.*, 'these data get fed back into that system, to serve as the raw material for action-research sequences: diagnosis, prescription of changes, implementation, and evaluation' (1982, p.86).

This action research cycle, adapted for the purposes of managing change, has developed into the OD cycle, which has become a core framework for organisational development approaches to change. It is described in detail in Chapter 4, and can be an integral part of any the interventions that follow in subsequent chapters; however, any OD process that does not contain some variation on this cycle in its design and delivery is unlikely to be robust.

Organisational learning

As noted above, a key feature of OD is that it not only aims to improve an organisation, but also to change the organisation into one which is continually reflexive and self-examining. The growth of organisational learning as an approach to organisational change and transformation has this objective at its heart. Organisational learning is founded on the theories of individual learning, such as the well-known work of Kolb and the development of his classic learning cycle (Figure 1.1; Kolb, 1984).

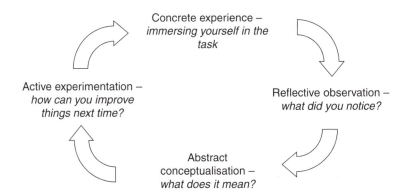

Figure 1.1 The organisational learning cycle.

Embedding continuous learning into an organisation as an outcome, as a set of processes and as a prevailing culture has been shown to be a complicated challenge. Among the several suggested reasons for this is that 'learning' is often interpreted too narrowly, focusing on solving problems or correcting mistakes, with an emphasis on changing the cause-and-effect relationship between actions and outcomes. Argyris (1991) illustrates this tendency in organisations with the simple analogy of a thermostat. When the temperature gets too hot or too cold, the thermostat automatically switches itself on or off to compensate. Argyris describes this sort of response to a problem as '*single-loop learning*', whereby a problem is detected, action is taken to resolve the problem and work resumes – until the problem arises again. Single-loop learning thus reinforces existing norms, practices and values.

In a cycle of '*double-loop learning*', the emphasis is on understanding the reason for a problem as well as identifying the problem itself. In Argyris' example of the thermostat, a double-loop learning approach would be to, 'ask "Why am I set at 68 degrees?" and then explore whether some other temperature might more economically achieve the goal of heating the room' (Argyris, 1991, p.99). Asking the key question 'why?' in an organisation opens up the possibility that the organisation, or the people within it, may need to adapt their practice, behaviour and values in response. Double-loop learning is therefore based on challenging current norms and questioning current practice, adapting these where it is both necessary and possible (*see* Chapter 10 for more on addressing values).

A third level of learning, '*deutero learning*' (or 'learning how to learn'), enables an organisation to anticipate change by proactively embedding learning processes into the culture (Argyris and Schon, 1978). This creates a climate where internal critical reflection and self-examination is combined with ongoing evaluation of the external environment to develop a proactive organisation that is prepared to respond to whatever the future may hold. It is at this third level that organisational learning becomes very closely aligned to the values and principles underpinning organisational development. It also raises a key question about potential OD interventions, that is, how will this proposed intervention help this organisation to 'learn how to learn'?

Nonetheless, organisational learning approaches put the individual centre stage. As Senge (1990) puts it: 'organizations learn only through individuals who learn. Individual learning does not guarantee organizational learning. But without it no organizational learning occurs' (p.139).

Sensemaking in organisations

Weick (1995) provides an accessible introduction to the notion of sensemaking: 'Active agents construct sensible, sensable ... events. They "structure the unknown"... How they construct what they construct, why, and with what effects are the central questions for people interested in sensemaking' (p.4). This emphasis on construction places sensemaking firmly in the tradition of social constructionism discussed in the Introduction to this collection. As Weick puts it, 'sensemaking is about authoring as well as reading' (p.7); for him, it involves creation as much as discovery. Unlike Morgan and his metaphors (*see* below), however, Weick means us to accept sensemaking non-figuratively; 'sensemaking ... may have an informal poetic flavor, that should not disguise the fact that is literally just what it says it is' (p.8).

Box 1.2 summarises the seven distinguishing features of sensemaking discussed by Weick (1995). He describes the expression 'how can I know what I think until I see what I say' as a 'recipe' through which each of these seven properties can be parsed (and the seven statements that result are in the quotation marks in Box 1.2).

Box 1.2: Weick's seven properties of sensemaking

1 It is grounded in the importance of sensemaking in the construction of the identity of the self (and of the organisation); 'who I am as indicated by discovery of how and what I think'.
2 It is retrospective in its focus on sensemaking as rendering meaningful lived experience; 'to learn what I think, I look back over what I said earlier'.
3 It recognises that people produce at least part of the environment (e.g. the constraints and opportunities) within which they are sensemaking; 'I create the object to be seen and inspected when I say or do something'.
4 It stresses that sensemaking is a social process undertaken with others; 'what I say and single out and conclude are determined by who socialized me and how I was socialized, as well as by the audience I anticipate will audit the conclusions I reach'.
5 It argues that sensemaking is always ongoing in that it never starts and it never stops (even though events may be chopped out of this flow in order to be presented to others); 'my talking is spread across time, competes for attention with other ongoing projects, and is reflected on after it is finished, which means my interests may already have changed'.
6 It acknowledges that sensemaking is typically based on cues, where one simple and familiar item can initiate a process that encompasses a much broader range of meanings and implications; 'the "what" that I single out and embellish as the content of the thought is only a small proportion of the utterance that becomes salient because of context and personal dispositions'.
7 It is driven by plausibility rather than accuracy; 'I need to know enough about what I think to get on with my projects but no more, which means that sufficiency and plausibility take precedence over accuracy'.

Derived from Weick, 1995, pp.61–2.

The importance of Weick's work to OD is that it emphasises the potential for changing the way in which organisational pasts, presents and futures are constructed by organisational members. In particular, he argues that 'occasions for sensemaking are themselves constructed' (p.85) and may be particularly common where people reach a threshold of dissatisfaction that previous patterns of sensemaking are unable to reduce (this idea links closely to that of 'the tipping point' – a context especially propitious for OD interventions – that recurs in this book).

Images of organisations

In his influential writing on organisations, Morgan (1986) has identified eight distinct metaphors through which organisations can be read and understood (or, in Weick's terms, made sense of). He argues that the premise on which his work builds is 'that our theories and explanations of organizational life are based on metaphors that lead us to see and understand organizations in distinct yet partial ways ... many of our taken-for-granted ideas about organizations are metaphorical ... by using different metaphors to understand the complex and paradoxical character of organizational life, we are able to manage and design organizations in ways that we may not have thought possible before' (1986, pp.12–13). The important part of Morgan's argument for our purposes is that drawing on new or unfamiliar metaphors can help managers – potentially with the support of OD practitioners – to make their organisations different from the ways that they have been before, i.e. judicious use of metaphors can guide action and not just analysis. Given that its distinctive aspect appears to be promoting reflection and learning, any OD process that does not pinpoint and challenge the metaphors that currently govern organisational behaviour – and offer alternatives – would appear to be missing an important component.

Morgan's eight metaphors are summarised in Box 1.3. The potency of his argument can be illustrated by the apparent link between some of these metaphors and the interventions described in Chapters 5 to 12. For example, service improvement (Chapter 5) seems to view the organisation predominantly as a machine, psychodynamic theory (Chapter 6) as a psychic prison and open systems theory (Chapter 7) as an organism. This may suggest that managers and clinicians selecting an OD practitioner should seek out one whose intervention is based on a metaphor unfamiliar to the organisation which is to be the subject of the process, or who is able to work competently across a range of metaphors and interventions. It also carries the implication that OD practitioners require a range of theoretical constructs and modes of intervention which they deploy in a thoughtful and disciplined fashion.

Box 1.3: Morgan's eight metaphors

- Organisations as machines
- Organisations as organisms
- Organisations as brains
- Organisations as cultures
- Organisations as political systems
- Organisations as psychic prisons
- Organisations as flux and transformation
- Organisations as instruments of domination

Derived from Morgan, 1986.

Whole systems thinking

Another key characteristic that most OD processes need to demonstrate is the way in which they will impact on 'whole systems thinking'. At a metaphorical level, this view conceptualises organisations as living organisms or ecosystems that are constantly evolving. Core to this thinking is that the parts making up the 'whole' are autonomous, capable of acting for themselves, but at the same time interdependent, since the actions of one will impact on the others. This leads to an approach to organisational change which concentrates on understanding and improving the relationships, connections and meanings that join the parts up into a whole.

A whole systems approach to organisational change and organisational development starts with the assumption that tackling complex, multidimensional problems is beyond the ability of any one individual or agency. Breaking the problem down into its component parts is a conventional way of trying to understand such problems, but often fails as an effective way to improve things. Whole systems working takes an alternative approach, viewing these complex problems as 'issues for an interconnected system to tackle together' (Pratt *et al.*, 1999, p.3). Chapter 7 of this volume explores these ideas in much more depth.

Why is organisational development currently so popular in healthcare?

Possible reasons for the heightened profile, growing importance and unmistakable popularity of OD in the contemporary NHS remain somewhat opaque. Claims made within the 'strategic' OD movement that it can align complex internal features of a system with challenging external demands may provide part of the explanation. The allure of an approach to change which creates organisational success through such alignment is no doubt powerful to policy makers, politicians and managers alike, especially when it seems to have been effective in the private sector. Since 1997, OD in healthcare has to some extent become a servant in support of local implementation of national policy; this context raises some very particular challenges for OD which the next chapter examines in detail.

At this point, however, it is only necessary to recognise that some uncomfortable tensions are emerging as a result of this connection between OD and the 'modernisation' of the NHS. The NHS Plan was designed as a ten-year strategy and was arguably fertile ground for an approach to change grounded in organisational development. The nature of the changes proposed for the NHS resonated closely with many of the features of organisations which had effectively used OD to bring about effective change in other sectors (French *et al.*, 2000). Central to OD's effectiveness elsewhere, however, has been the long-term and strategic nature of the change effort. To bind an OD process with highly specified government targets, to interrupt it constantly with short-term performance checks and to disrupt it frequently with significant innovations in social structure (for example, the changes in organisational accountabilities represented by financial flows and payment by results) is proving to be potentially counter-productive in the NHS. The apparently slow progress that results has consequences: it casts doubt on the change processes being used; causes nervousness about their likely success; and calls into question the commitment and competence of those trying to bring about organisational transformation. Further, the model of OD predominantly adopted by the Modernisation Agency – the major deliverer of OD to the NHS under New Labour – has itself tended to favour one set of interventions over others and, arguably, a set that is less likely than those others to create a 'changing organisation' rather than just a 'changed organisation'. The evidence that might support this contention is examined in Chapter 13.

Nonetheless, the challenges facing the NHS will only increase as time goes on and the search for ways to realise significant – indeed transformational – change will continue. One of the reasons that OD currently exerts such influence in healthcare is that organisations facing such challenges and changes will look for external succour from OD gurus promising solutions to apparently intractable obstacles (or insurmountable opportunities, as they are now widely known in the NHS). Much of the literature promoting OD interventions and practitioners is compellingly aspirational, often drawing more on the language and images of lifestyle magazines than academic journals. At the same time, OD continues to hold considerable promise and potential for contributing to a modern, dependable NHS for the 21st century. As this chapter has highlighted, in order to gain the optimal benefit of OD, it is vital to remain focused on its core purpose and its distinct contribution, while being aware of some its limitations as explored in the Conclusion to this book.

Perhaps one question would help to clarify whether OD can bring about the real and lasting change required by current NHS policy. Is 'modernisation' merely about creating improved and specific NHS performance in the short to medium term or is it also about creating a health and social care system which is continually reflexive and responsive for the future? The current policy context does not suggest the latter as the prime driver or key desired outcome. In other words, modernisation is not necessarily the same as transformation. Unless this changes, the current popularity of OD in the NHS may be relatively short-lived. A better understanding and a different perspective on OD may thus be central to transforming the NHS and thus securing the future of a publicly funded health service in the UK. This is a theme to which the book returns in both Chapter 13 and its Conclusion.

One final reason for the apparent popularity of OD also needs to be examined. Deriving from its origins in the human relations and action research schools, there is a tendency among many OD practitioners to adopt a moral stance, which is well expressed by Carnevale (2003): 'Human development matters in OD and work is seen as an activity that holds great promise for persons to actualise themselves. Organizations and their human resources are intimately related in the OD view and must collaborate for mutual gain. These ideals may seem beyond reach in reality, but consider the alternative ...' (p.123). In this secular age, OD practitioners who adhere to such views can take on the mantle of organisational missionaries, proselytising in pursuit of the betterment of the human condition. This is potentially attractive to many hard-pressed managers, especially those charged with raising the morale of their clinical colleagues. However, it seems to us to be little more than a form of organisational alchemy, promising more that it can possibly deliver and inevitably leading to disappointment. The apparent attraction of the OD practitioner as latter-day priest or witch doctor is discussed further in the Conclusion to this volume.

Conclusion

This chapter has attempted to place the current popularity of organisational development in the NHS into a historical, conceptual and practical context. The interwoven threads that have been traced and explored represent a complex overall picture of OD in healthcare. Knitting together the various strands over several years has led to a melée of ideas, colour and texture which are not easy to interpret into a clear or distinct impression. It is easy to become too close to see the whole picture, or too distant to value the distinct threads that it is made up of.

While many definitions of OD have been developed over the years, it is the work to identify the distinct nature of OD which is perhaps most useful for practitioners and managers within healthcare organisations. The key features of OD discussed in this chapter help to reinforce its central themes. However, the overarching aim of not only improving organisational performance but also creating a continually reflexive and learning organisation or system emerges as the most salient point. It suggests that writers who have focused on action research, organisational learning, sensemaking, images of organisations and whole systems thinking have all made important contributions to delineating the characteristics of effective OD. In a policy context where multiple tools, techniques and approaches to change management are creating potential congestion, it is this focused objective and key characteristics that provide OD with its core purpose and clarify where it can offer its unique contribution.

References

Argyris C (1991) Teaching smart people how to learn. *Harvard Business Review*. **May–June**. 99–102.

Argyris C and Schon D (1978) *Organizational Learning: a theory of action perspective.* Addison-Wesley, Reading, MA.

Baumgartel H (1959) Using employee questionnaire results for improving organizations: the survey (feedback) experiment. *Kansas Business Review*. **12**: 2–6.

Beckhard R (1969) *Organization Development: strategies and models.* Addison-Wesley, Reading, MA.

Beer M (1980) *Organization Change and Development.* Goodyear Publishing, Santa Monica, CA.

Bennis W (1969) *Organization Development: its nature, origins and prospects.* Addison-Wesley, Reading, MA.

Carnevale D (2003) *Organizational Development in the Public Sector.* Westview Press, Cambridge, MA.

Cummings T and Worley C (2001) *Organization Development and Change.* South-Western College Publishing, Cincinatti, OH.

Department of Health (2000a) *Improving Working Lives Standard: NHS employers committed to improving the working lives of people who work in the NHS.* HMSO, London.

Department of Health (2000b) *The NHS Plan: a plan for investment, a plan for reform.* HMSO, London.

French W, Bell C and Zawacki R (2000) *Organization Development and Transformation.* McGraw-Hill, Singapore.

Golembiewski R, Proehl C and Sink D (1982) Estimating the success of OD applications. *Training and Development Journal.* **36**: 4.

Kolb D (1984) *Experiential Learning.* Prentice-Hall, Englewood Cliffs, NJ.

Levy A and Merry U (1986) *Organizational Transformation.* Praeger Publishers, New York.

Marrow A (1969) *The Practical Theorist: the life and work of Kurt Lewin.* Basic Books, New York.

Mintzberg H (1994) *The Rise and Fall of Strategic Planning.* Free Press, New York.

Morgan G (1986) *Images of Organization.* Sage, London.

Pratt J, Gordon P and Plamping D (1999) *Working Whole Systems: putting theory into practice in organizations.* King's Fund, London.

Senge P (1990) *The Fifth Discipline: the art and practice of the learning organization.* Doubleday, New York.

Trist E and Sashkin M (1980) Interview. *Group and Organization Studies.* **5**: 150–1.

Warner Burke W and Hornstein H (1972) *The Social Technology of Organization Development.* Learning Resources Corporation, Fairfax, VA.

Weick K (1995) *Sensemaking in Organizations.* Sage, London.

CHAPTER 2

The role of organisational development in policy implementation in healthcare

Perri 6 and Edward Peck

Introduction

The previous chapter suggested that part of the explanation for the increasing popularity among both politicians and managers of organisational development in healthcare is their perception that it can support the local implementation of national policy. But what is the nature of the problem with policy implementation that OD is being used to address? What are the lessons that OD commissioners and practitioners can learn from writers on policy implementation? What are the particular challenges that OD faces when used in the support of such implementation? These are some of the questions this chapter sets out to explore. In doing so, it draws on ideas discussed in more depth in 6 and Peck (forthcoming). However, the fundamental hypothesis of this chapter is that successful policy implementation is the result of effective organisational settlements between new central policy initiatives and established local organisational routines. Linking to the definition of OD developed in Chapter 1, it suggests that reflection on the nature of existing settlements and learning about ways in which they might be changed is the key task of OD in support of policy implementation.

Policy implementation – is there a problem?

In almost every country, there seem to be periods during which politicians in the governing party bemoan what they see as the inadequacy of the efforts made by the central civil service, by public sector professionals and by local statutory organisations to implement their policies. Ministers in the New Labour administration elected in the UK in 1997 and 2001 have complained, sometimes with apparent bitterness, of the ways in which the implementation of their policies have been frustrated. On occasions Prime Minister Blair blamed public sector staff for their resistance to change, speaking of the 'scars on his back' resulting from his efforts to persuade them to accept reform (Blair, 1999). On occasions, he hinted at sabotage. In 2002, for example, he talked of unnamed 'wreckers' seeking to undermine reform suggesting to many that he meant public sector workers, or at the very least, members of the public sector trades unions (Blair, 2002). At other times, he and his ministers shifted rather uneasily between talk of the progress with the ten-year programme of modernisation for the National Health Service (Milburn, 2002) and complaining of the slowness of the pace with which civil servants, professionals and local agencies were implementing their reforms. If there has been a problem for New Labour in getting its policies implemented – with its huge parliamentary majority, weak opposition and formidable communications machine, and where no other democratically elected authority had any mandate that might have restricted it – then we must surely look for explanations of Blair's frustration that lie not in political factors but within processes internal and external to the local organisations concerned. When these processes have been uncovered, it may prove possible to consider the potential role of OD in intervening in them.

Of course, achieving the implementation of national policy by local agencies has not just been a problem for New Labour, as the literature reviewed below demonstrates. However, the amount of faith that this administration has put in the power of supposedly evidence-based policy perhaps made their disappointment particularly marked. In health settings, this faith was partly derived from the influential four-stage framework for the adoption of evidence in medical practice articulated by Sackett and Haines (1995); the evidence-based approach assumes that ensuring implementation of new ideas is mostly a matter of effective dissemination of those ideas. Several research studies have found that this framework is not reflective of medical practice (e.g. Dawson *et al.*, 1998; Newman *et al.*, 2000; Smith and McClenahan, 2000), and we should not, therefore, anticipate that it will reflect the broader picture of organisational life.

However, the findings of the most extensive of these studies, undertaken by Fitzgerald *et al.* (1999), represents a comprehensive critique of the claims of evidence-based approaches to policy and practice in healthcare. In conducting their four case studies, the research team set out to examine the adoption of clinical change within the acute hospital sector, and to identify the scientific and non-scientific factors shaping this adoption. In summary, the most evidence-based change was the least adopted and the least evidence-based change was the most adopted. They suggest five key findings from this study and five implications for the process of effective policy implementation (some of which we would recognise as OD interventions). These are reproduced in Box 2.1. In essence, however, the research provides compelling support for the suggestion that it is in the processes of organising that the opportunities and obstacles to policy implementation lie. At the same time, it should be noted that Fitzgerald and colleagues describe an example of national policy – in this case significant innovations in the support of pregnant women before and during childbirth – being put into local practice, albeit that it was actively adapted and not merely passively adopted. This distinction between adoption (where national aspirations are complied with locally) and adaptation (where national aspirations are interpreted and adjusted locally prior to change taking place) is central to the argument about the role of OD in policy implementation developed in this chapter.

Box 2.1: The findings and implications of research by Fitzgerald *et al.* on evidence-based practice

Finding one   There was no strong relationship found between the strength of the evidence base and the rate of adoption of the innovation.

Implication   Linear models of implementation are seriously misleading and are likely to lead to serious implementation deficits.

Finding two   Scientific evidence is in part a social construction as well as 'objective' data.

Implication   There is no such entity as 'the body of evidence' but rather competing bodies of evidence available.

Finding three There are different forms of evidence differentially accepted by different individuals and occupational groups.

Implication   The inter-group issues also need to be addressed explicitly through the construction of linking bodies which bring the different groups involved in the implementation together, preferably within a learning environment and outside the busy daily routine.

Finding four   The data identify specific organisational and social factors which affect the career and outcome of clinical change issues.

Implication   The most effective implementation strategies may combine top-down pressure and bottom-up energy.

Finding five   The upper tiers of the NHS, healthcare purchasers, R&D and the general management process played only a marginal role in the change process.

Implication   There is a need to embed change within the professions themselves.

Summarised from Fitzgerald *et al.* (1999) by the authors.

This chapter explores some central theories about the organisational processes through which national policy is interpreted and adjusted before it is (perhaps and partially) implemented locally. It continues in the next section with a brief review of the literature on policy implementation, before exploring the issues for organisational development that seem to arise from this literature.

Lessons from policy implementation studies

In the 1970s, there was a period of intense focus on policy implementation, which began with the famous work of Pressman and Wildavsky (1973). The title of their book is instructive: *Implementation: how great expectations in Washington are dashed in Oakland or, why it's amazing that federal programs work at all, this being the saga of the Economic Development Administration as told by two sympathetic observers who seek to build morals on a foundation of ruined hopes.* Reflecting on the experience in Britain some time later, Barrett and Fudge observed that, 'Government seems unable to put its policy into effect as intended, or finds that its interventions ... have unexpected or counter-productive outcomes' (1981, p.3).

As with these examples, much of this literature starts with an attempt to explain failure in policy implementation, often moving from descriptions of disappointments to prescriptions for progress. Many take one of two perspectives, representing either a 'top-down' or 'bottom-up' approach to actual and/or desirable policy implementation.

The 'top-down' method asks why frontline activity deviates from what the researcher reconstructs as the original intentions of the central policy makers. Writers in this tradition focus on such factors as:

- conflict over goals
- the 'private' interests of local agency managers or professionals (or, indeed, clients)
- inadequate resources
- weak or inaccurate causal assumptions about the effect of the proposed initiatives
- weaknesses of training or organisational ability
- lack of leadership
- institutional constraints, routines or habits, and so on.

For example, in their original edition, Pressman and Wildavsky (1973) explained the failure of the Economic Development Administration in Oakland by reference to the rational pursuit of their own 'private' interests by each of the agencies that had to be involved in the programme.

A strength of the tradition is its ability to claim that it asks the right democratic question; namely, has the will of the elected representatives of the people been carried out or has it been thwarted? However, its weakness is the converse of its strength; the approach must treat the realities of organisational culture which lead to local settlements (and thus deviations from original intentions) as a potential problem to be managed, and must be suspicious of anything that smacks more of adaptation than of simple adoption. Moreover, since policy decisions made centrally are themselves often complex compromises, it often hard to reconstruct a single self-consistent set of original intentions that would be shared by all those with a key stake in the original decision; indeed, identifying the set of original decision makers is difficult, since many policies require continuous central clarification or compromise involving shifting groups of stakeholders.

There is no single 'bottom-up' approach (Hill, 1997; Hill and Hupe, 2002), but the approaches share the commitment to starting from the question 'what actually happens once a policy is released to the care of local agencies and frontline staff?' (rather than the question 'how far has the will of the elected central policy makers been followed?'). They also have in common a presumption of some value in the local settlements identified. One group of writers (Hjern and Hull, 1982; Porter and Hjern, 1981) argue that, for all the weight of their democratic mandate, the preferences of elected representatives should not be decisive and that in most cases a wide range of both producer and consumer interests should have great and perhaps even equal weight (a view which, as we have seen, is not shared by politicians such as Tony Blair). Some, including famously Lipsky (1980), focused less on agencies than on the situation of individual professionals and the ways in which their coping mechanisms – under the constraints of their workloads, capabilities, aspirations and resources – define the extent of adherence to policy at a local level.

The 'bottom-up' tradition stresses both the inevitability of local agency and staff discretion and its desirability for generating motivation and for sustaining professional capabilities and local problem solving of the kinds that get anything done at all (whether or not what is done is a faithful recapitulation of the intentions of the centre). The approach emphasises the negotiated character of whatever is counted as implementation.

More recently, the trend has been towards finding syntheses of 'top-down' and 'bottom-up' approaches (Sabatier, 1986). It is accepted that top-down approaches, considered as prescriptions, produce all the usual distortions of central planning; and, considered as descriptions, overestimate the coherence of policy formulation and underestimate the importance of the micro-politics of local bargaining around the meaning of policy with frontline staff, service users and other stakeholders. Similarly, it is recognised that the bottom-up approaches are often equally guilty of the opposite sins. Prescriptively, they fail to recognise the powerful authority of the democratic mandate. Descriptively, they overgeneralise about the discretion available to professionals and frontline staff (Ham and Hill, 1993). Many commentators now follow Sabatier's argument that from bottom-up perspectives we should take the focus on the network of local actors engaged in strategic behaviour, and from top-down approaches we should retain the definition of the policy problem and the setting of the parameters of the policy solutions that will be acceptable.

It is important to stress that the claims of the more extreme bottom-up theorists, that the unanticipated and unanticipatable consequences of attempting to implement policy will mean that little can be achieved, reflect a fatalism that goes far beyond the evidence (*see* 6 *et al.*, 2002). The natural history of policy implementation is not simply a catalogue of inevitable fiasco (as the successful example in Fitzgerald's research and the case studies in some chapters of this book illustrate). These arguments are as implausible as the opposing extreme hierarchical arguments of some top-down theorists; they suggest that if only the centre would produce causally well-designed, internally coherent, adequately resourced policies, communicate them properly and hold to account those charged with carrying them out, while also giving them appropriate incentives, then implementation can in most cases be achieved as intended. In these circumstances, it is the role of managers – and OD practitioners – to create and/ or maintain organisational processes that confound the fatalists while containing the hierarchists.

Policy implementation studies: the messages for OD

So, what are the central lessons for OD from this brief review? The first is that policy implementation is, and has probably always been, problematic. Second, that elements of both top-down instruction (emphasising adoption) and bottom-up negotiation (emphasising adaptation) are going to be part of any effective approach to implementation. Third, that organisations are attempting to reconcile the central definition and boundaries of the policy – which may be underpinned by targets and inspectorates – with the local interpretations of networks of professionals and other stakeholders which will generate commitment and ownership to change. In attempting this reconciliation, senior managers may find themselves caught between the rock of politicians' objectives and the hard place of professionals' and local managers' or agencies' aspirations.

In these circumstances, it is scarcely surprising that OD interventions are viewed as important in achieving a balance between adoption and adaptation. Nonetheless, this represents a very particular, if increasingly common, context within which OD interventions are designed and deployed. It is one that brings to the fore the important question raised in Chapter 1: 'to serve whose interests are the OD interventions being delivered?'. For, very often, OD is called for by those at the centre who want to use it as a way of treating what are seen as blockages due to local organisational culture, either as an alternative to the imposition of sanctions (sacking chief executives or management teams, reorganising organisational boundaries and roles, substituting other agencies) or else as a last resort before such sanctions are used. On the other hand, where it is welcomed locally, many professionals and middle managers see it as a toolkit for developing more effective local negotiation processes for creative local problem solving around national expectations. This is a potential ethical dilemma addressed by many writers on OD. Carnevale (2003), for instance, argues that OD practitioners must negotiate a path between the objectives of managers and the aspirations of staff: 'change agents can do that or they can sell out to power' (p.120). At the very least, it may well be important to clarify for both central and local decision makers just what can reasonably be expected from OD interventions in supporting and sustaining policy implementation, and also to stress the importance of engaging local networks of stakeholders in any processes for change.

In exploring these issues, the broad argument of this chapter supports the bottom-up perspective to the extent that it represents a view of implementation as one of bargaining and settlement between conflicting interests. At the same time, and as the top-down perspective did, it also recognises the quite proper *asymmetric* character of the legitimate bargaining power of the various conflicting interests (and in particular the democratic mandate which is at the heart of the legitimacy of politicians' ambitions for reform).

It is probably not helpful, therefore, for organisational development practitioners working in health and social care services to make a simple choice between asking on the one hand: 'How, if at all, can the centre gets its way?' (the top-down question); and/or on the other; 'How can processes be identified that might, on average and over the long run, be more likely to produce better outcomes from the implementation processes, whatever the centre may have wanted originally?' (the bottom-up question). Rather, the appropriate question for practitioners – and for those commissioning their interventions – should perhaps be something more like: 'How can general strategies and practices be developed and institutionalised for coming to settlements between rival but asymmetrically legitimate conflicting interests, which recognise their legitimacy, the inequalities of that legitimacy and the empirically known constraints on achieving effectiveness either by simple demands from the centre for compliance or by allowing indefinite local freedom?' (the organisational process question).

This is an important question, and deserves a little unpacking. First, the OD interventions must be sufficiently generic that they are likely to work across a range of policy initiatives and organisational settings. Second, they have to offer the prospect of achieving a reconciliation between different interests, recognising that some of these may carry more power than others and that some are going to be arguing for contrasting approaches. Third, they have to build on the evidence that neither top-down nor bottom-up approaches, deployed by themselves, will deliver an acceptable outcome.

OD interventions as processes to enable policy implementation

If much of the current popularity of OD is due to its apparent importance in supporting policy implementation (as argued in Chapter 1), then it is incumbent upon OD practitioners to have an account of the overall role of OD in this area, regardless of the specific theoretical orientation of particular practitioners. The commissioners of OD in healthcare should expect no less. This section attempts to set out the areas that such an account should cover.

OD in support of policy implementation has two characteristics that are not typical of other contexts in which it might be deployed. First, there is generally a more or less clear outline of what success (adoption) might look like. This will be represented in policy documents, organisational objectives and inspection standards. Under New Labour, the level of detail contained in National Service Frameworks – and the rigour with which performance management processes pursue the local delivery of their objectives – probably represents the high-water mark to date of specificity in such national outlines in the UK. It is also noteworthy that a government committed to local compliance should have recognised – through the creation of the Modernisation Agency (MA) – that dissemination has to take many and varied forms in order to engage the local stakeholders who have to turn policy into practice (*see* Chapters 5 and 13 for more discussion of the MA). Second, there is inevitably local interpretation and adjustment that will have to take place (adaptation) to ensure that this outline is acceptable to stakeholders while being at least sufficiently recognisable to policy makers and inspectors. The focus on the generation of local solutions to local challenges through local engagement of local stakeholders – the common calling card of OD practitioners in other contexts – is, however, simply not adequate here.

In order to support policy implementation, therefore, OD has to assist organisations in two key tasks. At one level, organisations may need interventions to ensure sufficient *capabilities* within organisations and (increasingly) between organisations, and also just enough *willingness* among key players at least to acquiesce to, and not actively to obstruct, the use of those capabilities. At another level, organisations have to be able to connect the requirements of the new policy with the established routines of local organisation. The organisational settlement perspective seeks to account for both these elements.

Before detailing the argument contained in this perspective, it is necessary to introduce one more theoretical component. This relates to four styles of approaches to management in the public services, perhaps best articulated by Hood (1998), but summarised here in Figure 2.1.

Isolates: All we can do is:	*Hierarchy*: All we need to do is:
• stop trying to be so ambitious • go with the flow of organisational life • cope with the inevitable fiascos	• put in place proper regulations • create proper accountability upwards
Individualism: All we need to do is:	*Enclaves*: All we need to do is:
• create space and incentive for public entrepreneurs • create institutions to support learning from innovations • ensure contestability and competition	• create supportive work teams and professional networks • create space for service users to feel part of the community with the providers • emphasise the value of caring

Figure 2.1 Styles of public management (adapted from 6 (2001); *see also* Douglas (1992); Thompson *et al.* (1990)).

These four approaches to the management of public organisations are argued to be always present in every agency. Further, they are in constant negotiation with each other, and the predominance of any one style over the others will lead to dysfunctionality. A broad schema that mapped these four styles on to professional groups within the NHS might suggest, for example, that:

• nursing favours hierarchy
• hospital medicine is typified by enclaves
• psychologists are individualists
• general practitioners tend to be isolates.

This is a crude oversimplification included here only for the purposes of illustration. A finer-grain analysis is presented below in relation to the implementation of *Changing Childbirth* (DoH, 1993).

With these four styles in mind, the organisational settlement perspective (Thompson *et al.*, 1990, 1999) proposes, therefore, the following eight hypotheses.

1 The appropriate standard against which we should judge what is done in the name of implementing a policy is neither strict fidelity to original intentions nor local participatory commitment regardless of whatever gets done, but is itself a compromise of creative local problem solving within the framework of the general goals set by the centre.
2 In achieving this compromise, processes of reflection and learning are supported by which organisations gain in relevant *capabilities* and sustain *willingness* for implementation and commitment to those broad goals.
3 For this, sustaining capabilities and willingness calls for settlement making between all of these styles (hierarchy, enclave, individualist and isolate), accepting the principle of requisite variety.
4 In the absence or the excess of any one of these organisational styles, the result is likely to be some kind of disorganisation; for example, demotivation through over-regulation or lack of motivation due to insufficient mutual support.
5 Constraining these tendencies to different kinds of disorganisation requires a process of checking each of the styles, in order to ensure that each is balanced by the others.
6 This means that the timing and design of OD interventions are crucial. Ideally, they need to be timed to take place at those points in the trajectories that threaten disorganisation at which the relevant people can recognise the risks and where they can see the importance of checking those processes (what is called elsewhere in this book 'the tipping point').
7 Striking settlements of the kind that sustain the requisite variety of institutional styles takes place in ritual processes. The interest of OD, therefore, lies in the ritual order through which its practitioners can define the arena for negotiating settlements and specify processes of, for example, stirring commitment to action.
8 Rituals for striking settlements must, like every conflict resolution or conflict containment process, involve various forms of intervention, where the development of alternative future scenarios and the articulation of alternative versions of the organisational past take place. That is, at its best, OD sustains collective sensemaking and thus supports settlements between rival meanings.

On this account, the task of the OD practitioner is to construct opportunities for organisations and their stakeholders to reflect on the robustness of current organisational settlements between these styles, and the interests that they represent, and to facilitate ways of enabling them to learn about how these settlements may be changed. In many ways, the 'linking bodies' of Ferlie and Fitzgerald are examples of interventions – of new rituals – attempting to enable alternative futures to be imagined. Furthermore, there are strong connections here with the chapters in Part 2 (e.g. with the notion of crafting strategy discussed in Chapter 8 and with the storytelling techniques introduced in Chapter 12).

In order to demonstrate that *capabilities* and *willingness* are not abstract notions, let us return to consider in more depth these 'linking bodies'. They represent innovations in the *capabilities* of organisations to structure opportunities for new interprofessional relationships in support of encouraging the *willingness* of those professionals to embrace change: 'our data stress the importance of the local – and often multi-disciplinary – professional groups in shaping or "mediating" the flow of knowledge into practice ... the development of mechanisms to promote active boundary spanning, dialogue and joint learning' (Ferlie *et al.*, 2000, p.101). In other words, they are advocating the creation of new structures and processes to enable new forms of collective sensemaking.

However, Fitzgerald and her colleagues are researchers in organisational behaviour not practitioners in organisational development. They imply that creating and facilitating such groups is unproblematic, and much of the second part of this book is an exploration of why it is not. Nonetheless, these researchers' insights into the importance of structures, processes and sensemaking in developing *capabilities* and *willingness* does demonstrate the potential centrality of OD to effective policy implementation.

It is now time to turn to the other level, that is, the requirement to incorporate the demands of new policy into the established routines of local organisation. If the concepts of *capabilities* and *willingness* focus on the more human and cultural aspects of the organisation, this second level is more concerned with the structural aspects of the organisation and with those dimensions that might deliver sustainability of innovation. Of course, and as Chapter 10 argues, culture and structure are inextricably interlinked. However, and merely for the purposes of clear presentation of the argument, they are distinguished here.

On this account, organisations constitute social structures (e.g. policies, procedures, rules) which allocate time and resources to specific areas of organisational concern (and thus not to others) subject to incentives and constraints. Effective policy implementation – and in particular its maintenance over time – is a process of shaping the sensemaking in organisations in order that the settlements produced by the *capabilities* and *willingness* of individuals and groups are routinised into these policies, procedures and rules of the organisation. Failure to embed innovation into the everyday sensemaking of the organisation (and therefore into the priorities to which it commits attention, time and money) will leave it very vulnerable to neglect and decline.

Let us return again to the most successful example of policy implementation described by Fitzgerald and Ferlie in their work, *Changing Childbirth* (DoH, 1993), to illustrate some of these rather abstract concepts. The reason that some form of 'linking bodies' were central to the sensemaking that underpinned local implementation – and it was very much adaptation rather than adoption – of this government initiative lies in the disparate nature of the stakeholders. To return to the framework outlined in Figure 2.1, the competing interests debating the appropriate local response to this new policy could be characterised as:

- the hierarchists, hospital nursing officers and middle managers, often in close association with obstetricians (whose collective ascendancy in the organisational

settlement had arguably led to the perceived problems which *Changing Childbirth* was intended to address)
- the enclavists, the local members of the Natural Childbirth Trust (NCT)
- the individualists, the local community midwives
- the isolates, the local general practitioners.

The change in *capability* that was being sought by *Changing Childbirth* and its local supporters related to the authority of community midwives, in collaboration with GPs, to take on (or, in the view of more radical midwives, take back) the responsibility for the care of pregnant women without the formal oversight of a consultant obstetrician. The *willingness* that was necessary related to the nursing and managerial hierarchy and the obstetricians concerned accepting this (re)assertion of professional autonomy on behalf of community midwives. At a second level, that relating to organisational meaning, the new sensemaking that was being pursued by the NCT and the midwives sought to redefine pregnancy and childbirth as natural events in the lives of women that should be under their control and that of their (female) supporters rather than a medical condition necessitating supervision by a (frequently male) obstetrician.

Presumably, it was in the 'linking bodies' observed by Ferlie and Fitzgerald that the new settlements – the policy implementation which they report – were negotiated. Or, in other localities, not; either because this implementation process was not adopted and/or the enclaves and individualists were not sufficiently strong to challenge the hold of the hierarchy (it is perhaps interesting to note that their research took place in north London and its contiguous shire counties where the influence of the NCT and community midwives might have been particularly strong). Almost ten years on, the House of Commons Health Committee (2003) reported disappointingly on progress; for instance, they stated that on two key ambitions of *Changing Childbirth* (DoH, 1993) there was still a long way to go before 30% of women have a midwife as their lead professional and 75% of women know the person who delivers them prior to being admitted for labour.

Of course, this may mean that progress towards these targets was more advanced in some parts of the country in 1998 than it was in 2003. As organisational settlements are constantly being renegotiated, it may be that the hierarchists have regrouped and it would be difficult to argue that the NCT has the profile now that it enjoyed ten years ago. Perhaps this latter point reflects a broader change in women's views on childbirth as a central issue for active feminism; certainly the health committee presents some striking statistics about the choices that women want to be able to make (i.e. that 50% want access to epidural pain relief). This potential change in the influence of parties to the organisational settlement – and in the aspirations of the people whose interests they claim to represent – sheds a new light on the vexed issue of sustainability of innovation. Inconsistency in sustaining innovative approaches in response to national policy is frequently presented as a failure of *capacity* and/or *willingness* by local managers and clinicians. On this account, such inconsistency may be further adaptation in the light of changing circumstances, whether or not national policy has caught up with such changes; yesterday's innovation may be tomorrow's old hat. This topic of sustainability –

which has become central to the concerns of the MA – will be revisited in both Chapter 12 and the Conclusion.

The nature of health policy and its implementation

Perhaps it is time to reflect more broadly on the nature of healthcare and health policy, and how this may influence implementation. There is a well-developed argument that the public services are especially challenging settings within which to pursue change, and its contours are summarised in Boxes 2.2 and 2.3.

Box 2.2: Factors inhibiting change in the public services in comparison with the private sector

- Absence of economic markets for outputs, reliance on governmental appropriations for financial resources
- Extensive oversight by government, courts, regulators and other agencies
- Greater political attention from an attentive public and considerable pressure from political groups to influence decisions
- Greater public scrutiny of administrative decisions where the public sees a 'right' to access to information and coverage of events not usual in the private sector
- Greater ambiguity of goals

Derived from Carnevale, 2003.

Box 2.3: Factors inhibiting public sector managers from leading change

- Public managers have less decision-making discretion because of a thicket of institutional constraints
- Public managers have weaker control over subordinates because of civil service tenure realities, a greater degree of unionisation in the government sector and alliances subordinates may establish with outside interests
- The red tape and other features of ideal-type bureaucracy inhibit action
- Public managers have less opportunity to develop and control reward and incentive structures than their private counterparts

Derived from Carnevale, 2003.

The factors identified in these two boxes may resonate with health and social care managers, but not all of them are as self-evident as they appear. For instance, providing healthcare might seem at first sight to be highly structured by policy. In fact, often the reverse is true. There is lack of clarity about what ministers really want because, as Carnevale (2003) recognises, politicians must appeal to many constituencies, and public and service users' expectations can change quickly and unpredictably. Indeed, with changing technologies – for example, fertility treatments and cosmetic surgery – the public's definition of health itself changes. It is often very difficult to know what organisations and their senior managers are supposed to implement, and interpreting the information and signals available requires going far beyond 'the evidence'. Field and Peck (2003) argue that just such ambiguity has undermined the commitment of local NHS managers to pursuing strategic relationships with the private sector. Finally, as acknowledged in MacMillan's famous phrase about 'events, dear boy, events' being the most difficult thing to deal with, the world is full of surprises.

Faced with such uncertainty, ambiguity and surprise, in practice healthcare managers cannot be endlessly inventive. They must fall back on a repertoire of more or less stock interpretations of the events and the problems that they face, of the intentions of other people (such as more senior policy makers and clients and colleagues in other organisations) and, indeed, of their own *capabilities*. This concept of repertoire is explored further in Chapter 3, and the broadening of managers' personal repertoires is presented as being one of the key contributions of OD, both in its theories and its interventions.

However, sensemaking is undertaken socially, not alone. Further, the sensemaking process must encompass stories about the past. Policy initiatives in health – no matter how innovative – come into a setting with a long and contested history. Perhaps more than in any other context, ambitions for change in healthcare have to coalesce into narratives of organisational traditions (March, 1994, pp.206–19). These narratives, in particular in the form of doctors, have long-standing advocates, for example the narrative of clinical autonomy being beyond the reach of political or managerial imposition. In these circumstances, current policy innovations may have to be distanced from those predecessors which organisational members remember as damaging or discredited. This is perhaps especially important in healthcare, as policy – in terms of both structure and process – seems to operate on a relatively short time frame for the recycling of ideas. Furthermore, in hospital consultants and GPs, the NHS possesses 'street-level bureaucrats' (Lipsky, 1980) with resources of personal intelligence, professional organisation and public prestige that are still unmatched by frontline staff in any other public service.

Conclusion

This chapter has explored the specific challenges that OD has to address when its interventions are deployed in support of policy implementation. It has suggested that OD is attempting to support healthcare organisations – and in particular their senior managers – in achieving a balance between the adoption of policy desired by policy makers and the adaptation of policy desired by stakeholders, and between all the basic institutional styles that shape organisational structure and culture. In doing so, it has argued that OD has to provide rituals for sensemaking, in order to enable the growth of *capabilities* and *willingness* among managers and professionals while at the same time ensuring that the emerging local interpretation is routinised into the social structures of the organisation.

Of course, these points do not tell us which theoretical interventions will be most appropriate in specific contexts. However, they do map out the issues that interventions will have to address if they are to support effectively the local implementation of national policy.

Acknowledgements

The authors would like to thank Suzanne Tyler for her insights into the development of maternity services over the past ten years.

References

6 P (2001) New Labour's project: 'modernisation' and the challenge for health management. Paper given at the Institute for Applied Health and Social Policy and Royal College of Psychiatrists joint conference *Managing mental health services in the modernised NHS in England*, 17 May, Macclesfield, Cheshire.

6 P, Leat D, Seltzer K and Stoker G (2002) *Towards Holistic Governance: the new reform agenda*. Palgrave, Basingstoke.

6 P and Peck E (forthcoming) *Beyond Delivery: policy implementation as organisational settlement*. Palgrave Macmillan, Basingstoke.

Barrett S and Fudge C (eds) (1981) *Policy and Action: essays on the implementation of public policy*. Methuen, London.

Blair T (1999) Speech to the British Venture Capitalists Association, 6 July, London.

Blair T (2002) Speech to Labour Party Spring Conference, 3 February, Cardiff.

Carnevale D (2003) *Organizational Development in the Public Sector*. Westview Press, Cambridge, MA.

Dawson S, Sutherland S, Dopson S and Miller R (1998) *The Relationship Between R and D and Clinical Practice in Primary and Secondary Care: cases in adult asthma and glue ear*. North Thames NHSE, R&D Committee, London.

Department of Health (DoH) (1993) *Changing Childbirth: (Part 1) Report of the Expert Maternity Group, and Part 2: Survey of good communication practice in maternity services*. HMSO, London.

Douglas M (1992) *Risk and Blame: essays in cultural theory*. Routledge, London.

Ferlie E, Fitzgerald L and Wood M (2000) Getting evidence into clinical practice: an organisational behaviour perspective. *Journal of Health Services Research and Policy*. 5(2): 96–102.

Field JE and Peck E (2003) Public-private partnerships in healthcare: the managers' perspective. *Health and Social Care in the Community*. 11(6): 494–501.

Fitzgerald L, Ferlie E, Wood M and Hawkins C (1999) Evidence into practice: an exploratory analysis of the interpretation of evidence. In: A Mark and S Dopson (eds) *Organisational Behaviour in Health Care: the research agenda.* Macmillan, Basingstoke.

Ham C and Hill M (1993) *The Policy Process in the Modern Capitalist State.* Harvester Wheatsheaf, Hemel Hempstead.

Hill M (1997) Implementation theory: yesterday's issue? *Policy and Politics.* **25**(4): 375– 85.

Hill M and Hupe P (2002) *Implementing Public Policy.* Sage, London.

Hjern B and Hull C (1982) Implementation research as empirical constitutionalism. In: B Hjern and C Hull (eds) *Implementation Beyond Hierarchy,* special issue of *European Journal of Political Research.*

Hood C (1998) *The Art of the State: culture, rhetoric and public management.* Oxford University Press, Oxford.

House of Commons Health Committee (2003) *Provision of Maternity Services.* TSO, London.

Lipsky M (1980) *Street Level Bureaucracy: dilemmas of the individual in public services.* Russell Sage Foundation, New York.

March J (1994) *A Primer on Decision Making.* Free Press, New York.

Milburn A (2002) Redefining the National Health Service. Speech to the New Health Network, 15 January, London.

Newman K, Pyne S, Leigh S, Rounce K and Cowling A (2000) Personal and organisational competencies requisite for the adoption and implementation of evidence-based health care. *Health Services Management Research.* **13**(2): 97–110.

Porter D and Hjern B (1981) Implementation structures: a new unit of administrative analysis. *Organisation Studies.* **2**: 211–27. Reprinted in abridged form in M Hill (ed.) (1993) *The Policy Process: a reader,* pp.248–65. Harvester Wheatsheaf, Hemel Hempstead.

Pressman J and Wildavsky A (1973) *Implementation: how great expectations in Washington are dashed in Oakland or, why it's amazing that federal programs work at all, this being the saga of the Economic Development Administration as told by two sympathetic observers who seek to build morals on a foundation of ruined hopes* (2e). University of California Press, Berkeley.

Sabatier P (1986) Top down and bottom up approaches to implementation research: a critical analysis and suggested synthesis. *Journal of Public Policy.* **6**: 21–48. Reprinted in abridged form in M Hill (ed.) (1993) *The Policy Process: a reader,* pp.266–93. Harvester Wheatsheaf, Hemel Hempstead.

Sackett D and Haines R (1995) On the need for evidence-based medicine. *Journal of Evidence-based Medicine.* **1**(1): 5.

Smith L and McClenahan J (2000) Evaluation of the Purchaser-led Implementation Programme. In: D Evans and A Haines (eds) *Implementing Evidence-based Changes in Healthcare*. Routledge, London.

Thompson M, Ellis R and Wildavsky A (1990) *Cultural Theory*. Westview Press, Boulder, CO.

Thompson M, Grendstad G and Selle P (1999) *Cultural Theory as Political Science*. Routledge, London.

CHAPTER 3

Organisational development and the 'repertoire' of healthcare leaders

Deborah Davidson and Edward Peck

Introduction

Over the past 20 years, first management and then leadership have become central to government-driven initiatives to deliver public service reform, initially with the introduction of the concepts of general management and internal markets in the 1980s (e.g. DoH, 1983, 1989) and subsequently with the 'modernisation' of the NHS in the 1990s (DoH, 1997a). In this chapter, we examine this growing policy focus on management and leadership and, in particular, the construction of leadership as a key tool for change, by mapping and analysing the leadership paradigms being used in health and social care. We then explore some of the outcomes of this construction – for instance how leadership for change is interpreted and enacted in the public service domain – by looking at specific examples in community care services. This exploration leads the chapter to consider how, if leadership is to be a key intervention for bringing about public service reform, current leadership theories need to be developed in light of public service experience. Next, we suggest how leadership might be developed to have more local organisational impact and identify expertise and experience in the theory and practice of organisational development as a central component of the 'repertoire' of leaders in healthcare. We conclude that there is an important link to be made between this 'repertoire' of OD frameworks and the notion of sensemaking that has emerged as an important theme in Chapters 1 and 2 of this volume.

Context

Up until the late 1990s, the word 'leadership' appeared infrequently in policy pronouncements whereas between 1998 and 2001 it featured in over 70 DoH documents and circulars. For most of the 1990s, government was still influenced by the hierarchical managerialism of the mid-1980s, and especially the introduction of general management following the Griffiths report (DoH, 1983), and effort was first focused on improving public service management (Harrison *et al.*, 1992) and then on attempts to introduce an internal market. However, during the 1990s, the influence of economic and social changes – and the related ambitions of a New Labour government – placed increased demands and new expectations on public services in the UK. These pressures for reform were identified by one influential central government department (Performance and Innovation Unit, 2001) as being:

- increased demand for public sector problem solving, particularly in relation to cross-cutting issues, such as social exclusion and the environment
- enhanced expectation of seamless, personalised services, so that even where many agencies are involved services meet the needs of the user rather than the organisational convenience of the providers
- assumptions of far greater porousness between sectors, as delivery of many public services now involves elements of the public, private and voluntary sectors
- greater expectations of continuous improvement, innovation and learning
- growing challenges of coping with a more complex political and institutional architecture which includes devolved administrations, regional bodies and the European Union.

These pressures were seen to 'create a need for highly effective leadership and a requirement for new leadership skills' (Performance and Innovation Unit, 2001, p.11), and suggested that the government shifted from focusing on management to accepting the premise that leadership was now the key intervention to deliver reform. Although the issues highlighted by the Performance and Innovation Unit (PIU) were equally applicable to healthcare, their primary focus was local government reform, and as such, it was felt that a specific focus was needed to address the modernisation of the NHS and thus the DoH established the Modernisation Agency (MA). The MA viewed leadership development as a core concept in bringing about service improvement and, in turn, established the NHS Leadership Centre to develop leaders at every level of the service. It set up a large number of leadership development activities initially targeted at organisational leadership – chief executives, chairs and board-level executives – with subsequent programmes targeted at both individual clinicians and teams of professionals. The importance of – and investment in – leadership development and research across the public services confirms that the government views effective leadership as a central intervention in the achievement of service reform.

However, leadership has meant many things to many people over the years. As a consequence, it is important to place these recent policy initiatives in the context of the development of leadership theory over the past 50 years. To do so, we need to understand how leadership theories and models have been influenced by changes in organisations' forms and functions as well the impact of global economic and social developments.

The evolution of leadership theory

Definitions of leadership have been reviewed several times since the mid-1950s (for example: Morris and Seeman, 1950; Shartle, 1956; Bass, 1960; Stogdill, 1975). More recently, Bass (1990) gives a summary of leadership which establishes the close connection between this concept and the account of OD (focusing on reflexivity and learning) provided in Chapter 1, arguing that:

> leadership is an interaction between two or more members of a group that often involves a structuring or restructuring of the situation, perceptions and expectations of the members. Leaders are agents of change – persons whose acts affect other people more than other people's affect them. Leadership occurs when one group member modifies the motivation or competencies of others in the group ... any member of the group can exhibit some amount of leadership and the members will vary in the extent to which they do so (p.19).

Since the early 1900s, there has been an evolution of leadership theories and models and in the following sections we take a brief look at some of the major approaches that have emerged.

Great man and trait theories

Much of the literature initially focused on the leadership of 'great men', where examples tended to be military or political leaders (e.g. Woods, 1913). These studies were influenced by Galton's earlier study (1869) of the hereditary background of great men. The organisational forms being led in these cases were very large systems requiring command and control and obedient followership to achieve goals in a uniform process. In the early 1920s, theorists continued to examine the idea of inherent traits and, in particular, which traits distinguished leaders from other people and the extent of those differences (for example: Bernard, 1926; Tead, 1929). However, as the context for leadership research changed from military and political leadership to other human systems (for instance athletics, education and the local community), the identified leadership traits that seemed to be required started to differ. As a result, pure trait theory fell out of favour. Stogdill's critique of trait theory (1948) concluded that both the person and the situation (*see* the next section) had to be included to explain the emergence of leadership; nonetheless many current policy initiatives (e.g. organisational franchising in healthcare where an apparently successful chief executive in one trust is given responsibility for another that is perceived to be failing) show that trait theory (and to some extent 'great man' theory) remains a significant factor in the thinking of politicians.

Personal-situational theories

In direct contrast to trait theorists, *situational* theorists suggested that leadership styles are adopted as a response to the demands of a given situation and, therefore, situational factors will determine who will emerge as a leader. Furthermore, these theorists suggested that great men were a product of the particular situation that required them to emerge at the time (e.g. Schneider, 1937). However, it was still recognised that there remained some personality factors that did make a difference and therefore trait theory could not be dismissed completely. This led to the evolution of *personal-situational* theories, which argue that in any given case some of the variance in what happens is due to the situation, some due to the person, and some due to the combination of both the person and situation (Bass, 1960).

Humanistic theories

Returning from World War II, some psychologists and social scientists brought back a renewed energy and determination to understand the impact of such events, including the ways in which they affected leadership behaviours. In addition, with the postwar creation of large nationalised industries – including the NHS – they saw opportunities to apply this knowledge to improving industrial relations between management and employees. This was partly predicated on the belief that it would be a serious omission not to consider how psychological processes – whether individual or system based – influence the way in which services are structured, organised and delivered. These writers began to acknowledge that leadership was also contingent on interpersonal relations (Likert, 1961), individual motivation (Maslow, 1954), the interdependence between individuals and the organisation (Blake and Moulton, 1965), and the fit between individual and organisational needs (McGregor, 1966).

Interaction and social learning theories

The 1950s and 1960s were an era of relative global stability and economic predictability in which postwar industrialisation developed, public services expanded, and key concepts of business and managerialism emerged (e.g. Drucker, 1954; *see* Chapter 9). This led to the development of three new approaches: *reinforced-change theory* (Bass, 1960), which focused on the observed effort of one member in a group to change the motivation, understanding or behaviour of other members; *path-goal theory* (House, 1971), which suggested that the successful leader shows the follower the rewards that are available and the paths (behaviours) through which the rewards may be obtained; and *contingency theory* (Fiedler, 1967), which focuses on task-oriented and relations-oriented leadership.

Transactional and transformational leadership

Nonetheless, personal-situational-based approaches remained the predominant paradigms until the worldwide economic down turn of the 1970s. Organisations found themselves in a new era of continuous change as they needed to downsize and/ or merge to survive global market forces. In addition, the introduction of new technologies, including IT, challenged them to operate across traditional boundaries and pursue new forms of organising, such as networks (*see* Agranoff and McGuire, 1998). These challenges persist to the present day. Whereas yesteryear's leaders operated, therefore, in a world of relative stability and predictability, today's leaders have to enable organisations to adapt to, and to be capable of working in, a world of constant challenge in a rapidly moving environment.

This has led to the development of new paradigms for leadership. Two are particularly important: *transactional* leadership (Kotter, 1990); and *transformational* leadership (Bass, 1985). The following quote, from a writer who is the predominant theorist of leadership in UK public services, explains the distinction between of the two modes of leadership:

> Leadership has experienced a major reinterpretation from representing an authority relationship (now referred to as management or Transactional Leadership which may or may not involve some form of pushing or coercion) to a process of influencing followers or staff for whom one is responsible, by inspiring them, or pulling them towards the vision of some future state ... this new model of leadership is referred to as Transformational Leadership because such individuals transform followers. Although this model of leadership is still hierarchical, it nevertheless recognises that leaders are seen as having to 'earn' their influence from staff and colleagues ... The new model of Transformational Leadership represents a paradigm shift, from a model of leadership in which followers are seen as relatively passive recipients of the leadership process, to one in which they are perceived as constituents of the leader (Alimo-Metcalfe, 1998, p.7).

Kotter (1990) provides a practical illustration of the task areas for which each mode might be appropriate, illustrated in Table 3.1.

Table 3.1 Transactional and transformational leadership modes

Transactional (management) produces degrees of predictability and order	Transformational (leadership) produces changes – often to dramatic degree
• Planning and budgeting • Organising and staffing • Controlling and problem solving	• Establishing direction • Aligning people • Motivating • Inspiring

Reproduced from Alimo-Metcalfe, 1998.

Most writers agree that organisations require both transactional (managerial) and transformational (leadership) approaches, and that staff should ideally be competent in both. Indeed, if artistic creation is 90% perspiration (for example, the understanding of your materials and preparing them appropriately for your task) and 10% inspiration (Harrison, 1979), then effective change in healthcare may be a similar mix of management (for example the putting in place of and following through on performance review procedures) and leadership.

However, the shift in focus from management in the 1980s to leadership in the 1990s seems to suggest that this balance may have been lost. This is evident in current health and social care policy by the lack of reference to 'management' in policy documents. This trend is also mirrored in recent leadership frameworks developed for public services in the UK, which have gained much currency in health and social care systems, and which are central to much of the recent documentation emanating from the Leadership Centre.

The major shared implication of these new leadership paradigms is that healthcare managers and clinicians need to lead complex adaptive systems that operate as a series of networks with multiple stakeholder interests while placing service users at the centre. Leadership is neither longer only viewed as 'leaderness' – the traits or characteristics of an individual – nor just as the context or situation within which skills and styles need to be exercised. Rather leadership is seen as a *process* that is dynamic, non-linear, and is created between leaders, followers and other diverse stakeholders within the context of organisations, systems and networks.

In these circumstances, how does government conceptualise leadership? In the next section, we look at the current leadership frameworks predominantly used in health and social care and analyse how they might achieve these aspirations. The subsequent section then looks at how government views the operationalisation of leadership through the policy implementation process and whether this is likely to deliver the intended change.

Conceptual frameworks on leadership used in public services in the UK

In this section, we examine some of the leadership frameworks currently used in public services. The PIU has developed its own approach to leadership which focuses on the individual and organisation, as in the *humanistic theories* discussed by Blake and Moulton (1965). The NHS Leadership Centre has commissioned a Leadership Qualities Framework (DoH, 2001), which seems to have as its underlying concepts *path-goal theory* (House, 1971) and *contextual leadership*. The MA draws heavily on the *transformational leadership* model articulated by Alimo-Metcalfe (1998) and the *emotional intelligence* model described by Goleman (1998).

The NHS Leadership Qualities Framework (DoH, 2001) was initially aimed at NHS chief executives but is being adapted to cover other roles. It consists of three dimensions and 15 scales. It is shown in Table 3.2.

The Transformational Leadership Questionnaire (TLQ), a 360° feedback instrument, was published following one of the most comprehensive investigations into leadership across the public and private sectors in the UK (Alimo-Metcalfe, 1998). The framework is based on a model of leadership that includes three dimensions with 14 scales, and is shown in Table 3.3.

Table 3.2 The NHS Leadership Qualities Framework

Setting direction	Personal qualities	Delivering the service
• Seizing the future • Intellectual flexibility • Broad scanning • Political astuteness • Drive for results	• Self-belief • Self-awareness • Self-management • Drive for improvement • Personal integrity	• Leading change through people • Holding to account • Empowering others • Effective and strategic influencing • Collaborative working

Reproduced from the DoH, 2001.

Table 3.3 Transformational Leadership Questionnaire (TLQ)

Leading and developing others	Personal qualities	Leading the organisation
• Showing genuine concern • Enabling • Being accessible • Encouraging change	• Being honest and consistent • Acting with integrity • Being decisive • Inspiring others • Resolving complex problems	• Networking and achieving • Focusing effort • Building shared vision • Supporting a developmental culture • Facilitating change sensitively

Reproduced from Alimo-Metcalfe, 1998.

A significant difference between the TLQ and the NHS Leadership Qualities Framework is their divergent conceptual bases. The TLQ was developed using a repertory grid format deployed to survey people working in the field of health and social care, with attention paid to previous and current paradigms of leadership theory (although the TLQ has since been tested in the private sector and the leadership competencies required were found to be comparable). The NHS Leadership Qualities Framework has its origins in a comparison of existing frameworks in the health sectors in the UK and USA and from existing models in business, commerce and industry. More specifically, policy implementation approaches in public services feature as a central influence on its design. In the language of Chapter 2, the TLQ could be seen as 'bottom up' and the Leadership Qualities Framework as 'top down'.

The third framework is that described by Goleman (1998), which evolved from the findings of two major surveys of parents and teachers about the emotional competencies of children (Achenbach and Howell, 1989). In addition, a survey of American employers revealed more than 50% of their workforces lacked motivation to keep learning and improving in the job (Harris Education Research Council, 1991).

Goleman's framework includes two dimensions, five competency areas and 25 dimensions. The framework is shown below in Table 3.4.

Table 3.4 Emotional competence framework

Personal competence		Social competence	
Self-awareness	• Emotional awareness • Accurate self-assessment • Self-confidence	Empathy	• Understanding others • Developing others • Service orientation • Leveraging diversity • Political awareness
Self-regulation	• Self-control • Trustworthiness • Conscientiousness • Adaptability • Innovation	Social skills	• Influence • Communication • Conflict management • Leadership • Change catalyst • Building bonds • Collaboration and cooperation • Team capabilities
Motivation	• Achievement drive • Commitment • Initiative • Optimism		

Adapted from Goleman, 1998.

A fourth framework, which was not explicitly developed in the PIU report on strengthening leadership in the public sector (Performance and Innovation Unit, 2001), but has been constructed here for the purposes of comparison, consists of eight personal characteristics and seven organisational actions. This is presented in Table 3.5.

Surprisingly, none of these four leadership frameworks addresses a key feature of policy for health and social care services, that is the need to focus on achieving outcomes for service users and responding to their experiences. This policy imperative would suggest an additional demand on public services which should be reflected in the frameworks, that is to 'improve the responsiveness of services by giving people at a local level the power to make decisions about the range of services that are needed' (DoH, 1998, p.6).

In addition, there is a strong contrast between the three frameworks developed exclusively for the NHS and the more generic PIU public service approach. None of the

Table 3.5   Public sector leadership

Personal characteristics	Organisational actions
• Think carefully about roles • Give responsibility to others • Communicate values, vision and priorities • Motivate and bring the best out of others • Be willing to learn • Be tough and not shy from conflict • Be clearly focused on end goals • Convince staff that short-term difficult transitions will lead to improvements in the long run	• Recognise the complexity of modern organisations • Focus on defining and communicating visions and strategy • Ability to bring the best and most out of staff • Keeping sight of the service that is provided to the public • See the importance of making wider connections • Ability to work well with other organisations and achieve common goals • Partnership, collaboration and cooperativeness with other organisations

Developed by the authors from Performance and Innovation Unit, 2001.

former frameworks focuses on partnership working, while the latter emphasises this aspect. Given the multi-agency environment in which contemporary health and social care agencies operate, we also therefore need to consider the work of Greig and Poxton (2001), who suggest that eight new competencies are required for leading in partnerships. These are shown below in Table 3.6. These dimensions illustrate a dynamic relationship between the individual capabilities a leader needs to have and the organisational actions a leader needs to take. In particular, they suggest a re-orientation in the ways in which a person takes up their leadership role towards an emphasis on keeping in touch with the core purpose of the organisation and the services.

Taken together, these frameworks constitute a major, not to say a rather intimidating, set of characteristics for leaders in healthcare; it is scarcely surprising that many managers and clinicians feel a need to book themselves onto leadership development programmes! Nonetheless, they demonstrate the amount of thought

Table 3.6   Leading in partnerships

Individual capabilities	Organisational actions
• Negotiation, not direction • Influence, not control • Adaptability • Diplomacy • Networking	• User responsiveness • Focus on outcomes • Multiple accountabilities

Reproduced from Greig and Poxton, 2001.

(and money) that has gone into establishing leadership as a – if not the – central tool for the local delivery of national policy in health and social care. Furthermore, they identify that skills in organisational development and change are now seen as crucial in the repertoire of effective leaders. For instance:

- leading change through people (Table 3.2)
- supporting a developmental culture (Table 3.3)
- adaptability (Table 3.4)
- recognising the complexity of modern organisations (Table 3.5)
- influence (not control) (Table 3.6).

This idea of leadership 'repertoire' is developed further below. First, however, given that leadership is seen by government as such a key intervention for bringing about public service reform, we will briefly examine how leadership is interpreted and enacted locally in the policy implementation process by examining case studies within the field of community care.

The interpretation and enactment of leadership in local policy implementation

In recent policy documents, especially in National Service Frameworks (NSFs), we can see that the responsibility for local delivery of national policy is placed on individuals through the appointment of specific roles such as senior managers or clinicians, local champions or project managers, who are designated to lead projects and processes of change. Typically, these individuals are located within the context of collective inter-agency fora (such as partnership boards, joint committees, stakeholder groups and collaboratives) that reflect the wider partnerships required for implementation. This is illustrated in Table 3.7.

Table 3.7 Arrangements for leadership of delivery of policy in three client groups

Services	Individual roles	Collective bodies
Mental health	LIT lead	Local implementation teams
Learning disability	Lead officer	Partnership boards
Older people	LIT lead	Local implementation teams

Evidence from a recent survey (Davidson *et al.*, 2003) in the mental health field on the establishment of policy implementation leaders (LIT leads) and inter-agency partnership fora (local implementation teams, LITs) for implementation of the National Service Framework for Mental Health (DoH, 1999) suggests that there are difficulties in implementing both the individual and inter-agency leadership models promoted by policy makers. These difficulties can be summarised in seven key areas.

Establishing and embedding local leadership

The evidence of the survey suggested that little clarity about the role was provided to support people in undertaking such significant leadership duties and that the time set aside for carrying out the leadership task was often very limited and frequently combined with other substantial posts. The vast majority of individuals were not provided with a role description and/or clear objectives and consequently their interpretation of the role produced a very diverse picture spanning both operational and strategic tasks. At the same time, continuous organisational change meant that there was little continuity, with many LIT leads reporting more than three substantive job changes in five years and, therefore, occupying the implementation leadership role for only short periods of time.

Leadership capabilities and management actions

The survey examined respondents' perceptions of their roles and their performance in those roles in terms of leadership capabilities and management actions. Respondents were asked to rank a series of seven leadership capabilities in terms of importance to their LIT role. The seven leadership capabilities were:

- initiating ongoing adaptation and change
- being courageous, taking risks, tackling interpersonal tensions
- enabling others to act (inspiring; motivating; coaching; giving authority)
- engaging with people, responding to problems, and making decisions
- utilising insight into behaviour (self and others)
- being principled personally and professionally
- exerting influence and exercising authority (with host organisation and other organisations).

As with the leadership capabilities, respondents were asked to rank seven management actions in terms of their importance for their role. They were then asked to rate the extent to which they had executed each action. The management actions examined were:

- service redesign
- financial planning
- formulating and assigning tasks
- coordinating
- problem solving
- performance management of NSF targets
- evaluating outcomes.

The findings showed that greater importance was given to the more facilitative management processes than to those that could be seen as requiring authority, managing tensions and exercising political skills. Not dissimilarly, influencing, persuading and managing differing agendas were ranked as the least important processes. This suggested that insufficient importance was attributed to some of the more transformational leadership skills, such as exercising authority, challenging and influencing, and engaging with differing agendas (Alimo-Metcalfe and Alban-Metcalfe, 2003). The leadership capability 'utilising insight into behaviour (self and others)' was ranked as the least important capability and was given a low rating for the extent to which respondents had demonstrated the capability. This seems to contrast significantly with the aspects the MA might perceive as important, given their promotion of the emotional competence framework.

Implementing policy

Policy implementation mostly related to the development or redesign of individual services rather than to a more strategic overview or whole-systems redesign. Furthermore, a substantial number of respondents listed tasks relating to the processes that underpin policy, such as the development of planning and commissioning structures, the production of a broad financial plan, a workforce plan or a plan for specific service design. It is also interesting that a substantial number of respondents mentioned tasks relating to 'meeting NSF reporting requirements' in this context. In addition, the most frequently cited obstacle was a lack of resources for developing services and problems that could be seen as reflecting inter-agency or partnership difficulties. A substantial proportion indicated that a major obstacle in implementing the NSF was the emphasis placed on meeting the requirements of the central monitoring of the NSF and having to demonstrate the attainment of targets that were centrally determined, rather than focusing on local outcomes.

Establishing effective inter-agency partnership fora

Respondents were asked to rank seven functions of the LIT according to the degree of importance given to each function by their LIT. They were then asked to rate the extent to which their LIT had made progress in relation to each function. The functions examined were:

- service mapping, planning and redesign
- financial resource planning and allocation
- workforce planning and development
- partnership building and working
- knowledge management and information systems development
- utilising clinician and practitioner experience in service development
- achieving better outcomes for service users.

They were also asked to rank six LIT processes according to the degree of importance accorded each process by the LIT. The processes examined were:

- cooperating with each other (focus on the strategic/common task)
- effective communication and information-giving processes
- inclusiveness of members (and others as needed)
- influencing and persuading (each other/member organisations)
- managing rivalries and differing agendas
- openness and transparency (in decision making).

Although respondents ranked 'cooperating with each other' and 'openness and transparency' as the most important LIT processes, the survey results also indicated that 'partnership working issues' were seen as a major obstacle to progress. In this context it was interesting to note that 'influencing and persuading' and 'managing rivalries and differing agendas' were the two processes to which the least importance was attributed. This may have suggested that the LIT leaders were reluctant to deal directly with more challenging and dynamic issues and that the very positive relationships reported between the LITs and their member organisations were founded on the avoidance of tensions which ultimately need to be addressed for the LITs to function effectively. Another indication of LIT functioning perhaps being less straightforward than reported stemmed from the relatively low rating accorded the ability of LIT members to commit resources to LIT activities. This supported the view that the LIT leaders were unable to address difficult issues that required them to engage in political behaviour.

Power and authority

Recent guidance from the National Institute for Mental Health in England (NIMHE, 2003) stated that a LIT should 'usually be chaired by a senior manager of a statutory service ... for example, a PCT Chief Executive or Director of Social Services, and will usually be a member of the Local Strategic Partnership Board where one exists' (p.18). However, findings indicated that only 19% of LIT chairs were either an NHS chief executive or a director of social services, suggesting that the level of seniority and political influence in the local system may not be at the level required. In addition, they showed that LIT leads appeared to be drawn principally from the ranks of middle managers, suggesting that they may not have the senior status and political influence required for this role.

Accountability

There was considerable variation in the responses in relation to accountability, with little clarity or consensus. This was in stark contrast with the expectation of NIMHE (2003) that LITs should be clear about their accountability in terms of governance arrangements, limits to authority and links with broader planning processes.

User outcomes

Two rather surprising, and apparently contradictory, findings emerged in relation to outcomes for service users. Although respondents attached great importance to 'achieving better outcomes for service users', there was evidence to suggest that they were not necessarily clear how this might be achieved given the low ranking accorded evaluating outcomes as a management action. The obvious question was how LITs could know whether they were achieving better outcomes for service users unless outcomes were evaluated. Perhaps the importance attached to outcomes for users again reflected a 'socially acceptable' response. Alternatively, the vision may have been genuine but evaluation of its achievement was precluded by the evident focus on national targets and performance management requirements.

Discussion

While leadership is viewed as a key intervention for service improvement, the findings summarised above seem to suggest that there are a number of key structural, capacity and capability difficulties in leadership delivering the changes being promoted by policy makers. Leadership, rather than being the solution to the challenges of service reform, seems almost to have become a local problem that needs reconsideration both in its formulation and in its relation to local delivery mechanisms. It appears that, in order to enable managers and clinicians to lead complex adaptive systems that operate as a series of networks with multiple stakeholder interests while placing service users at the centre, attention needs to be focused on strengthening system capacity and individual capability to engage with and lead processes of development. In other words, if they are to represent an effective OD intervention, then local leaders need much more familiarity with the theory and practice of OD.

Linking this discussion back to Chapter 1, and expressed in organisational development terms, the survey suggests that LITs are functioning within a 'single-loop' learning process; they are able to adapt and make adjustments to maintain performance only within the scope of their existing practices and norms of behaviour, precluding any questioning or amending of ineffective functioning. If the more difficult issues facing the LITs are to be addressed, a double-loop learning process will be required to both maintain and improve performance (Argyris, 1999).This would involve reconstructing basic aspects of the LITs' functioning. To do this, LIT leaders will be required to promote shifts in LIT members by helping them to achieve some degree of insight and develop motivation to change (Schein, 1992). In addition, if we accept that it is individuals – acting as agents of organisations – who produce the behaviour that leads to learning and therefore to change (Argyris, 1999), then a dynamic relationship and exchange has to take place between LIT leaders and members with active followership as well as active leadership required (Obholzer and Roberts, 1994).

If LITs need to function within a double-loop learning process predicated on a dynamic relationship between LIT members, leaders and followers, and new leadership competencies are required to work in partnership in this environment, then responses to the survey indicate that the culture of working in mental health services has to change. In particular, the low rankings accorded 'being courageous, taking risks, tackling interpersonal tensions', 'utilising insight into behaviour (self and others)', 'influencing and persuading', and 'managing rivalries and differing agendas' are a strong indication that current leadership approaches are unlikely to represent the effective OD intervention that the government envisages.

Implications for the role of OD in the growth of leadership theory and practice

How then do current leadership theories and models need to be developed in light of this public service experience? The organisational challenges in health and social care policy implementation processes point to the notion of 'repertoire', the idea that the characteristic of a good leader is her or his ability to tune their responses to the context in which they are operating in order to deliver an effective outcome.

At first sight, this notion of 'repertoire' might seem like a resurrection of a situational approach to leadership, suggesting that different situations demand different kinds of leadership that require the individual to adapt his or her style to those different situations. While this model does relate closely to some of our thinking, the concept of 'repertoire' leadership has a broader range of dimensions which can be summarised under three headings:

- **intellectual** – the theories and concepts available to the person to inform their personal and organisational responses
- **psychological** – the understandings that the person has of her or his behaviours and relationships with others, and the extent of her or his insight into and use of them
- **performative** – the range of observations and behaviours the person can call upon to enact leadership in the system.

In addition to the three dimensions of repertoire, we also suggest there are three related 'mechanisms' through which repertoire can be exercised:

- use of **multiple aspects of the self** which are brought to the fore by different demands and situations (and where the challenge of leadership is to select the aspect of self that will have the most impact) in contrast to the reliance on the so-called essential self (the 'I' of 'I think therefore I am')
- use of **emotional intelligence**, of being sensitive to the needs and responses of oneself and others as a way of linking performance to integrity and credibility
- use of the **physical enactment** of the performance, that is, body language, posture, speech, assessments of impact on an audience, etc.

Argyris C (1999) *On Organisational Learning* (2e). Blackwell Publishing, Oxford.

Bass B (1960) *Leadership, Psychology, and Organizational Behaviour*. Harper, New York.

Bass B (1985) *Leadership and Performance Beyond Expectations*. The Free Press, New York.

Bass B (1990) *Bass and Stogdill's Handbook of Leadership Theory, Research and Managerial Applications* (3e). The Free Press, New York.

Bernard L (1926) *An Introduction to Social Psychology*. Holt, New York.

Blake R and Moulton J (1965) A 9,9 approach for increasing organizational productivity. In: M Sherif (ed.) *Intergroup Relations and Leadership*. Wiley, New York.

Davidson D, Field J and Thomas K (2003) *Supporting Leadership and Organisational Development in Mental Health Local Implementation Teams*. HSMC (University of Birmingham), Birmingham.

Department of Health (1989) *Working for Patients*. HMSO, London,

Department of Health (1997a) *The New NHS: modern, dependable*. The Stationery Office, London.

Department of Health (1997b) *Patient and Public Involvement in the New NHS*. The Stationery Office, London.

Department of Health (1998) *A First Class Service*. The Stationery Office, London.

Department of Health (1999) *National Service Framework for Mental Health*. The Stationery Office, London.

Department of Health (2001) *NHS Leadership Qualities Framework*. http://www.nhsleadershipqualities.nhs.uk/ (accessed 28 April 2004).

Department of Health and Social Security (1983) *NHS Management Inquiry*. HMSO, London.

Drucker P (1954) *The Practice of Management*. Harper and Row, New York.

Fiedler F (1967) *A Theory of Leadership Effectiveness*. McGraw-Hill, New York.

Galton F (1869) *Hereditary Genius*. Appleton, New York.

Goleman D (1998) *Working with Emotional Intelligence*. Bloomsbury Publishing, London.

Greig R and Poxton R (2001) From joint commissioning to partnership working – will the new policy framework make a difference? *Managing Community Care*. 9(4): 32–8.

Harris Education Research Council (1991) *An Assessment of American Education*. Harris Educational Research Center, New York City.

Harrison A (1979) *Making and Thinking*. Wheatsheaf, Brighton.

Harrison A, Hunter D, Marnoch G and Pollitt C (1992) *Just Managing: power and culture in the NHS*. Macmillan, Basingstoke.

House R (1971) A path-goal theory of leader effectiveness. *Administrative Science Quarterly.* **16**: 321–38.

Kotter J (1990) *A Force for Change: how leadership differs from management.* Free Press, London.

Likert R (1961) An emerging theory of organizations, leadership and management. In: L Petrullo and E Bass (eds) *Leadership and Interpersonal Behaviour.* Holt, Rinehart & Winston, New York.

Maslow A (1954) *Motivation and Personality.* Harper, New York.

McGregor D (1966) *Leadership and Motivation.* MIT Press, Cambridge, MA.

Morris R and Seeman M (1950) The problem of leadership: an interdisciplinary approach. *American Journal of Sociology.* **56**: 149–55.

National Institute for Mental Health in England (NIMHE) (2003) *The Capable LIT.* http://www.nimhenorthwest.org.uk/news/CapableLITJuly2003.pdf (accessed 28 April 2004).

Obholzer A and Roberts V (eds) (1994) *The Unconscious at Work: individual and organisational stress in the human services.* Routledge, London.

Performance and Innovation Unit (2001) *Strengthening Leadership in the Public Sector.* The Cabinet Office, London.

Schein E (1987) *Process Consultation, Vol II: Lessons for managers and consultants.* Addison-Wesley Publishing Company, Wokingham.

Schein E (1992) *Organizational Culture and Leadership.* Jossey-Bass, San Francisco.

Schneider J (1937) The cultural situation as a condition for the achievement of fame. *American Sociology Review.* **2**: 480–91.

Shartle C (1956) *Executive Performance and Leadership.* Prentice-Hall, Englewood Cliffs, NJ.

Stogdill R (1948) Personal factors associated with leadership: a survey of the literature. *Journal of Psychology.* **25**: 35–71.

Stogdill R (1975) *The Evolution of Leadership Theory.* Proceedings, New Orleans Academy of Management, pp.4–6.

Tead O (1929) *Human Nature and Management.* McGraw-Hill, New York.

Weick K (1995) *Sensemaking in Organisations.* Sage, London.

Woods F (1913) *The Influence of Monarchs.* Macmillan, New York.

CHAPTER 4

The organisational development cycle: putting the approaches into a process

Deborah Davidson

Introduction

Chapter 1 introduced organisational development (OD), explored a variety of definitions and suggested that for the purposes of this book it would be understood as representing activities designed and delivered to enhance reflexivity and learning in an organisation. The chapter also noted that approaches to undertaking OD in healthcare are diverse, which clearly is a strength, but also sometimes rather ad hoc, which just as clearly is not. Effective OD is rooted in systematic thinking about a process within which its interventions can take place. Although healthcare agencies frequently deploy more or less elaborate project management techniques to oversee the achievement of specific projects (arguably more focused on delivering 'changed organisations' than 'changing organisations'), especially where they are required to deliver against targets to very tight deadlines, they are not necessarily as familiar with the more iterative and sophisticated approaches to process planning that OD demands. Iles and Sutherland (2001) point out that traditional project management is useful in '... situations in which there is a defined beginning and end, and in which a discrete and identifiable set of sub-tasks must be completed' (p.70); as the chapters in Part 2 of this book will demonstrate, most OD does not have these clearly defined boundaries.

However, the creation and sustenance of profound (transformational) or even significant routine (transactional) change cannot be achieved through project management alone. Richer processes are required – within which project management is only one element – to enable the identification and the refinement of the interventions that are necessary to renegotiate, for instance, organisational settlements between disparate interests (see Chapter 2). This chapter suggests a process – the OD cycle – within which such identification and refinement can take place. It argues that it is helpful to have a 'map' that can help guide us through a process of change while neither specifying the exact interventions that should be used nor suggesting that the process will unfold in exactly the way that it is envisaged at the beginning. Furthermore, underlying the processes discussed in this chapter is a belief in a concept fundamental to any effective OD approach; that of engaging organisational stakeholders' active participation so as to build ownership of and support for the innovations in practice that emerge.

In laying out this OD cycle, I will look at the overall organisational development process in order both to set out what a commissioner of OD might expect from an OD practitioner and to provide some food for thought about the potential tasks for that commissioner (or the person leading the process from within the organisation) as the work progresses (and thus the capabilities and competencies that they may need to fulfil them). As I describe the OD cycle, the chapter will also provide some suggestions about the types of technique that could be included at each of the first four stages. I start by returning to the roots of organisational development already discussed in more depth in Chapter 1, this time focusing on the ideas that led to the establishment of the OD cycle.

The origins of the organisational development (OD) cycle

In going back to the origins of OD, the most important concept for this chapter is that of action research, which can be traced back to Lewin (1946, 1948). Lewin's thinking is central to much of our knowledge of social change, particularly in groups, and '... has had a more pervasive impact on organisational development, both direct and indirect, than any other person's' (Burke, 1994, p.41). His 'three steps' model (Lewin, 1946, 1951, 1958) – Unfreezing, Movement and Refreezing – was one of the earliest attempts to map out a process of change. This construct was later expanded by Lippitt *et al.* (1958) to encompass five phases in order to illustrate that the completion of one phase and the starting of another would frequently not be consecutive but concurrent. Their elaboration of Lewin's model was mostly in the phase that focused on 'working toward change' – Lewin's 'Movement' – which for them had three subphases.

1 *Clarification*: collecting and analysing data to provide understanding of the organisation and of the issues that need to be addressed.
2 *Examination*: establishing the focus for change (intentions) and path (actions) to achieve this, and determining the nature of support and motivation within the organisation to start this process.
3 *Transformation*: of intentions into actions through implementation.

Further adaptations of the action research approach to adapt it specifically for organisational development purposes were undertaken by French (1969), Kolb and Frohman (1970), Frohman *et al.* (1976), Schein (1980), and Bushe and Shani (1991) (for a review of these, *see* Burke, 1994). Drawing from each of these theoretical and practical developments, a generic model for planned change can be derived. For the purposes of this chapter, I will use Kolb and Frohman's (1970) term the 'OD cycle' to describe this generic model and it is presented in Figure 4.1.

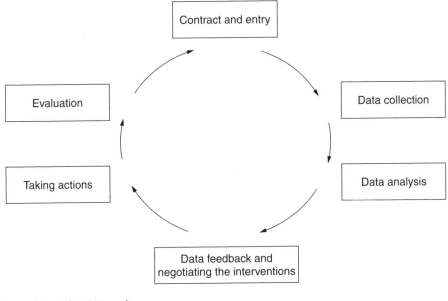

Figure 4.1   The OD cycle.

Figure 4.1 suggests there are six phases to the OD cycle:

- entry and contracting
- data collection
- data analysis
- data feedback and negotiating intervention(s)
- implementing interventions
- evaluation.

While these phases are depicted as discrete stages, and the cycle as a whole process appears linear, experience of using it with complex and emergent processes of change prove that it is as applicable in those situations as it is with more simple and predictable processes of change. In use, the relationship between the stages has to involve overlap, (re)iteration and the flexibility to respond to surprises. I will now describe each of the first four phases and, for each, its main function, the type of activities that might be adopted during that phase, and the processes and dynamics the change agent needs to consider.

The change agent

First, however, it is important to briefly address the role of the 'change agent'. In some organisations, the performance management or human resource (HR) role incorporates OD, whereas in others it is added on to the responsibilities of a board-level director. Alternatively, a relatively junior member of staff – whether clinician or manager – is expected to lead service 'modernisation' (*see* Chapter 3 for discussion of the experience of these staff in the mental health context). Whatever the corporate arrangements, most managers and many clinicians now combine responsibilities for achieving specific changes with their regular duties, and there is an increased involvement of all levels of staff in the process of change. In these circumstances, the role of change agent is not necessarily a clearly defined or established role and it follows that more people and teams need to have the skills and knowledge required to engage with, and bring about, change. As a consequence, therefore, the terminology and concepts that were originally developed from the perspective of an 'external OD consultant' are now just as relevant to an 'internal' manager or clinician identified as responsible for leading change, whether or not the process adopted involves external interventions. Box 4.1 provides one set of competencies that have been prescribed for change agents.

Box 4.1: Fifteen competencies of change agents

Goals

1 Sensitivity to changes in key personnel, perceptions, and contexts and the way these impact on goals for change.
2 Clarity in goal setting, defining the achievable.
3 Flexibility in responding to changes outside the project manager's control, possibly requiring major shifts in goals and management style.

Roles

4 Team-building abilities, to bring together key stakeholders and establish effective working groups and to clearly define/delegate respective responsibilities.
5 Networking skills in establishing and maintaining contacts.
6 Tolerance of ambiguity, being able to function comfortably, patiently and effectively in an uncertain environment.

Communication

7 Communication skills to transmit effectively the need for changes in project goals and individual tasks.
8 Interpersonal skills, including listening, collecting information, identifying others' concerns, managing meetings.
9 Personal enthusiasm in expressing plans and ideas.
10 Stimulating motivation and commitment in others.

Negotiation

11 Selling plans and ideas to others by creating a desirable and challenging vision of the future.
12 Negotiating with key players for contributions of resources, changes in procedures, resolutions of conflicts.

Managing up

13 Political awareness, identifying potential coalitions, balancing conflicting goals and perceptions.
14 Influencing skills, gaining commitment from potential sceptics.
15 Helicopter perspectives, standing back and taking a broad view of priorities.

Edited from Buchanan and Boddy, 1992.

The six phases

Entry and contracting

This phase can be summarised as:

- identifying the stakeholders
- determining the conditions of the working relationship
- setting mutual expectations
- establishing ground rules for behaviour
- ensuring acceptance by all involved (Weisbord, 1984).

Whether acting as internal or external change agent, the first task for the leader of change process is to identify the stakeholders that need to be involved. This is important for two reasons. First, as no department, service or organisation is a closed system that operates in isolation from other departments, services or organisations, it is crucial to be confident that change in one part of the system is sensitive to and influenced by other parts of that system. The theoretical concept behind this idea is open-systems theory (von Bertalanffy, 1950), which was used by Miller and Rice (1967) to conceptualise organisations as living systems with a permeable boundary across which there are regulated transactions with their environment. Vega Roberts and Jane Keep describe open systems theory in more detail in Chapters 6 and 7. Therefore, processes of change need to take account of the 'whole system' and to ensure that people who work within the interconnected parts have their views incorporated into the subsequent collection and analysis phases. Getting some of these basics wrong at the beginning often means that the overall interventions end incompletely or unsatisfactorily.

Second, it is also important to determine the nature and context of the working relationships within which interventions will be designed and delivered. Whether the change agent is an OD practitioner, frontline clinician, HR manager or board-level director, he or she will need to ascertain a number of factors before starting to collect and analyse data. These factors might include: clarifying and negotiating the expected outcomes; the extent of resources (financial and human) available; and the timescales within which change needs to occur. More basically, it is important to establish the identity of the client for the OD process (*see* Figure 4.2), and this may be influenced by the nature of the interventions envisaged, and complicated by this process involving various forms of intervention with different individuals or parts of the system taking place simultaneously (for example, for mentoring, the client is the individual manager being mentored; for recommendations about structural recon-figuration, the client may be the organisational board).

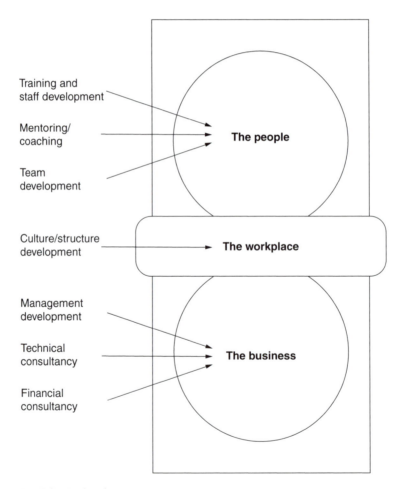

Figure 4.2 Who is the client?

This question about the identity of the client is not as straightforward as it may first appear. Who defines the initial parameters of the brief? Who chooses the change agent? Who negotiates the contract and who pays the bill? Whose interests does the proposed project serve? Furthermore, the client may change over time (as the original structural change is supported, for example by subsequent mentoring of new postholders).

In my experience, the agreement between the change agent and client should be at least as focused on establishing the nature of relationship (e.g. mutual expectations) as on the deliverables. Nonetheless, both the personal and contractual aspects should enable clarity to emerge about a number of aspects:

- shared understanding of the issue/problem
- expectations of mutual responsibilities in tackling the problem
- mutual commitments of resources, e.g. time, money, people
- ground rules for relating to one another
- the first steps
- when and how the review will occur.

However, although a formal outline of design, process and outcomes may be required before any OD contract is awarded, it is important to retain some flexibility about all of these components as the programme unfolds.

Data collection

This phase includes mapping the organisational structures, processes and relationships within the organisational system and within the external world. In many respects, the techniques for collecting data are similar to, and draw on, methodologies from evaluative research (*see* Gill and Johnson, 1991, Easterby-Smith *et al.*, 1991 for accessible discussions of the ones summarised below). Areas for data collection might include the following.

- **Analysis of organisational documentation:** information gathered, for instance from annual reports, public leaflets and minutes of management meetings.
- **Audit data:** information derived from routine data sources within the organisation (for example on staff turnover or complaints by department) or generated by activities in support of the OD project, using ideas such as process mapping, examined in Chapter 5, or cultural assessment, introduced in Chapter 10.
- **Survey responses:** information drawn from the annual staff survey, responses to specific initiatives looking at areas deemed problematic or undertaken in support of the OD project.
- **Focus groups:** more or less structured sessions with staff to establish and explore their perspectives, perhaps using some of appreciative inquiry approaches described in Chapter 11 or the storytelling techniques discussed in Chapter 12.
- **Group event:** again, more (stakeholder conference) or less (open-space event), structured sessions which bring together large numbers of staff and/or stakeholders to examine pre-set questions (stakeholder conference) or broader themes (open space event).

- **Interviews:** structured or semi-structured interviews with organisational members, potentially involving key personnel across different layers and disciplines in the organisation and also people from other stakeholder organisations in the local system, including service users and carers.
- **Observation of meetings:** watching key organisation events, for example board meetings.

There are a number of issues for both the commissioner and change agent to bear in mind during data collection.

- There is often an assumption that organisations know what their problems are and what needs to be done (this is not entirely false, but ...).
- The presenting problem is not always where the organisation most pressingly requires intervention and support.
- The collection of data is itself an intervention (e.g. convening a focus group of staff to discuss the effectiveness of the senior management team will both draw their attention to the issue and start to develop their shared ideas about what could be different).
- The way that data are collected both shapes and is shaped by the framework for analysis that it is proposed to use and will be influenced by the theoretical orientation of the collector (as Chapter 3 argues, 'believing is seeing').

Data analysis

Data analysis requires a framework within which the change agent can make sense (both for self and others) of the data. This framework will serve to select and to highlight certain aspects of the data (in particular those where the change agent judges that interventions are both desirable and possible) at the expense of others. Furthermore, the framework may be one that the change agent brings to the work (that is it may be overtly theory-based) or alternatively may appear to arise from their consideration of the data itself (that is it may be covertly theory-based). In most cases, it will be some combination of the two. One example of the former, derived from Rice (1963), has the following components.

- **Task:** using the concept of primary task, identifying those activities that the organisation is required to carry out for its development and survival.
- **Formal structures:** examining the roles, tasks, boundaries, authorities and accountabilities of individuals and groups.
- **Management processes:** establishing key processes, including strategic planning, budgetary control, communication and recording of information, delegation and decision making.
- **Personnel processes:** exploring levels of recruitment and retention, terms of employment, terms of remuneration, etc.
- **Culture and relationships:** assessing consensus or hierarchical processes, individuality or joint working, dependence or autonomy, etc.

- **Informal structures:** reflecting on social contact within and outside of the department, groupings or cliques, etc.

Clearly, the wider the repertoire of the change agent (the more beliefs through which s/he can see), the broader and more insightful the analysis is likely to be. As Morgan (1989) puts it 'if you only have a hammer, every problem tends to become a nail' (p.14). Indeed, one potential framework for analysis is that provided by the metaphors of Morgan (1986), which are summarised in Chapter 1. Another is the six-box diagnostic model of Weisbord (1976) reproduced in Figure 4.3.

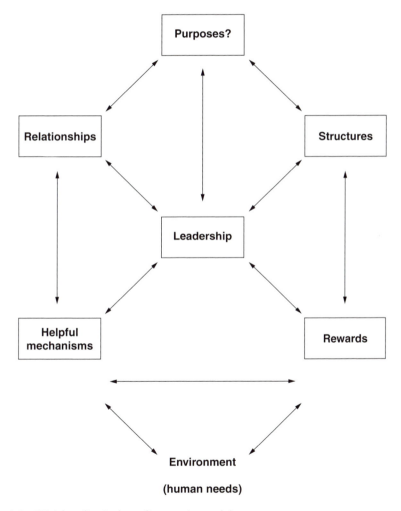

Figure 4.3   Weisbord's six-box diagnostic model.

In truth, the literature is resplendent with such models (*see* Iles and Sutherland, 2001; Cummings and Worley, 2001). While an important aid to sensemaking, they can also serve to oversimplify the complex and dynamic nature of the situation.

Data feedback and negotiating interventions

In the cycle, data feedback is sandwiched between data collection/analysis and planning the interventions, but is also part of both. Feedback acts as a tool both for managing the transition from collecting information to planning action, and for modelling for the organisation ways to make sense of and work with the information gathered about the system. Nadler (1977) suggests that data – through collection, analysis and feedback – can be used for the specific purpose of planning intervention activities by:

- identifying the specific nature of problems
- discovering appropriate steps of action
- helping to decide how these steps can be implemented.

Working within a systems framework (*see* Chapter 7), he provides a working definition of feedback where he argues that it is a basic component of self-regulating systems. In its broadest form, feedback is any information about the system functioning which has the potential of being used to change the operation of the system. Viewing organisations as open systems, he views feedback as essential, enabling the correction of errors and the adaptation to environmental change. In social systems, however, such as healthcare agencies, feedback does not automatically achieve change in the systems' operations; the process of obtaining, interpreting and using feedback information is important in creating such change. Since organisations often ignore feedback or do not make an effort to use feedback effectively, OD activities serve an important function in facilitating feedback processes. In Chapter 2 of this volume, it is suggested that it is feedback at the 'tipping point' that can have the most impact on organisations' commitment to pursuing change. Anticipating Chapter 8, it is also important to note that complexity theory further illuminates aspects of feedback. For present purposes, it is only necessary to note here that when humans interact in response to feedback it will produce a number of effects, the cumulative consequences of which may be difficult to predict. In these circumstances, data feedback is, in itself, a major intervention in a system, and one that requires sensitive planning and execution. Handled well, such information can be a powerful motivating force in bringing about change where it is seen as plausible, presenting new yet recognisable pictures of the organisation. Of course, feedback which is inconsistent with the current perceptions or beliefs of individuals and groups can create anxiety, and for change to take place such data must be perceived as valid and accurate; that is, it must possess psychological safety (Schein and Bennis, 1965).

There are a variety of ways of giving feedback:

- verbal feedback (informal)
- working note (semi-formal)

- workshop/stakeholder conference (semi-formal)
- letter (formal)
- report (formal).

Inevitably, feedback may be incremental and constant, for instance where meetings with staff draw on data from surveys, but at some stage the change agent will want to engage the organisation in something that signals the move from data collection/analysis towards the design of interventions.

Most of these approaches will be familiar, but the working note perhaps requires more introduction. Miller (1995) suggests that it is an interim account of observations and findings which gives people a chance to check on the change agent's enquiry and ideas about the future, on the basis that the more fully people are involved in designing and implementing what happens next, the more committed they will be to making positive changes happen. It can look at the differences between what Lawrence and Robinson (1975) call the normative primary task (what an organisation ought to be doing), the existential primary task (what they believe they are doing) and the phenomenal primary task (what the organisation seems to be unconsciously performing). The working note can be usefully employed to offer working hypotheses about why these differences are occurring and provide options for addressing them. Above all it is a tool for generating a dialogue between the organisation and the change agent in order to bring about a more comprehensive understanding of the issues that need to be addressed so that action plans may be developed and decisions may be taken.

Of course, these action plans – the description of the interventions – will be specific to the context of the organisation and the change agent, and these will drawn from the range of 'schools' of OD discussed in Part 2 of this volume. In these circumstances, it would be inappropriate to say anything more here about the fifth phase (taking actions). Furthermore, as each author in Part 2 has been invited to discuss evaluations of the interventions based on their frameworks – and Chapter 13 is entirely given over to discussion of the evidence available from such evaluations – it is not necessary to say anything here about the sixth phase (evaluation), beyond noting that it should be concerned with both the content (what was being achieved) and the process (how it was being achieved). Overall, one aim of any evaluation should be to involve the organisation in a reflexive process where participants are able to reflect on and learn from the change experience as part of the ambition to create 'changing organisations' rather than 'changed organisations'.

Conclusion

This chapter has introduced the OD cycle and suggested that it is an important part of any OD project regardless of the theoretical orientation of the change agent. It is to those theories and their accompanying interventions that this book will now turn in Part 2.

References

von Bertalanffy L (1950) The theory of open systems in physics and biology. *Science*. 3: 23–9.

Buchanan D and Boddy D (1992) *The Expertise of the Change Agent: Public Performance and Backstage Activity*. Prentice-Hall, Hemel Hempstead.

Burke W (1994) *Organization Development: A process of learning and changing* (2e). Addison-Wesley, Reading, MA.

Bushe G and Shani A (1991) *Parallel Learning Structures: increasing innovation in bureaucracies*. Addison-Wesley, Reading, MA.

Cummings T and Worley C (2001) *Organization Change and Development*. South-Western College Publishing, Cincinnati, OH.

Easterby-Smith M, Thorpe A and Lowe A (1991) *Management Research: an introduction*. Sage, London.

French W (1969) Organisation development: objectives, assumptions and strategies. *California Management Review*. 12: 23–34.

Frohman M, Sashkin M and Kavanagh M (1976) Action research as applied to organization development. *Organization and Administrative Sciences*. 7: 129–42.

Gill G and Johnson P (1991) *Research Methods for Managers*. Paul Chapman Publishing, London.

Iles V and Sutherland K (2001) *Organisational Change: a review for health care managers, professionals and researchers*. National Co-ordinating Centre for NHS Service Delivery and Organisation R & D, London.

Kolb D and Frohman A (1970) An organization development approach to consulting. *Sloan Management Review*. 12(1): 51–65.

Lawrence W and Robinson P (1975) *An Innovation and Its Implementation: issues of evaluation*. Tavistock Institute of Human Relations, Document No. 1069, London.

Lewin K (1946) Action research and minority problems. *Journal of Social Issues*. 2: 34–46.

Lewin K (1948) *Resolving Social Conflicts*. Harper, New York.

Lewin K (1951) *Field Theory in Social Sciences*. Harper, New York.

Lewin K (1958) Group decision and social change. In: N Maccoby, T Newcomb and E Hartley (eds) *Readings in Psychology*. Holt, Rinehart and Winston, New York. pp.163–226.

Lippitt R, Watson J and Westley B (1958) *Dynamics of Planned Change*. Harcourt Brace, New York.

Miller E (1995) Dialogue with the client system: use of the 'working note' in organizational consultancy. *Journal of Managerial Psychology*. 10(6): 8–17.

Miller E and Rice A (1967) *Systems of Organisation: the control of task and sentient boundaries*. Tavistock Publications, London.

Morgan G (1986) *Images of Organization*. Sage, London.

Morgan G (1989) *Creative Organization Theory*. Sage, London.

Nadler D (1977) *Feedback and Organization Development: using data-based methods*. Addison-Wesley, Reading, MA.

Rice A (1963) *The Enterprise and Its Environment*. Tavistock Publications, London.

Schein E (1980) *Organizational Psychology* (3e). Prentice-Hall, Englewood Cliffs, NJ.

Schein E and Bennis W (1965) *Personal and Organizational Change Through Group Methods: the laboratory approach*. Wiley, New York.

Weisbord M (1976) Organizational diagnosis: six places to look for trouble with or without a theory. *Group and Organizational Studies.* **1**: 430–47.

Weisbord MR (1984) Client contact: entry and contract. In: RJ Lee and AM Freedman (eds) *Consultation Skills Reading*, pp.63–6. NTL Institute Publications, Arlington, VA.

Part 2

Organisational Development in Healthcare: introducing the models

CHAPTER 5

Service improvement

Lynne Maher and Jean Penny

Introduction

This chapter reflects some of the learning of the healthcare improvement journey jointly undertaken by the NHS Modernisation Agency (MA) and local healthcare teams. The pace of this journey has been fast and achievements outstanding in terms of large system change in an organisation comprising over 1.2 million employees. This journey is summarised in Box 5.1.

Box 5.1: Service improvement – the journey so far

1997	2004
Few isolated quality projects	Extensive activity in every part of the NHS
Handful of individuals with experience in service improvement	Thousands of staff trained in service improvement techniques
Limited evidence of what works	Strong evidence with outstanding improvements in access and quality
No national focus or international profile	Improvement at the heart of the NHS Plan and established as world leader in the field

Reproduced from Fillingham, 2004.

Service improvement lies at the centre of the NHS Modernisation Agency's work to support change that results in improvements in healthcare for NHS patients and staff. It is a term deployed broadly to describe many different tools and techniques that are used by NHS teams to:

- better understand their system including the human relationships within it
- identify areas for improvement
- plan and test changes

- implement new systems
- create a culture which supports and sustains the gains made and stimulates continuous learning and improvement.

The term 'service improvement' can mean different things to different people depending on an individual's role, responsibilities, experience and needs. To a clinician, it may mean the introduction of evidence-based practice and better clinical outcomes. To a manager, it may mean the achievement of improved access and a reduction in waiting times. To a patient, it may mean a better 'customer' experience with more choice and involvement in their care. The common theme linking all these different interpretations of service improvement is that they all involve change. We must, however, bear in mind that 'not every change is an improvement but certainly every improvement is a change and we cannot improve something unless we change it' (Goldratt, 1990, p.10).

The goal of improving services is to achieve a higher-quality experience for patients than the NHS is currently achieving. There are already many examples of high-quality care, which provide patients with an excellent experience, and it must be our overall intention to provide this level of care to all patients while constantly seeking ways in which we can further improve. Everyone should appreciate that 'this higher level of quality cannot be achieved by further stressing current systems of care. The current system cannot do the job, trying harder will not work. Changing systems of care will' (Institute of Medicine, 2001, p.4).

Over recent years, experienced improvement practitioners in healthcare have recognised that, while there is not a simple step-by-step approach to change that will always work, there is a helpful formulation of the process of service improvement which suggests a logical sequence of actions:

- understand the problems and needs from the perspectives of patients and staff
- develop aims and measures
- test ideas for improvements
- ensure those improvement are sustained and spread.

This chapter elaborates on these actions, drawing on the extensive experience of the MA. First, however, it is essential to establish the mind-set of an effective service improver.

Improvement thinking

So what does a clinician or manager need to do to make service improvements? Plsek (2002), after interviewing and working with a group of NHS leaders, suggests that they must be able to:

- see whole systems and any counter-intuitive linkages within them
- bring in the experiences and voices of patients, carers and staff
- seek to translate evidence into practice
- expose processes to mapping, analysis and redesign
- apply engineering concepts of flow, capacity, demand and waste reduction

- encourage flexible, innovative rethinking of processes and systems
- facilitate active local improvement, innovation and reflective practice
- set up measurement to demonstrate impact and gain insight into variation
- work constructively with the human dimension of change
- sustain past improvement and drive for continuous improvement
- spread improvement ideas and knowledge widely and urgently.

This is a challenging list, and not one for which most clinicians and managers will have been prepared. Developing an understanding of, and gaining confidence in using, improvement tools and techniques does not occur by accident. It requires purposeful effort by staff working in healthcare to draw on a range of skills and knowledge that often lies outside their experience and professional training and development. Healthcare staff need to be encouraged and enabled to develop the skills to improve their part of the service and to work with others to improve the whole service as determined by the perspective of the patient. The most effective way of introducing staff to improvement tools and techniques is through practical, work-based learning, where they can use, experiment with and practically apply the theory.

Experienced improvement practitioners have described the knowledge they have had to draw on in four interrelated and equally important domains. This framework, presented in Box 5.2, is seen as 'a novel combination of approaches to service change that combines modernist and postmodernist positions' and as offering 'something new to our understanding of change in the complex world of health care provision' (Clarke *et al.*, 2004, p.85).

Box 5.2: The body of knowledge that supports building the discipline of improvement in health and social care.

Domain of knowledge	Including knowledge of
• Involving users, carers, staff and the public	• effective techniques for recognising, involving, valuing and incorporating the views of users, carers, staff and the public
• Personal and organisational development	• psychological principles for self-awareness • psychological principles for the work of multidisciplinary teams • psychological principles for the work and culture of organisations • communication methods and mechanisms • facilitation skills for working with groups • principles of adult learning

- Systems and process thinking

  - the current place, role and function of the service to be improved within the patient or support process and its current place, role and function within the whole care system
  - the effect of matching capacity and demand
  - the impact of variation
  - the redesign opportunities

- Initiating, sustaining and spreading improvement in daily work

  - local and national context, politics and strategies
  - project and programme management techniques
  - key factors for sustaining improvement gains
  - ways of evaluating outcomes
  - techniques for ensuring minimum risk and maximum patient safety
  - approaches to encouraging the adoption and spread of improvements

Adapted from Penny, 2003.

This body of knowledge is, to a significant extent, the subject of this book. Other chapters deal with essential elements of service improvement illustrated in Box 5.2. For example, working with individuals, groups and teams is dealt with in Chapter 6, systems theory in Chapter 7, and chaos theory, complexity and emergence in Chapter 8. It should be stressed that this chapter should be read within the context of this broader body of knowledge, which together underpins service improvement. Within this chapter, we intend to focus on the following aspects.

- Key tools and techniques of service improvement including:
  - involving patients and their carers in improving health services
  - setting aims, measures and testing improvements/change ideas
  - systems and process thinking
  - creative thinking and ideas generation.
- Lessons learnt in sustaining and spreading change.
- Lessons learnt from experience of using improvement tools and techniques.

Key tools and techniques of improvement

Involving patients and their carers

The primary motivation for service improvement should be the needs of the patients for whom we are caring. This is reflected in the NHS Plan, which states that 'our aim is to redesign the system around the patient' (DoH, 2000, p.57). The NHS has been criticised for what can be described as a paternalistic method of care during which patient involvement, as active partners, has not always been a primary focus. This has resulted in comments such as: 'People in Britain forget that the health service is their service not just the professionals' and 'Often professionals forget to treat patients as people first, not just as patients' (Bradford Health Community Newsletter, 2004, p.4). These comments should be viewed in parallel with the many positive messages that are also received by healthcare staff; however, they indicate that there is a great need to involve patients in designing care systems that really work for their needs.

Patients' needs do vary a great deal from condition to condition, and even within the same medical condition, depending on the often unique perspectives of the patients, healthcare organisations and the communities within which they reside. Different needs and different types of care may well require different approaches to involving patients in the process of improvement. The focus of attention for the change process might be a particular stage of the patient's journey or it might be their whole experience of the healthcare process. While acknowledging that the patients' journey from illness to health will differ, there are approximately seven stages, which are generally recognisable and applicable:

- feeling something is wrong
- seeing someone in the NHS
- assessment and diagnosis to find out what is wrong
- initial treatment and management
- continuing treatment and care (including rehabilitation, long-term management, and palliative care)
- discharge and follow-up
- living with the condition, staying well and maintaining quality of life.

The Improvement Leaders' Guide to involving patients and carers (Modernisation Agency, 2002a) describes a variety of methods and suggests that:

> patients should be involved at all stages of the improvement process, including discovering needs for improvement, designing improvements and learning from the outcomes of improvement efforts. Involvement is about truly creating working partnerships, not 'doing to' or even 'doing for', patients. Agreed courses of action may be undertaken by patients themselves, by staff team members or jointly by both, reinforcing the point that ideally everybody should be considered to be members of the same team (p.15).

The Pursuing Perfection programme is an international initiative which aims to radically improve the quality of healthcare. Its approach to patient involvement is to create close partnerships with patients that result in the development of promises to patients based on what they do and do not want. The Pursuing Perfection team has highlighted that 'patients may often understand their condition better than the health care professionals treating them. By creating genuine partnerships with patients, professionals can tap into this abundance of expertise' (Modernisation Agency, 2002b, p.6).

Setting aims, measures and testing change ideas

There is a common-sense approach to improvement that we all use in both our work and home lives. Mostly it is subconscious, but there are even more significant gains when it is consciously applied. This common-sense approach contains five steps:

- Step 1: choose an aspect that needs to be improved.
- Step 2: measure it quickly.
- Step 3: intervene and change something.
- Step 4: measure it again.

If the desired improvement is not achieved, repeat steps 3 and 4, and then:

- Step 5: when satisfied return to step 1 and focus on something else.

The fundamental elements in this approach are: setting the aim; measuring for improvement; and testing out change ideas. It is these aspects of the service improvement challenge that are now explored. The model for improvement was first developed by Shewhart (1931) and represents all the fundamental elements contained in three questions supported by a framework for testing improvement/change ideas (*see* Figure 5.1).

Question 1: What are we trying to accomplish?

To answer this question, an aims statement is needed to focus on a problem or a challenge causing concern for patients and staff. It is important to really understand what the problem or challenge is and its relationship to the process and system that it lies within. A risk at this stage is to think that you know exactly what the problem is and develop an aim and implement a plan for change, only to discover later that the original challenge has been misunderstood.

Many healthcare staff have cited process mapping as the most valuable tool to use in creating this understanding. This tool is now used widely by many organisations to better understand a variety of systems and processes. When applied to healthcare it can provide a detailed representation of each stage of the patient's journey, identify all of the staff groups involved in that journey, and illustrate who does what to the patient and when that happens. Process mapping provides a real opportunity to bring together multidisciplinary teams. It provides a common reference point for all those involved in the process and, in doing so, fundamentally improves communication and understanding. Process mapping is described in more detail later in this chapter.

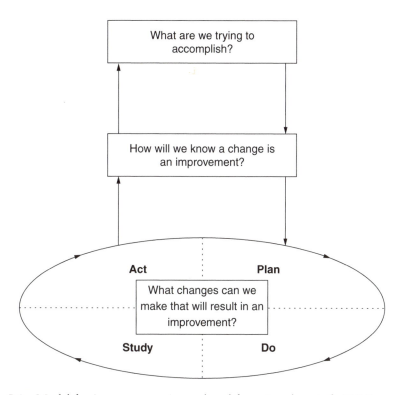

Figure 5.1 Model for improvement (reproduced from Langley *et al.*, 1996).

An aims statement is vital to identify, articulate and communicate the desired outcome. It should be written in such a way that it is clear and unambiguous, and in sufficient detail that the staff involved can really understand what is expected. '*Improve the patient process*' is an example of a poor aims statement as it is open to different interpretations and does not provide enough explicit detail for anyone to really understand the focus of the desired improvement.

A good method to use when writing the aims statement is to define it so that it says what patients and their families can expect. An example of an aims statement stated in such a way is: '*We aim to give you the best chance of getting home quickly, to be able to do what you want, after the safest, most effective and pain-free treatment from the moment you break your hip, and to try and stop it happening again.*' This aims statement, from the work of a Pursuing Perfection project, is in the style of a promise to patients who have a fracture to their neck of femur. Note that the scope of this aim involves the whole process as the patient would see or experience it; from the moment they break their hip through to the preventative element of stopping it happening again. Its intentions are clear and unambiguous and are written in plain English rather than 'professional jargon'. When defined in such a way, the aims statement will lead to a number of specific work or target areas. For example, using the aim as stated above:

- 0% of our patients will have a wound infection
- 100% of our patients will achieve or be above their pre-admission level of activities of daily living.

At this early stage it is important to ensure that clinical and managerial leaders support the aim and that it is aligned with the strategic goals of the overall organisation. It is also crucial to involve patients and staff to get everyone in the group engaged in process mapping to really pinpoint where the challenges lie and where they would like the changes to start.

Question 2: How do we know a change is an improvement?

Much data is collected in healthcare and some of it is not helpful in terms of measuring improvements. The focus here is on the few specific key measures that really demonstrate an improvement to staff and patients, rather than measures created for external judgement or for league tables. It is useful if the measures are incorporated into the improvement aim statements or work/target areas as indicated above.

One approach is to develop measures that can be displayed as 'run' charts or 'time series' graphs. This is where the measure is displayed on the vertical axis against a measure of time (e.g. hours or days on the horizontal axis). The commonly used temperature chart is a good example of a run chart used in everyday healthcare. Run charts provide a simple yet effective visual display of progress and they show the exact point in time that things start to improve. This is vital as healthcare systems are complex and are often influenced by many changes both from internal and external sources at the same time. It is important to understand which specific intervention really made a difference. Run charts will also show if the situation has not improved or in fact is getting worse!

Some examples of useful measures to reflect improvement include:

- number of days/hours of waiting time between two defined points in the patient's journey
- number of hospital and patient cancellations for appointment or admission
- the level of wound infection for a specific group
- number of patients who do not attend at admission.

Question 3: What changes can we make that will result in the improvement that we seek?

Everyone should be encouraged to contribute ideas for improvement, inspiring staff to think creatively and involving patients and their carers in order that they can say what would really make things better for them. When a number of change ideas have been identified, systematically work through each one to see if it fits with the aims statement. This will result in a list of change ideas from which the team need to choose the ones most likely to achieve the aspiration for improvement. Follow with plan–do–study–act (PDSA) cycles and test whether the change ideas work in practice and whether implementation will actually result in the desired improvement to the healthcare process or journey.

PDSA cycles to test change ideas

Plan–do–study–act (PDSA) cycles are one of the most useful tools in the armoury of the service improver. They are described in detail by Langley *et al.* (1996). The PDSA cycle has been used as a framework to support improvements within both health and business contexts. It was initially tested systematically in England within the Cancer Services Collaborative Programme in 1999 and proved so effective it has since been adopted as an important tool to support many other healthcare improvement efforts. The PDSA cycle has been particularly valuable in testing change ideas on a small scale; for example, starting with one patient in one clinic on one day. This has facilitated a high level of staff involvement and low level of risk in comparison with other large-scale change efforts such as early examples of business process re-engineering which were sometimes perceived as culturally at odds with NHS values (*see* Chapters 9, 13 and the Conclusion to this volume for more discussion of BPR). Box 5.3 summarises the PDSA cycle.

Box 5.3: A summary of the PDSA cycle

Plan: Be very clear about the objective of the test cycle, the reason for testing and what is expected to happen. Specify exactly what is to be measured and what is planned: who will do what, when, where and how?

Do: Carry out the plan and document what happens. Do this by testing on a small number of patients. Record what happened that was expected, what happened that was not expected, and what was seen and heard.

Study: Analyse what happened. Look at the data by comparing what was predicted and what actually happened. What did you and your colleagues learn?

Act: Discuss with your colleagues and decide: continue with the change idea and collect more data; modify the idea; or test a different change idea.

Remember that it is necessary to be successful with at least five patients but this may not be sufficient. So keep going to build up data and evidence over time until all involved are confident that the change really will make an improvement.

There will be some change ideas on which everyone agrees, and that are simple to implement and will unequivocally result in an improvement. If this is the case, it is perfectly acceptable to just make the changes; however it is still important to undertake some reflection to ensure that they have had the desired effect and have not impacted negatively on any other part of the patient pathway.

For other changes, those that are more complex and less consensual, the advice is 'don't try to do it all at once'. It is helpful to start small, e.g. with one patient in one clinic with one clinician. Initially, it may be most productive to work with those colleagues who want to be involved and use early successes as the basis on which to approach others. Creating ownership by involving others in the planning and working out of the specifics of a service improvement is important, as is not getting attached too early to any one idea. The best method is to test a number of change ideas before implementing any change. The importance of allowing time to actually carry out test cycles cannot be emphasised enough; this includes time to stand back, look at the whole picture, learn what the impact has been and reflect on what that means for future test cycles of change.

One word of caution is necessary. Some people react negatively to a high volume of test cycles that do not result in any implemented change. While there is no hard-and-fast rule about how many cycles should be tried before a change is implemented, one should be aware that endless cycles are not productive and if this becomes the case the initiative should be reassessed. Box 5.4 illustrates the way in which the PDSA cycle can apply in an everyday example.

Box 5.4: Example of the PDSA cycle in use

Example: The regular measuring, displaying and acting on the data on a patient's temperature chart

You have a patient with a raised temperature. Her temperature is being measured and recorded hourly.

- You **plan** according to your objective, which is to bring the temperature down. You decide which drug/treatment you will give, based on your clinical knowledge or the advice of colleagues and anticipate the effects.
- You **do** by giving the drug/treatment according to the correct regime and continue to measure and record on the chart.
- You **study** the results and look for improvement. Does the temperature come down, stay the same or go up over the next few hours?
- You **act** appropriately according to the data on the temperature chart; either continue or change your intervention.
- You then repeat the cycle as many times as necessary.

Systems and process thinking

Process mapping and analysis

Process mapping is a key starting point to any improvement project, large or small, as it enables a greater understanding of exactly what happens to the patient and who does what in the process of care. The *Improvement Leaders' Guide to Process Mapping, Analysis and Redesign* states that it is 'one of the most powerful ways for multidisciplinary teams to understand the real problems from the patients' perspective, and to identify opportunities for improvement' (Modernisation Agency, 2002c, p.16). The *Improvement Leaders' Guide* goes on to list more benefits of process mapping including:

- an opportunity to bring together multidisciplinary teams and create a culture of ownership, responsibility and accountability
- an aid to help plan effectively the testing of ideas that are likely to have the most impact
- a chance for generation of brilliant ideas especially from staff who really know how things work
- an end product, the process map, which is easy to understand and highly visual.

When mapping the process the team needs to define a clear start and end point to the process that they want to improve (*see* Box 5.5). Each step in between those two points is considered and 'mapped' at the level of one person doing one thing to one patient at one time. The map should demonstrate what actually happens, not what ought to happen nor what is thought to happen.

Box 5.5: Example of the boundaries of a process map

Specific area of concern:	outpatient department for first specialist appointment
Start of the process:	when the patient is advised by the GP they need to see a specialist
End of the process:	when the patient has had a specialist consultation

---

Key indicators within the map will help to identify where 'bottlenecks' are in the process. Bottlenecks are the stages in the process that cause waits and delays and are identified by a large volume of patients queuing before the stage or long waiting times. Managing the bottleneck is an important first step and can often be improved by either reducing demand or by increasing the capacity of the bottleneck. The concept of bottlenecks is well described by Goldratt and Cox (1993).

Other information gained by the analysis of a process map, which helps to prioritise specific areas of work, includes:

- approximate time between the first and the last step
- number of times the patient is passed from one person to another (for example receptionist, nurse, doctor, diagnostic technician, nurse, doctor, porter)
- number of different steps or stages in the process
- approximate wait time between each step
- approximate time taken for each step or task
- steps that add no value for the patient (imagine that you or your parent or your child is the patient and decide which steps add nothing to the care being received)
- problems for patients (what do patients complain about?)
- problems for staff (what do staff complain about?).

Undertaking process mapping is often enlightening for staff who may never have examined the process in so much detail and were not aware of all the different steps and stages the patient has to negotiate. By asking those involved the following four simple questions a significant number of potential change ideas will be generated.

- What is the purpose of each step or task? Why does it happen?
- Does the step or task have to be done in that location?
- Is this the best order of doing things?
- Is that the right person doing that task? Could someone else do it?

Measuring and managing variation in a process

Understanding process variation is key to improving performance and quality. All processes vary and this variation can be attributed either to common causes (and thus normal and expected variation) or to special causes (that produce unusual or unexpected variations). These two forms of cause are exemplified in Box 5.6.

Box 5.6: Variation – common cause and special cause effects

The time taken for a journey from home to work each morning will vary. This is due mainly due to **common causes**, which are normal or expected causes of variation, e.g. volume of traffic, pedestrians crossing the road, etc. However, there are also **special causes** that result in a far longer than expected journey, e.g. punctures, road traffic accidents, abnormal loads on the roads.

It would not be appropriate to react to a **special cause** as it is unlikely to happen again. You may, however, choose to improve your journey time and reduce the **common causes** of variation by changing your route to work or the time you set off.

Statistical Process Control (SPC) is a statistical tool used to plot, demonstrate and measure the amount and type of variation in a process over time. It builds on the 'run' chart method of demonstrating improvement described earlier in this chapter. This tool allows:

- the impact of any changes made to the process to be assessed
- immediate action if a process is going out of control
- continuous monitoring to see if improvements are being sustained
- reporting by exception once a process is stable until other improvements are implemented to further improve the system.

Processes and systems

Understanding and improving healthcare processes is important in improving the outcomes and experiences for patients; however, processes do not exist in isolation. Processes are the fundamental parts of systems and all systems are part of bigger systems, which in turn are part of even bigger systems, etc. (*see* Chapter 7). The *Improvement Leaders' Guides to Working in Systems* (Modernisation Agency, 2002d) illustrates this by using an example of the London Underground, which 'is made up of lots of different processes such as the ticketing processes and the different underground lines. Everything needs to work together as a system for things to run smoothly and you know the effect if one part, such as the Central line, breaks down!' (p.10). It, in turn, is part of the bigger system of transport in London.

It is essential to understand processes in terms of where they fit within a wider system. Capra (1996, 2002) describes systems in terms of structures, processes and patterns where:

- **structures** refers to the geography and layout of facilities and equipment, organisational maps showing roles, committees, working groups, etc.
- **processes** refers to the patient journey, educational processes, financial processes, etc.
- **patterns** refer to patterns of behaviours, patterns of conversations, patterns of clinical outcomes and the patterns of anything that can be counted, such as waiting lists, prescribing patterns, patterns of demand, etc.

The three component parts that make up systems are highly intertwined and interconnected, and improvement cannot be achieved by making changes in just one part of the system; making changes to the structure of a healthcare organisation without changing the supporting processes or underlying patterns of behaviour will rarely result in sustainable improvements (and this is also the argument that is developed in more depth in the Conclusion to this volume). This notion also starts to describe the basis of understanding healthcare as a complex system, which is more fully discussed in Chapter 8.

Creative thinking and ideas generation

Recent literature from the Department of Trade and Industry (DTI) states that within the UK there are sectors that lead the world in innovation: aerospace; pharmaceuticals; biotechnology; financial services; and many of the creative industries. However, overall UK innovation performance seems to be, at best, average compared to our major competitors and there is a need to improve our understanding of innovation and ability to innovate in order to provide world-class products and services in the future (DTI, 2003).

The NHS has a strong history of innovation within medical technologies and has demonstrated some innovative approaches to service redesign over the past seven years. However, there is limited evidence that creativity and innovation are established within healthcare organisations as a way of doing business, that is as a fundamental part of thinking and acting. In particular, there is little evidence of creativity and innovation being systematically applied to healthcare processes (Maher and Plsek, 2003).

The development of a culture of innovation in healthcare has become a strategic imperative. The NHS Plan (DoH, 2000) identifies a series of challenging targets, the achievement of which depends on significant transformation of working practices and organisational processes. In recent years, the health service has been very successful in introducing change based on 'improvement methods'. This has resulted in outstanding improvements to services and patient care but does not go far enough to close the gap between where we are now and where we need to be in order to deliver world-class health services. In many cases, our current improvement efforts result in what we can describe as 'first-order change', where the improvement effort results in an improvement but often represents more of, or less of, the same thing, rather than a fundamental or innovative difference in the way care is provided (in the language of Chapter 3, too much change has been transactional instead of transformational).

Innovation methods, by definition, build on and are integrated with improvement methods, enabling teams to challenge fundamental assumptions about current care-delivery methods. These methods have the potential to provide a 'missing link' in a comprehensive toolkit to support NHS modernisation. The goal is to build on learning from previous change initiatives to create second-order change, enabling radical rethinking and transformation of services (*see* Figure 5.2). There is a clear link here to the ideas around single- and double-loop learning introduced in Chapter 1.

Innovation occurs following the generation of creative ideas. These ideas can be generated using specific tools and techniques in a deliberate and directed way. It is important to remember that creative ideas only have real value when they are implemented and can be demonstrated to have made a positive impact on the healthcare setting. The *Directed Creativity* Cycle developed by Plsek (1997) provides a useful framework to follow from the point of a first observation of an area of concern through the generation and selection of ideas to the implementation and evaluation of the impact made (*see* Figure 5.3).

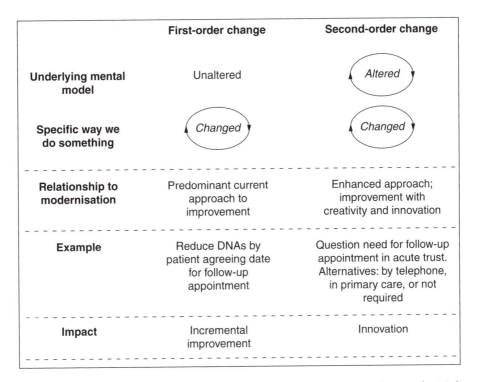

	First-order change	Second-order change
Underlying mental model	Unaltered	Altered
Specific way we do something	Changed	Changed
Relationship to modernisation	Predominant current approach to improvement	Enhanced approach; improvement with creativity and innovation
Example	Reduce DNAs by patient agreeing date for follow-up appointment	Question need for follow-up appointment in acute trust. Alternatives: by telephone, in primary care, or not required
Impact	Incremental improvement	Innovation

Figure 5.2 First- and second-order change (adapted from Langley *et al.*, 1996 by Maher and Plsek, 2003).

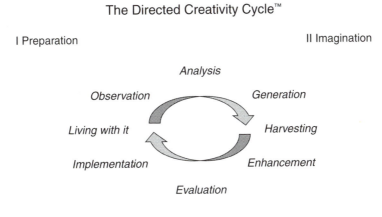

The Directed Creativity Cycle™

I Preparation   II Imagination

Analysis

Observation   Generation

Living with it   Harvesting

Implementation   Enhancement

Evaluation

IV Action   III Development

Figure 5.3 The Directed Creativity Cycle (reproduced from Plsek, 1997).

Beginning at the 9 o'clock position on the cycle in Figure 5.3:

- We **live in the world** every day just like everyone else, but creative thinking begins with careful **observation** of that world coupled with thoughtful **analysis** of how things work and fail. These mental processes create a store of concepts in our memory.
- Using this store, we **generate** novel ideas to meet specific needs by actively searching for associations among concepts.
- We then **harvest** a few of the many ideas generated and work to further **enhance** them before we subject them to a final, practical **evaluation**.
- But it is not enough just to have creative thoughts; ideas have no value until we put in the work to **implement** them.
- Every new idea that is put into practice (that is, every innovation) changes the world we live in, which restarts the cycle of observation and analysis.
- The Directed Creativity Cycle can be further divided into four phases of preparation, imagination, development and action.

A central barrier that needs to be overcome is that many people do not consider themselves to be creative. The reverse is true. We all have the potential to be creative and there are many tools and techniques that we can use to help to support the generation of creative ideas, which can lead to implementation of innovative methods for the provision of improved healthcare services.

Lessons learnt in sustaining and spreading change

Over recent years there has been a significant increase in the number of change and improvement efforts within healthcare services. These initiatives have demonstrated the existing ability and further potential to provide better ways of delivering healthcare, such as reductions in waiting, increase in safety, improvements in patient flow through the system, and so on. This increase has been achieved through a combination of staff acquiring skills and then consciously and deliberately applying them within health services with a passion and determination for change. These attributes have contributed greatly to the current improvements within healthcare services. However, there are two major frustrations being experienced by health and social care staff: sustainability of the improvements; and spread, or dissemination, of the improvements.

Sustainability is about being able to hold the gains made during the improvement initiative, evolving them as required and definitely not going back to the old ways of working. This aspiration supports the notion of a continuous improvement cycle rather than a situation where even the new process becomes stagnant over time and makes further improvement difficult.

Spread is the extent to which the learning that takes place in any one part of an organisation is actively shared between and acted on by all parts of the organisation. It is the ambition of the MA that improvement knowledge generated anywhere in the healthcare system needs to become common knowledge and routine practice across the whole healthcare system (Modernisation Agency, 2002e).

Spread

The approaches to improvements currently being undertaken in the UK healthcare system are focused on achieving large-scale and transformational change. *The NHS Plan* (DoH, 2000) promises 'a revolution in patient care' (p.60) over the next ten years, and Bevan *et al.* (2003) call for 'a situation where every patient and family can expect optimal care' (p.2). The challenge is to understand how improvement can move from 'isolated islands' to become widespread across the whole of the NHS.

An early approach used by the MA was that of spread by scaling up. This entailed piloting improvement projects with a small number of organisations and then sequentially 'spreading' the programme to larger numbers until a point was reached where every organisation or health community was involved. This approach has been successful up to a point. Indeed, every organisation or health community have teams of staff who have been involved in, and possess skills around, improvement techniques. However, they typically operate as separate improvement initiatives or teams rather than as a whole organisational or systemic joined-up approach. What appears to be lacking is the understanding of how to move towards a critical mass of improvers working together across the whole health system.

The MA has commissioned an extensive review of the literature on spread and sustainability. This draws some clear messages about the attributes of the innovation (or change), the behaviour of individual adaptors, the nature of communication and influence, and the various structural and sociological features of the organisation and its wider environment (Greenhalgh *et al.*, 2004). Greenhalgh's work complements the findings of the Research into Practice Programme, which undertook in-depth studies into spread and sustainability of two distinct improvement programmes (Modernisation Agency, 2002f,g).

A third approach comes from Bate *et al.* (2003), who have explored the similarities between the mechanisms by which social movements (such as environmental or peace movements) develop and the process of change in organisations (and this is also a link that is explored in the case studies in Chapter 2 and the Conclusion). There are connections to be drawn with Gladwell's (2000) concept that messages and behaviours can spread like epidemics, and when applied to the positive actions of people this relates to a social movement. Gladwell describes three characteristics of epidemics:

- contagiousness
- that little causes can have great effect (a central concept of complexity theory)
- that change happens not gradually but at one dramatic moment (he names this last characteristic the 'tipping point', and it is an idea that recurs in other chapters in this book).

Clearly, therefore, there is a huge focus on this vital element of improvement. Practically, where dissemination or spread has been seen to happen, one important factor that always appears to be present is an emphasis on respect and good relationships between individuals. This may be considered an oversimplification, but it is a very good place to start.

Sustainability

The word 'sustainability' is used frequently and is linked to many aspects of life, such as the environment and economic growth. It has been particularly linked to globalisation and the concern about the impact of so-called 'destructive technologies, which result in ever greater levels of environmental damage' (AtKisson, 2001, p.11).

Sustainability is considered here in the context of holding the gains achieved through improvement efforts, evolving them as required and not going back to the old ways of working. This does assume that the improvement process has confirmed that the new way of working does result in an improvement, which has demonstrated benefits to key groups such as patients, staff and the organisation. Greenhalgh *et al.* (2004) noted that the evidence on sustainability of innovations in health service delivery was difficult to disentangle from that on change management and organisational development in general. This, added to the ambiguity of the meaning dependent on which form of intervention was foremost, creates complexity around the whole topic.

An effusion of communication and excitement usually accompanies the launch of an improvement initiative. As the work progresses, demonstrating the achievement of goals and improvements, a similar amount of fervour is experienced. In addition, many initiatives have 'formal ends', and a celebration of the hard work and achievement ensues. The process just described is exactly as it should be; however, what happens next is important. Too often this is 'nothing' or, even worse, a withdrawal of some or the entire supporting infrastructure that surrounded the change process. This infrastructure can be, for example, in the form of special attention from senior management, a project lead with dedicated time or resources including training and measurement systems. Added to this is the omission that role descriptions, policies and other systems have not been changed to support the con-tinuance of the new process; 'The challenge for sustainability is not starting improve-ment, but continuing after the initial enthusiasm has gone' (Øvretveit, 2003, p.7).

After examining improvement projects approximately one year after their formal end, Ham *et al.* (2002) concluded that, if change initiatives are to achieve continued improvement, they 'will only succeed if the same effort is put into their sustainability as their launch' (p.xv). They identified that around a third of improvement projects within their study had failed to sustain the gains that had been made and, in fact, had to some degree reverted to the previous way of working.

Evidence from business and industry outside of health cites rates of non-sustain-ability of their change efforts as high as 70–80% (Daft and Noe, 2000). While it is important to recognise that learning can be taken from every change initiative, even if it has not been sustained, a question has to be raised about the amount of effort, commitment and resource that has been focused on such initiatives and the overall value gained for health services if such a large number do not continue.

Like spread, the study of sustainability has been undertaken from a number of different approaches, and consequently different models and methods have been developed internationally. Maher *et al.* (2003), intrigued by the findings of Ham *et al.* (2002), have subsequently undertaken a study into the key factors which affect the likelihood of sustainability. The focus of this work is within the NHS, with information gathered from both the available literature and individuals and teams who are involved in change for improvement. A model has been developed consisting of ten factors, which provide a framework for improvement teams to work within from the beginning of their improvement initiative and continuously to the end. The model (*see* Figure 5.4) is currently being 'field tested' within the NHS, but early responses are encouraging, including specific feedback reflecting how, by using the model, change leaders have been able to set systems in place that they previously would not have thought of establishing.

While there is no definitive answer to the question of how we spread or disseminate sustainable change of healthcare improvement, there is a significant amount of work being undertaken. Emerging evidence suggests that spread and sustainability are significantly influenced and affected by the local culture and context for change, as well as the level of positive relationships within a healthcare organisation or system.

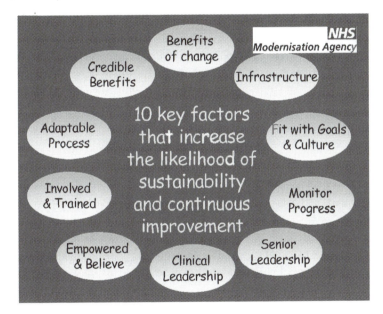

Figure 5.4   A framework for sustainability (reproduced from Maher *et al.*, 2003).

Conclusion

Much progress has been made in service improvement achieving better healthcare for patients, typically resulting in shorter waiting times, streamlined care processes, increased choice and more involvement of patients as partners in their care. It is recognised that many of the improvement initiatives in healthcare over the past five years have been heavily influenced by political aspirations for reform through policy documents such as *The NHS Plan* (DoH, 2000) (discussed in greater detail in Chapter 1), which trailblazed the formation of the Modernisation Agency.

The MA has supported healthcare staff to better understand the systems within which they work, including the importance of human relationships. Using tried-and-tested tools and techniques, teams and individuals can identify areas for improvement, plan and test changes, and implement new systems. The result is often patients with improved experiences of care.

Much has been learnt about the complexity of structures, processes and patterns that influence relationships and cultures within organisations and this has supported the implementation of improvement initiatives. However, we must close the gap in our current understanding of how to create cultures that support and sustain the gains made and stimulate continuous learning and improvement. Experience has shown that the primary motivation for service improvement should be the needs of the patients for whom we are caring, and by focusing on this we are able to better understand what needs to improve. To achieve change for improvement that both sustains and leads to continual improvement, individuals and teams must use a combination of the 'softer sides' of organisational development and the human dimension of change and the 'harder sides' of tools, techniques, measurement and project management.

The next phase must embed this philosophy at all levels of our complex healthcare system and demonstrate how it complements professional values and knowledge. It will involve the development of organisational environments and cultures conducive to service improvement along with methods to build improvement and learning into everyday practice.

References

AtKisson A (2001) *Sustainability is Dead – Long Live Sustainability*. Accessed from www.AtKisson.com on 31 December 03.

Bate P, Robert G and Bevan H (2003) The next phase of health care improvement: what can we learn from social movements? *Quality & Safety in Health Care*. **13**: 62–6.

Bevan H, Corrigan C and Plsek P (2003) *NHS Modernisation: making it mainstream: a commentary on the research report*. Modernisation Agency, unpublished paper.

Bradford Health Community Newsletter (2004) *Raising the Bar: pursuing perfection in Bradford*. **Issue 1**: 1.

Capra F (1996) *The Web of Life: the new scientific understanding of living systems*. Anchor Books, New York.

Capra F (2002) *The Hidden Connections: integrating the biological, cognitive and social dimensions of life into sustainability*. Doubleday, New York.

Clarke C, Reed J, Wainwright D, McClelland S, Swallow V, Harden J, Walton G and Walsh A (2004) The discipline of improvement: something old, something new? *Journal of Nursing Management*. **12**: 85–96.

Daft R and Noe R (2000) *Organisational Behaviour*. Harcourt, London.

Department of Health (2000) *The NHS Plan: a plan for investment, a plan for reform.* The Stationery Office, London.

Department of Trade and Industry (2003) *Innovation Report – Competing in the Global Economy: the innovation challenge.* The Stationery Office, London.

Fillingham D (2004) *The Future Development of NHS Modernisation.* Presentation to Modernisation Leaders Conference, 1 April, London.

Gladwell M (2000) *The Tipping Point: how little things can make a big difference.* Abacus, London.

Goldratt E (1990) *Theory of Constraints.* North River Press, Massachusetts.

Goldratt E and Cox J (1993) *The Goal.* Gower, Aldershot.

Greenhalgh T, Robert G, Bate P, Kyriakidou O, Macfarlane F and Peacock R (2004) *How to Spread Good Ideas: a systematic review of the literature on diffusion, dissemination and sustainability of innovations in health service delivery and organisation.* NHSSDO Programme, London.

Ham C, Kipping R, McLeod H and Meredith P (2002) *Capacity, Culture and Leadership: lessons from experience of improving access to hospital services.* Health Services Management Centre School of Public Policy, University of Birmingham, Birmingham.

Institute of Medicine (2001) *Crossing the Quality Chasm, A New Health System for the 21st Century.* National Academy Press, Washington, DC.

Langley G, Nolan K, Nolan T, Norman C and Provost L (1996) *The Improvement Guide: a practical approach to enhancing organisational performance.* Jossey-Bass Publishers, San Francisco, CA.

Maher L, Gustafsen D, Evans A and McManus L (2003) *A Framework to Support Sustainability of Improvement in the National Health Service.* Modernisation Agency, unpublished paper.

Maher L and Plsek P (2003) *Enabling Innovation through Creativity to Transform Healthcare.* Modernisation Agency Management Board, November, unpublished paper.

Modernisation Agency (2002a) *The Improvement Leaders' Guide to Involving Patients and Carers.* Ancient House, Ipswich.

Modernisation Agency (2002b) *An Introduction to Pursuing Perfection: raising the bar in health and social care locally and internationally.* Ancient House, Ipswich.

Modernisation Agency (2002c) *The Improvement Leaders' Guide to Process Mapping, Analysis and Redesign.* Ancient House, Ipswich.

Modernisation Agency (2002d) *The Improvement Leaders' Guide to Working in Systems.* Ancient House, Ipswich.

Modernisation Agency (2002e) *The Improvement Leaders' Guide to Sustainability and Spread.* Ancient House, Ipswich.

Modernisation Agency (2002f) *Sustainability and Spread in the National Booking Programme.* Summary Report No. 2, Leicester.

Modernisation Agency (2002g) *Spreading and Sustaining New Practices: sharing the learning from the Cancer Services Collaborative.* Summary Report No. 3, Leicester.

Øvretveit J (2003) *Making Temporary Quality Improvement Continuous: a review of research relevant to the sustainability of quality improvement in healthcare.* Unpublished paper.

Penny J (2003) *Building the Discipline of Improvement in Health and Social Care: summary of progress October 2002–October 2003 and recommendations.* Modernisation Agency Management Board, unpublished paper.

Plsek P (1997) *Creativity, Innovation and Quality.* American Society for Quality, Wisconsin.

Plsek P (2002) *Framework for the Leading Modernisation Programme.* Modernisation Agency, unpublished paper.

Shewhart W (1931) *Ecomomic Control of Quality of Manufactured Product.* Nostrand Reinhold, Princeton, NJ.

Further reading and websites

http://www.modern.nhs.uk/improvementguides

Visit this website for full access to the following guides.

Series 1
Process mapping, analysis and redesign
Matching capacity and demand
Measurement for improvement

Series 2
Involving patients and carers
Managing the human dimensions of change
Sustainability and spread

Series 3
Building and nurturing an improvement culture
Working with groups
Redesigning roles
Working in systems

For more on creativity contact: paulplsek@DirectedCreativity.com

CHAPTER 6

Psychodynamic approaches: organisational health and effectiveness

Vega Zagier Roberts

Introduction

The term 'psychodynamic' conveys the link between two ideas: 'psycho-', deriving from the Greek word *psyche,* meaning soul or mind and forming words relating to mental processes; and 'dynamic' from the Greek *dynamis,* meaning strength or power, used in physics and other fields to denote forces 'causing energy, motion, action and change'. Thus, the study of psychodynamics is the study of mental forces operating in and between individuals and systems in ways that affect their thinking and behaviour.

Practitioners of psychodynamic approaches to organisational development (OD) vary both in their theoretical orientation and in their practice. This chapter is based on one particular tradition developed at the Tavistock Institute of Human Relations from the late 1950s onwards, which combines concepts and insights from psycho-analysis with ideas and practices from the social sciences, open systems theory and group relations training. Crucially, this 'school' attends not only to emotional and unconscious forces within organisations as they affect individuals and groups in the workplace, but also to structures, organisational design, the division of labour, the distribution and exercise of authority, and the processes and activities through which work is carried out. At the outset it is important to make clear that the commonly held belief that psychodynamically informed consultancy in organisations is necess-arily 'touchy-feely', focusing chiefly on interpersonal relationships or individuals, is a misperception. Indeed, some of the earliest projects of the Tavistock Institute were in such 'hard-headed' environments as coal mining and factories (for descriptions of these see Trist and Murray, 1990; also the account of the work of Jaques in Chapter 9 of this volume). Now often referred to as 'systems-psychodynamics', this tradition continues to be applied in a wide variety of organisations, often in combination with other OD approaches.

Nonetheless, with some of its roots in what was originally a clinical discipline, systems-psychodynamics consultancy is often concerned with improving organisational 'health'. The misunderstanding that arises is that this refers mainly to the psychological state of individuals and groups, whereas in fact the focus is on what is 'healthy' or 'unhealthy' in the structure and functioning of work systems. As I shall demonstrate, organisational health is as much about effectiveness as about morale or stress levels. Indeed, I would argue that the opportunity to do a good job is the greatest source of job satisfaction and workforce wellbeing.

This chapter will first set out the theoretical underpinnings of a systems-psychodynamics approach to OD before moving on to describe some of the tools and techniques deployed by practitioners working in this 'school'. It then outlines some uses, misuses and limitations of the approach before looking at evaluations of its impact.

Theoretical underpinnings

Concepts from psychoanalysis

The unconscious: anxieties and defences

The cornerstone of psychodynamic thinking is the assumption that there is an unconscious, that is, a part of our mental life which is hidden and affects us in ways that we are not aware of. While it is easy to demonstrate that there are thoughts and memories lodged in our brain but out of conscious awareness – for example, when we suddenly remember a forgotten name or telephone number – psychoanalytic theory proposes that particular aspects of our experience become unconscious as a way of protecting us from anxiety and pain.

Like 'unconscious', the word 'anxiety' is part of our everyday language, generally referring to a disturbing emotional state evoked by anticipating a threatening future event. In the workplace, staff have many conscious anxieties, such as fear of redundancy, worries about a patient who may die as a result of some failure on their part, and so on. They are then likely to take certain actions in order to manage or reduce these anxieties, such as mobilising their trade unions or setting up elaborate protocols to prevent errors (and there may be links here to the account of 'street-level bureaucrats' given in Chapter 2).

However, Sigmund Freud, and many of those developing his ideas subsequently, put forward the notion that some anxieties are unconscious. For example, we may have impulses which we consider unacceptable such as wanting to hurt someone we love or harbouring sexual feelings towards a parent or child. If these feelings were to be fully conscious, they could pose a threat to our sense of ourselves as loving and generally decent people and therefore the feelings are pushed out of awareness through the use of defence mechanisms. These include, among others, denial (the feelings do not exist), projection (the feelings belong to someone else), rationalisation, idealisation and intellectualisation (*see* Freud, 1966).

The application of these ideas to organisations builds on the work of the psycho-analyst Melanie Klein. Klein (1959), basing her work on infant observation as well as the analyses of adults, proposed that the newborn infant is initially unable to perceive and relate to others as whole people. She has good experiences which she attributes to a 'good mother' towards whom she has loving feelings, and bad experiences which she experiences as coming from a 'bad mother' whom she hates and attacks with screaming and biting. Klein called this way of interpreting the world the *paranoid-schizoid position*: 'paranoid' because the cause of distress and anxiety is perceived as coming from outside oneself; and 'schizoid' because of the splitting of others into good and bad.

As the infant matures physically and emotionally, she gradually learns that the good and bad mother are one person whom she both loves and hates, that is, she becomes capable of *ambivalence* or mixed feelings towards the same person. This is accompanied by guilt and remorse for attacks on her. Klein called this the *depressive* position, because the nature of the anxiety shifts away from paranoid to depressive concerns about damage one has caused. If the baby can tolerate these depressive anxieties, she can continue to mature, and the guilt and remorse lead to taking responsibility for the impact one has on others, and to the need and desire to make reparation. These are the source of generosity, altruism and creative productivity throughout life. However, if the guilt and remorse are too extreme to bear, there is a retreat to the paranoid-schizoid position, using splitting, denial and projection to locate badness 'out there' rather than within oneself. Klein referred to these two states of mind as 'positions' rather than stages, because throughout life we oscillate between these two positions, depending on the strength and nature of our anxieties and other factors.

So what does all this have to do with organisations? In his ground-breaking paper 'On the dynamics of social structure', Jaques (1953) proposed that 'one of the primary cohesive elements binding individuals into institutionalised human association is that of defense against anxiety' (pp.420–1). Within social structures, including organis-ations, individuals and groups take up unconscious as well as conscious roles. He gives the example of the first officer of a ship who 'is regarded by common consent as the source of trouble' (p.426) for everything that goes wrong. This serves on the one hand to relieve everyone else of persecuting anxiety, and on the other allows the ship's captain, on whom all lives depend, to be idealised as a reliable protector. This kind of splitting is characteristic of the paranoid-schizoid position. While it may be useful aboard ship, it is often dysfunctional in organisations, leading to blaming, scapegoating and a reduction in realistic problem-solving capacities.

Probably the best-known of the early Tavistock consultancy interventions in healthcare systems is Isabel Menzies' work with a teaching hospital, described in her classic paper: 'Social systems as a defense against anxiety: an empirical study of the nursing service of a general hospital' (1960). The presenting issue was a request for help in planning the training of student nurses in order to reconcile the conflicting needs of student nurses on the one hand and patient care on the other. There was a very high level of student drop-out and they also had high sickness rates. Menzies postulated that the nature and intensity of the anxieties inherent in nursing work – the intimate involvement with human pain, distress and death – had led to the development of organisational defences. Examples of such defences included splitting up the nurse–patient relationship by allocating nursing tasks for each patient to a number of different nurses and constant rotation of nurses to different wards, denial of the significance of the individual by depersonalising patients ('the liver in bed 5'), promoting detachment from feelings, and reducing the potentially unbearable sense of responsibility for life-and-death decisions through elaborate systems of checks and counter-checks and through ritualised task-performance.

These defences came at a high cost, both to the organisation encumbered by an inflexible system which made it difficult to respond adequately to constantly shifting demands, and to individual student nurses who were deprived of the kind of meaningful interactions with patients that had drawn them to the profession in the first place. As Menzies Lyth (1979) puts it:

> Defence systems are in the end likely to be anti-supportive to staff. This is not only because they reduce their level of performance and their satisfaction from it, but also because they tend to their personal diminution. Comments about such personal diminution were common among the nurses at the teaching hospital; they were grieved by it and felt unsupported in their efforts to discharge their responsibilities efficiently (p.273).

Every kind of work has its own particular anxieties, related to the nature of the work, and each work system develops structures which defend against anxiety. Obholzer and Roberts (1994) suggest that our health service might more aptly be called the 'keep-death-at-bay' service in that one of its functions is to manage societal anxieties about death, illness and disability. Thus, in addition to the anxieties associated directly with the work, the health service is used as 'a collective unconscious system to shield us from the anxieties arising from an awareness of illness and mortality' (Obholzer and Roberts, 1994, p.171) by giving hope of ever-longer life.

Defences are essential if we are not to be overwhelmed by anxiety; the question is whether existing defence systems in an organisation are working, and at what cost. As Obholzer and Roberts (1994) put it:

> Walk into one or another [hospital] and you will probably be bowled over by the horror of the place. Mention it to a regular member, however, and they will not know what you are talking about … What they are expressing is a denial, or a repression, of the substance of your observation. This flight from reality happens gradually and largely unconsciously. In the process of inducting new members, the group unconsciously gives the message, 'This is how we ignore what is going on – pretend along with us, and you will soon be one of us' (p.174, parentheses added).

A systems-psychodynamics approach to OD generally involves an assessment of the client organisation to identify the nature of the anxieties and the prevailing social defence system(s). This can open the way to finding more effective and less costly alternatives, as illustrated by the scenario in Box 6.1.

Box 6.1: Interdisciplinary conflict in a hospital

At Shady Glen, a hospital caring for very impaired elderly people, there was constant conflict between the ward-based nursing staff and the specialist therapists – speech, occupational and physiotherapists – who were based in specialist departments and visited the wards or removed patients to work with them. The senior management team wished to set up a project to study and improve the quality of life for patients, which would require collaboration between these two groups, and invited two external consultants to work with them. Because of the depth of ill feeling between the groups, these consultants decided to work with them separately, one with the ward managers and the other with the heads of the different specialist therapies, before trying to work with them together.

The therapists were young, fairly autonomous and full of therapeutic zeal, though frustrated by what they perceived as the nurses undermining and sabotaging their rehabilitative efforts, for example by not having patients ready on time for their appointments or by cancelling groups. The therapists were very enthusiastic about the project and generated a stream of new ideas for ways to improve the quality of patients' lives. Gradually discussions ground to a halt as they anticipated that the nurses would prevent any of these ideas being put into practice. Meanwhile, the ward managers' group held back from the project, saying very little in meetings beyond that they had 'seen it all before' and that 'as usual' they would be blamed for the lack of change. Most of them had worked in this hospital for a long time, devoting themselves to maintaining the patients in the best physical condition possible: clean, well-fed, free of bedsores and protected from injuring themselves. They felt both the therapists and the senior management team were unrealistic about what was possible for patients, and had no idea how much back-breaking labour was involved in keeping the patients safe and well.

One way to understand the situation presented in Box 6.1 is in terms of the different social defence systems operated by the two groups. The work with frail, demented elderly people stirs up unconscious anxieties about our own eventual ageing and dependency, and also about our relationships with parents and grandparents, for example about whether we have cared for them well enough in their old age. In this particular setting, where patients rarely left except to be buried, there were also inevitably repressed anxieties about how to do a good-enough job or indeed to make much difference at all. The nurses' insistence that any rehabilitative work was unrealistic served to defend them against potentially unbearable feelings of disappointment and failure. The therapists meanwhile held all the therapeutic optimism, defending against feelings of failure by blaming the nurses for preventing them from carrying out rehabilitative work. This allowed them to hold on to fantasies about the potential results of their interventions, if only they were 'allowed' to implement their ideas. Thus each group used the other unconsciously to hold their own split-off, denied and disowned feelings as a way of making their experience of the work more bearable. However, this paranoid-schizoid mode of functioning impaired the abilities of both groups to work effectively, let alone to collaborate in providing the optimal quality of life for the patients. Ironically, these defences – designed to protect staff from painful feeling – actually reduced job satisfaction, thus making the experience of working at Shady Glen even more painful.

Containment and listening to unconscious communication

What potentially makes depressive position anxieties tolerable is *containment*. In individual development, this comes from the capacity of the infant's caretakers to respond appropriately to the baby's communications. In the pre-verbal phase, communication is largely through *projective identification*, a psychological process whereby the feelings of one person are projected 'into' another who identifies with them. A calm and psychologically available mother can 'hear' the baby's communication because she can allow his or her distressed feelings to get inside her without herself becoming excessively disturbed by them. She can then 'metabolise' the projected feelings so that the baby is no longer overwhelmed by them. In contrast, a harassed, pre-occupied or over-anxious mother may feel persecuted by the baby's crying and rush to action – for example stuffing a bottle in his mouth – or she may distance herself from the child, or even punish him for making her feel inadequate.

Unconscious communication through projective identification is universal. It is the basis of empathy, that is, the capacity to 'read' another person's feelings accurately through allowing oneself to be emotionally in touch with them. This enables us to respond with 'emotional intelligence' (Goleman, 1996) to those around us, containing their anxieties (making them more bearable) rather than pushing them away or retaliating. In the workplace, managers are potentially a major source of containment as staff project the difficult feelings stirred up by their work into them. If the manager can tolerate these projections and reflect on them, he or she is likelier to respond in ways that reduce anxiety, so that staff regain the capacity to think and behave in a work-oriented way. But, like the harassed mother, the pre-occupied or over-burdened manager may well be unavailable to provide this containing function, as illustrated by the example in Box 6.2.

Box 6.2: The harassed manager

Peter was the newly appointed head of a learning disabilities directorate in disarray. There were very high levels of staff sickness, huge numbers of complaints from patients and carers, and constant serious incidents requiring investigation by senior management. The unit was generally regarded as failing both clinically and financially, and was under constant scrutiny.

By the end of his first year he had succeeded in putting sound systems in place so that the directorate was meeting all of its targets and serious incidents had almost stopped. Instead of feeling pleased with his achievement, he felt exhausted and very irritable with his staff, whom he felt were making incessant unnecessary demands on him, calling him at night to ask advice on minor matters they 'should' be able to handle without him. It required constant effort not to 'leak' his irritation and shut himself away from them.

Peter was familiar with the concept of projective identification and during a period of sick-leave was able to consider how his own state of mind might be an unconscious communication from his staff. This enabled him to think about the constant drain on them of looking after clients who were so highly dependent and so rarely gave them a sense of significant success. Over the next few months he initiated new kinds of conversations with team leaders and staff about the stresses of the clinical work itself, and together with them put in place some new practices and support systems to address these. The out-of-hours calls fell dramatically and Peter found a renewed sense of challenge and interest in his job.

In this example, the staff projected both their own depressed exhaustion and their competence into Peter. He contained and identified with these projections, joining the staff in their belief that only he had the competence to make decisions. However, the cost of this was an extremely high level of dependency on him, with the result that his health suffered. In many similar situations, managers defend themselves unconsciously from this dynamic by 'volleying back' the projections which can then get acted out by the staff in the form of neglect, mistakes or even minor (and occasionally major) acts of abuse. Alternatively, staff may turn the unwanted feelings inward, which can contribute to low job satisfaction, absenteeism, high staff turnover, accidents or serious untoward incidents.

Concepts from open systems theory

A living organism can survive only by exchanging materials with its environment, that is, by being an open system. This requires having an external boundary, a membrane or skin, which separates inside from outside. This boundary must be solid enough to prevent leakage and to protect the organism from disintegrating, but permeable enough for the necessary exchanges with the environment to take place. The simplest living system is a single cell; in more complex organisms, there will be a number of open systems operating simultaneously, each performing its own specialised functions but coordinated with the activities of other systems so as to serve the needs of the organism as a whole.

The work of Lewin (1947) in applying these ideas to human systems was extended and developed by Miller and Rice (1967) to provide a framework for studying the relationships between the parts and the whole in organisations, and also between organisations and their environment.

The primary task

An organisation as an open system can be schematically represented as in Figure 6.1. The box in the centre represents the system of activities required to perform the task of converting inputs into outputs, for example turning leather into shoes.

Figure 6.1   Schematic representation of an organisation as an open system (adapted from Miller and Rice, 1967).

Obviously, most enterprises have many different kinds of input and output. A shoe factory, for example, besides taking in the raw materials required to make shoes, also takes in information from the environment and uses it to produce financial plans and marketing strategies. It is likely to have different departments such as production, sales and personnel, all of which need to be coordinated. How to allocate resources, and how to prioritise among the organisation's various activities, is determined by its *primary task*, defined by Rice (1963) as the task it must perform in order to survive.

In human service organisations, one might define inputs as 'people in state A' and outputs as 'people in state B'. For example, a hospital takes in people who are ill and its main intended output is people whose health is improved enough so as not to require inpatient care. Clearly, a hospital has many other tasks such as training, research and so on, and therefore many subsystems with different inputs and outputs. In theory, the task of each, however large or small, contributes in some way to the task of the system as a whole. However, often the tasks of subsystems are experienced as competing or even contradicting one another. Even in a relatively small healthcare system like Shady Glen Hospital, described earlier, the competing task definitions guiding the work of the different professional groups caused significant problems. In the ever-larger healthcare organisations, relating the tasks of subsystems to each other and to a sense of common purpose is becoming more and more challenging. Despite its limitations in complex systems, the concept of the primary task remains extremely useful. A clear task definition can provide a kind of yardstick by which staff and managers can continually evaluate whether or not they are on course and whether the design of the system, its boundaries and working practices remain appropriate.

Management at and of the boundary

Just as living organisms need a membrane which is neither too permeable nor too impermeable, so organisational systems need boundaries which regulate transactions with the environment and between subsystems. This regulation is a core function of management. For example, a ward manager needs to ensure that staffing levels and other resources match the number and needs of patients on the ward. If too many patients are admitted, or essential supplies run out, the ward system can no longer perform its task. For this reason, the open systems model locates the manager at the boundary of the system they manage (*see* Figure 6.2).

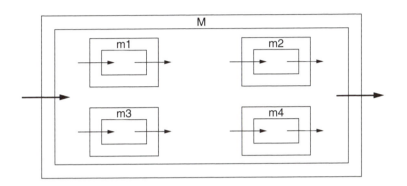

Figure 6.2 Management of multiple systems of activity within an organisation (reproduced from Roberts, 1994)

Note: The smaller boxes represent discrete task-systems, each with a boundary managed by m1, m2, etc. The larger box represents the overall enterprise, managed by M. In conventional organisational terms, M is the line manager of the four Ms.

This position *at* the boundary of the system enables the manager to be in contact both with the external environment and with the internal state of the system. This includes being in touch with the emotional state of the staff he or she manages in order to provide the necessary *containment* of conscious and unconscious anxieties, as described in the previous section. The manager who loses this boundary position, either by being drawn too far into the system, or by being too cut off from it, can no longer manage effectively.

Bringing the two theoretical strands together: systems-psychodynamics

Task and anti-task

Menzies Lyth (1979) suggests that when the primary task becomes too difficult, or when it is inadequately defined, task performance may implicitly slip into anti-task behaviour. If we refer back to the example of Shady Glen, it was the impression of the external consultant team that the nurses behaved as if their task was to keep the patients as safe and well as possible for as long as possible. While this led to commendable standards of nursing care, it also led to a number of practices that were not in the patients' best interests, such as discouraging mobility lest they hurt themselves and keeping their personal belongings under lock and key, and, as a result, the environment was excessively institutional. The nurses felt that they would be blamed if any physical harm came to their patients, and ward protocols evolved to prevent this rather than to enhance patients' wellbeing. The more complex and psychologically demanding task of balancing the tension between patients' safety and their quality of life was thus avoided.

The design of work systems

Boundaries around subsystems within organisations serve a number of functions. They help to identify who is inside and who is outside the system, thus fostering a sense of group and also individual identity: 'I am a member of team X which has a task to which I contribute'. Thus, they enable us to create mental maps of the system(s) of which we are a part.

However, boundaries may be drawn in such a way as to support an anti-task. For example, at the start of the consultation to Shady Glen, the therapists were managed from within their respective departments, entirely separate from the ward system, which was staffed and managed by nurses. At a later stage, therapists were integrated into multidisciplinary ward teams. The new boundary gradually shifted everyone's mental maps. Therapists began to think of themselves primarily as members of a ward team, rather than of the speech or occupational therapy or physiotherapy department, and nurses came to regard the therapists as 'one of us' rather than as outsiders visiting – and even disrupting – the ward.

Box 6.3: Redesigning a mental health system

Cannon Fields, the Community Mental Health Centre (CHMC) for Northwest Woodham, was one of three CMHCs set up to provide mental health services in the community as part of a programme to close wards at Woodham Hospital. The team, most of whom had previously worked at the hospital, was very committed to creating a service where clients would flourish, developing social and independent living skills. Its members regarded the hospital as rigid and oppressive, and based its programme on the intention to be as different from it as possible, with patients (now called clients) free to choose which therapeutic activities they would attend.

Relations between the centre and C ward at the hospital, to which Northwest Woodham residents were admitted when they needed inpatient care, were antagonistic. Cannon Fields staff considered attending ward rounds a dreaded chore, and left as soon as the round was over, as if contact might contaminate them with something they had been lucky to escape.

The formal task definition of Cannon Fields was 'to provide a comprehensive mental health service to the adult population of Northwest Woodham', a task which could only be undertaken together with C ward. However, it was as if their implicit task definition had become to be a superior alternative to hospital care, as different from the hospital as possible. This as-if or anti-task was supported by the management structure. Community psychiatric care was managed as a system quite separate from, and even in competition with, the hospital system (*see* Figure 6.3a).

Subsequently, the entire county mental health system was sectorised so that each of the three localities had a single manager overseeing both inpatient and community-based care (*see* Figure 6.3b). The new boundaries matched and supported the task of providing a comprehensive and integrated mental health service to each catchment area. Patients could then be more readily seen as a shared responsibility, whether they were at any given moment in the hospital or in the community, and the rivalry between the CMHC and the ward lessened. Ward rounds became a central activity for the staff of Cannon Fields as well as of C ward, involving their working together at assessing and meeting the needs of their joint clients.

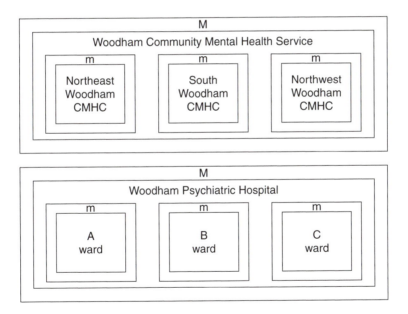

Figure 6.3a Organisation of Woodham Mental Health Services before restructuring (adapted from Obholzer and Roberts, 1994).

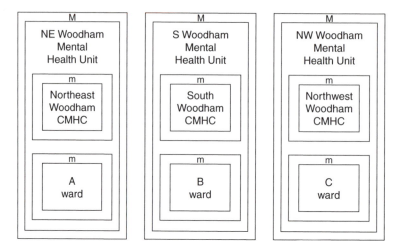

Figure 6.3b Organisation of Woodham Mental Health Services after restructuring (adapted from Obholzer and Roberts, 1994).

Interventions: tools and techniques

Most traditional psychodynamically informed therapies are based on the idea that understanding the unconscious as well as the conscious determinants of their experience enables patients to integrate previously disowned parts of the self. This integration frees psychic energy previously used to keep these parts of the self unconscious, so that the patient enjoys a greater capacity to be productive and creative, to engage in meaningful relationships and to enjoy life. The therapist provides a contained setting where the patient comes to feel safe enough to face aspects of themselves which were previously too threatening or painful to allow into consciousness.

However, organisational clients, whether these are large departments, small teams or even individuals seeking help with workplace dilemmas, are not patients, and psychodynamically oriented consultants are not in the therapist role. This is a crucial distinction. On the whole, consultants do not deliberately attempt to surface unconscious material, nor do they interpret it directly. What is transferred from therapeutic practice is not so much what consultants do but how they think and how they take up the consulting role. Four key features are set out in the following paragraphs.

'Listening with the third ear'

This is a particular kind of listening, not only to what is said but to what is being communicated at other levels; what is unsaid may be unconscious. For example, Halton (1994) describes working with a team under threat of closure which started a conversation about euthanasia. On the surface, the team was still fighting for survival, but the talk of euthanasia could also be understood as a communication about wanting to be put out of their misery. However, what is unsaid is not necessarily unconscious but may for some reason be unsayable. For example, a management team was talking angrily and defensively about a recent Commission for Health Improvement (CHI) inspection; what could not be said was that some of them were in full agreement with the report and even glad that some shortcomings had come to light. When external consultants can listen in this way, they may be able to help the client work on critical issues that previously felt too dangerous to name.

Using one's own feelings as data

This is another kind of psychoanalytically informed listening, sometimes described as listening to 'the music behind the words' or 'parallel process'. It is based on the idea that the consultant's feelings are not just their own, but may mirror the client's out-of-awareness emotional state and therefore serve as essential information about what is going on under the surface. An example is provided in Box 6.4.

Box 6.4: The music behind the words

At an awayday with an eating disorders unit to consider how to change their management structure, every comment made by the external consultant seemed to be appreciated as illuminating and useful. In the last session this changed, and suddenly everything she said was rejected. This was initially very puzzling, as she felt she was mainly summarising what they had been telling her all day. She became increasingly irritated, reminding them insistently of the evidence supporting her comments, and the team became increasingly hostile. Only when she was able to wonder if she was being 'given' an experience of what it is like to work with patients with eating disorders, who alternately swallow everything in sight and then either vomit or refuse to take in any food, could she engage with them again.

Without directly interpreting, she stopped trying to 'force-feed' her ideas and instead wondered with them about the stresses of working with their hostile and rejecting patients. This opened the way for the unit to think about how to use the new management structures to support staff in containing the difficult feelings stirred up by the work.

Some people listen to themselves in this way naturally, which may be the basis of intuition. However, it is also a skill that can be learned and practised, not only by consultants and therapists, but by managers and others in the workplace, adding richly to the other sources of data on which they base their actions and decisions.

Staying in role

It is worth noticing in the previous vignette (Box 6.4) that the consultant was already getting information about the core dynamics of the work of the eating disorders unit in the morning, when her every word was eagerly taken in. However, her pleasure at feeling she was doing good work led to her not realising this until the interaction became unpleasant. Clients' idealisation of a consultant is just as anti-task as wholesale rejection; both can derail the consultancy work and pull the consultant out of role. When consultants meet with negativity, they may act out the feelings put into them rather than using them as information. When they have too glowing a rapport with their clients, they become vulnerable to colluding in avoiding the difficult issues that need to be named and addressed.

To be effective, consultants need to be on the boundary of the system they are consulting to. This includes being non-judgemental, modelling curiosity about how things are and why, rather than taking sides, and containing anxiety (their own as well as the client's). While arguably these are attributes of all good consultants, psychodynamically informed consultants pay particular attention to the unconscious dynamics which can pull them off the boundary, for example, into oversympathising with a team who feel victimised by an unfeeling senior management, or alternatively overidentifying with managers and trying to 'fix' a recalcitrant team.

Providing conditions that facilitate growth and change

As described above, work groups develop defence systems to prevent being overwhelmed by anxiety. These systems may be healthy and effective or they may be dysfunctional, but in either case provide some psychological equilibrium. Any change invariably evokes anxiety and will therefore threaten this equilibrium to some degree. At times, the level of anxiety reaches such a pitch that staff may lose touch with their own competence, authority and power. Psychodynamically informed OD can provide the containment needed for staff to recover their capacity for effective work, as illustrated in Box 6.5.

Box 6.5: A team under threat

Bluebells was a school within a paediatric unit. It was regarded as highly innovative in its work with children with chronic debilitating illnesses. Now its founder, Irene, was leaving, as was the deputy, and it seemed unlikely that they would be replaced for some time. The team was demoralised and extremely worried about the future, anticipating that they would become vulnerable to cuts in funding and staffing. Irene was concerned that the programme she had worked so hard to build might collapse in the face of the drop in team morale, and asked me to facilitate an awayday to help the team plan how to manage the interim between the departure of the old leadership and the appointment of the new head and deputy.

At the outset of the day, the team seemed overwhelmed by issues of threat and loss – it was as if this was all they could think or talk about. When the consultant suggested that the changes might also provide some people with new opportunities, the staff who were staying on became almost manic, calling themselves 'the takeover gang', joking about getting the keys to the safe and how they would be able to pass on to new staff all the tasks they most disliked. Throughout the day, the team oscillated between feeling so dependent on Irene that they could not think about how to manage the next few months, and at other times so excited about the new opportunities ahead that the difficulties were virtually forgotten. As the day went on, they became calmer and more thoughtful, and finally were able to confront the issue that had been avoided ever since the departures had been announced, namely who among them would apply to act up as head and deputy. Only when their anxieties about how to manage rivalry and competition among themselves could be addressed were they able to focus on how to run their programme during the transition. By the end of the day they had begun to find solutions for many of the challenges ahead, and the mood was subdued but confident. Summarising the day, one teacher commented, 'Those of us who are staying are the future backbone of the school'. The team seemed to have shifted to a new position, neither fearing they might collapse into a 'spineless heap' when Irene and the other senior staff left, nor seeing themselves as an all-powerful 'takeover gang'.

The interim period before a new head was appointed was even longer than anticipated, lasting nearly a year, and was well managed by the staff. Morale remained high, and a school inspectors' report just before the new head arrived commended Bluebells highly for its work.

In the example in Box 6.5, Irene had built a stable, highly competent and cohesive team who together had created the successful Bluebells programme. However, her departure stirred up anxieties about latent rivalry in the team. To avoid dealing with these, the team focused on the external 'enemy', the senior managers who they imagined would take advantage of the hiatus to cut their programme. This successfully maintained harmony among team members, but also exacerbated their feelings of helplessness and vulnerability to the point that they were temporarily unable to engage in realistic problem solving. The awayday with an external consultant provided sufficient safety and containment to confront the deepest anxieties which in turn enabled the team to recover their competence.

Thinking systemically

At the core of a systems-psychodynamics approach to working with organisations is the assumption that whatever the presenting issue it needs to be understood systemically. Consultants are often presented with 'problem' individuals or teams who are identified as the cause of organisational difficulties, and indeed the covert consultancy assignment may be to 'sort them out'. However, as Obholzer (2003) puts it, it is 'absolutely essential to see individuals, or roles or subsets, as different but interconnected parts of the whole. Any "individual" presentation thus always, and first and foremost, needs to be seen as a systemic symptom and addressed at that level' (p.156). This is illustrated in the vignette in Box 6.6.

Box 6.6: A 'failing' pilot project

Jonathan, the manager of a well-established drug-dependency service, was having great difficulty managing his two newly appointed outreach workers. The main work of the team was clinic-based, staff seeing clients at set times for counselling, medical appointments and prescribing methadone. In response to concern about hard-to-reach clients, those who might not be accessing services because they could not 'fit' into this model, funding had been found to set up a two-year pilot drug-outreach project for two outreach workers who were to try to seek out potential clients in youth clubs and other local venues with a view to providing a more accessible service.

The outreach workers missed many supervision sessions and rarely attended team meetings. Jonathan saw them as resistant and difficult individuals and was considering starting disciplinary proceedings. In the meantime, he felt uncertain whether the team should continue providing an outreach service as there was little evidence it was effective.

In this scenario, while the two workers' personalities were doubtless part of the problem, construing the problem simply in terms of individuals provides limited options and prevents one from tackling the systemic issues. For example, the outreach service could be seen as an implicit criticism of the clinic, which had failed to reach the young drug-abusing population. One might then see the wish to blame and extrude the outreach workers as a group avoidance of the painful limitations of the traditional treatment programme. Furthermore, even clinic clients often sabotaged their treatment by missing appointments or supplementing their prescriptions with street drugs, and even those team members who attended supervision and team meetings were ambivalent about being managed and did not always adhere to rules and policies. Locating untreatability in those drug users not formally registered as clients of the services, and resistance to management in the outreach workers, may have served unconsciously as a way of maintaining the clinic as a 'good' and safe place, while 'badness' was located outside.

This way of thinking opens up new options for managing the problem. For example, the structure of the pilot project, treating outreach as an activity entirely separate from the core work of the clinic, might have been one source of difficulty. How might the service 'own' the outreach work, both its failures and potential successes? Might it be more effective for clinic staff to have mixed caseloads including some outreach work rather than having two identified specialists working apart from the rest? Alternatively, might recruitment and induction have been handled differently so that the outreach workers were more integrated with the core service from the outset?

Interventions: consulting to organisational change – a case study

---

Box 6.7: Preparing for merger

Three teams providing different kinds of day services to mentally ill people across a small county were to be merged into a single county-wide service. Team A was a day hospital staffed by nurses and occupational therapists, providing a time-limited rehabilitation programme. Team B was a resource centre staffed mainly by group and family therapists, providing a range of insight-oriented therapies. Team C was a day centre providing social activities for a more chronic client group. The vision for the new service was that this much larger team would be able to be more flexible in setting up small local mini-services responsive to particular needs in particular areas, rather than clients travelling long distances or having to fit into whichever service was nearest.

There was huge resistance to the project in all three teams, and senior management brought in a small OD team to support the merger process. The consultants first met with each team separately and during this time discovered two significant things. One was that each team had many misconceptions about the others, and tended to denigrate them. The other was that all three teams believed that a major driving force for the change was senior management's wish to get rid of Team C which was perceived to be too 'institution-alised' in its practices. Each said this privately to the consultants, but it was never said in public.

There was considerable pressure to push the change through as quickly as possible. However, the consultants felt it was essential to provide space for people to share their losses and anxieties, to understand each other's practices and to learn about each other's strengths. Only then could they begin to engage in thinking together about how to build something new and meaningful. The process was slow at first, but over a period of several months most of the staff from all three teams were able to invest in the new system. Within a year the service had become a model for innovative day care, highly regarded by both service users and senior management, and a source of great pride to its staff.

I would like to consider this case study from three points of view: first, issues around the design of change efforts; second, issues around loss and mourning; and third, issues around containing anxiety during periods of major change.

Conscious and unconscious factors in designing change efforts

Most change efforts appear to be rational enterprises. Someone has examined a particular system and found it lacking in some way, or there is a government directive which needs to be implemented and a new system has been designed to meet this need. However, all designs – whether designing a new building, a new social programme or a new organisational structure – have irrational as well as rational elements. Colman (1975), a professor of psychiatry with extensive experience of teaching and consulting to architects, and Bexton (1975), a professor of architecture, have identified some of the irrational factors which come into play in designing change, and which contribute to the widespread disappointment (ifnot actual failure) of the final results. They propose that every design has three components:

- conscious: what is said to be the intended purposes and outcome
- covert: what is known (at least to some) but unacknowledged in public, including political factors, ambitions and dreams
- unconscious: purposes that influence design but are unknown to those involved.

The conscious aims of the change described in Box 6.7 were to create a more flexible, accessible and user-responsive service across the county. A covert aim (known to all but never mentioned in a public forum) was to eliminate the institutional practices of Team C. Team B believed that another covert aim was to dismantle its psychodynamic programme which had long been a source of envy to other mental health services in the area. Identifying unconscious aims is inevitably more speculative, but over time it seemed to the consultants that one unconscious aim in this design was to get rid of the clients of Team C (who were the most chronic and least likely to improve group). The new design would probably mean that some of the clients would learn to use the new service and develop new skills, but many would not be able to make the change and would disappear, relieving people of the uncomfortable sense of achieving very little from working with them. Enabling participants in change processes to recognise and talk about some of the covert and unconscious elements in change design can be very helpful in reducing the suspiciousness and even paranoia which often undermine the implementation of change.

Change and loss

Every change involves loss which requires space for mourning. At the same time, every change brings new hope for the future. One might draw an analogy with the experience of having a bereavement while pregnant. Studies undertaken by the Tavistock Perinatal Unit in the 1980s (Bourne and Lewis, 1984; Lewis and Casement, 1986) suggest that women in this situation generally cannot manage simultaneously the two psychological tasks of mourning and preparing for the new birth, and that often mourning is neglected, with potentially serious long-term consequences. In organisations, these two experiences tend to be split up among different subgroups, described by Marris (1974) as 'tribes'; a pro-change tribe trumpeting the advantages of the impending 'birth', while the anti-change tribe holds all the feelings of loss and may be unable to see any benefits. In this way, ambivalence is avoided; each tribe holds one side of the emotional experience on behalf of the whole system. However, those expressing resistance to change on behalf of others may become quite marginalised and alienated as the change is driven forward in a way that fails to take the losses into account. When feelings of loss are respected, and space is made for working through these feelings, change processes are likelier to succeed and to produce fewer casualties.

In the story told in Box 6.7, Team A was the most enthusiastic about the change, while Teams B and C held the feelings of loss and expressed the resistance. However, over the course of the consultation, Team A was able to recognise and acknowledge significant losses for themselves which they had previously denied. This helped to shift the dynamic and free members of Teams B and C to recognise ways in which they might gain from the proposed change. This shift played a major part in enabling staff from all three teams to begin to own and shape the new system. Furthermore, as Marris (1974) points out, the essential work of grieving is about reconstructing meaning, that is detaching one's sense of purpose from the past and reformulating it so that it enables one to engage with the present and future. In this way, a sense of continuity of self and meaning can be restored. This requires valuing the past. A significant aspect of the preparation for merger in this case study involved the three teams sharing their stories and finding ways to connect values from the past with the plans for the future (an example, perhaps, of the social nature of sensemaking described in Chapter 1).

Containing anxiety during change

Organisational change also inevitably involves the dismantling of existing social defence mechanisms which unleashes the anxiety these previously contained. In the example above, Team C's 'institutionalised' practices were one way of managing the anxieties inevitably stirred up by working with severely mentally ill people; so were Team B's highly structured therapeutic programme and Team A's focus on rapid throughput. The change therefore led not only to conscious fears about loss of cherished working practices or status, but also to unconscious and primitive fears about annihilation as aspects of each team's previous identity were taken away. The consultancy intervention could be seen as providing a 'transitional container' (Amado and Ambrose, 2001) to manage anxieties in the interim period.

The change described in Box 6.7 was on a relatively small scale, involving fewer than 50 staff. However, similar dynamics occur in very large-scale changes as described, for example, by Krantz (2001). He categorises change efforts in terms of how 'primitive' or 'sophisticated' they are, where primitive refers to the use of organisational defences such as denial, splitting and projection, and sophisticated to the more integrated functioning of the depressive position 'where the anxieties attending deep change are sufficiently contained to prevent the emergence of destructive disarray or scapegoating' (p.139). In Krantz's view, a major indicator of the level of sophistication of a change effort, and also a major contributor to its success, is the degree of investment the organisation makes to providing containment during the change process, how realistic they are about the time needed to bring about the change, and how capable they are of respect and concern for those who may be hurt or damaged by the change.

Uses, misuses and limitations of psychodynamically informed approaches

A major limitation to the effectiveness of psychodynamically informed interventions in healthcare systems comes from the nature of many of the projects which often focus on 'soft' issues like stress and morale, divorced from issues of structure or effectiveness. For example, a project to study stress in junior doctors in A&E departments involved three external consultants working with three groups of such doctors in three different hospitals. While evaluation of the project, based on before and after questionnaires, indicated some decrease in stress levels, the design of the project precluded any systemic intervention. Any benefit was therefore limited to those junior doctors who actually participated in the study rather than to those who came after them, and there was no impact on the functioning of the A&E department as a whole.

Some of this can be laid at the door of the practitioners themselves, particularly those who come from clinical backgrounds. Their internal model may be one of 'treating' symptoms, so that they fail to attend sufficiently to systemic issues of task, roles and work design. At its worst, this can lead to causing harm. Menzies Lyth (1990) warns that psychoanalytically oriented consultants often:

> ... go into an institution to conduct sensitivity or support groups, usually for 'carers' like nurses or social workers. Their aim is to increase the sensitivity of the carers to their clients and themselves and help them bear the stress of their work ... the problem is that the carers often return to a work situation where roles, structures and work culture are changed minimally, if at all ... people become disappointed, frustrated and disillusioned. Attitudes change back in defense against these feelings, and in line with the demands of the institutional system. Or people can no longer tolerate the system and leave. The consultants and what they stand for may be discredited (pp.468–9).

Some of the difficulty stems from the combination of lack of awareness in commissioners of how to make the best use of this kind of consultancy and consultants' failure or inability to engage key stakeholders sufficiently before embarking on an intervention. This is illustrated by the case study in Box 6.8.

Box 6.8: A contract for post-merger culture building

Following the merger of two health trusts, a team of consultants was invited to assist with building a new culture of participation. Their initial proposals, involving work with all levels of the organisation, were rejected on the basis that all posts above the level of team leaders were occupied on a temporary basis as the full senior management structure had still to be worked out. The intervention therefore comprised a number of learning sets, bringing together team managers from across the county.

Learning sets met monthly over approximately one year, and because all participants came from within one organisation, they were able to set up a number of problem-solving projects, for example developing systems for smoother transition of patients between day care, inpatient and outpatient services. It was hoped that as senior managers were appointed, they would engage in dialogue with the learning sets, inviting them to join in working on some of the 'hard' issues facing the new trust, such as the overspend resulting from high drug bills and employment of agency staff. However, the new managers saw the purpose of the learning sets as providing support for team managers during the period of transition, and the sets were disbanded once the new structure was in place.

Thus, in the end, the learning set benefited the members, their teams and their patients, but failed to impact significantly on the wider system. Some participants who had joined sceptically, but wanting to believe the rhetoric of the new trust about mobilising frontline expertise to tackle 'the big problems', retreated back into a cynicism even greater than before the merger.

It is not only underestimating the potential of psychodynamic consultancy which is the problem, but the deeply ingrained underestimation of the capacity and desire of 'frontline' staff to contribute to strategic problem solving. More than 40 years after Menzies' study of nursing we still see the projection of responsibility upwards and irresponsibility downwards, as if staff are capable only of local concerns. For example, in some recent work by the author with a new primary care trust to develop its Professional Executive Committee (PEC), it proved very easy to 'develop' the clinical representatives. However, it proved very difficult to develop genuine collaborative dialogue between them and executive board members of the PEC on strategic matters. The desire to change this is present – we hear endlessly about empowerment and participation – but it still happens relatively rarely. Perhaps this is because any health service is suffused with issues of dependency: patients who comply with treatment because of an implicit promise that this will give them the best chance of restored health; and clinical disciplines with strong hierarchies which implicitly promise to protect juniors from anxiety and blame if they comply with decisions from the top.

Evaluating outcomes: impact on organisational health and effectiveness

In order to evaluate outcomes systematically, criteria need to be identified from the outset as part of the diagnostic and design phases (*see* Chapter 4), and in collaboration between client and consultant. In practice, this happens relatively rarely. Often there is a small budget, used to buy an 'off-the-shelf' solution, such as a staff support group, an awayday or consultancy to an individual, and evaluation is never considered. Where larger-system interventions are commissioned, evaluation, if any, is likely to be done as a separate piece of work, often by consultants other than those providing the intervention, and usually written up for the insight (or reassurance) of the client rather than for publication. Even when there is no formal system for measuring impact, consultants usually attempt some evaluation of the effectiveness of their own intervention, both through reviewing the work themselves and inviting feedback from the client. However, as Chapter 13 points out, devising measures that can link process to outcomes confidently is complex, and proving that a particular change is linked to a specific intervention is problematic. There are numerous descriptive case studies specifically about the impact of systems-psychodynamically informed interventions (*see*, for example, Menzies Lyth, 1988; Miller, 1993; Trist and Murray, 1990) but no published empirical research.

One formal evaluation study that has been undertaken jointly by the client and consultant organisations was of a three-year intervention by the Tavistock Clinic in a large social services department (which at this stage remains confidential). The consultants met with senior managers in social services to agree the aims of the intervention, and then with the evaluation researchers to incorporate these into the research instruments. The researchers used quantitative measures based on questionnaires before and after the interventions, as well as qualitative interviews. This study has not yet been completed, but preliminary findings indicate significant positive impact both in team functioning and also at an organisational level on a number of parameters. These included: greater clarity about organisational purpose(s); more realistic engagement with clients; a shift towards shared leadership and problem solving; and reduction in intra- and intergroup conflict. Evidence from the study converged in highlighting that attention should be drawn to the following three areas:

- clarity about the task of the organisation
- clarity about the authority structure
- the opportunity to participate and contribute.

Given that much of the evaluation research focused on changes in individual wellbeing, it is fascinating that participants identified these three areas as key. This supports the central premise of this chapter, namely that organisational 'health' depends more on developing healthy social structures and effective ways for staff to relate their own particular work to the broader organisational purposes, than on providing support for stress to individuals or teams. The systems-psychodynamics approach to working with organisations always keeps these issues in view. Even when consulting to individuals, the focus is on understanding inter-related roles and issues of task, boundaries and authority structure; it is essentially an organisational intervention which enables people to renegotiate their roles and exercise authority more effectively.

Conclusion

The psychodynamic strand of the systems-psychodynamics approach described in this chapter is fundamentally about enabling people at all levels in organisations to use their full capacities, neither projecting these on to others (as described in the vignette in Box 6.2) nor taking flight into unrealistic omnipotent fantasies (as described in Box 6.1). In particular, this means employees exercising their authority fully and appropriately, without either lapsing into an exaggerated sense of help-lessness or becoming authoritarian. This fits with current national and local initiatives to promote shared leadership and empowerment. Further, at the heart of this approach is the endeavour to foster a spirit of enquiry, a culture of curiosity in place of a culture of blame. Organisational work in this tradition is always a collaborative enterprise between clients and consultants who learn and problem solve together, never a 'doing to' the client by 'experts'. Thus it is well placed to contribute to OD with its core task of developing the learning capacities of organisations, as defined in Chapter 1.

Psychodynamically informed OD work brings into view the irrational elements of organisational life, the 'emotional undertow' (Obholzer, 2004), which can contrib-ute to the kinds of disappointment and failure described in Chapter 2 with regard to implementing policy. Such insight can be invaluable, but it is not enough. Indeed, used in isolation, psychoanalytic approaches to organisational work will at best have little impact; at worst they can actually cause harm by surfacing issues that cannot be adequately dealt with, or by 'pathologising' individuals and organisations.

This chapter describes one model for combining psychodynamic insights with other approaches, namely using concepts from open systems theory in order to attend to issues of organisational structure and the design of change, but it is not the only one. OD practitioners trained in very different disciplines can enrich their work by adding a degree of psychodynamic understanding to their 'toolkit'. Indeed, it has been argued (James and Jarrett 2003) that any OD practitioner (and arguably any clinician, manager or leader), however 'expert', needs this kind of understanding in order to work successfully with the complex challenges they face. They evocatively refer to this as 'extending the consultant's band-width' (or repertoire in the language of Chapter 3). Similarly, any psychoanalytically grounded consultant undertaking projects to bring about organisational development and change needs to be aware of and able to use ideas and practices from among the range of other approaches described in this book.

All too often, psychodynamically informed consultancy is 'given' to teams or individuals as a gift or in response to a request to provide 'support' for stressed staff teams or prescribed as a 'treatment' for 'symptoms' such as conflict or resistance to change. While consultants can and do provide supportive containment, it is essential not to overlook the fact that the greatest source of support for workers in any organisation is the containment provided by having a clear task definition that is both feasible and meaningful, and roles and boundaries designed in a way that support task performance. The 'health' and effectiveness of organisations depends on developing systems and structures that make best use of the rich human resources within them. It is in this area that the approach introduced in this chapter has most to offer.

References

Amado G and Ambrose A (2001) *The Transitional Approach to Change. Karnac Books, London.*

Bexton W (1975) The architect and planner: change agent or scapegoat? In: A Colman and W Bexton (eds) *Group Relations Reader 1.* Grex, Sauslito, CA.

Bourne S and Lewis E (1984) Delayed psychological effects of perinatal deaths: the next pregnancy and the next generation. *British Medical Journal.* **289**: 147–8.

Colman A (1975) Irrational aspects of design. In: A Colman and W Bexton (eds) *Group Relations Reader 1.* Grex, Sauslito, CA.

Freud A (1966) *The Ego and the Mechanisms of Defense.* International Universities Press, New York.

Goleman D (1996) *Emotional Intelligence.* Bloomsbury Publishing, London.

Halton W (1994) Some unconscious aspect of organizational life: contributions from psychoanalysis. In: A Obholzer and VZ Roberts (eds) *The Unconscious at Work: individual and organisational stress in the human services.* Routledge, London.

James K and Jarrett M (2003) The elusive 'dream team': CEO or consultant fantasy? *Organisational and Social Dynamics.* **3**: 61–82.

Jaques E (1953) On the dynamics of social structure: a contribution to the psychoanalytical study of social phenomena deriving from the views of Melanie Klein. Reprinted in: E Trist and H Murray (eds) (1990) *The Social Engagement of Social Science, Volume 1: The Socio-psychological Perspective.* Free Association Books, London.

Klein M (1959) Our adult world and its roots in infancy. In: A Colman and M Geller (eds) (1975) *Group Relations Reader 2.* AK Rice Institute Series, Washington, DC.

Krantz J (2001) Dilemmas of organizational change: a systems-psychodynamics perspective. In: L Gould *et al.* (eds) *The Systems-Psychodynamics of Organizations: integrating the group relations approach, psychoanalytic, and open systems perspectives.* Karnac, London.

Lewin K (1947) Frontiers in group dynamics, Parts I and II. *Human Relations.* **1**: 5–41; **2**: 143–53.

Lewis E and Casement P (1986) Inhibition of mourning by pregnancy: a case study. *Psychoanalytic Psychotherapy.* **2**(1): 45–52.

Marris P (1974) *Loss and Change*. Routledge and Kegan Paul, London.

Menzies I (1960) Social systems as a defense against anxiety: an empirical study of the nursing service of a general hospital. *Human Relations*. **13**: 95–121.

Menzies Lyth I (1979) Staff support systems: task and anti-task in adolescent institutions. In: *Containing Anxiety in Institutions: selected essays*. Free Association Books London.

Menzies Lyth I (1988) *Containing Anxiety in Institutions: selected essays*. Free Association Books, London.

Menzies Lyth I (1990) A psychoanalytical perspective on social institutions. In: E Trist and H Murray (eds) *The Social Engagement of Social Science, Volume 1: The Socio-psychological perspective*. Free Association Books, London.

Miller E (1993) *From Dependency to Autonomy: studies in organization and change*. Free Association Books, London.

Miller EJ and Rice AK (1967) *Systems of Organisation: the control of task and sentient boundaries*. Tavistock Publications, London.

Obholzer A (2003) Some reflections on concepts of relevance to consulting and also to the management of organizations. *Organisational and Social Dynamics*. 3(1): 153–64.

Obholzer A (2004) Personal communication.

Obholzer A and Roberts V (1994) The Unconscious at Work: individual and organizational stress in the human service. Routledge, London.

Rice A (1963) *The Enterprise and Its Environment*. Tavistock Publications, London.

Roberts V (1994) The organization of work: contributions from open systems theory. In: A Obholzer and V Roberts (eds) *The Unconscious at Work: individual and organizational stress in the human services*. Routledge, London.

Trist E and Murray H (eds) (1990) *The Social Engagement of Social Science, Volume 1: The Socio-psychological Perspective*. Free Association Books, London.

Further reading

DeBoard R (1978) *The Psychoanalysis of Organizations: a psychoanalytic approach to behaviour in groups and organizations*. Tavistock Publications, London.

French R and Vince R (1999) *Group Relations, Management and Organization*. Oxford University Press, Oxford.

Gabriel Y (1999) *Organizations in Depth*. Sage, London.

Hinshelwood R and Skogstad W (2000) *Observing Organisations: anxiety, defence and culture in health care*. Routledge, London.

Hughes L and Pengelly P (1997) *Staff Supervision in a Turbulent Environment: managing process and task in front-line services*. Jessica Kingsley Publishers, London.

Kets de Vries M (and Associates) (1991) *Organizations on the Couch: clinical perspectives on organizational behaviour and change.* Jossey-Bass, Oxford

Klein E, Gabelnick F and Herr P (1998) *The Psychodynamics of Leadership.* Psychosocial Press, Madison, CT.

Websites

For training in leadership development and consultancy skills based on systems-psychodynamics:

- Cassel Hospital Training and Consultancy Service: www.thecasselhospital.org/training.htm (for courses for health service managers look under 'Management')
- Tavistock Clinic and UEL Diploma and MA 'Consultation and the organisation: psychoanalytic approaches' (course code D10): www.tavi-port.org/departments/c_coursesandproftraining/tavicourses/COURSES_tavistockcourses_D10.htm

For conferences and other learning events in systems-psychodynamics and leadership:

- International Society for the Psychoanalytic Study of organisations (ISPSO): www.ispso.org/
- Grubb Institute for Behavioural Studies: www.grubb.org.uk
- Tavistock Institute of Human Relations: www.tavinstitute.org

CHAPTER 7

Systems theories and their applications

Jane Keep

Introduction

This chapter introduces 'systems' theories as a framework for conceptualising and practising OD, and looks at their applications in the workplace within the NHS. It outlines some of the tools and techniques that arise from this way of thinking and working, highlights the practical application using a composite case study within the NHS context and suggests some of its challenges. It starts from the same definition of OD provided in Chapter 1 which focuses on the enabling of organisational reflexivity and learning. However, as systems theories are closely linked to ideas around learning organisations, there is also discussion of systems theory as a method of supporting such learning.

The term 'systems theory' is much used and covers a wide range of meanings and interpretations so that, although the term is generally familiar, people's understanding of it may vary widely. The question this chapter sets out to answer is: 'What is systems theory and how does it apply to the working world of health service leaders, managers and clinicians attempting organisational development?'

Systems theory – the language

In any OD process, the first clarification to be made relates to the language – the jargon – in which it is to be described; clarity is crucial in order to create a 'level playing field' between stakeholders. So, it is important at this point to offer some working definitions. As with any concept that has a range of authors and commentators, the language of systems theory could feel ambiguous without some definitions. The mélange of quotes and perspectives from key authors in this chapter will give the essence of the theory; nonetheless, here is an overview of some of the terms more frequently used.

System

An obvious place to start is with some definitions of the word 'system':

- 'denotes interdependency or interaction of components or parts, and an identifiable wholeness or gestalt' (Sinclair, 2001, p.1531)
- 'a group or combination of interrelated, interdependent, or interacting elements forming a collective entity' (Sinclair, 2001, p.531)
- 'an organised, unitary whole composed of two or more interdependent parts, components, or subsystems, and delineated by identifiable boundaries from its environmental supra system' (Kast and Rosenzweig, 1985, quoted in French and Bell, 1990, p.52).

Connecting 'system' with 'theory', Wilson and Rosenfeld (1990) state that, 'in any organisation, the multitude of parts and processes are so interrelated and so interdependent that a small change in one part necessitates changes and adaptations in other parts' (p.315).

Systems theory

Based on these accounts of 'system' that emphasise wholeness, parts and inter-dependence, a working definition of 'systems theory' could be: *a powerful analytical construct in the study of organisations (that is, a way of thinking and applying thought), that suggests the concept of an organisation (or many organisations) having interrelated parts (systems) and/or being interconnected.* Moving from 'systems theory' into another widely used term, 'systems thinking', Sterman (2001) suggests 'systems thinking' is 'the ability to see the world as a complex system, in which we understand that "you can't do just one thing" and that "everything is connected to everything else"' (p.9). As a consequence:

> systems thinking managers know that simple solutions are bound to fail when pitched against complex problem situations. They are willing to struggle with more complicated ideas that, at first acquaintance, may be more difficult to understand. They hope to emerge from this engagement with systems thinking better equipped to cope with complexity, change and diversity. This hope is based on the fact that systems thinking is holistic rather than reductionist and, at least in the form of critical systems thinking, does everything possible to encourage creativity (Jackson, 2003, p.XV).

The roots of systems theory as a 'construct' for organisational analysis can be seen in biology, engineering and the physical sciences. For example, as a biological concept, it was used to help understand the adaptation of organisms in eco-systems; it seems to provide resonant metaphors for our understanding of the way organisations function (as in Morgan's (1986) organisation as organism, *see* Chapter 1). Systems thinking and theories can thus be applied to our understanding and interpretation of life in health service organisations; for example, to the (only apparently) 'simple' task of booking outpatient appointments or the more obviously complex process of introducing a new system of pay and reward for a group of staff. These examples are explored in more depth below.

Overall, systems theory can be used both as a guide to making sense of what is observed in organisational life (that is, to help diagnose and analyse what is happening and thus to identify a place to start with organisational development) and also as a guide to the OD interventions best placed to move the organisation towards 'better' performance. One of the opportunities for systems thinking to assist managers 'comes from using the different approaches in combination' (Jackson, 2003, p.xvii); as a result, this chapter next gives an overview of definitions, perspectives and approaches.

Systems theory explored – the emergence of systems theory as a 'construct'

First off, because of the many metaphors used in writing on systems theory (at least when it is applied to organisational theory and development), it is important to locate this theory in the tradition of social constructionism (*see* Introduction). Metaphors matter because language matters: 'as a central constitutive element of language, metaphors often play an important part in determining how we think and act in the world. They provide mental pictures that are highly graphic, enabling the transformation of words from a context in which their use is literal to a context in which they provide an analogy' (Palmer and Dunford, quoted in Oswick and Grant, 1996, p.7). Hence, throughout this chapter, the overarching metaphor is around organisations as systems (or subsystems) within which there are many other metaphors which derive from a number of intellectual traditions in science over the past 200 years. Morgan's (1986) seminal work on metaphors is introduced in Chapter 1 of this volume and critiqued in the Conclusion, and there is a related discussion of the importance of 'resonance' in the selection of metaphors for organisational analysis in Chapter 12.

To go back to definitions, if a system is a 'complex whole the functioning of which depends on its parts and the interactions between those parts' (Jackson, 2003, p.3) we can see that there is a challenge here to the conception of the organisation as machine. From a scientific perspective, the 'traditional scientific method for studying such systems is known as reductionism. Reductionism sees the parts as paramount and seeks to identify the parts, understand the parts and work up from an understanding of the parts to an understanding of the whole' (Jackson, 2003, p.3). In looking at systems in this way, however, we could miss the interactions between the parts. Jackson (2003) suggests an alternative to reductionism: 'holism considers systems to be more than the sum of their parts' (p.3). However, notions of 'holism' – and thus the guiding principles of systems theory – are taken from a range of scientific sources. Inevitably, these sources emphasise different aspects of the system. Three of these are biology, engineering and physical sciences; each is briefly introduced in the following paragraphs with one example of the contribution to organisational theory that has been drawn from these fields.

For instance, biologists seek to understand whole organisms; this is difficult if they are merely looked at in a 'reductionist' way that reduces them to the sum of their parts. Biology stresses that any organism is capable of making internal changes so that it adapts and survives in different environments and the notion of 'homeostasis' (self-adjustment in search of stability) has become important for organisational theory (Ackoff, 1999; Sherwood, 2002; Flood, 1999).

In engineering, Wiener's work (*see* Jackson, 2003) argued that the 'new science' of cybernetics (the science of control and communication in the animal and machine) dealt with general laws that governed control processes whatever the system under consideration, and discussed the notion of negative feedback (that is, feedback that suggests that something is problematic in the relationship between component parts of a system and/or with its environment and seeks correction). Communication becomes central to systemic equilibrium. Highlighting the contrasting insights of this source of systems thinking to organisational theory to those derived from biology, Morgan considers it a distinct metaphor for organisations (that is, as brains).

Physical sciences have also been a major source of metaphors, in particular in the complexity theories of the 'new science' which are discussed at length in Chapter 8. Complexity theory (for example, *see* Gleick, 1987) introduced the idea of the self-organising system, bringing order from disorder and identifying patterns in apparently random behaviour. The weather system is often cited as a good example of patterning:

> A cloud masses, the sky darkens, leaves twist upward, and we know that it will rain … all these events are distant in time and space, and yet all connected within the same pattern, each has an influence on the rest, an influence that is usually hidden from view. You can only understand the system of a rainstorm by contemplating the whole, not any individual part of the pattern' (Senge, 1990, p.6).

Although Morgan does not really do justice to the organisation as complex system, his discussion of the 'new science' is included in a chapter that once again has a distinct metaphor: organisation as flux and transformation.

All of these scientific traditions have been influential on writers and practitioners of OD. As Wilson and Rosenfeld (1990) note: 'systems theory, originally a theory of organism survival and adaptation in the biological sciences, has proved a very powerful analytical construct in the study of organisations' (p.315). It is the biological metaphor that is the predominant focus of this chapter because it is the most important to OD alongside ideas derived from complexity science (which are dealt with in detail in Chapter 8). In particular, this chapter will focus on 'open systems theory' connected to the notion of homeostasis around living organisms, which has been related by writers such as Armstrong (1991) to behaviour and motivation in organisations.

What are the core elements of systems theories?

'The more we study the major problems of our time, the more we come to realise that they cannot be understood in isolation. They are systemic problems, which means that they are interconnected and interdependent' (Capra, 1996, quoted in Jackson, 2003, p.3). If we accept this underlying rationale behind the emergence of systems theory, what is common among the theorists? First, the core elements of systems theory are summarised by Ackoff (1999) as:

- 'A system is a whole consisting of two or more parts that satisfies the following five conditions:
  - the whole has one or more defining properties or functions
  - each part in the set can affect the behaviour or properties of the whole
  - there is a subset of parts that is sufficient in one or more environments for carrying out the defining function of the whole; each of these parts is necessary but insufficient for carrying out this defining function
  - the way that each essential part of a system affects its behaviour or properties depends on (the behaviour or properties of) at least one other essential part of the system
  - the effect of any subset of essential parts on the system as a whole depends on the behaviour of at least one other such subset'
- thus 'a system is a whole that cannot be divided into independent parts without loss of its essential properties or functions' (pp.5–8).

Second, and building on this core, what are the shared lenses through which systems theorists (for example, Checkland, 1988, 1994; Senge, 1990) and broader organisational theorists (for example, Wilson and Rosenfeld, 1990; French and Bell, 1990; Rummler and Brache, 1995) see organisations? Among the characteristics they identify are the following – organisations:

- have the potential to 'go wrong'
- have management, leadership and practitioners' roles that could be problematic
- are multifaceted
- have multiple parts and processes
- have interrelationships
- have interdependencies
- have a sense of connectivity that is often undisclosed, unnoticed or ill considered
- are all part of a 'system'
- are a 'system' within larger systems
- when adapted or developed in one part have a 'knock on' effect in another part of the same organisation (intra) or on a wider system among organisations (inter)
- can be closed or open systems
- are complex
- have hidden dynamics (of many sorts; for instance, see those discussed in Chapter 6).

Third, a distinction that is useful for organisational purposes is between the notions of dynamic complexity and combinatorial complexity. If, for example, we worked scheduling airline flights there is one kind of complexity based on the many different combinations of available stands, landing and take-off slots, etc., we would have to consider before making decisions. This is known as 'combinatorial complexity' (Sterman, 2001), where the factors, although numerous, are presumed to stay the same over time. If we look at healthcare organisations, however, we see a different type of complexity because they are both evolving and interconnected; this can be described as 'dynamic complexity'. Taking this a step further, Sterman (2001) suggests that dynamic complexity arises because systems are:

- constantly changing
- tightly coupled and interacting
- governed by feedback
- influenced by history
- self-organising
- adaptive
- characterised by trade-offs.

Fourth, I want to return to an idea covered briefly earlier in this chapter and re-introduce here a distinct type of 'thinking'. Ackoff (1999) suggests managers require a change in the way they think, and what is thought about when thinking, in order to make the most of the insights of 'systems' theory. He argues that what is required is:

> synthetic thinking, which provides better understanding of complex systems than analytical thinking does. Synthetic thinking is a way of thinking about and designing a system that derives the properties and behaviour of its parts from the functions required of the whole. The whole has properties that none of its parts have. Analysis of a system reveals *how* it works but synthetic thinking is required to explain *why* it works the way it does. Systems thinking integrates the two (p.21).

This makes the distinction between knowing (how to questions) and understanding (why questions).

Fifth, another pertinent aspect of systems theory is to consider thought patterns and how we use these to conceptualise (or make sense of) our workplace. In the work of Senge (1990), for instance, these are called mental models. Mental models 'are conceptual structures in the mind that drive cognitive processes of understanding. They influence people's actions because they mould people's appreciation of what they see' (Flood, 1999, p.22). Checkland (in his work on 'soft systems' methodology in 1994) highlights the importance of the mental models that managers use to make sense of their worlds. A key part of the rationale behind 'soft systems' methodology is that the social construction of our world views is filtered through many mental models; this applies as much to how organisations, organisational processes and managerial tasks are viewed as any other aspect of our life. Senge (1990) discusses mental models as being 'deeply ingrained assumptions, generalisations or even pictures or images that influence how we understand the world and how we take action' (p.8). There is a strong link here to the accounts of sensemaking given by Weick (1995).

Finally, a brief distinction around soft systems (as mentioned above in the work of Checkland, 1994) and hard systems is pertinent to demystify all of the terms commonly used today to describe 'systems'. Checkland (1994) helpfully summarises this distinction as:

> hard systems thinking assumes that the world is a set of systems (i.e. is systemic) and that these can be systematically engineered to achieve objectives. In the soft tradition, the world is assumed to be problematic, but it is also assumed that the

process of inquiry into the problematic situations that make up the world can be organised as a system. In other words, assumed systemicity is shifted: from taking the world to be systemic to taking the process of inquiry to be systemic (p.80).

(*See also* Checkland, 1983, 1985.)

Systems theories in the workplace

So how do we apply systems thinking? And what is in it for managers? Sterman (2001) argues that 'Systems dynamics is fundamentally interdisciplinary ... because we apply these tools to the behaviour of human as well as technical systems, systems dynamics draws on cognitive and social psychology, organisation theory, economics and other social sciences' (p.10). There are many possible practical uses of systems theories, as well as different theoretical approaches, within each perspective. Generally, though, systems theory can be used in developing organisations, understanding power, structuring organisations, implementing policy, managing operations and mapping consequences. Some of the more specific uses are as follows:

- diagnosing individual and group behaviour
- examining system fits and power relations
- diagnosing environmental relations
- establishing systems for learning in organisations.

To help understand the application of systems theories, there are a number of classifications that Jackson (2003) makes between some of the systems approaches. There is not the space to describe these approaches in detail; however, Jackson's four clusters of approaches provides one useful guide around their potential use within organisational settings and these are summarised in Box 7.1.

Box 7.1: Jackson's clusters of systems approaches

Type A: Improving goal seeking and understanding variability – involves deploying 'hard systems' thinking, organisational cybernetics and complexity theory; 'developed because of the failure of reductionism to cope with problem situations exhibiting increased complexity and turbulence' (p.45).

Type B: Exploring purpose – involves strategic assumption surfacing and testing, interactive planning and 'soft systems' methodology; 'aims to assist managers improve the way in which they decide what purposes their enterprises should pursue and achieve a measure of agreement around those purposes' (p.135).

Type C: Ensuring fairness – involves critical systems heuristics, and team synergy and integrity; 'aims to assist managers improve their enterprises by ensuring fairness, because of the failure of functionalist and interpretive systems approaches to give appropriate attention to ensuring the proper participation of all stakeholders in taking decisions and to addressing the disadvantages faced by some groups in and affected by organisations' (p.211).

> **Type D**: Promoting diversity – involves post-modern systems thinking; 'aims to assist managers improve their enterprises by promoting diversity ... seeking to make a space for suppressed voices to be heard' (p.253).
>
> Adapted from Jackson, 2003.

Systems theory and learning organisations

Many writers on organisational learning and knowledge management have used notions of systems thinking and working (such as Senge, 1990 and Collinson and Parcell, 2001) to inform their work. As the phrases 'learning organisation' (during the last decade particularly) and 'knowledge management' (more recently) are common concepts within the NHS, it is worth outlining these in brief because they can also be practised by using systems approaches. This connects straight back to the definition of organisational development offered at the beginning of this book; the idea that one outcome of effective OD is the enhancement of the capacity of the organisation to make further changes in the future.

Senge (1990), in his influential work *The Fifth Discipline*, introduces 'systems thinking' which he sees as a 'conceptual framework, a body of knowledge and tools that has been developed ... to make patterns clearer to help us see how to change them effectively' (p.6). This, in essence, is his fifth discipline, which he highlights because it is 'much harder to integrate new tools than simply apply them separately. But the payoffs are immense' (p.12). The other important aspects of this 'fifth discipline' lie in the growth of the learning organisation through:

- personal mastery (managers and leaders consistently realising the results that matter most deeply to them)
- building shared vision (unearthing shared pictures of the future that foster genuine commitment and ownership rather than compliance)
- team learning.

Importantly, Senge's work also looks at how structure influences behaviour (*see* Chapter 9), and, in turn, how patterns of behaviour influence outcomes of organisational development, and hence the need for a 'shift of mind' using various tools.

Pedlar *et al.* (1991) have written extensively on the learning company and the theory behind single- and double-loop learning (*see* Chapter 1). Initially their work outlined 11 features that characterise a learning company:

- the learning approach to strategy
- participative policy making
- informating (information and IT being used to inform and help everyone to understand what is going on and to empower people rather than to have control over them)
- formative accounting and control
- internal exchange (among operational units and departments)

- reward flexibility
- enabling structures
- boundary workers as environmental scanners
- inter-company learning
- learning climate (continuous improvement/developmental)
- self-development opportunities for all.

In more recent work, Burgoyne (1999) drew up a list of things that needed to happen for the concept of continuous learning to become a reality. He identified the main factors as being:

- companies being more aware of internal politics
- managers being clearer about where collective learning processes take place and where the consequent collective knowledge is located
- strategies to enable collective learning to occur in the fragmented and loosely coupled forms taken by many organisations and
- dealing explicitly with the issue of achieving synergy among stakeholders and tackling conflict between them.

Both the early and more recent conceptions of learning companies draw extensively on systems theory; indeed factors such as internal politics, collective learning processes, synergy, participative policy making and inter-company learning are all subsystems within an overall organisational system.

Systems theory and knowledge management

Increasing in pertinence over recent years, arguably supporting growth and innovation, knowledge management (KM) as a theory has itself had to take a 'soft systems' approach; it is a process of inquiry as well as a way of organising. At its most basic, KM is an umbrella term for mobilising the flow of information and knowledge from people to people (the connection factor: people to expertise) and people to knowledge (the collection factor: people to information). Collinson and Parcell (2001) quote a definition of KM: 'it is not about creating an encyclopaedia that captures everything that anybody ever knew. Rather it is about keeping track of those who know the recipe, and nurturing the culture and the technology that will get them talking' (p.14). This definition shifts the emphasis from knowledge libraries to placing more value on thinking and ideas and finding ways to increase mobility of knowledge and understanding. Collinson and Parcell (2001) suggest that:

> it is about capturing, creating, distilling, sharing and using know-how. That know-how includes explicit and tacit knowledge. Know-how is used as shorthand for know-how, know-what, know-who, know-why and know-when. It's not about books of wisdom and best practice, it's more about the communities that keep know-how of a topic alive by sharing what they know, building on it and adapting it to their own use (p.8).

They argue that KM is a holistic model, 'it's more than the sum of the parts' (p.8), and thus located squarely within the realm of systemic theory. It is a practical approach that combines a number of systems and processes under one umbrella (and which is discussed further in Chapter 13 in relation to healthcare).

Forrester (quoted in Boyett and Boyett, 1998) concludes: 'People are interconnected, many such loops are intertwined, through long cascaded chains of action, each person is continually reacting to the echo of that person's past actions as well as to the past actions of others' (p.8). Boyett and Boyett (1998) take from this synthesis that 'our systems theorists argue that the world is a loopy place where cause and effect go around and around like a long winding spring of causality. Nothing ever really begins or ends; there is just cause, effect, cause, effect, for eternity' (p.106). Thus, individuals, organisations, learning and systems theory are connected, interconnected and, indeed, interdependent in the warp and weft of organisational life, particularly as organisations work to build capacity and capability, to continuously improve the quality of services, to make efficiency savings and gains, and to continue to pioneer with expanding technological capacities.

Applying systems approaches – tools and techniques

As with all OD frameworks, tools and techniques derived from 'systems' approaches are numerous. Many of these tools and techniques can be described as 'n' step models, in that they describe a series of steps or actions that can be taken to take the manager or clinician from A to B on their OD journey. A basic premise of this chapter is that in undertaking any organisational development it is important to define the following two key stages (which is a simplification of the OD cycle presented in Chapter 4).

1 A process of sensemaking, diagnostics, leading towards a working analysis of the issue or finding the place to start. This recognises that undertaking diagnostics, or initial analysis, is also an intervention in its own right. In addition, this can also form the beginning of the evaluation as goals and objectives may be set here too.
2 A series of further interventions either to continue the analytical and diagnostic pathway (if the defined end point is to have understood or made sense of something) or to intervene into a subsystem, system or series of systems using a series of tools or techniques to evoke or enable the required change.

Systems theory is most pertinent around the first phase, in diagnosis and in constructing a frame for sensemaking – understanding the nature of 'things' – rather than being used as a particular intervention to solve problems themselves. In essence, using a systems approach is a way of framing one's thinking. As Checkland (1994) suggests, it involves moving from taking the world to be systemic to taking the process of inquiry to be systemic.

Organisational analysis and diagnosis – taking a systems approach

French and Bell's (1990) 'organisational subsystems' looks at an initial organisational analysis through describing organisations 'in systems terminology' (p.54). French and Bell consider both organisations as subunits (departments/divisions,) as well as the organisation as consisting of a number of significant interacting variables that cut across or are common to all subunits. They identify:

- task subsystem: 'subdivision of the total work to be performed into those tasks and subtasks that need to be accomplished by organisation members to produce the end product' (p.55)
- technological subsystem: 'consists of tools, machines, procedures, methods and technical knowledge' (p.55)
- structural subsystem: 'highly influenced by the technical subsystem and consists of task groupings, such as units, departments or divisions. Interrelated with such task groupings is the design of the work flow, that is where a partially completed product goes next and so forth' (p.55)
- human social subsystem: 'can be viewed as consisting of four aspects: the skills and abilities of organisational members, the leadership philosophy and style, a formal subsystem, and an informal subsystem' (p.55)
- goal subsystem: 'consists of one or more (usually several) interrelated superordinate objectives or goals, usually set forth in the organisation's charter or mission statement, plus the subgoals of units and programmes stemming from or forming the superordinate goals' (p.55)
- external interface subsystem: 'consists of data sensing and gathering, resource procurement, and outplacement or exchanges of outputs for resources; environmental influencing; and responses to external demands' (p.55).

These provide a useful approach to organisational development based on the premise that 'organisational subsystems exist in a highly interdependent state' (French and Bell, 1990, p.56). French and Bell (1990) also suggest that:

the initial vehicles for organisation development efforts tend to be the human social and the structural subsystems, that is the communications and feedback systems and the attitude and sentiment components of the informal system. However, these become vehicles for confronting problems in any of the major organisational subsystems (p.56).

Systems theory in use

If systems theory is accepted as a fruitful analytical construct within organisations, then what sort of cases from within the NHS could be explored using this construct? I explore two in Box 7.2.

Box 7.2: Applying systems theory

1 Booking an appointment – a task

Take the task of booking an outpatient appointment for a patient which, at face value, is a rational and linear exercise, and something that could (in principle) be controlled and managed. But how many practitioners (and indeed patients or carers) would describe their experiences of this 'simple' procedure as one that was (well) managed, or controlled, or that produced the desired outcome?

2 Pay reform – a project

Take a more complex project, for example the introduction of a new system for pay and reward to achieve harmonisation of working hours and annual leave among a group of radiographers. How simple or easily controlled or managed is this project?

Each of these cases can be explored either in a unidimensional manner or within a multidimensional 'systems theory' construct. For example, seemingly conventional classical management models and theories of organisations reaffirm that organisations can manage themselves and that they can collectively pursue and achieve organisational goals through leaders and managers who deploy rational and linear decision making to help achieve these goals. However, this approach may be too simplistic, or, at least, may be too simplistic most of the time for most of our goals.

If we take case 1 (the 'simpler' of cases from the two examples), the types of things that could go 'wrong' during this task are, for instance, that the IT operating system may be faulty, the 'operator' may mishear or misread some of the information, or the consultant may see control of his own appointment schedule as a central facet of his organisational authority. Further, the administrator may make the appointment in isolation from a number of other interdependencies such as: whether the patient's notes will be available in that place at that time; whether the tests or x-rays results will be back for that appointment; and whether the patient's transport will be able to complete all its 'pick ups' allowing enough time for the patient's arrival in outpatients (and so on).

If we take case 2 (the more complex project from the two cases), the types of things that could 'complicate' the outcome range from not recognising that some working hours or annual leave arrangements may have been adapted 'locally' in a department or organisation to suit particular service delivery needs or to meet certain waiting time targets, to failing to appreciate that these adjustments may have been made on an individual basis in an attempt to provide more convenient working conditions to ensure staff retention or form part of the psychological and social 'contract' with staff. Added to which, change in these working hours may leave some elements of the service depleted or patients' needs unmet.

As these examples illustrate, there are many challenges for managers in achieving systemic change.

> One of the reasons the manager's role remains obstinately problematic stems from our less-than-adequate thinking about the context in which managers perform, namely the organisation. Some basic systems thinking indicates that if we adopt a limited view of organisation then the conceptualisation of the manager's role will inevitably also be rather threadbare (Checkland, 1994, p.76).

Looking in more detail at case 2, a 'pre-design' analysis was undertaken within the organisation to ascertain the elements within each subsystem (and whether these were in fact the key systems) and the major priorities to be addressed within these elements, including the discussion of clear problems and also the identification of any 'wicked problems' (that is, problems that have previously proved irresolvable due to the complex and/or obscure links between cause and effect). Under each subsystem, there was an analysis of the following.

- The external interface subsystem (external demands, environmental influences, etc.): policy drivers, national labour market issues, national professional issues within the radiography profession, national service redesign issues, international and national recruitment, national (and local) funding available to make the changes.
- Task subsystem: listing each of the tasks required to undertake the project, from the initial analysis, project planning and scoping, to diagnosing and preparing a number of options, piloting one or more of the options after 'road testing' on paper first, testing out financial modelling and workplace redesign issues.
- Technological subsystem: looking at the actual work undertaken by the radiographers, the work required, where technology plays a role in their working lives as well as where technology plays a role around organising working hours and paying the radiographers (e.g. electronic staff records, rota systems, the national (and local) IT strategy and infrastructure).
- Goal subsystem: scoping the goals and aims of the radiographers, the managers, the patients and users of the radiography services, the national professional organisations and the trade union/professional association perspectives.
- Structural subsystem: looking at the working structure, roles and tasks of the radiographers, the way the department is structured, pay structures, reward management structures, the way the patient pathway could be re-engineered, the support structures.
- Human social subsystem: the formal and informal rewards, the issues around equity, equality, diversity, the working life and quality of this for radiographers, the attitudes of the radiographers, their managers and other staff in the department, general issues of leadership style and philosophy now and those that are desired for the future.

Involving all key stakeholders at the outset – in this 'pre-design' stage – enabled the OD practitioner to work in partnership with stakeholders and thus gave the exploration 'integrity'. By questioning the various systems and subsystems at this stage, a better understanding of the multifaceted and complex task that lay ahead was nurtured in all those involved. Steps could be then put in place to look deeper into the key priority areas which had been jointly identified and which had the potential of a longer-term feel rather than a shorter-term 'fix'. Participants all learnt a number of important lessons from the project and these are summarised in Box 7.3.

Box 7.3: Learning derived from the application of systems theory in the case examples

- Working with values and integrity builds relationships and support.
- Systems are highly complex and even looking at them separately they were very difficult to analyse but the interdependencies became much clearer by looking at them together.
- Doing a piece of pre-work prior to some further analysis felt more sustainable in the long run rather than rushing to some early conclusions.
- Using a conceptual model helped to support early thinking and gave more opportunity to prepare for the journey ahead (preparing was felt to be more key than planning).
- Using any theoretical approach, even with practical guidance, is not fail-safe, and trial and error, process review and evaluation serve to build a learning and development process.

Limitations of systems theory

Boyett and Boyett (1998) summarise some insights from their synthesis of writing on the learning organisation which seem helpful as broader insights and challenges for systems theory.

- There are no right answers ... just a variety of potential actions, each of which will produce some desired consequences and some unintended consequences' (p.119).
- There is no way to break a system into parts and fix them separately as systems have integrity; and you must treat the whole not just the individual parts.
- Cause and effect often are not closely related in time and space.
- The most obvious solutions may not work at all (but sometimes they do!).
- Many apparent dilemmas may not be either/or choices.
- While people like to blame others for their difficulties, problems in a system are often caused by people within it and not by some outside force.

Beyond those general warnings, it seems difficult to see many limitations to systems thinking. Perhaps, there is a danger that some projects that could have been relatively discrete will either spiral out of control or grind to a halt as more and more potential connections and consequences are identified. On the whole, however, the appeal of taking a systems approach to OD seems both intuitively comfortable and theoretically robust.

Conclusion

In order to understand, explore, investigate, diagnose and plan OD interventions, consideration of organisations as systems, and using systems thinking and perspectives as a guide, seems to offer the prospect of a better account of the very complex operating environment in which we all now find ourselves. While this chapter has introduced a range of approaches, it is important to appreciate that some writers and practitioners in this field (for example, Bate *et al.*, 2003) are moving on to broader 'dynamic' perspectives, such as social movement theory (*see* Chapter 2 and Conclusion for examples of the connection between social movements and OD) in order to be able to see the workplace in a three-dimensional way. Any journey in life that involves change is complex; there are no right or wrong answers or easy solutions. However, reflective, evidence-based practice can enable us to move from short-term approaches to change to ones that build and sustain capacity and willingness to move forward. This chapter has shown how 'systems' theory can play an important part on such journeys.

References

Ackoff R (1999) *Re-creating the corporation: a design of organizations for the 21st Century*. Oxford University Press, Oxford.

Armstrong M (1991) *A Handbook of Personnel Management Practice*. Kogan Page, London.

Bate P, Robert G and Bevan H (2003) *The Next Phase of Health Care Improvement: what can we learn from social movements?* Modernisation Agency, unpublished paper.

Boyett J and Boyett J (1998) *The Guru Guide: the best ideas of the top management thinkers*. John Wiley & Sons, London.

Burgoyne J (1999) Sign of the times. *The Learning Organisation People Management*. 3 June: 39–43.

Checkland P (1983) OR and the systems movement. *Journal of the Operational Research Society*. **34**: 661–75.

Checkland P (1985) From optimizing to learning: a development of systems thinking for the 1990s. *Journal of Operational Research Society*. **36**: 757–67.

Checkland P (1988) Soft systems methodology: an overview. *Journal of Applied Systems Analysis*. **15**: 27–30.

Checkland P (1994) Systems theory and management thinking. *American Behavioral Scientist*. **38**(1): 75–91.

Collinson C and Parcell G (2001) *Learning to Fly: practical lessons from one of the world's leading knowledge companies*. Capstone Publishing, Oxford.

Flood R (1999) *Rethinking the Fifth Discipline: learning within the unknowable*. Routledge, London.

French W and Bell C Jr (1990) *Organization Development: behavioural science interventions for organization improvement* (4e). Prentice Hall International Editions, London.

Gleick J (1987) *Chaos: the making of a new science*. Abacus, London.

Jackson M (2003) *Systems Thinking: creative holism for managers*. John Wiley & Sons, London.

Morgan G (1986) *Images of Organization*. Sage, London.

Oswick C and Grant D (1996) *Organisation Development: metaphorical explorations*. Pitman Publishing, London.

Pedlar M, Burgoyne J and Boydell T (1991) *The Learning Company: a strategy for sustainable development*. McGrawHill, London.

Rummler G and Brache A (1995) *Improving Performance: how to manage the white space on the organization chart*. Jossey-Bass, San Francisco, CA.

Senge P (1990) *The Fifth Discipline: the art & practice of the learning organization*. Century Business, London.

Sherwood D (2002) *Seeing the Forest for the Trees: a manager's guide to applying systems thinking*. Nicholas Brealey Publishing, London.

Sinclair J (2001) *Collins Concise Dictionary for 21st Century*. HarperCollins, London.

Sterman J (2001) System dynamics modeling: tools for learning in a complex world. *California Management Review*. 43(4): 8–25.

Weick K (1995) *Sensemaking in Organisations*. Sage, London.

Wilson D and Rosenfeld R (1990) *Managing Organizations: texts, readings and cases*. McGraw Hill, London.

Websites

- The site of the Systems Dynamics Group at MIT: www.sysdyn.mit.edu/
- The site for the System Dynamics Society: www.albany.edu/cpr/sds/
- A site devoted to the *Fifth Discipline Fieldbook* and *The Dance of Change*: www.fieldbook.com
- A site that focuses on systems change around healthcare can be found at: www.natpact.nhs.uk.cms/116.php

CHAPTER 8

Emergence, complexity and organisational development

Kieran Sweeney

Introduction

This chapter explores the nature of complexity, describes its principal characteristics, non-linearity and inherent uncertainty, and illustrates its key processes, sensitivity to initial conditions, self-organisation and co-evolution. Drawing on examples from the author's own background in general practice in the UK, the chapter reflects on how organisational theorists currently deploy the principles of complexity to understand organisational change and the ways in which OD practitioners, managers and clinicians can draw on this understanding when deciding how to achieve such change in healthcare organisations. The chapter contrasts and then compares linearity (the basis of the scientific method) with non-linearity (the basis of complex systems) in the context of organisational theory. The two are complementary, the chapter concludes, not dichotomous. Balancing linearity and non-linearity appropriately when devising a process for organisational development is a key challenge for managers and leaders. Command and control can no longer occupy a dominant role in organisational policy. In the 21st century, managers must learn to live with uncertainty.

Reductionism

For nearly two centuries, science was the cornerstone of the dominant intellectual paradigm in the Western world. Rational reductionism, which characterised the scientific model, vastly extended the ability of human beings to make sense of the world. Its key principles are linearity and predictability. Phenomena are described in terms of their parts, are thought to be regulated by a small number of core laws, and are presumed to change in a smooth and predictable manner. Historically, the central figure contributing to this way of thinking was Isaac Newton. His discoveries in mathematics and physics created a seductive, clockwork universe in which one developed increasing confidence in determinism and predictability. Regularity became part of our being, and we based our knowledge on this comforting predictability.

The success of the scientific method extended well beyond the fields in which it originated. Drawing on the scientific paradigm, Adam Smith and David Ricardo advanced the laws of economic interaction (Fukuyama, 1993), and sociology and politics also tried to become sciences. This linear paradigm reached its zenith towards the middle of the twentieth century, where it was applied to modernisation theories of third world development, international relations and public policy (Geyer, 2001). Influenced by the success of the scientific paradigm, planners, politicians and social scientists at this time held, albeit without justification, that stable relationships existed between cause and effect. As a consequence one could scale up, for example in economics, from an individual model of self-interest to a macro-economic policy predicated on self-interest (Fukuyama, 1993).

We organised our work around similar beliefs too. The machine metaphor for Newton's universe was translated into a desire to understand the structure and parts or all systems, and to build organisations on that basis. As early as 1911, Taylor (1911), (and *see also* Chapter 9) published his theories of scientific management, with its underlying model of the organisation as a machine. The importance of mechanical metaphors cannot be underestimated (as argued by Morgan, 1986). Even up to the 1990s, these deeply embedded beliefs were expressed in the management predilection for such interventions as business process re-engineering (Hammer, 1995).

Linearity and organisational development in the NHS

In the UK, the National Health Service embraced this Taylorist approach enthusiastically, but only after an initial period, spanning its first quarter century, of management by diplomacy (Harrison, 1988). The command and control approach in the NHS, recalling the wartime circumstances during which hospitals were first brought under central control, is epitomised in the far-reaching *Hospital Plan for England*, devised in the 1960s, but not implemented for another decade (HMSO, 1962) and which has left the NHS with the inheritance of numerous small hospitals with which it is (arguably) burdened today. Similarly, by the early 1970s, healthcare policy gurus agreed that the administration of the NHS was in need of an overhaul, but their solution in the form of the *Grey Book* (HMSO, 1972) further testifies to the confidence at that time in linear, algorithmic solutions to what were truly complex problems. The *Grey Book* adopted a rigid, centralised approach to resolve the administrative confusion in the NHS. But its insensitivity to local context exposed its inherent weaknesses almost as soon as its recommendations were implemented (Kember and Macpherson, 1994) and the structural reorganisation that it underpinned generally viewed as a failure (Klein, 1989). These two major – and flawed – attempts at OD in the NHS based on rational and linear assumptions should alert us to the need for more flexible and sensitive approaches.

But they were not to be the last such initiatives. Coming into office in 1979, the Conservative government's preference was to devise solutions in line with their market-driven philosophy. The then Prime Minister, Margaret Thatcher, commissioned the managing director of Sainsbury's, Sir Roy Griffiths, to examine the ways in which NHS resources were deployed, with the aim of securing better value for money. He was deeply critical of the lack of managerial accountability, and deplored what he saw as a pervasive system of management by consensus. 'If Florence Nightingale were carrying her lamp through the corridors of the NHS today,' Griffiths wrote, 'she would almost certainly be searching for the people in charge' (DHSS, 1983). His enquiry stressed 'the clear similarities between NHS management and business management' (DHSS, 1983). In retrospect, the Griffiths report again exposes the inherent weakness in predicating an explanatory model for a complex system like the NHS on linear thinking. As we shall see later in this chapter, Griffiths' contemporaries in mathematics and biology could have told him that systems just do not work in that way.

Over a decade later when Robinson and Le Grand (1994) evaluated another set of NHS reforms, they were simply unable to say whether their impact was positive or negative. The reasons for taking their appropriately balanced position become increasingly interesting in the light of our greater understanding of systems which are both complex and adaptive (Battram, 1998). 'There are rarely simple answers to simple questions,' the authors said, 'usually because the questions are not actually simple' (Robinson and Le Grand, 1994). In their concluding commentary to their interesting evaluation, Robinson and Le Grand (1994) paint a picture of inherent uncertainty, unpredictability and sudden changes of direction in the NHS, which stymied all but the best-crafted local plans, and left the innocent taxpayer wondering how the increasing amounts of money allocated to the NHS were actually being dispersed.

The development of a non-linear paradigm

Throughout the course of the twentieth century, as the spectacular advances of the scientific model were still unfolding, another intellectual tradition was emerging, based on two key characteristics: non-linearity and organising relations. A non-linear effect occurs when the output is disproportionate to the input. Perhaps the most frequently referred to example is the butterfly effect, described by the meteorologist Edward Lorenz, where 'a butterfly flapping its wings over the Amazon leads to a hurricane on the other side of the world' (Lorenz, 1963). Organising relations refers to the importance of understanding how constituent elements in any system interact with, adapt and evolve in relation to each other. Their importance was first described by the mathematician Henri Poincaré. 'The aim of science,' Poincaré (1958) wrote, 'is not things in themselves, but the relation between things. Outside these relations there is no reality knowable.' The product of this paradigm, and its relevance to this chapter, is located in our present understanding of complex adaptive systems. This term refers to a *system* – that is the coming together of parts, their interaction and sense of purpose – which is *complex* – that is functions with a large number of elements interacting richly – and can *adapt* – the elements can co-evolve as a result of their interaction (Plsek, 2000). While it is not the remit of this chapter to trace the development of the non-linear paradigm in detail (an excellent review can be found in Capra, 1996) it is important to recognise some of the key contributions which gave rise to our present understanding of complex adaptive systems, as these have had a substantial influence on the contemporary theory and practice of organisational development. Two features of complex systems are worth reporting in some depth: the nature of self-organising behaviour; and sensitivity to initial conditions.

Self-organisation

Self-organising behaviour refers to the tendency within complex systems for patterns of observable, coherent behaviour to emerge from what initially appear to be random interactions. This was first observed by two chemists, Belousov and Zhabotinski, in a really simple chemical reaction (which you can, if you wish, reproduce for yourself). They took a simple mixture of citric acid, sulphuric acid and potassium bromate, placed it in a shallow dish and stirred. Bright blue dots appeared and spread; red dots then appeared in the centre of the blue dots, forming an expanding series of blue and red rings; when these rings ran into each other, they did not superimpose on top of each other or mix, but formed more intricate red and blue circular patterns. This was the first, and still the most easily reproducible, example of spontaneous formation of patterns emerging from initial chaos (Cohen and Stewart, 1994).

Its implications were recognised by Nobel prize-winning chemist Ilya Prigogine (1998) in his observations about entropy; this can loosely be understood as the amount of disorder in a system which is running down. The conventional, Newtonian view was that the amount of entropy was increasing: that was the basis for his Second Law of Thermodynamics. What Prigogine did was to measure not just the amount of entropy in a system, but also what happened to it. He found that deterioration in systems was not inevitable: they could exchange entropy for energy. The disruption or disequilibrium in a system associated with entropy need not lead inevitably to dissipation (or equilibrium, the equivalent of dynamic death). Prigogine attached the term 'dissipative structures' to those systems that could give up their original structures to recreate themselves in new forms; they had, said Prigogine, the ability to self-organise. Self-organisation operates through positive feedback within a system. In a biological complex system, activity which confers an advantage on the system, or causes it to behave positively, tends to augment the influence of those agents or activities associated with the desired state through positive feedback. Over time, the system will preferentially weight the input of agents whose actions provide positive output, thus establishing repeating patterns of behaviour, which the system expresses as stable characteristics.

So what, one might ask? Well, self-organising behaviour is a fundamental feature of complex adaptive systems. All biological systems are self-organising: ants exhibit self-organising behaviour when they build their anthill; and birds are self-organising when they flock. Self-organising is pervasive in human systems. The economic system self-organises when stock market trends (for example, a rush to buy gold) respond to currency fluctuations in the market. Since complex adaptive systems are pervasive in biological, human, and organisational communities, it is important to understand the nature of self-organising behaviour in order to know how those systems work (Cilliers, 1998).

Sensitivity to initial conditions

Advances in computing during the third quarter of the twentieth century allowed scientists to explore the nature of complex systems in greater and greater detail. When exploring non-linear equations, especially equations with several variables which were solved simultaneously, it became clear that the most minute difference in the value of one of the variables at the beginning of a computation could make a huge difference as those equations were solved iteratively, as one would do to describe mathematically the evolution of a complex system over time. The classic example of this is found in early attempts to model weather patterns.

In 1963, Edward Lorenz was working on weather systems, exploring how they could be modelled mathematically to determine the extent to which the behaviour of such complex systems could be predicted. He identified three variables which seemed crucial to convection (the tendency for hot air to rise), and ran a series of equations, plotting each of these variables over time, substituting slightly different values for each of the variables as he progressed (Lorenz, 1963). The computer he was using stored numbers in up to six decimal places, but printed them out to only three. On one occasion, Lorenz entered the value 0.506 for one of the variables, which was the figure, printed out from the computer's memory, of the more precise value for this variable, namely 0.506127. While he assumed that this difference was negligible, what he observed was that the system evolved subsequently in a markedly different way. Even this small difference, one part in 10 000, proved crucial in altering the system's development.

Lorenz's modelling revealed that in complex systems, prediction, other than over a very short range, was impossible. The tiniest alteration in one of the values – for example changing a value at the third or fourth decimal place – could have a dramatic effect on the direction of the system. Complex systems are extremely sensitive to their initial conditions.

In organisational development, the equivalent of sensitivity to initial conditions is typically called 'receptive context'. Put simply, a receptive context is a prerequisite for organisations, as complex adaptive systems, to produce coherent behaviour, to self-organise and to co-evolve. It originates in the framing of potentially shared activities, which all constituents in an organisation recognise as mainstream business, and therefore worthy of focused collaborative action. From this perspective, a receptive context consists in an anticipation that coherent behaviour will emerge; it requires leadership to initiate the co-creation of patterns of such behaviour, and the ability of the agents in the system to interact, through a set of shared values or sense of purpose, to sustain that behaviour (Sweeney, 2003a). These ideas are central to OD interventions derived from emergence and complexity.

OD and the non-linear paradigm

Stacey's 'crafting' strategy

The description of complex systems above continuously stresses the importance of rich interaction between the agents in any complex system. In relation to human systems, this interaction is expressed through the conversations the participants conduct with each other about the system. The organisational theorist Ralph Stacey has described the nature and importance of this interaction in human complex systems. 'The modelling of complex systems,' Stacey (2001) asserts, 'demonstrates the possibility that interaction between entities, each entity responding to others on the basis of its own organising principles, will produce coherent patterns with the potential for novelty in certain conditions.' Stacey's thesis here is that the interaction between agents in a system, which constitutes the processes of communication, is the essence of a complex adaptive system. The analogy is important, Stacey holds, because interaction through complex communication can be thought of as a self-organising process with the property of emergent coherence.

The power of this insight, according to Stacey, suggests that there is 'no reason to look for some kind of underlying blueprint, plan or predetermined mechanism, other than the interaction itself to explain coherence in human action with its character-istics of continuity and potential transformation' (Stacey, 2001). In organisational terms, the way participants in a system communicate, interact and co-evolve inter-personally is crucial to the development of the system. This has important impli-cations for OD interventions.

Let us briefly return to the work of Ferlie and his colleagues (2000), discussed in Chapter 2, who present powerful research evidence for the limitations of the rational and linear model of change. To recap, they discovered that the innovation supported by the most evidence was the least adopted in the NHS and the innovation supported by the least evidence was the most adopted. They concluded that different forms of evidence are accepted to varying extents by disparate individuals and occupational groups and suggested that these differences need to be addressed explicitly through the construction of linking bodies, which bring together the individuals and groups involved in the implementation. Interestingly, this suggestion links closely with the argument by Stacey that the task of managers is to devise opportunities for organ-isational members to 'craft' strategy.

This distinction, between linear and non-linear approaches, has been part of the debate about the nature of strategy which has been taught in business schools since their inception. The rational approach is associated, for example, with the SWOT analyses of Ansoff (1988), who advocated a rigorous description of skills and resources within a company, a robust analysis of the external operating environment and a matching of the two in the context of clear strategic purpose. This has been called the 'deliberate' approach to strategy to contrast it with the 'emergent' approach of Mintzberg and van der Heyden (1999).

Comparing what managers said was their strategy with what they actually did in practice, Mintzberg and others came to the view that the key skill of the strategist was pattern recognition, their most important attributes were intuition and a detailed knowledge of local working practices and practitioners ('how things work round here'), and their most important contribution the ability to recognise and respond to unexpected changes as they occurred. Managers cannot command and control, and to think they ever could was unreasonable.

Stacey's agreement/certainty matrix

The earlier description of complex adaptive systems stresses the importance of the interaction between the components in a complex system, that is the organising relations within the system. To understand the nature of such interaction, it is important to be clear, in as much as one can, about what actually are the components of the system, and what the nature of their interactions might be. In the OD context, this implies that a local context for the creation of the linking bodies or stakeholder conferences (or whatever) needs to be established. In this regard, Stacey (1999) has produced a valuable contribution with his agreement/certainty matrix shown in Figure 8.1. In this matrix, the vertical axis represents *agreement*, that is the extent of the clarity about the components of a system, and the extent of consensus between the agents about the nature of an issue arising within that system. *Certainty*, represented by the horizontal axis, is an indication of how sure one can be about the cause-and-effect linkages within the system. Where a manager or OD practitioner is operating close to certainty, they can usually draw on prior experience of a similar

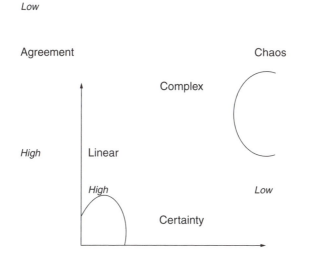

Figure 8.1   Stacey's agreement/certainty matrix (reproduced from Stacey, 1999).

issue or experience in the past to inform action. Where the lines intersect, at the bottom left-hand corner, participants are both entirely agreed about the attributes of the system and about the nature of the causal linkages between them and this can be described as the zone of linearity.

New or unexpected situations, however, force the agents far from certainty, i.e. towards the right of the horizontal axis. Where neither agreement about the attributes of the system exists nor certainty about the nature of the interconnections is available, this can be characterised as the zone of chaos. Complexity, and the area where interventions drawing on emergence are most applicable, lies between these two zones of linearity and chaos.

For OD, the value of this visual matrix lies in clarifying which intervention might best be suited to address issues located at different places within the notional space. For example, when operating in the linear or simple zone, classic rational strategies like business process re-engineering or total quality management can be effective. In the zone of chaos, these will not help; indeed they may be harmful. Here, it is best to look for patterns by continuously communicating with other agents in the system before applying any coherent strategy. It is in the zone of complexity, however, that most of the issues facing large organisations reside.

Build networks, enhance communication, work collectively and allow direction to emerge are the guiding management principles here (Wheatley, 2001). This is the zone where self-organisation operates, and where organisations need to diminish the need for rigid structures, and become agile, reactive and flexible. The emphasis is on minimising strategic rigidity, preferring rather more fluid processes, in which, for example, small teams within organisations are created in response to new and ever-changing needs – and then disbanded once that need has been addressed. This is what the Swedish manufacturing company Oticom did in a major destructuring of its entire corporation (Pinchot and Pinchot, 1996). In an attempt to respond more swiftly and flexibly to the changing environment in which they operated, employees literally gave up their office space and furniture, swapping these for mobile essentials, a cell phone, laptop and file cart on wheels. So did the chief executive, who located himself in marketing, finance or HR, depending on where an immediate need had arisen (Pinchot and Pinchot, 1996).

Critical to sustaining this adaptability is the flow of information, combined with its dispersal and deployment within the organisation. For organisations, this means seeking out information from all available sources, for example strategists, partners, frontline staff, even rivals. The principle behind this information flow is actually to maintain disequilibrium, that is to keep the organisation continuously changing, just, as it were, off balance. Balance means equilibrium, and equilibrium means organisational dissipation, atrophy and death. Willett (1999) describes the transformation of the US chemical manufacturer Buckman Laboratories, which reorganised its company's work practices around an open distributed approach to information. One of the company's employees, challenged by some technical information needed to close a business deal, made use of the recently developed company intranet to request advice. He received, within hours, a range of replies from the company's centres in six countries. Not only did this information help him secure the deal, but his technical query spawned a further conversation between some of the respondents about the issue which grew into an ongoing conversational resource – a neat example of self-organisation (Willett, 1999).

This picture, of organisations constantly responding to change, is not meant to convey an impression of organisations as passive, helpless victims, awash in a turbulent sea of unpredictability. Organisations have to accept that the environment is unpredictable, but they retain their stability from a deeper clarity about who they are and what they do. This is what Wheatley (2001) calls self-referencing. Self-referencing, Wheatley argues, is the key to facilitating orderly change in an ever-changing environment. To do this, organisations develop and rely on a clear sense of their own identity, a composite of their values, competencies, experiences, successes and failures. Paradoxically, the environment in which organisations operate gains overall stability from the impact of numerous local changes. This is the principle at the heart of the stability of ecosystems, where, Jantsch (1980) points out, the more freedom in self-organisation, the more order there is.

Relational dynamics

There has been increasing interest in the past two decades in the application of the principles of complex systems to organisational change in both the commercial sector (Wheatley, 2001) and healthcare (Plsek, 2000). Wheatley (2001) contextualises her interpretation of complexity for organisational change consistently within the intellectual developments described above. Her interpretation of the principles of complexity is particularly informed by quantum physics. Quantum physicists can identify a range of subatomic particles, Wheatley explains, but these cannot truly be understood in isolation; they are particles in an intermediate state sustained within a network of interactions (Zukav, 1979). 'Physicists can plot the probability and results of these interactions, but no particle can be drawn independent from the others,' she observes (Wheatley, 2001).

Wheatley brings these notions together in a new model of change management predicated on relational dynamics. In stark contrast to the widely espoused Western values of individualism, competition and a mechanistic view of life, Wheatley exhorts us to accept that there is nothing independent of relationships. These relationships are expressed in the need to trust others, to be involved in changes that affect us as individuals, to participate in meaningful work and to be recognised for our contribution. She cites examples in large commercial companies where large-scale successful transformational change has been guided by the principles of complexity. For example, the Dupont chemical plant in West Virginia reorganised its relationships not just with regulators, but with local communities, to learn how better to develop its safety profile, and communicate these efforts successfully, in a process of co-evolution with its partner agents in the community system.

Applying complexity to healthcare

Recently, Plsek (2000) has incorporated the principles of complex adaptive systems into his vision of how the US healthcare system should develop in the 21st century. Like Wheatley and Stacey in their writings on the commercial sector, Plsek focuses on the importance, in healthcare systems, of the connections and interactions between components of the system. 'A healthcare system,' Plsek (2000) writes, 'is a macro-system. It consists of numerous micro-systems (doctor's offices, hospitals, pharmacies and so on) that are linked to provide comprehensiveness of care.' Plsek distinguishes mechanical from adaptive systems: 'In mechanical systems, we can predict what the system will do in great detail. In complex adaptive systems, the parts (which in a healthcare system include human beings) have the ability to respond to stimuli in fundamentally unpredictable ways. For this reason, emergent creative behaviour is a real possibility' (Plsek, 2000). Plsek's conclusion is that complexity provides a new paradigm to guide an understanding on how organisations work in healthcare.

Plsek frames this new paradigm, in the context of healthcare, in what he calls a set of simple rules for complex systems. Here, he is drawing on the surprising finding from research into complex adaptive systems that the application of a small number of simple rules can lead to complex innovative behaviour. For example, thinking in terms of simple rules has led to a greater understanding of many biological systems, such as the flocking of birds, schooling of fish and predator–prey relationships (Stewart, 1989; Battram, 1998; Plsek, 2000). Plsek (2000) has devised a set of simple rules for the US healthcare system in the 21st century, contrasting them, in Table 8.1, with what the equivalent approach from a previous linear system might have been.

Table 8.1 Simple rules for the 21st century US healthcare system

Former linear approach	New complexity approach
Healthcare based on episodic office visits	Care based on continuous healing relationships
Variability driven by professional autonomy	Care customised according to patient needs and values
Professional-centred care	Patient-centred care
Information located in medical record	Knowledge is freely available and shared
Decision making based predominantly on experience	Evidence-based decision making
Do no harm seen as individual's responsibility	Safety an inherent feature of the system
Secrecy is necessary	Transparency is necessary
System reacts to needs	System anticipates needs
Cost reduction is sought	Waste is continuously diminished
Preference given to professionals' roles over the system	Cooperation and collaboration among professionals a priority for the system

Adapted from Institute of Medicine, 2001.

Within the UK healthcare system, the principles of complex adaptive systems have been reframed by Fraser *et al.* (2003) within the notion of 'agility'. An agile system is one that can respond rapidly to a changing environment and markets. The importance of rich interaction, a key feature of complex adaptive systems, is stressed; agile commercial organisations draw on their relationships with suppliers, partners and customers to improve their practices. Using flexible working patterns and virtual teaming, agile companies can, it is asserted, deliver products more swiftly, with better quality and at lower cost.

The principles of agility, set out in Box 8.1, strongly evoke the key characteristics of complex adaptive systems, namely receptive context, self-organisation and co-evolution. There are examples in the UK NHS where these principles of agility have been applied to healthcare organisations, for example in the redesign of older people's services in London (Jones *et al.*, 2003).

Box 8.1: Attributes of agile systems applied to healthcare

- Rapid change over (for example in the use of operating theatres)
- Doing today's work today (the basis of advanced access in general practice)
- Cooperative rescheduling carried out with partners, stakeholders, patients and carers
- Flexibility, particularly in the constitution of teams
- Synchronised scheduling
- Care coordinated around a specific patient, not as part of mass customisation

Adapted from Yarrow *et al.*, 2003.

Within the past five years, the principles of complexity have been applied to a greater variety of organisational contexts. For example, non-linear models have also been proposed as the basis for education of healthcare professionals (Fraser and Greenhalgh, 2001). Others have described the advantages of understanding organisational change from the perspective of complexity (Zimmerman and Plsek, 1998; Plsek and Wilson, 2001; Kernick, 2002). The development and embedding of clinical governance at the level of primary care trusts has been described in terms of complex systems (Sweeney and Mannion, 2002; Sweeney, 2003b). Finally, Hassey (2002) has proposed a theoretical model for understanding the consultation in general practice based upon the non-linear principles of complexity.

Connecting linear and non-linear approaches

The argument in this chapter supports the view that the principles of complexity offer an additional perspective to help understand organisational development in healthcare. This proposition is careful to frame complexity as a complementary commodity, not something to replace all that went before, nor something completely radical which denies the importance of the linear paradigm alongside which it has developed.[1] Relating the two intellectual traditions in this way carries interesting theoretical and practical implications for OD practitioners. The theoretical implications of reflecting on the potential complementarity of linear and non-linear paradigms has implications for our worldview, for the framework of evidence that we construct to populate that worldview, and for the explanatory model which is created as a product of that worldview and its framework. Put another way, this alignment of the two traditions challenges the conventional wisdom from which the explanatory model that supports most current theories of organisational change is constructed. While on the one hand, they can be contrasted, and represent different (but overlapping) worldviews, they can also be seen as complementary, their combination helping to extend our understanding of change.

As an illustration of this argument, we can consider the Stacey diagram referred to above as a unified notional space, in which the choice of OD intervention reflects how certain we can be about the attributes of the system (the agreement axis) and the way in which these attributes interact (the certainty axis). This allows us notionally to subdivide the Stacey space into a linear zone, near the lower left corner, at the intersection of agreement and certainty, and complex zone at the edge of chaos, as shown above. Zimmerman and Plsek (1998) have described how different management approaches can be deployed for issues that are located on various positions on the Stacey space. Four examples developed from the perspective of healthcare organisations are given below, and illustrated in Figure 8.2.

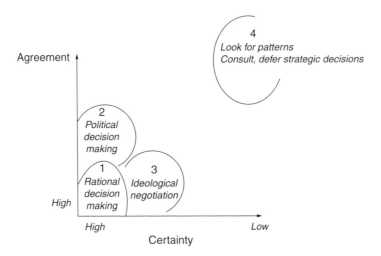

Figure 8.2 The Stacey matrix developed by Zimmerman and Plsek (1998).

---

[1] For those interested in the mathematics of this, linearity is a mathematical subset of non-linearity, where, in the non-linear equation, $x = a^n + c$, 'a' is constant and $n = 1$.

Rational decision making

This is the area in which an organisation may feel it is clear both about the attributes of the system and how those attributes will interact. The system can operate in a linear manner, drawing on experience and expertise to feel confident about prediction. An example in healthcare might be the implementation of a National Service Framework (NSF). Here, the agents in the system (healthcare professionals and managers) are apparently clear about the attributes of the system (the parameters of the framework) and are confident, based on arguably good evidence, about how the system will proceed once the framework is implemented (there will be better, more systematic care for patients). OD practitioners can, therefore, draw on simple re-engineering processes, such as those described in Chapter 5, and the like, to guide management in setting out what has to be done, by whom, by when, in alignment with a pre-determined plan, based on understanding of similar situations in the past.

Political decision making

In this domain, there is considerable certainty about how outcomes are achieved, but much less agreement about which outcomes (attributes) should be considered. This is the area of negotiation and compromise. The recent negotiations in the NHS leading to a new contract for general practitioners is an example where this was the appropriate strategy. In these negotiations, it was obvious what the out-come would be; the government was intent on developing and implementing a fresh contractual relationship with family doctors. But what were to be its content, the obligations of each party, the accountability processes and so forth? While negotiations between the government of the day and doctors have been going on for over 150 years, in these circumstances neither side could deploy pre-determined plans; there was no blueprint (a strict timetable, maybe, but no blueprint) and the outcome – a service-based contract where remuneration reflected the level of service to patients – was an emergent (and largely welcome) outcome of the discussions (NHS Confederation, 2003).

Ideological negotiation

Here, the aim will be to head towards a shared future state, without necessarily agreeing in advance how that state might be reached.

One of the key interventions of the OD process in asylum closure in the 1990s was a series of stakeholder conferences used in the design of service models that would replace the asylums. In many respects, these conferences – which brought together representatives of all of the interest groups around mental health services – were the linking bodies that Ferlie and his colleagues (2000) recommend. In this case, however, the stakeholder conferences involved users, carers and voluntary sector staff as well as the range of professional disciplines. In addition, they were carefully designed and facilitated in order to give particular power to the voices of the service users in the articulation of their needs on the assumption that: first, it would be difficult for professionals, especially psychiatrists, to deny in public the veracity of these views; and, second, that these needs would not be met most effectively by the asylums given the alternatives starting to emerge in the research literature. Furthermore, they took place in a context in which the overall goal – hospital closure – was clear and broadly consensual, and within a process where there were regular opportunities for local interest groups to interact, but there were no pre-determined views about the specific content of the particular local strategy (I owe this example to the editor, and *see* the Conclusion for further reflections on the closure of the asylums).

The edge of chaos: looking for patterns

Here, there is neither agreement about the attributes of the system, nor any certainty about how the system might proceed. For instance, the promotion of patient choice – uniquely, it could be argued, at least in the initial seven years of New Labour interventions in the NHS – is a policy where the present government is responding to lack of agreement about the attributes (e.g. the legitimacy of the private sector as a provider to the NHS) and a lack of certainty about how to proceed (e.g. mutual government and service frustration with targets) by attempting to introduce a new pattern onto the system; that is they are introducing a deliberately destabilising factor into the healthcare arena without trying to specify the specific consequences that it might deliver through, for example, articulating detailed targets. If New Labour holds its nerve in this approach – a big if – then this initiative could create the most profound transformation in the relationships, for instance, between the public and professionals and between secondary care and primary care since 1948, but in ways that may very difficult to predict or control.

Linear and non-linear strategies seen as rational and emergent

Hadridge (2004) has offered a way of resolving the creative tension involved in recognising these two approaches to strategy, that is linear (or rational) and non-linear (which Hadridge calls emergent). He theorises that the two approaches can be considered as two axes of strategy, each axis representing a continuum of rationality or emergence; within the space defined by the two axes, one can 'plot' various characteristics of OD strategies. His diagram is shown in Figure 8.3.

If we consider each axis separately, the higher up the rational axis the more linear a strategy can be, and the further to the right along the emergent axis the more non-linear. Hadridge's contribution has been to help us conceptualise OD strategies as combining these two characteristics in differing proportions. Visualising the balance of OD interventions in this way can help managers envisage prospectively how a strategy might combine the two characteristics, and it may also help retrospectively

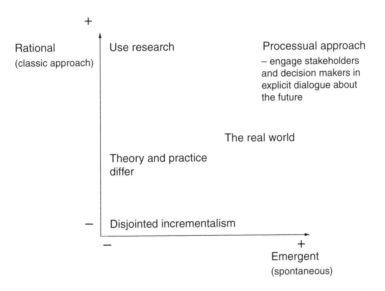

Figure 8.3 Combining rational and emergent approaches to strategy (adapted from Hadridge, 2004).

by allowing us to reflect on why a particular OD approach that did not encompass this balance might have failed.

Consider the following examples from healthcare to illustrate these points. The implementation of a NSF, referred to above, must be evidence based to justify its clinical imperatives. Because it is argued to be so firmly rooted in robust evidence, and relates to such a key clinical area, it is able to carry the support of the practitioners who are charged with implementing it; thus, a rational, linear approach to implementation is more likely to be successfully deployed.

Now, consider the current controversy surrounding the supposed link between autism and the combined vaccination to protect children against mumps, measles and rubella (MMR). In brief, the safety of the vaccine has been called into question by a single paper (which has more authors in its title than patients in the study) which proposed that vaccinating children with the combined MMR jab might increase their risk of developing autism (Wakefield *et al.*, 1998). Following a large number of media reports of the principal warning in the paper, that MMR may cause autism, vaccination rates have fallen from almost universal to, in some areas, less than two-thirds of the target population (Goldacre, 2003). In response, the Department of Health has continued to cite the scientific research to support its rational linear approach to resolving the dilemma. The problem is, however, that their interlocutors in the debate (mostly mothers of young children) are not responding to this strategy; in terms of Stacey's representation (Figure 8.2) above, they find themselves towards the right on the certainty axis. Hadridge's matrix (Figure 8.3) helps us see that, in the real world, strategic approaches to these issues need to balance emergence and rationality, and that what he calls a processual approach – engaging stakeholders through conversation – might stand a greater chance of success.

Consider, finally, an example of what Hadridge calls disjointed incrementalism. Gaming, a strategy used by some healthcare organisations to subvert imposed targets (in this case imposed by the DoH), is an example of this. The recent report on the state of the ambulance service in England and Wales published by the Commission for Health Improvement (CHI) (2003) contained two interesting examples of such gaming. Ambulance services were required by the DoH to hit a target which demonstrated that, in a specific proportion of calls, their crews arrived at the scene within a specified time (eight minutes). Accident and Emergency departments, to whom the crews often transported their patients, had their own target, that is to see all patients within four hours. Some ambulance crews 'gamed' the first target by failing to turn on their stop clocks until they felt they were about eight minutes away from their target. Their colleagues in the Accident and Emergency departments encouraged ambulances to form queues outside their departments, not disgorging their patients until they were able to be seen, thus achieving their waiting times target. In Hadridge's terms, this strategy was neither rational or emergent; it was rather a response to a target which some perceived to be unfair but where failure to achieve it might carry a high price.

Case study: the management of an AIDS epidemic in Brazil

Although research into complex systems has been conducted for over half a century, there are few examples in the healthcare or OD literature where an analysis of large-scale transformational change has been undertaken from the perspective of complex adaptive systems. One such example, however, shows clearly how regarding a problem as complex rather than complicated radically altered the options which emerged for policy and intervention. The case in question describes Brazil's approach to its AIDS epidemic in the 1990s (Gloubermann and Zimmerman, 2002).

In the 1980s Brazil had one of the worst infection rates for AIDS in the world (Darlington, 2000). With an accelerating infection rate for the virus far in excess even of that in South Africa, coupled with an annual per capita income of less than $5000, the World Bank predicted disaster, calculating that Brazil would have 1.2 million cases of AIDS by 2000 (World Bank, 1997). In fact, in that year, 0.5 million cases were reported to the World Health Organization (WHO), an infection rate of 0.6%, compared to South Africa's 25% (WHO, 2002).

The World Bank's (1997) predictions on the global AIDS epidemic make for pretty gloomy reading, but Glouberman and Zimmerman's (2002) careful analysis reveals how the Bank's prediction was predicated on linear modelling of the issue, leading to the development of complicated, rather than complex, assumptions, from which the apocalyptic picture emerged. Here are some of the assumptions in the World Bank's report which demonstrate their linear conceptual framework in relation to the AIDS epidemic.

- Effective treatment, in the form of antiretroviral treatment, is too demanding of clinical services in poor and developing countries.

- Poor countries rapidly realise that they cannot sustain the cost of effective treatments so they concentrate exclusively on prevention.
- Even if drug treatment was available for some AIDS patients, the ill-educated and barely literate people who are typical of the AIDS patients in poor countries could not possibly manage their own complicated drug regimes.
- The way to implement effective prevention is to scare people, for instance fear of death will limit the spread of the disease.
- Effective prevention still results in huge losses to the current adult generation, and its benefits will take two or three generations to accrue.
- An integrated programme of prevention and treatment in combination is beyond the organisational capacity of poor and developing countries.

This is what the Brazilian authorities actually did (Glouberman and Zimmermann, 2002).

- They gave the drugs away free. They took a risky decision to manufacture their own generic brands of the antiretroviral preparations. By 2000, eight of the 12 available preparations were produced generically in Brazil. Thus, the costs of treatment came in at between 65% and 90% less expensive than in the USA (on whose figures the World Bank had based their calculations).
- They used treatment as a part of the prevention strategy, figuring that, when people know that they will receive treatment free, they will be more willing to attend for therapy. Those who attended received preventive advice, subsequently spread the word to the close communities in which the disease was rife (an intriguing example of self-organisation) and felt their decisions were being reinforced as the progression of their symptoms slowed down. A self-perpetuating positive feedback loop had emerged.
- The Brazilian authorities accepted poor literacy and numeracy in their target population as a challenge and developed a huge number of creative ways of tackling it. Doctors and nurses co-opted other healthcare workers, lay people and patients themselves to produce their own ideas of how to get the key messages across. Drawings of food were used to remind people when to take the pills and arrangements were made for food to be provided free through schools and churches, thus giving a further point for compliance messages to be reinforced. Humour became a key ingredient of billboards advertising free condoms.
- The Brazilian government seized on the AIDS epidemic as an opportunity to strengthen its healthcare infrastructure rather than simply seeing it as the reason for their failure to control the problem. They deployed over 600 pre-existing non-governmental and community organisations to access hard-to-reach groups, and established a network of over 130 testing and counselling centres (Centre for Disease Control, 2000).

From the perspective of complexity, what the Brazilian government did was to accept and make use of the messiness in its healthcare system and maximise the connectivity in the informal, social and community relationships which they knew existed but were not displayed on any organisational chart. They knew they had a receptive context, that is a focus on potentially shared activities (the care of AIDS patients) which all constituents agreed was mainstream business (no one was in any doubt the country faced a catastrophe). As a result, the system self-organised. For example, AIDS patients redefined their informal groups as patient groups receiving treatment and preventive advice, while churches and other non-governmental organisations became actively involved as agents of the healthcare system. In summary, as Gloubermann and Zimmerman (2002) put it, they reframed complicated questions as complex challenges: 'Who can we afford to treat?' became 'How can we reduce the cost of treatment so we can provide it for everyone?' and 'What infrastructure do we need and from what existing service will we take the money to pay for it?' became 'Where and what are the pre-existing informal arrangements that we can deploy as part of an emerging infrastructure and how can we strengthen them?' Complicated became complex, pre-determined became emergent, a shortage of resource was redefined as a potential abundance. It became, in the words of Rosenberg (2001), 'a well organised, well formulated programme that works because the government has managed to integrate the whole society'.

Planning, responding and reflecting: time, emergence and OD

Planners have to plan. Managers have to manage. Both have to learn from past successes and failures the better to inform future policy. This implies three stages of strategic process: prospective, real time and reflection. Isles (2004) has applied the thinking about emergence to the evolution of organisational strategy in these three stages.[2] Running a large organisation obliges managers to have a plan, that is to identify a set of critical issues the organisation must address and to implement a programme to address those issues. There simply must be a prospective element to strategy and this is where a classic rational approach is best suited. But in real time, those managers need to be able to expect the unexpected, to adapt and evolve with circumstances as they emerge in sometimes unforeseen ways, and to be sufficiently agile to respond to changes in circumstances.

In health, for example, services may be redesigned, activities enlarged, skill mix re-configured; managers have to be ready to address these new challenges. This agility will consist of the processes of self-organisation and co-evolution. There needs to be sufficient flexibility in an organisation to allow policies to emerge through an empowering, permission-giving environment, where all participants feel they can contribute to strategic processes by trying out new ways of working on a small scale; small enough not to destabilise the organisation if they fail but easy enough to scale up should they be successful. In her analysis, Isles (2004) identifies storytelling as the principle medium for effective retrospection (*see* Chapter 12 for more on storytelling).

---

[2] Drawing on Mintzberg's work, Isles in her paper distinguishes between rational, spontaneous and emergent strategic approaches. Here, I continue to use the terms emergent and rational to distinguish two approaches.

With a rational strategy, managers will have evidence to compare what was planned with what actually happened. Weaving together the elements of recent strategic history into a coherent story is a sensemaking process (*see* Chapter 1 for an introduction to this concept), which allows the organisation to justify itself to stakeholders, understand better 'how things work round here' and thus be better prepared for future challenges. This attention to the temporal element of OD interventions – planning for the future, responding in the present and reflecting on the past – is an inherent strength of the model predicated on complexity and emergence which I have described in this chapter.

Limitations

Complexity is not a panacea. It is, however, more than a passing OD fad. Its main limitation, for the moment, is the struggle complexity enthusiasts in OD have when replying to the perfectly reasonable question 'So what?'. There is little empirical evidence of complex systems developing in organisations, and almost none which have been described either prospectively or in real time (although case studies from the Department of Health Modernisation Agency's Pursuing Perfection programme, of transformational change in healthcare communities, are currently underway). While there will have to be substantive evidence of the benefits of such a shift for OD theory, the nature of such proof is itself contested. How can one know, in the UK NHS, that a particular outcome in an organisation was attributable to the organisation's acceptance of complexity theory and its willingness to run itself as a complex system? This is the hoary old chestnut of attributability, itself a key element of a linear chain of causes and effects which complexity seeks to challenge. In a complex system, predicting what outcome will emerge from which input, and when, is not simple, and may only be discernible in retrospect. Not only will the 'burden of proof' need to be reframed, in order to reveal the benefit of assessing organisational change from the perspective of complexity, but the nature of the evidence which constitutes such proof will have to be redefined too. Narrative will increasingly become the currency of understanding how complex systems work and needs to be recognised as the principal tool for effective retrospection. The collation of such work-based stories will come to constitute the basis on which organisations define and redefine themselves in response to an ever-changing environment (Stephenson, 2003).

The inherent unpredictability within complex systems poses substantial new challenges for managers. At worst, they might be seen to have responsibility for a system over which they have little control. The challenge for such managers lies in balancing clarity of vision – that is robust framing of the system, what it wants to do, what its values are, what competencies it can deploy – with light touch to implementation which effectively allows the system to create its own detail within the overall framework. This is what self-referencing calls for (Wheatley, 2001), and it will be a central challenge for managers of complex systems. The imperative is for managers to frame a set of potentially shared activities, which embrace the aspirations, values and culture of an organisation, and which all the constituents accept as core business.

How can we learn from complex systems? Their characteristics – emergence, co-evolution and self-organisation – seem to be highly context-specific, rendering the generalisability so beloved of the scientific paradigm elusive. Transferability is the aspiration, not generalisability. This means identifying and learning from other 'systems' which share sufficiently similar contexts for comparisons to be meaningful. In some cases, this will mean literally transferring some agents from one system to another; a visit (by bus) by residents from one deprived estate in the southwest of England to another similar estate which had managed to turn itself around resulted in the adoption, by the former, of some of the activities successfully implemented by the latter (Stutely, 2004, personal communication). Buddying, mentoring and secondments constitute other mechanisms for transferring learning. The shift towards accepting an approach to OD based on complex adaptive systems requires the adoption of a different worldview and the development of a different body of knowledge to make sense of that worldview. It will produce, as a result, a different explanatory model for sensemaking in organisations.

Conclusion

The rise of science in the twentieth century created an intellectual paradigm which has been hugely influential and has come to be applied to areas well beyond its original domain. The principles underpinning this paradigm – linearity and predictability – formed the cornerstone of policy making in politics, economics, organisational development and even international relations. Early in the twentieth century the discovery that non-linear systems were pervasive in nature focused attention on the implications of accepting an inherently non-linear (and therefore unpredictable) basis for understanding systems in general. Out of this, our present understanding of complex adaptive systems has evolved. Within the past two decades, management theorists have become interested in the potential application of complexity to strategy. In this chapter I have proposed that a fresh and extended understanding of organisational change can be informed by regarding linearity and non-linearity as complementary, by balancing both in appropriate proportions in formulation of strategy and by accepting that both can be expressed simultaneously as organisations change. In the 21st century, policy makers, managers and clinicians will need to learn to live with uncertainty, assisted by OD practitioners versed in its theory and practice.

References

Ansoff I (1988) *Overview of Strategic Behaviours*. Wiley and Sons, New York.

Battram A (1998) *Navigating Complexity*. The Industrial Society, London.

Capra F (1996) *The Web of Life*. Doubleday, New York.

Centre for Disease Control (2000) *Centre for Disease Control Daily News*. Cited 22 September 2000 (www.ama-assn.org/special/hiv/newsline/cdd/091800g3.html).

Cilliers P (1998) *Complexity and Postmodernism*. Routledge, London.

Cohen J and Stewart I (1994) *The Collapse of Chaos*. Penguin Books, Harmondsworth, Middlesex.

Commission for Health Improvement (2003) *A Report on the Ambulance Service in England and Wales*. CHI, London.

Darlington S (2000) *Brazil Becomes Model in AIDS Fight*. 7 November 2000 (www. aegis.org/news/re/2000/re001107.html).

DHSS (1983) *NHS Management Enquiry (Griffiths Report)*. Department of Health and Social Security, London.

Ferlie E, Fitzgerald L and Wood M (2000) Getting evidence into clinical practice: an organisational behaviour perspective. *Journal of Health Services Research and Policy*. 5(2): 96–102.

Fraser S and Greenhalgh T (2001) Coping with complexity: educating for capability. *British Medical Journal*. 323: 799–802.

Fraser S, Conner M and Yarrow D (eds) (2003) *Thriving in Unpredictable Times: a reader on agility in health care*. Kingsham Press, Chichester.

Fukuyama F (1993) *The End of History and the Last Man*. Penguin, London.

Geyer R (2001) *Beyond the Third Way: the science of complexity and the politics of choice*. Paper presented to the Joint Session of the ECPR, Grenoble, April.

Gloubermann S and Zimmerman B (2002) *Complicated and Complex Systems: what would successful reform of Medicare look like?* Discussion Paper 8, Commission on the Future of Health Care in Canada, Montreal, Canada.

Goldacre B (2003) Never mind the facts. *Life* section, *The Guardian*, 11 December.

Hadridge P (2004) Personal communication.

Hammer M (1995) *The Re-engineering Revolution*. Harper Business, New York.

Harrison S (1988) *Managing the NHS: shifting the frontier?* Chapman and Hall, London.

Hassey A (2002) Complexity and the clinical encounter. In: K Sweeney and F Griffiths (eds) *Complexity and Healthcare: an introduction*. Radcliffe Medical Press, Oxford.

HMSO (1962) *A Hospital Plan for England and Wales*. HMSO, London.

HMSO (1972) *Report of the Working Part on Medical Administrators (The Grey Book)*. HMSO, London.

Institute of Medicine (2001) *Crossing the Quality Chasm: a new health system for the 21st century*. National Academy Press, Washington, DC.

Isles V (2004) *Developing Strategy in Complex Organisations*. NHS Confederation, London.

Jantsch E (1980) *The Self-Organising Universe*. Pergamon, Oxford.

Jones V, Layton A, Andrews J, Adam R, Beaton A, Strahan K and Fraser S (2003) The journey to agility: case studies for improving the care of older adults in London.

In: S Fraser, M Conner and D Yarrow (eds) *Thriving in Unpredictable Times: a reader on agility in health care*. Kingsham Press, Chichester.

Kember T and Macpherson G (1994) *The NHS A Kaleidoscope of Care – conflict of service and business values*. Nuffield Hospitals Provincial Trust, London.

Kernick D (2002) Complexity and healthcare organisation. In: K Sweeney and F Griffiths (eds) *Complexity and Healthcare: an introduction*. Radcliffe Medical Press, Oxford..5

Klein R (1989) *The Politics of the NHS*. Longman, London.

Lorenz E (1963) Deterministic non-periodic flow. *Journal of Atmospheric Sciences*. **20**: 130–41.

Mintzberg H and van der Heyden L (1999) Organigraphs: drawing how companies really work. *Harvard Business Review*. **September–October**. 77(5): 87–94.

Morgan G (1986) *Images of Organization*. Sage, London.

NHS Confederation (2003) *The New GMS Contract: investing in general practice*. NHS Confederation, London.

Pinchot G and Pinchot E (1996) *The Intelligent Organisation: engaging the talent and initiative of everyone in the workplace*. Berrett-Koehler, San Francisco, CA.

Plsek P (2000) *Crossing the Quality Chasm: a new health system for the 21st century*. National Academy Press, Washington, DC.

Plsek P and Wilson T (2001) Complexity, leadership and management in healthcare organisations. *British Medical Journal*. **323**: 746–9.

Poincaré H (1958) *Science and Value*. Dover, New York.

Prigogine I (1998) *The End of Certainty: time, chaos, and the laws of nature*. The Free Press, New York.

Robinson R and Le Grand J (1994) *Evaluating the NHS Reforms*. King's Fund Institute, London.

Rosenberg T (2001) Look at Brazil. *New York Times Magazine*. 28 January: 26–54 (www.accessmed-msg.org/msf.accessmed/accessmed2.nsf/iwpList4).

Stacey R (1999) *Strategic Management and Organisational Dynamics: the challenge of complexity*. Financial Times, London.

Stacey R (2001) *Complex Responsive Processes in Organisations*. Routledge, London.

Stephenson M (2003) *Narrative Analysis in Multi-national Organisations*. Presentation to Complexity Conference, Complexity In Healthcare Group, University of Exeter, September.

Stewart I (1989) *Does God Play Dice?* Penguin, London.

Stutely H (2004) Personal communication.

Sweeney K (2003a) *Complexity and Explanatory Models*. Presentation to the European Quality in Practice (EquiP) Conference, 14 November, Heidelberg.

Sweeney K (2003b) Progressing clinical governance through complexity: from managing to co-creating. In: D Kernick (ed.) *Complexity and Organisations*. Radcliffe Medical Press, Oxford.

Sweeney K and Mannion R (2002) Complexity and clinical governance: using the insights to develop the strategy. *British Journal of General Practice*. **52**(supplement): 4–9.

Taylor F (1911) *Principles of Scientific Management*. Harper and Brothers, New York.

Wakefield A, Murch S, Anthony A, Lunnell J, Casson D, Malik M, Berelowitz M, Dhillon A, Thomson M, Harvey P, Valentine A, Davies S and Walker-Smith J (1998) Ileal lymphoid nodular hyperplasia, non-specific colitis, and pervasive developmental disorder in children. *Lancet*. **351**: 637–41.

Wheatley M (2001) *Leadership and the New Science*. Berrett-Koehler, San Francisco, CA.

Willett C (1999) Knowledge sharing shifts the power paradigm. In: M Maybury, D Morey and B Thuraisingham (eds) *Knowledge Management: classic and contemporary works*. Massachusetts Institute of Technology Press, Cambridge, MA.

World Bank (1997) *Confronting AIDS: public priorities in a global epidemic*. (www.worldbank.org/aids-econ/confrontfull/summary.html)

World Health Organisation (2002) *Archives: The World Health Report 2000*. World Health Organization, Geneva.

Yarrow D, Fraser S and Tennison B (2003) Planning and scheduling: maintaining flow in adaptive systems. In: S Fraser, M Conner and D Yarrow (eds) *Thriving in Unpredictable Times: a reader on agility in health care*. Kingsham Press, Chichester.

Zimmerman B and Plsek P (1998) *Edgeware: insights from complexity science for healthcare leaders*. VHA, Irving.

Zukav G (1979) *The Dancing Wu Li Masters*. Bantam, New York.

Further reading

A useful primer to introduce anyone interested to complexity is:

- Battram A (1998) *Navigating Complexity*. The Industrial Society, London.

A more complete and eminently readable account of the development of complexity is:

- Capra F (1996) *The Web of Life*. Doubleday, New York.

Some good stories about the application of complexity to healthcare organisations can be found in:

- Zimmerman B and Plsek P (1998) *Edgeware: insights from complexity science for healthcare leaders*. VHA, Irving.

A more theoretical analysis of the potential application of complexity to the US healthcare system is:

- Institute of Medicine (2001) *Crossing the Quality Chasm: a new health system for the 21st century*. National Academy Press, Washington, DC.

Finally, an accessible introduction to complexity and healthcare:

- Sweeney K and Griffiths F (eds) (2002) *Complexity and Healthcare: an introduction*. Radcliffe Medical Press, Oxford.

Websites

- Health Complexity Group: www.healthcomplexity.net

This is the site of the Health Complexity Group for whom the author is a researcher. It contains some useful articles and background information on complexity.

- Tufton Group (Complexity in Primary Care Group): www.complexityprimary care.org

This is the website of a group of healthcare researchers and practitioners, initially from primary care, but now including representatives from all sectors of healthcare.

- Plexus Institute: www.plexusinstitute.com

A useful source for books, articles and stories about complexity.

- Santa Fe Institute: www.santafe.edu

This site is managed by the Santa Fe Institute, acknowledged world leaders in complexity.

Editor's note: the editor regrets the lack of page references in the text of this chapter but these were not available from the author.

CHAPTER 9

Working with structure

Murray Anderson-Wallace

Introduction

From its formation in 1948 – and especially since 1974 – the NHS has undergone numerous structural changes in repeated attempts to improve the organisation and delivery of its services. As a consequence, many managers and clinicians consider organisational reconfiguration and organisational development (OD) as being almost synonymous. In any discussion of OD, innovations in social structure (that is, the rules and accountabilities of organisational life) would play a legitimate part; in healthcare, perhaps, they loom particularly large.

A brief résumé of this history will help make this point (*see* Klein, 2001, for a detailed account). For instance, as early as 1962 the Porritt report criticised the three-part separation in the provision of healthcare (between hospitals, general practice and local authorities) and called for a more unified structure. Later that decade, the Salmon and the Cogwheel reports produced proposals aimed at reforming aspects of the nursing and medical professions, respectively, in order to improve coordination and performance and to encourage more clinicians into managerial roles. Several plans for significant structural change fell by the wayside in the early 1970s until, in 1974, major reorganisation of the NHS introduced new tiers of management in the form of regional and area health authorities. Within five years, however, a Royal Commission into the NHS criticised the complex organisational and managerial structures created by the 1974 reforms and, in 1982, a further restructuring took place in an attempt to simplify organisational arrangements.

Throughout the 1980s, political discontent with the performance of the NHS increased, as did the search for better organisational solutions. In the belief that the prevailing consensual approaches to management had failed, general management was introduced in the mid-1980s following the pointed critique of the management of the NHS contained in the Griffiths report. The limited impact of the imposition of this enhanced hierarchy (Harrison *et al.*, 1992) led to the NHS White Paper *Working for Patients*, which heralded the introduction of a more market-based approach (typically known as the purchaser/provider split) and the creation of NHS trusts and GP fundholding. On the whole, these provider trusts adopted fairly traditional functional and directorate-based structures, in the case of the latter, making renewed attempts to engage clinicians in the management of the organisation.

With the election of a Labour government in 1997, another White Paper signalled the end of the internal market, and the characteristics of 'modernisation' started to emerge, including, for example, an emphasis on standards, inspection and partnership working between health and social care (6 and Peck, 2004). This partnership initiative was one manifestation of the increasing interest in network approaches to the delivery of healthcare, also represented by the collaboratives of the Modernisation Agency (MA) (*see* Chapters 5 and 13). The turn of the 21st century saw further significant structural change in the NHS with the advent of primary care groups (PCGs) and then their rapid aggregation into primary care trusts (PCTs), with 'Shifting the Balance of Power' leading to additions to their role alongside the abolition of district health authorities and the creation of strategic health authorities (SHAs). More recently still, the first foundation hospitals have been founded, bringing further innovations in both the accountabilities of and rules surrounding the providers of tax-funded healthcare.

There have been numerous influences on these structural reforms. Some have been imported from outside healthcare, such as alterations over time in the view of the most effective balance between hierarchy, markets and networks in the provision of public services (*see* Goodwin *et al.*, 2003). Some are more specific to healthcare, such as the most appropriate method for involving clinicians in management. Yet others are hybrids, most notably the oscillation between critical mass (and thus viability) and localness (and thus responsiveness) that have become two opposite poles on the continuum of NHS reconfiguration (without either being consistently defined).

There is little evidence for the continued structural change having the desired impact; indeed political disappointment with the last round of reforms usually prompts the next. Fulop *et al.* (2002) discuss the failure to achieve the objectives, and the significant disruption to service development, of NHS trust mergers. Wilkin *et al.* (2003) fail to find any basis for assuming that, beyond a certain point, bigger is better when it comes to primary care organisations (PCOs). Peck *et al.* (2002) are lukewarm about the benefits of health and social care integration. Moreover, evidence from the private sector also suggests that the costs of significant structural changes are rarely recovered and that the benefits that are expected are hardly ever realised (*see* Field and Peck, 2003).

Yet in the face of all this, structural change still tends to be an almost inevitable response when things are not working as hoped. So, perhaps the time has come then for us to ask ourselves some serious questions about the purposes and promises of structural intervention as a method for organisational development, and to consider whether our developmental repertoires in this regard are in need of a renaissance?

In this chapter, I will explore what the term 'structure' has come to mean by looking at the ideas and methods supporting the deployment of structural innovations as a means of developing organisations. I will also allude to some of the benefits and limitations of these ideas in relation to OD in today's NHS.

Stories of structure ...

The term 'organisational structure' has been widely used over a long period to denote a wide range of institutional processes that are said to help define organisations. In particular, the term has tended to focus on functional hierarchies and roles along with notions of authority, accountability and responsibility. It has always been strongly connected with the establishment of rules, the procedures for making them and the methods used for monitoring them. More recently the term has also been used in relation to new organising forms such as network organisations (e.g. matrices and collaboratives), although the emphasis on role definition, accountability and responsibility continues to be prevalent (OPM/SERO, 2002).

  To better understand these definitions and their origins, it is worth spending time looking at some of the dominant approaches to structure drawing on the work of a number of the key management theorists and the tools and techniques that their work has spawned. These compelling narratives from the history of management offer a route into understanding the way in which our organisations have been developed when it comes to structure and perhaps also to illuminating some alternative accounts that might be available for future use.

Ancient or modern?

The primary lens through which we view organisations today – that is, in Morgan's (1986) terms, as a machine – is often thought to be relatively new, with the modern or classical concepts of organisation having only been around for the past 200 years or so. But for some management historians (for example Mooney, 1939), the key concepts of management science have a much longer pedigree, comprising of three universal principles:

1 hierarchy
2 functional division of labour
3 coordination.

On this argument, these principles have been evident in the organisational activities of civilisations as far back as the Ancient Greeks. Furthermore, some historians (for instance Urwick and Brech, 1953) contend that mankind has, since the beginning of civilisation, always aimed at being more efficient and ordered, suggesting perhaps that these key principles speak to some profound human need. Furthermore, first the church and then the army, both major influences on the structure of the NHS (especially in the development of nursing), strove to keep these ideas alive during the medieval and early modern period. However, while these roots seem to take us back almost to the beginnings of human history, apparently showing us how influential certain basic management principles have always been in our existence, it was not until the scientific revolution that the proper tools for building the discipline of management were provided.

Scientific management

The nineteenth century tends to be seen as the era of managerial awakening, where the first explicit references to management science appear to have been made. During this period, in the USA for example, the advent of the railroads made the management of organisations a full-time task for the first time. Due to the geographically dispersed nature of the system, personal surveillance of business transactions by owners became much more difficult. Inadequate methods of communication made it impossible for information to be passed back to the centre in time for it to make all of the decisions and thus alternative structures had to be developed. The military model of administration and bureaucracy was adopted, leading to Cummings' (2002) observation that 'the modern enterprise is easily defined as having two specific characteristics; it contains operating units and it is managed by a hierarchy of salaried executives' (p.82).

For many, and as also noted in Chapter 8, the most significant advances in the modern science of management did not really come until 1911 when Taylor published his *Principles of Scientific Management*, which constituted the world's first universal theory of management. Frederick Taylor was a foreman at a US steelworks at the turn of the century and his early work was focused almost entirely on issues of work organisation and how to improve efficiency by application of scientific method. While the stories of Taylor's work are numerous, perhaps one of the most famous relates to the moving of pig iron (crude iron that comes in pieces called 'pigs' weighing about 92 pounds). It is worth briefly recounting this story as it encapsulates a number of the key principles of his scientific approach and, moreover, shows us the genesis of some of enduring features of management practice that still influence organisational structures today.

The task Taylor studied was quite simple: to take pig iron from the blast furnace and carry it up a plank on to a railway car. Taylor studied the men as they did this work and he determined that, based on prevailing practice, a good worker was able to move about 12 tons per day. Deploying some elementary biomechanical analysis of energy expenditure and task efficiency, Taylor calculated that a man should be able to move 47 tons a day. Taylor knew that simply telling the workers the new target would not achieve it. Even if they were willing, he was concerned that they would merely try to speed everything up and end up getting tired too quickly, with the possible result of moving even less than the original 12 tons. Based on his biomechanical analysis, Taylor knew that the only way to achieve 47 tons would be to walk at a certain measured pace, to carry the pig iron in a very specific way, to drink water at measured intervals and to take very frequent but very short breaks (whether the worker thought he wanted one or not). So he put the men to work on a stopwatch, and told them when to move, when to stop, when to drink, and even when and how to breathe. On the very first day, his first subject moved 47 tons.

A key lesson Taylor drew from this episode was that the worker himself did not have the means to work out the best way to do the job but merely did it the way it had always been done. So Taylor advocated a strong division of labour between management (thinking) and worker (doing). He defined the manager's job as being about fully understanding the worker's task and then devising – using the application of science – a method of doing it. Thereafter, the managerial challenge was to get the worker to do the job that way, and to ensure the correct, consistent and continued application of the method via careful policing. Alongside this, Taylor introduced a system of reward known as piecework, which meant that workers only got paid for what they achieved. Taylor felt that workers' attempts to do things their own way were detrimental to the company and indeed to themselves. Put simply, if they did not follow his method they would accomplish less and therefore get paid less.

Associates of Taylor included Frank Gilbreth, who was credited with the formal development of the time and motion study, and Henry Gantt (best known for the still popular planning chart that bears his name), who developed an approach to scheduling based on time rather than quantity, weight and volume. The work of these US-based pioneers was complemented and re-inforced in Europe by others, such as the French mining engineer Henri Fayol (1949) who identified 14 general principles of management and a set of five universal functions, namely planning, organising, directing, coordinating and controlling. In many ways, these still appear strikingly contemporary, and are summarised in Box 9.1.

Box 9.1: Fayol's five functions of management

1 To forecast and plan: 'examining the future and drawing up the plan of action'
2 To organise: 'building up the structure, material and human, of the undertaking'
3 To command: 'maintaining activity among the personnel'
4 To coordinate: 'binding together, unifying and harmonizing all activity and effort'
5 To control: 'seeing that everything occurs in conformity with established rule and expressed command'

Edited from Pugh and Hickson, 1971.

The work of these early pioneers enabled the move away from the highly personalised and often repressive autocracies that preceded them. The idiosyncratic and unpredictable behaviours of owners were replaced by the explicit standardised methods and rules based on this science. It is clear to see how their work provided the assumptions about structures which became such an enduring feature of twentieth-century organisations; indeed the 'organisation in our heads' is still heavily influenced by the principles of classical management theory (*see* Box 9.2). The notions of unity of command and span of control, for instance, are still influential in OD interventions today.

Box 9.2: Some principles of classical management theory

- **Unity of command:** an employee should receive orders from only one superior
- **Scalar chain:** the line of authority from superior to subordinate, which runs from top to bottom of the organisation
- **Span of control:** the number of people reporting to one superior must not be so large that it creates problems of communication and coordination
- **Division of work:** management should aim to achieve a degree of specialisation designed to achieve the goal of the organisation in an efficient manner
- **Authority and responsibility:** attention should be paid to the right to give orders and to exact obedience and an appropriate balance between authority and responsibility should be achieved.
- **Discipline:** obedience, application, energy, behaviour and outward marks of respect in accordance with agreed rules and customs
- **Subordination of individual interest to general interest:** through firmness, and constant supervision

Edited from Morgan, 1986.

The ideal-type bureaucracy

Another key contributor to the field is Max Weber, the German sociologist whose seminal work, *The Theory of Social and Economic Organisation* (based on research conducted at the turn of the century but not published in English until 1947, almost 20 years after Weber's death), focused on the notions of what he described as the ideal-type bureaucracy. The bureaucratic coordination of human action, Weber suggested, was the distinctive mark of modern social structures and in order to study organisations, both in history and in contemporary society, Weber identified the characteristics of an ideal-type bureaucracy (Weber, 1947).

According to Weber, bureaucracies were structures designed according to rational principles in order to efficiently attain specific goals. Highly specialised 'offices', as he called them, were ranked in hierarchical order, with information flowing up the chain of command and directives flowing down. The operations of the organisation were characterised by impersonal rules that explicitly stated duties and responsibilities, standardised procedures and specified conduct of all office holders. All of these ideal characteristics had one and only one purpose, that is, to promote the efficient attainment of the organisation's goals (Aron, 1970).

Some writers wrongly claim that Weber invented the notion of bureaucracy and some others suggest that Weber's work has been seriously misinterpreted. Cummings (2002), for example, claims that only certain aspects of Weber's work were correctly understood at the time and that his investigations into bureaucracy were over-emphasised. In particular, he points out that Weber's position was strongly historically situated and that Weber argued that the bureaucratic form was, from a *technical* point of view, the most rational form of organising in the early twentieth century; that is to say, that the bureaucratic organisation exhibited technical superiority over other earlier forms but was driven by the particular values and context of his times which Weber himself described as dominated by victorious capitalism resting on mechanical foundations (Weber, 1947). Thus, one possible interpretation is that Weber described bureaucracy as an 'ideal type' in order to explain its growth in power and scope in the modern world rather than suggesting that it was *the* ideal type for all times. Nevertheless, the bureaucratic coordination of the action of large numbers of people became the dominant structural feature of many modern societies. It was only through the deployment of this device that large-scale planning and coordination was deemed to be possible, and it is important to note that the planning for the original NHS structure was taking place just at the moment that the theories of Weber were becoming known in the English-speaking world.

Taxonomies of structure

The search for a comprehensive rational account of organisational structure has continued to the present day, most famously in the early writings of Henry Mintzberg (1979, 1989). He posited five basic components of structure, albeit ones that differ in size and importance according to local environmental determinants. First, he describes the *operating core*, which consists of the personnel who undertake the basic work of the organisation related directly to service provision or operations. The second element is the *strategic apex*, which consists of the managers responsible for the overall direction of the organisation. Their task is defined as being to achieve the objectives of those who own or control the organisation and their primary functions are associated with supervision, resource allocation, planning and control of system design, conflict resolution and strategic decision making. They are also responsible for monitoring relations with the external environment and for formulating the organisation's strategy. The third component is the *middle line*. These are the managers who have formal authority and responsibility for connecting the operating core and the strategic apex. This middle line provides feedback up and down the hierarchy, makes some basic operational decisions and allocates some resources, although these are both undertaken within strict limits. Mintzberg also identifies two further components: *support staff,* who provide support for the line operations and manage boundary activities in order to reduce uncertainty and risk; and the *techno-structure,* which consists of the analysts and planners who act as control specialists evaluating and influencing the work of others in an attempt to increase levels of standardisation so reducing the level of skill required by the operating core.

Mintzberg's model also suggests the need for a high level of integration between the key components to be achieved through five coordinating mechanisms including: *mutual adjustment* – whereby the work is coordinated through direct informal communication between related personnel; *direct supervision* – a formal mechanism whereby an individual takes direct responsibility and authority for the work of others and for monitoring their work activities; and three forms of standardisation relating to *work processes*, where the content of work is specified and programmed, to *outputs* which ensure that the results of work conforms to predetermined standards and specifications, and to *skills,* which guarantees consistency of knowledge through appropriate training and recruitment practice.

According to Mintzberg, an organisation's structure – that is, the size and shape of the aforementioned components – is largely determined by the 'variety' of its environment. Both environmental complexity and the pace of change determine this environmental variety, and he identifies four types of basic organisational form that he claims are associated with four combinations of complexity and change (*see* Table 9.1). Of course, this focus on the environment takes us close to the concerns of Chapter 7, and the metaphorical idea of organisation as organism.

Table 9.1 Environmental determinants of organisational structure

Environment variety = Complexity × Pace of change

	Simple	Complex
Stable	**Machine bureaucracy** Standardised work process and outputs	**Professional organisation** Standardised skills and norms
Dynamic	**Entrepreneurial start up** Direct supervision	**Adhocracy** Mutual adjustment

Adapted from Mintzberg, 1979.

Mintzberg's model, as Cummings (2002) points out, was considered by many to have come close to a universally agreed upon framework for classifying organisational structures. Nonetheless, and even though Mintzberg was attempting to get beyond the mechanistic-modern forms of organising, his model is arguably still just 'a more comfy-looking ... hierarchy' (Cummings, 2002, p.145) that would still be immediately recognisable to Taylor, Fayol and Weber. Indeed, the search for such an overarching model is itself a very modernist project (notwithstanding that it may produce some useful tools for the OD toolbox).

The requisite organisation and stratified systems

Any historical account of the development of structural innovations in organisational development would not be complete without some reference to Elliot Jaques, the Canadian-born psychologist and psychoanalyst who is best known (although perhaps not well enough known) for his stratified systems theory and the notion of the requisite organisation. Jaques was a founding member of the Tavistock Institute of Human Relations and an early contributor to the field of organisational development through his work on T-groups and other approaches to group dynamics.

However, perhaps his most significant work was conducted at the Glacier Metal Company, an engineering enterprise employing some 5000 people in London (Jaques and Brown, 1965).

While a great deal can be said about Jaques' work (*see* Craddock, 2002), in short, he claims to have discovered that natural hierarchies assert themselves wherever human beings organise themselves to fight or to work. People are most effective in his view when organised into clear and accountable hierarchies with well-specified managerial and subordinate roles. Jaques (1997) identified the 'requisite organisation', the idea that a well-designed organisation is one which is structured so that the numbers of managerial layers are consistent with these natural boundaries, and which has the appropriate role relationships in terms of accountabilities and authorities. Moreover, he asserts that such managerial hierarchies are the most natural form for large groups of people and that, stratified correctly, they enable the release of energy and creativity and make the most of people's given capabilities.

Jaques (1997) places great emphasis on the importance of the presence of three critical managerial accountabilities. These relate to managers being accountable for: the outputs of their staff; for sustaining a team capable of producing those outputs; and for exercising effective managerial leadership which he defines as setting direction for staff and getting them to work in that direction. In order for managers to discharge these accountabilities, Jaques (1997) claims they must have four minimum authorities: a veto over the appointment of an unacceptable staff member; decision-making power over the assignment of tasks; authority over (not simply recommending) personal effectiveness appraisals and merit rewards; and finally, the authority to decide to initiate removal of a staff member from the team (not necessarily the authority to dismiss the person from the organisation). Everyone is considered to be accountable for his or her own personal effectiveness within a given role, the boundaries of which set limits on behaviour and action and, hence, also imply certain freedom of behaviour within those limits. Remaining within those limits, he contends, ensures tranquil interactions. Conversely, conflict emerges when people push beyond these limits.

Jaques defines work as the exercise of judgement and discretion in order to carry out a task which is defined as an assignment to produce an output of specified quantity and quality by a given time and with allocated resources within prescribed limits of action and behaviour. This implies absolute clarity of purpose, and the use of unequivocal policies and procedures which must be followed. The complexity of tasks can differ, and Jacques argues that a simple measure of complexity is provided by the time span of discretion; that is, the longest of the maximum target completion times of the tasks or task sequences in a role. Broadly speaking, the longer the time span of discretion the more complex the tasks and the more challenging the role. Jaques also theorises that role complexity does not increase in a continuous way but in a discontinuous or step-wise manner. Using the time span measure of role complexity, he proposes that these discontinuities appear at time spans of 1 day, 3 months, 1 year, 2 years, 5 years, 10 years, 20 years and 50 years. These breaks in role complexity form the natural boundaries between managerial levels or 'strata' in a managerial hierarchy, regardless of political, social, economic and cultural differences.

To explain the cause of the development of these strata, Jaques links them with categories of mental processing capability. He proposes that the complexity of mental processes develops in a hierarchy of stages. Furthermore, there is a correspondence between a person's current category of complexity of mental processing (which in his view can be objectively determined through scientific testing) and the highest-level work role (stratum) which that person has the potential capability to carry. To be capable of operating successfully in a particular role (at a particular stratum), a person must have: the right level of complexity of mental processes; a commitment to the type of work; the necessary skilled knowledge; and an absence of what he calls any negative temperamental traits. Once again all of these can and should be identified and measured using specific scientific methods. Problems in an organisation can arise, according to Jaques, either when a person is in role at a level higher than his or her current capability (causing stress) or at a level below his or her current capability (producing frustration) or when there are too many or too few layers.

Jaques' work has inspired a plethora of tools for stratification, role design, job analysis and capability development. Admirers of his stratified systems theory (SST) claim his work represents a comprehensive body of insights that explains organisational activity in the way Adam Smith described economic systems or Sigmund Freud explained the mysteries of the human psyche. Other see his work as a prime example of the nineteenth-century and early twentieth-century glorification of the 'scientific' solution to human problems, the ultimate expression of Mintzberg's 'machine bureaucracy' dominated by command and control in which all direction, division and allocation of work is derived from the top and broken up through successive functional layers. Much of Jaques' work certainly appears to directly contradict many currently fashionable management doctrines which tend to stress the importance, for example, of teamworking and networks. Jaques has been quoted as saying that he believes that teamwork has totally undermined the importance of effective managerial leadership and that such approaches are not merely misguided, but fundamentally, disastrously, and perhaps even dangerously, wrong (Ross, 1992).

Jaques' work has a particular historical connection with the NHS as it was used to inform the NHS reorganisation in 1974. On the positive side, this was a bold attempt to adopt a theory-led approach to major organisational reconfiguration. On the negative side, the approach was criticised for creating an overly complex system hidebound by the elaborate rules contained in the so-called *Grey Book* (again, *see* Klein, 2001); whether this was more a failure of theory or of application is difficult to ascertain. Nonetheless, it may explain why many of Jaques' ideas – such as the time span of discretion – are relatively well known within the NHS and why newer organisational fashions – such as self-managed teams – struggle to establish themselves.

Business process re-engineering and horizontal structures

Business process re-engineering (BPR) emerged during the early 1990s as a technique for (allegedly) effecting radical organisational change; 'the fundamental analysis and radical redesign of business processes to achieve dramatic improvement in critical contemporary measures of performance such as cost, quality, service and speed' (Hammer and Champy, 1993, p.xii). In short, BPR aimed to map and analyse workflow both within and across functions in order to then restructure organisations in line with efficiency of processes rather than efficiency of tasks. In so doing, Hammer claimed that the inherent notions of the mechanistic industrial paradigm were being rejected and that he and his colleagues had overcome the problems associated with the 'taking apart and simplification of task into meaningless slices' (p.26) by replacing hierarchical functional structures with horizontal process structures.

In this horizontal structure, work is organised around a small number of key core processes – or workflows – that explicitly link the activities of employees to the needs both of suppliers and of end users so as to improve performance and satisfaction in all three domains. Work and the management of work are performed by self-managed teams rather than by individuals and, while not without hierarchy, the new structures tend to be flatter than traditional functional structures. Decision making and resource allocating focus on continuous performance improvement, with information handling occurring 'just in time' and career progression taking place within the process rather than within the function, thus tending to move individuals towards being generalists rather than specialists. While individual reward structures might also be in place, compensation also relates to team performance against a range of key performance indicators (KPIs) which, while quantitative, tend not to be purely measures of financial performance. The evaluation of KPIs is also usually directly linked to end user satisfaction.

Leadership in this horizontal structure is still considered to be vitally important and thus teams are assigned ownership of each core process, but notions of self-management and empowerment are seen as central. The rationale behind this concept is simple. In BPR, those who participate in the process are considered to know best and, if so motivated, have the most to contribute to improvements in productivity and quality. Furthermore, within the self-managed team framework, decisions can be made and acted upon quickly without interrupting critical workflows. So, horizontal structures, unlike functional structures, combine rather than separate managerial and non-managerial activities wherever possible. Teams are empowered to evaluate and act on information whenever, however, wherever and with whomever they need to, and in so doing become the real managers of the process.

In the UK healthcare context, one of the most well-known examples of the application of BPR was the initiative undertaken at the Leicester Royal Infirmary (LRI) during the mid to late 1990s. Initially developed as national pilot site for BPR in the NHS, the project was the first substantial attempt to apply the theory and practice in the UK public sector (Bowns et al., 1999). In line with BPR principles, the aims of the project were ambitious and aimed at creating dramatic and discontinuous performance improvement through radical redesign of key processes and systems. An initially strong adherence to the classical BPR methodology gave way, however, to a more incremental and continuous approach to redesign (albeit that the ambitious aspirations of its champions remained).

The evaluation of the LRI project seems to suggest that some clear benefits in terms of service redesign and financial savings were achieved, but quantitative measures suggested that the impact of re-engineering in performance terms was less dramatic than anticipated in the original project business case. In short, the evaluation argues that the project was evolutionary rather than revolutionary and that change was transactional rather than transformational. Overall, the impact of individual projects on patient care was variable, although some valuable service improvements were noted and indeed sustained (Bowns *et al.*, 1999; McNulty and Ferlie, 2002).

The LRI initiative appears to demonstrate that the value of BPR as a tool to create radical organisational change in the public sector remains, at best, unproven. Nevertheless the legacy of BPR in other initiatives (such as process mapping) is not without merit and is discussed extensively elsewhere in this book (*see* Chapters 5 and 13). Furthermore, it has spawned a burgeoning, if arguably rather uncritical, literature on self-managed teams (for example, *see* Silverman and Propst, 1996; Mischenko, 2002).

Network organising

The macro conditions increasingly apparent in the world (accelerating change, increasing organisational complexity, rising of 'consumer' power and choice, blurring of boundaries between specializations, etc.) seem to point us towards more interdependent ways of organising that transcend traditional boundaries and that appreciate 'the complex, living and responsive nature of human existence at work and its fluid, shifting, continuously changing orderliness' (Shotter and Cunliffe, 2002, p.2). Many commentators have argued recently that such approaches probably lie at the heart of successful organising practice in the globalised era (Pettigrew and Fenton, 2000; Hosking, 2002; Giddens, 1999; Anderson-Wallace *et al.*, 2000). Accordingly, strategic alliances, partnerships and multi-organisational networks have become prevalent as a response to these conditions and are increasingly seen as common 'structures' for organising. Indeed, networks have been heralded by Pettigrew and Fenton (2000) as the organisational form for the 21st century (in contrast, presumably, to either hierarchies or markets). However, getting the most out of these sorts of new arrangement requires effective collaboration across the boundaries of hitherto deliberately separated functions, professions and traditions (Anderson-Wallace *et al.*, 2001). The World Health Organization (WHO) offers a definition of networks as 'a grouping of individuals, organisations and agencies organised on a non-hierarchal basis around common issues or concerns, which are pursued proactively and systemically based on commitment and trust' (WHO, 1998, p.16).

The existence of networks as a mode of structuring service delivery within the NHS was first observed explicitly in the mid-1990s (Ferlie and Pettigrew, 1996), although arguably they pre-date this decade (for example in the community mental health teams that started to appear in the early 1980s; *see* Peck and Parker, 1998). They are perhaps currently best exemplified by the concepts of 'managed clinical networks' and 'integrated care pathways' as means of responding to the need for better coordinated services across institutional boundaries. The NHS in Scotland was an early adopter of the concept of managed clinical networks following the Acute Services review of 1998 in which it was suggested that an actively orchestrated process of network construction could bring a variety of benefits, including the achievement of the policy objective of greater vertical and horizontal integration of care delivery in the NHS in Scotland (Scottish Office, 1998). These managed clinical networks were seen as distinct from the more informal networks referred to earlier and were defined as linked groups of professionals and organisations from primary, secondary and tertiary care, working in a coordinated manner, unconstrained by existing professional and organisational boundaries, to ensure equitable provision of high-quality, clinically effective services (NHSiS, 1999). Elsewhere in the NHS, the development of clinical networks has been said to offer the opportunity to develop and deliver fast and predictable improvements in patient care (OPM/SERO, 2002) and as a method for connecting complex agendas of change across agencies. From a managerial perspective, it is suggested 'the largely self organising networks offer a third way between the stable but slow moving hierarchy and bureaucracy and the creative yet uncontrollable market' (Attwood et al., 2003, p.152).

Networks often arise, and sustain, because their members (individuals or agencies) recognise that through a pooling of resources (whether this be time, money, skills, know-how, contacts, facilities) more can be achieved, and sometimes more efficiently, than through the efforts of members acting alone. Whether established organically or deliberately, networks tend to thrive on voluntarism, a passion for making things happen, flexibility and the ability to see and respond to localised needs (Anderson-Wallace et al., 2003).

When managers try to manage networks, as has been the case in the NHS more recently, there may be a need to exercise different and sometimes challenging repertoires of managerial activity which can at times feel counter-cultural. In particular, it seems important to be clear about what differentiates network organising from other institutional if widely cast (regional or national) bureaucracies in order to derive maximum value from these new arrangements. For example, in networks members may identify (have a sense of belonging) with local service issues and thus accountability tends to be local and outwards rather than centralised and inwards. Connected with this, the aims and objectives of the network tend to be locally validated (or arise locally) and the appropriate policy-making style is light, collaborative and enabling. Communication, which is seen as the primary management process and competence in networks, takes place with a view to helping others to do things rather than policing them (Huxham and Vangen, 2000), and members tend to talk about what they have achieved, what they are trying to do and what support they need, rather than talking about what cannot or must not be done. In terms of strategy, network members are more likely to gravitate towards the emergence of 'what needs doing' rather than following a preordained and abstract design, plan or procedure. As a result, variety in network situations tends to be abundant because solutions are more locally situated and this diversity is seen as evidence of responsiveness rather than deviation from the standard. Learning takes place through constant sharing of local acts of improvement within 'communities of practice' rather than through the imposition of bureaucratic 'recipes' or 'manuals'; as people tend to be valued for their local knowledge, competence and resourcefulness, the need for external expert knowledge and direction from the centre is reduced (*see* Bate and Robert, 2002, for a thoughtful discussion of the benefits of a voluntaristic approach to 'communities of practice' in contrast to what they perceive as the implicitly hierarchical nature of the initial 'collaboratives' established by the MA; *see also* Chapter 13 of this volume).

The extent to which these innovative practices can co-exist and interact with the traditional governance arrangements and organisational structures of the NHS is still unclear. As the OPM/SERO (2002) report seems to point out, unless we manage to change the organisational and managerial shape of the NHS to receive and support networks, then they may well do more harm than good, both because of the failure to derive best value from these network arrangements and also because of the risk of unaccountable and unsustainable decisions and actions which have inevitable systemic effects.

Critique

It is clear that Taylor, Fayol and the other exponents of scientific management have been massively influential on our thinking about the design and development of our organisations, and remain so today. Building on Weberian models of bureaucracy, and the benefits of hierarchy and fixed spans of control as ways of enhancing authority, the scientific approach spawned a variety of methods that revolutionised productivity and efficiency in many industries during the early part of the last century. Perhaps as you have read my account of their work, you will have sensed the strength of these ideas when placed in the context of their time; indeed there is little doubt that when they first appeared their contributions were clearly progressive. Their continued influence is ubiquitous in the prescriptions of most policy documents on, and in the interventions of many practitioners in, healthcare organisations; it is but a short step from Drucker's (1954) management by objectives to New Labour's performance management, and from Taylor's skilled workers to the NHS Leadership Centre's role competences (*see* Chapter 3). In another example, the popular 'PRINCE' methodology for project management is in many respects merely an update of the pre-World War II Gantt chart. As I noted earlier: 'the organisation in our heads is a bureaucracy'; our sensemaking about our workplaces is still heavily reliant on the apparent certainties that lie in their social structure.

However, when positioned against the backdrop of the 21st century and the challenges presented by the globalised era the unproblematic reliance on these mechanistic-scientific models and tools seems both oversimplistic and unsophisticated. Mintzberg may have given these basic ideas a more flexible form and connected the structure of organisations to environmental determinants; nevertheless, his model was still based on the same fundamental set of underlying principles. Jaques could be said to have integrated scientific rigour and psychological humanism (*see* Chapter 1) in provocative and radical ways; however, his uncompromising system was felt by some to be nothing more than a form of managerial totalitarianism (and is generally regarded as having failed in application in the NHS in the 1970s). Hammer and

Champy (1993) claimed that BPR marked the end of industrial revolution and of the organisations that were designed for it. The process-centred organisation would, he declared, end narrow jobs, supervisory management, traditional career paths and feudal cultures, and usher in a new era of flexibility and radical change. While there is no doubt that BPR had a massive impact – and was used extensively across the private sector during the 1990s – Hammer and Champy seem to have rather over-stated what BPR could achieve. Attempts to break down functional specialisms and rigid hierarchies have had limited success and cost thousands of middle management jobs while lining the pockets of the big management consultancies (Micklethwaite and Wooldridge, 1996). Notions of self-management and continuous improvement were arguably used to make employees internalise methods of control that were formerly exercised though hierarchy. Certainly, in terms of the application of BPR in the NHS, McNulty (2002) suggests that one of the most substantive contributions that the evaluation of the LRI initiative made was the way in which it countered the hype about the possibility of effecting the 'big bang' changes in organisational structure through the application of BPR.

As Morgan (1986) points out, much organisation theory has become locked into a form of engineering, pre-occupied with relations between goals, structures and efficiency. In his view, one of the most basic problems of modern management remains the way in which the mechanical way of thinking has become so deeply ingrained in the everyday conceptions of organisation, thus making it very difficult to organise in any other way. Much managerial practice still appears to be trapped within the mechanistic and bureaucratic languages of control, efficiency, planning and direction.

So how might we account for the dominance of these ideas over such a long period of time? Cummings (2002) attributes the continuance of the mechanistic-scientific orientation, at least in part, to the general absence of a critique of the underlying assumptions of the modernist foundation of organisation and management. I am tempted to agree with Cummings (2002) that the dominant narrative of the mechanistic-scientific approach to structure – its legacy and language – is well overdue for critique; perhaps a good place to start is with a reappraisal of the notion that management science is somehow an inherent aspect of human nature and civil-isation. I am not contesting the fact that a continuous accumulation of knowledge about this universal object we call management has taken place, but I am asking what difference it would make if we saw that process as a historically situated construction rather than an inherent truth about the world.

Cummings (2002) presents us with a significant challenge, claiming that our current stories about organisation structure (and thus our abilities to act and innovate) are predicated on a contingent view that prevailed during the early part of the twentieth century. He goes on to point out that it is based on a history that was constituted by men who had very particular aims and interests and that rather than representing a gradual building of knowledge from past to present, management scholars and practitioners in the early twentieth century used the past to legitimatise politically expedient practice in their present. Thus, scientific management strongly mirrored the overarching themes of modernism through its attention to bureaucratic rationality, efficiency and the pursuit of truth. It is perhaps this symmetry that helped to ensure that this form of organisational knowledge would come to be regarded as imperative, helping to turn it into the fastest-growing tertiary education subject in just a few short decades. A self-referential network of bodies – including the American Management Schools (which established the curriculum for management students) and the American Management Association (which explicitly sought to determine the universality of management's basic functions) – further emphasised the importance of the field, its primary approach and its dominant vocabulary. Of course, it is just such grand narratives which post-modernism seeks to challenge, to which I now want to turn in my conclusion.

Conclusion

As has been well illustrated in this chapter, the received wisdom about how organisations should be structured to best effect derives primarily from an era where centralised rule making and control worked well enough. However, the growing interest in and legitimacy of more collaborative structures and processes seems to suggest that the already overextended capacity of the 'bureaucracy' may be almost exhausted. As Gergen (1992) points out, while the era of modernist organisation theory may be in decline, it is by no means exhausted; a great deal of research and practice is still carried out in its name. However, he goes on to note that these approaches seem to have lost some of their sense of 'lived validity' as the benefits to be gained from the tradition diminish and the 'yearning for alternatives' becomes more evident.

It is perhaps only in the past few years that a more concerted effort to redefine ideas around management and organisational structure has begun to emerge and gain credibility. The idea of organisations as relatively reified and concrete features of the social world – groups of people, ideas and physical artefacts integrated for the purposes of achieving some set goal – is now being seen as increasingly problematic (Boje *et al.*, 1996). As a consequence, rather than conceiving of organisations substantively as entities embedded in artefacts such as policies, structures and buildings, organisations are increasingly being viewed as more relationally constructed, with their meaning being seen as residing in the contexts and occasions where they are created and enacted by members.

Of course, this view is clearly connected with post-modern frames of thinking which emphasise 'an incredulity toward the metanarrative' (Lyotard, 1979, p.xxiv) and point towards what Giddens (1990) describes as a 'new and distinct social order' (p.26); an order that involves a break from the past. The approach does not reject key notions such as responsibility, accountability and authority, but it does position them differently as emergent, situated, temporary and partial rather than fixed, universal, certain and permanent.

A very significant challenge clearly lies in managing activities in these more collaborative arrangements, as people find themselves having to make sense of practices that sometimes turn our organisational and managerial experience on its head. Moreover, in the NHS, people are attempting to enact these practices in the context of a wider system that remains largely bureaucratic and hierarchical in its nature. I do not claim to have *the* answer for these dilemmas. However, it does seem clear that the largely individualistic and scientific traditions still dominate, and yet they have never been more challenged. The space afforded by working with issues of structure alone seems increasingly limited, and as managers, clinicians and practitioners concerned with ways of developing organisations in the 21st century, we must expand rather than narrow our methods and our vocabularies to respond to the demand of these times.

Acknowledgements

I am particularly grateful to my colleagues Chris Blantern and Tom Boydell of Inter-Logics, whose words and ideas have made a major contribution to this chapter. I would also like to thank Elizabeth Gould, Phil Glanfield and Dr Fiona Adshead for the various and continuing conversations which helped to give form and shape to many of the ideas in this chapter. The editor also made some useful comments and contributions.

References

6 P and Peck E (2004) 'Modernisation': does New Labour have a distinct signature in public management? *International Journal of Public Management.* 7(1): 1–18.

Anderson-Wallace M, Blantern C and Lejk A (2000) Advances in cross boundary practice. In: T Taillieu (ed.) *Collaborative Strategies and Multi-Organisational Partnerships.* Garant, Leuven.

Anderson-Wallace M, Blantern C and Kristensen J (2001) Post-modern approaches to cross boundary interventions. In: D Perdue and M Stewart (eds) *Understanding Collaboration.* University of West of England Press, Bristol.

Anderson-Wallace M, Blantern C and Gould E (2003) Getting the net working. *Proceedings of the 10th International Conference in Multi Organisational Partnerships, Alliances and Networks.* University of Strathclyde, July.

Aron R (1970) *Main Currents in Sociological Thought II.* Anchor Books, New York.

Attwood M, Pedler M, Pritchard S and Wilkinson D (2003) *Leading Change: a guide to whole systems working.* The Policy Press, Bristol.

Bate S and Robert G (2002) Knowledge management and communities of practice in the private sector: lessons for modernising the National Health Service in England and Wales. *Public Administration.* 80(4): 643–63.

Boje D, Gephart R and Thatchenkery T (eds) (1996) *Postmodern Management & Organization Theory.* Sage, London.

Bowns I, McNulty T and Ferlie E (1999) *Reengineering Leicester Royal Infirmary: an independent evaluation of implementation and impact.* Sheffield Centre for Health and Related Research, Sheffield.

Craddock K (2002) *Requisite Leadership Theory: an annotated research bibliography.* Columbia University Press, Columbia.

Cummings S (2002) *ReCreating Strategy.* Sage, London.

Drucker P (1954) *The Practice of Management.* Harper and Row, New York.

Fayol H (1949) *Industrial and General Administration.* Pitman, London.

Ferlie E and Pettigrew A (1996) Managing through networks: some issues and implications for the NHS. *British Journal of Management.* 7: 81–99.

Field J and Peck E (2003) Mergers & acquisitions in the private sector: what are the lessons for health and social services? *Social Policy & Administration.* 37(7): 742–55.

Fulop N, Protopsaltis G, Hutchings A, King A, Allen P, Normand C and Walters R (2002) Process and impact of mergers of NHS trusts: multicentre case study and management cost analysis. *British Medical Journal.* 325: 246–9.

Gergen K (1992) Organisation theory in the postmodern era. In: M Reed and M Hughes (eds) *Rethinking Organisations; new directions in organisation theory and analysis,* pp.209–26. Sage, London.

Giddens A (1990) *The Consequences of Modernity.* Stanford University Press, Stanford, CA.

Giddens A (1999) *The Runaway World.* Profile Books, London.

Goodwin N, 6 P, Peck E, Freeman T and Posaner R (2003) *Managing Across Diverse Networks of Care: lessons from other sectors (policy report).* NHS Service Delivery and Organisation R&D Programme, London.

Hammer M and Champy J (1993) *Re-engineering the Corporation: a manifesto for business revolution.* Nicholas Brearly, London.

Harrison S, Hunter D, Marnoch G and Pollitt C (1992) *Just Managing: power and culture in the National Health Service.* Macmillan, Basingstoke.

Hosking D (2002) *Constructing Changes: a social constructionist approach to change work (and beetles and witches).* Katholieke Universiteit, Brabant.

Huxham C and Vangen S (2000) Ambiguity complexity & dynamics in collaboration. *Human Relations.* 53(6): 772–805.

Jaques E (1997) *Requisite Organization: a total system for effective managerial organization and managerial leadership for the 21st century.* Cason Hall and Co, Gloucester, MA.

Jaques E and Brown W (1965) *Glacier Project Papers.* Heinemann, London.

Klein R (2001) *The New Politics of the NHS.* Prentice Hall, Harlow.

Lyotard J-F (1979) *The Post Modern Condition; a report on knowledge* (translated by Bennington G and Massouri B). University of Minnesota Press, Minneapolis.

McNulty T (2002) Contested affordance of a corporate change programme. Paper presented to the 3rd European Conference on Organisational Knowledge, Learning & Capabilities, April, Athens.

McNulty T and Ferlie E (2002) *Reengineering Healthcare: the complexities of organizational transformation.* Oxford University Press, Oxford.

Micklethwaite J and Wooldridge A (1996) *The Witch Doctors.* Heinemann, London.

Mintzberg H (1979) *The Structuring of Organization.* Prentice-Hall, Englewood Cliffs, NJ.

Mintzberg H (1989) *Mintzberg on Management.* The Free Press, New York.

Mischenko J (2002) A framework for self-managed teams. *Community Practitioner.* 75(6): 218–22.

Mooney J (1939) *Onward Industry: the principles of organisation.* Harper and Row, New York.

Morgan G (1986) *Images of Organisation.* Sage, London.

NHSiS Management Executive (1999) *Introduction of Managed Clinical Networks in Scotland.* (MEL (1999) 10). Scottish Executive, Edinburgh.

OPM/SERO (2002) *NetWorks: resolving collateral issues associated with managed clinical networks.* Office for Public Management, London.

Peck E, Gulliver P and Towell D (2002) *Modernising Partnerships: an evaluation of Somerset's innovations in the commissioning and organisation of mental health services* (final report). Institute for Applied Health and Social Policy, King's College London.

Peck E and Parker E (1998) Mental health policy in the NHS: policy and practice 1979–1998. *Journal of Mental Health.* 7(3): 241–59.

Pettigrew A and Fenton E (2000) *The Innovating Organisation.* Sage, London.

Pugh D and Hickson D (1971) *Writers on Organizations.* Penguin, London.

Ross A (1992) The long view of leadership. *Canadian Business Magazine.* **May,** CB Media, Toronto.

Scottish Office (1998) *Acute Services Review Report.* Stationery Office, Edinburgh.

Shotter J and Cunliffe A (2002) Managers as practical authors: everyday conversations for action. In: D Holman and R Thorpe (eds) *Management and Language: the manager as practical author,* pp.15–37, Sage, London.

Silverman L and Propst A (1996) *Ensuring Success: a model for self-managed teams.* Partners for Progress and Quality Transformation Service, Madison, WI.

Taylor F (1911) *The Principles of Scientific Management.* Harper Row, New York.

Urwick L and Brech E (1953) *The Making of Scientific Management.* Pitman, London.

Weber M (1947) *The Theory of Social and Economic Organisation* (translated by Henderson A and Parsons T). Oxford University Press, Oxford.

Wilkin D, Bojke C, Coleman A and Gravelle H (2003) The relationship between size and performance of primary care organisations in England. *Journal of Health Services Research and Policy.* 8(1): 11–17.

World Health Organization (1998) *Health Promotion Glossary.* WHO, Geneva.

Further reading and websites

- On relational approaches to management and organisation: www.inter-logics.net and www.swarthmore.edu/SocSci/kgergen1
- On Henry Mintzberg: www.henrymintzberg.com
- On Gareth Morgan: www.imaginiz.com
- On Elliot Jaques: www.bioss.com and www.canadiancentre.com
- On management gurus: Micklethwaite J and Wooldridge A (1996) *The Witch Doctors*. Heinemann, London.
- On the history of scientific management: Cummings S (2002) *ReCreating Strategy*. Sage, London.

CHAPTER 10

Working with culture

Murray Anderson-Wallace and Chris Blantern

Introduction

Most people would agree that the modernisation of our public services involves some significant cultural change. Indeed, such change has been heralded as 'an essential part of the transformation' of the NHS over the coming years (DoH, 2002, p.1). Furthermore, transforming culture appears to be a key aspiration for partnerships between health and social care; for instance, the then Minister of State for Health stated that he wanted 'our organisations to work much more closely together, so we have talked repeatedly about a big culture change right across the care system, not just in social services but in the NHS too' (Hutton, 2000, p.1). But what is being referred to when this rallying call is made? What sort of change is imagined? Most importantly, in the context of this book, what OD interventions might prove useful to provoke such change?

The term 'culture' has its roots in the fields of sociology and anthropology. While an extensive discussion of these vast areas of study is beyond the scope of this chapter, the primary concepts shaping the term include an interest in: the methods through which meaning is made in groups (often referred to as systems of meaning); the way in which societies (from kinship groups to whole communities) organise themselves in relation to these systems of meaning; and the specific distinctive techniques that evolve for maintaining, reinforcing, developing and changing things within and between societies. It is well worth pointing out, however, that the lack of consensus within the fields of anthropology and sociology regarding the term 'culture' is mirrored in the field of organisational studies; a succinct definition of the term 'organisational culture' is not easily derived. As Scott and his colleagues (2003a) point out, several scholars have contributed to the literature on organisational culture that has appeared since the late 1970s and many have introduced new frameworks. As they go on to comment:

> there has been little agreement between scholars over the years as to what the terms 'organisation' and 'culture' mean, how each can be observed and measured or in

particular how different methodologies can be used to inform both practical administration and organisational change (p.1).

Of course, the term 'culture' also has a rich variety of meanings in our everyday language, including notions of behaviour, ideologies, languages, symbols of status, modes of politeness, prevailing beliefs and unspoken assumptions (to name but a few). It would be surprising if some, if not all, of these meanings did not also appear in our conception of organisational culture. Bate (1994), referring to the challenges of working with issues of culture, points out that those involved are 'constantly reminded of the Chinese saying that the more you know the more confused you become' (p.2). What follows in this chapter is an illumination of some of the key approaches and tools to working with culture; an overview of this vast and still growing area of theory and practice.

Stories of organisational culture

The term 'organisational' culture itself first appeared in the academic literature in 1979 (Pettigrew, 1979), but its constituent features can be traced to earlier literature on organisational analysis. By the 1970s, research in the field had already made some significant distinctions between organisations as 'rational, dispensable instrument for the production of goods and services and the organisation as a value-infused robust social institution' (Selznick, 1957, p.5). Moreover the view that by 'bringing people into association in the workplace, the mechanical organisation also gives birth to the dynamic social institution' (Selznick, 1957, p.7) was also becoming well established.

Brown's (1954) account of the formal and informal organisation parallels Selznick's analysis of the instrumental organisation and the value-infused institution in that both emphasised the 'emergence of an informal, socially organic organisation from bare blueprint of the formal organisational structure' (Scott *et al.*, 2003b, p.7). Brown is noted by Scott *et al.* (2003b) as having almost provided an early definition of organisational culture by proclaiming that:

> the culture of industrial groups derives from many sources; from class origins, occupational and technical sources, the atmosphere of the factory which forms their background and finally from the specific experiences of the small informal group itself. Some of its more important manifestations may be classified as (a) occupational language (b) ceremonies and rituals, and (c) myths and beliefs (Brown, 1954, pp.145–6).

It is worth noting that many of these early studies of organisational culture focus on the effects of the strong and idiosyncratic individuals who founded the organisations concerned; arguably this is when the links between notions of leadership and organisational culture were first made.

While a wide variety of conceptions of culture exist, Smircich (1983) suggests that two main perspectives have emerged. The first treats culture as a critical variable of organisation, in short a component part. The second treats culture as a 'root' metaphor for organising, a lens through which to view organisational life. It is to a consideration of these two conceptions that we turn next.

The 1980s witnessed the predominance of the critical variable approach. As the contemporary success of Japanese companies began to undermine the classical managerial belief that structure and technology were the only significant factors that contributed to organisational progress and success, the Western world of management (in particular the US companies which had fallen behind their Japanese counterparts in terms of quality control, competitiveness and growth) began to take an interest in notions of organisational culture. The critical variable approach proposed a direct correlation between organisational culture and organisational performance. It suggested that by analysing and actively manipulating this critical variable, improvements in quality and competitiveness could be achieved (Wilkins and Ouchi, 1983). On this account, transplanting the cultural strengths of one company (Toyota, for example) to another company (for instance, General Motors) would lead to the creation of a hybrid company where the introduction of similar cultures would lead to similar levels of output.

The critical variable approach further subdivided culture into independent variables and internal variables (for a detailed discussion of this distinction *see* Scott *et al.*, 2003b). When culture is viewed as an internal variable, organisations are seen as culture producing as well as culture consuming, and culture is defined as the social or normative glue that enables the organisation to cohere. In this so-called scientific view (although, as Scott and his colleagues point out, despite the 'scientific' label the approach lacked much in the way of robust research evidence to support it), culture tended to be seen as something that an organisation *had*; it became a 'component', rather like its strategies, systems and structures. Indeed McKinsey placed 'shared values' at the heart of the now famous 7-S framework (Peters and Waterman, 1982) and like the other 'S's, culture is treated as subsystem that affects the functioning and effectiveness of the overall organisational system. Strong, powerful and positive cultures became synonymous with unified, aligned and stable organisations; good cultures were those that were tightknit and demonstrated a high degree of commonality (Cummings, 2002). These were the features of the 'excellent companies' whose virtues were extolled by Peters and Waterman (1982).

Later, however, many of these companies fell on very hard times and thus the evidence to support the claim that the companies with so-called 'strong' cultures were ultimately more successful seems questionable. From their exhaustive study of the literature in healthcare, Scott *et al.* (2003b) conclude that 'empirical studies ... do not provide clear answers' (p.129) as to whether there is a link between organisational culture and organisational performance, while noting that the available research is small in quantity, mixed in quality and variable in methodology (thus making comparisons between studies difficult).

The association between this approach to organisational culture and the field of organisational development has traditionally been quite close (from Jaques, 1951, to Schein, 1990). This work has tended to focus on helping organisations to assess, analyse and question the espoused values and underlying assumptions under which employees operate, and, having done this, on suggesting interventions aimed at manipulating the culture to make it 'more receptive to change by facilitating the realignment of the total organisational system into a more viable and satisfying configuration' (Smircich, 1983, p.345). Numerous writers have produced classifications of culture to underpin these approaches. Of this proliferation of taxonomies – typically comprised of four elements – of cultural types perhaps one of the best known is that of Handy (1976), who suggests: the power culture; the role culture; the task culture; and the person culture. Other such taxonomies can be found, for example, in Pheysey (1993) and Schneider (1994). These taxonomies are popular, presumably because they make the concept of culture accessible and explicable to busy managers and clinicians.

The most commonly cited writer in this tradition is, however, Schein (for example 1985). Schein's theory specifies three layers: cultural artefacts; espoused values; and basic assumptions. Artefacts are the outermost layer, and are the most visible manifestations of culture, such as rituals and rewards. The second layer, espoused values, refers to those values used to justify behaviour and constitute the grounds on which alternative courses of action are justified. At the core lie assumptions, that is, the unspoken and often unconscious beliefs and expectations shared by individuals, binding together a potentially diverse group of organisational members. As Schein's framework is very influential, it is presented in a little more detail in Box 10.1.

Box 10.1: Schein's three levels of culture

Artefacts
These are the visible manifestations of culture:

- architecture and environment
- language
- technology
- style as embodied in clothing, manners of address, emotional displays, myths and stories told about the organisation, published list of values, observable rituals and processes of routine behaviour.

They may be easy to observe but more difficult to decipher and an observer may not be able to interpret what these artefacts mean in the organisation or whether they necessarily reflect important espoused values and underlying assumptions.

Values

- All group learning reflects some original values, that is, the 'what ought to be' as distinct from the 'what is'.
- Until collective action is taken by a group in response to a new task, issue or problem, and until members have observed the outcome of that action, a group does not have a shared basis for determining whether 'what ought to be' is a robust basis for 'what is and will be'.
- If the proposed solution works, and the group shares the perception of success, a process of cognitive transformation begins:
  - initially around a shared value or belief
  - ultimately into a shared underlying assumption (dependent on continuing success).

- Only values that are susceptible to validation, and continue to work reliably in solving the group's problems, will become transformed into underlying assumptions.

Assumptions

- More than rationalisations of the past or aspirations for the future, groups come to believe the underlying assumption as a truth about the world.
- Such assumptions are taken for granted and behaviour based on any other premise is inconceivable.
- These assumptions tend not to be debated or confronted and hence are difficult to change.

Adapted from Schein, 1985.

Can we see these three layers within healthcare settings? A recent briefing from the Department of Health Integrated Care Network (2004) suggests that:

> the fundamental cultural divide between health and social care is frequently claimed to be exemplified in the contrast between the 'medical model' and the 'social model' ... One cultural artefact of the 'medical model' is its emphasis on the rituals of diagnosis of the specific part of the individual patient that is perceived to be malfunctioning. This is underpinned by the espoused value of the predominance of the clinician's opinion over that of the patient. The underlying assumption is of the dependent nature of the patient in relation to the clinician. This is often contrasted with the 'social model' prevalent in social care where one cultural artefact is an emphasis on an assessment of the individual client within their wider social environment. This is underpinned by the espoused value of the importance of a dialogue between practitioner and client. The underlying assumption is of the independent nature of the client in active negotiation with the practitioner (p.5).

This may appear to be something of a parody, but its importance lies in it being a recognisable parody; the popularity of Schein's framework may lie in its ability to represent aspects of organisational experience that managers and clinicians recognise. Schein (1985) also connects the development of organisational culture with the life cycle of the organisation, suggesting that organisations undergo distinct stages of change, each of which is associated with a different culture serving different functions and susceptible to change in different ways. These changes mirror those of human existence and include birth and early growth, mid-life and maturity (for further details *see* Schein, 1985).

Within this approach, corporate and organisational culture is seen to function in four specific ways. First, it conveys a sense of identity for the organisation's members; second, it facilitates members' commitment to something larger than self; third, it enhances social system stability; and fourth, it provides a sensemaking device to guide behaviour. Meyerson and Martin (1987) argue that this is the 'integration' view of culture where it is an influence which promotes cohesion within organisations. Cultural artefacts, including management styles, are seen as powerful symbolic means of communication which can be used to 'build organisational commitment, convey a philosophy of management, rationalize and legitimate activity, motivate personnel and facilitate socialisation' (Smircich, 1983, p.345).

However, the key question for OD arising from these corporate culture theorists is whether corporate culture as an internal variable can be manipulated in predictable ways to influence the performance of the organisation? As Scott *et al.* (2003a) point out 'the research agenda that flows from this assumption and perspective focuses on how to change an organisation's culture in a way that brings it into line with management purposes' (p.18). They go on to suggest that by talking about corporate culture in this way, we risk losing sight of the possibility of multiple cultures, subcultures and indeed countercultures, which are actively competing to define the 'reality' or the nature of a situation (and this chapter returns to this theme below).

Partially based on their own OD work in the NHS, Bate *et al.* (2000) observe the poor track record of corporate cultural change programmes, pointing out that:

> such programmatic approaches to culture change rarely speak directly to people's concerns, purposes and aspirations and although a few mission statement and indoctrination sessions might change the senior management's perspective, they are unlikely to lead to sustainable changes in the way that people work, think and relate to each other (Bate *et al.*, 2000, p.198).

Parker (2000) comes to two conclusions from his consideration of the literature and of his own OD experience in healthcare. The first is that 'cultural management in the sense of creating an enduring set of shared beliefs is impossible' (p.228). On the other hand, he suggests that 'it seems perverse to argue that the "climate", "atmosphere", "personality", or culture of an organisation cannot be consciously altered' (p.229). So, a considered position might be that some manipulation of culture by managers is possible, but the impact may be limited and/or unpredictable.

According to Bate (1994), treating culture as a variable or an 'integrating mechanism' in this way suggests that 'it' (note how culture becomes objectified by the use of the definite article) is susceptible to control and manipulation by management and thus tends to promote what he calls the 'modular design & build approach' to OD. He likens this to 'the replacement of a faulty component in a TV set or the trading in of an old cooker for a new one' (Bate, 1994, p.12). In terms of OD interventions, he suggests this conception leads practitioners to search for cultural change programmes based largely on direct training or straightforward indoctrination. In summary, then, this approach is consistent with the scientific paradigm which assumes that the social world can be defined in terms of distinct interacting variables within a living subsystem, with organisational culture being seen as the product of a calculated human influence on the organisational environment.

In contrast, the root metaphor approach to culture offers us something really quite different. Here, organisations are seen as not *having* cultures in an objective sense but as *being* cultures. This marks a shift in focus from culture as a distinctive variable in organisational life to one where culture is the context for all organisational activity. Following this line of thought, Bate (1994), quoting Silverman (1970), points out that organisations are merely 'societies writ small' (p.12) and, therefore, culture becomes a metaphor for the total work organisation and not just one component of it. Cultures are thus synonymous with organisations; a lens through which to interpret organisational life processes rather than merely an aspect of them. However, the root metaphor conception, just like the critical variable one, is by no means homogenous. Many different perspectives are present in the literature, and three of these are briefly presented in the following paragraphs (*see* Further reading for more details of key texts).

The cognitive perspective, for example, studies culture as a shared system of ideas, knowledge and belief that is seen to provide a structure for knowledge that informs action and understanding (Smircich, 1983). Using a case study approach to examine members' 'theories in use', researchers have developed the notion of single- and double-loop learning to consider ways in which feedback on actions and learning can shift the sensemaking of organisational members (*see* Chapter 1 for more discussion of single- and double-loop learning and sensemaking).

The symbolic perspective draws attention to the power of organisational symbolism, of legends, stories, myths and ceremonies (Mitroff and Kilmann, 1976). Organisational culture is interpreted as symbolic discourse, and organisational rules and layouts, for instance, are seen as symbols. Drawing on healthcare examples, Scott *et al.* (2003a) suggest that the sector is 'loaded with symbolism' (p.20); for example, the wearing of uniforms and the display of accessories (e.g. stethoscopes), and the way that wards and waiting rooms are configured (for order and control, for access, for security, etc.). These material artefacts are seen as closely associated with the values and assumptions of the organisations concerned (consistent with Schein), but it is perhaps risky to take the meaning of artefacts at face value (do open plan offices always suggest a democratic workplace?). Thus, analysis using this model tends to focus on the ways in which participants make sense of these symbols (do open plan offices reduce requirements for costly office space and create an environment where employees are more easily observed?), and how such sensemaking influences behaviour. In particular, this approach takes an interest in how a collective sense of the organisation is maintained and developed.

The psychodynamic perspective views culture as the unconscious expression of psychological and psychodynamic processes. This approach is based on a belief about the underlying structure of the mind and is, in our view, intensely individualistic, although applications in organisational theory explore the impact of the unconscious on group and organisation culture (*see* Chapter 6).

This root metaphor notion leads to very different conclusions about OD practice. If organisations are viewed as cultures, then all organisational development is, de facto, cultural development. Anyone engaged in active change in organisations is involved, therefore, in cultural change. Strategies aimed at only changing the culture of the organisation – derived from the idea of culture as 'a thing' – should, according to Bate (1994), be avoided at all costs on the basis that these are strategies for developing something that does not exist; 'mythical strategies for mythical entities' (Bate, 1994, p.14).

As a consequence, any strategy for managing cultural (and thus organisational) development involves not the application of specific 'tools' or 'methods' to culture in isolation, but cultural change is what takes place among and between people in 'the patterns of connections and interpretation' (Meyerson and Martin, 1987, p.639).

Using this lens, the task for the developer is 'not to think *about* culture but to *think culturally*' (Bate, 1994, p.14, *emphases in original*). For Bate it is the concept of organisation that is produced, rather than the object of study, that makes the cultural perspective unique.

Our own practice adopts this increasingly common thought style (Fleck, 1979; Chia, 1995) and explicitly aims to integrate issues of culture, process and structure based on a relational approach to organising and managing (Blantern and Anderson-Wallace, 1999; Hosking, 2002). Within the approach, the relationship between culture and change is seen as complex, but one that can be more easily addressed when both are viewed as created, recreated and reinforced in the prosaic, day-to-day networks of conversation and interactions among people. Organising (as opposed to organisation) is viewed as a highly dynamic and live social process, and intervention is about making meaning and developing a critical consciousness of the connections between these meanings and the patterns of relationships and actions that they call forth. At the centre of this relational approach is a keen interest in the role of language and communication in human organising. Language is seen as playing a *constitutive* role rather than having a purely *representational* function. That is to say, social realities – and thus organisational realities – are viewed as being created in language and communication. They are social (co-)constructions between people.

On this account, organisations are understood as forms of cultural and communicative interaction; in effect, vast networks of dynamic, dialogic webs of meaning (Geertz, 1973). A belief in the reciprocal relationship between meaning and action is also central to the approach. In short, things (relationships, artefacts, plans, policies, procedures, professional practices, etc.) are seen to get their meaning from the way that they are used and, therefore, to understand what things mean involves focusing on them *in action* and *in context*.

Our interest in language and communication, however, goes beyond simply thinking that all we have to do to change things is to tinker with the words on the surface, for example by redesigning or prescribing the way people should speak. Change is seen as a *cooperated* activity in the constant dynamic negotiation created in collectives having dialogue around shared tasks. So, when it comes to organisational development work, we see this as most likely to be productive when associated with people's work tasks, where real issues are at stake, where there are real risks, real issues of power and real decisions to be made (rather than, for instance, in simulated environments such as open space events).

Tools and techniques

The methods associated with cultural change and developments are numerous, with a diverse array of tools involving various qualitative and quantitative techniques. As discussed earlier in this chapter, the choice of tools – and the way they are applied – differs depending on one's orientations towards both the notion of organisational culture and, indeed, one's purposes and ambitions.

From the scientific perspective, best represented by the internal variable school, cultural change is a rational and technical activity where certain inputs can be relied upon to produce certain outputs. The tools associated with this approach, therefore, tend to involve the careful administration of survey instruments designed to measure and compare key cultural characteristics of organisations. In a recent systematic review of quantitative measures of organisational culture that have either been validated and used in healthcare settings or appeared to have potential for use in such settings, Scott *et al.* (2003b) identify a total of 13 instruments (*see* Box 10.2). These measures varied in the extent to which they were grounded in the ideas of their authors or derived from their experience, global in scope or limited to specific subcomponents of organisational culture and in the extent to which their validity and reliability had been tested. The authors helpfully distinguish between typological and dimensional approaches: the former referring to assessments resulting in attribution of one or more 'types' of culture to an organisation (as in the taxonomies discussed above) and the latter describing the culture in an organisation in terms of its position on a number of continuous variables.

Box 10.2: Quantitative organisational culture measures

Typological approaches

- Competing Values Questionnaire
- Harrison's Organisational Ideology Questionnaire
- Quality Improvement Implementation Survey

Dimensional approaches

- Organisational Culture Inventory (OCI)
- Hospital Culture Questionnaire
- Nursing Unit Culture Assessment Tool
- Practice Culture Questionnaire
- MacKenzie's Culture Questionnaire
- Survey of Organisational Culture
- Corporate Culture Questionnaire
- Core Employee Opinion Questionnaire
- Hofstede's Organisational Culture Questionnaire
- Organisational Culture Survey

After Scott *et al.*, 2003b.

Scott and his co-authors (2003a) argue for the pragmatic selection of an instrument based on the purpose and context of any assessment. A global view requires a comprehensive multidimensional instrument, such as the Organisational Culture Inventory, while focused studies may require more focused tools, such as the Nursing Unit Cultural Assessment Tool, in order to examine the culture of a specific professional group. They identify four things to think about in utilising these measures:

- levels (i.e. are you looking at artefacts, values or assumptions?)

- triangulation (i.e. are you drawing messages following comparisons of data from various sources?)
- sampling (i.e. are you asking a representative number of staff?)
- analysis (e.g. are you going to explore the results by professional group or by geographical locality?).

Using Schein's definition of organisational culture, they suggest that instruments for assessing culture should be designed to elicit the 'normally unspoken assumptions which are formed through dynamic processes of work performance and socialisation and which guide behaviour of the organisational members imperceptibly' (Scott *et al.*, 2003a, p.130).

In their study of the lessons for mergers in health and social care from the private sector, Field and Peck (2003) suggest that the use of an instrument for cultural assessment (such as that developed by Tetenbaum, 1999) should be seen not so much as a tool for integration but as something to assist the understanding of difference between organisations and between professions within organisations. Such understanding, it is suggested, may enable parties to start to discuss what an alternative future might look like. Tetenbaum (1999) advocates the detailed analysis of cultures pre-merger as a means of establishing a new cultural identity for the merged organisation, and the Integrated Care Network (2004) paper presents a case study of the use of such an analysis in the process of the creation of a care trust.

Scott *et al.* (2003a) draw a number of interesting conclusions in their discussion on how organisational culture can be assessed and thus the value of such tools. First, they remind us of the highly contested nature of the concept, pointing out the wide variety of theoretical frames that have been used with varying degrees of success. Second, they emphasise organisational culture as a multiple phenomena, a 'coalition of patterns of meaning forged by human groups and subcultures' (p.59). With particular reference to the NHS, they also remind us that these patterns of meaning are not only produced by the organisations' employees but also – significantly and increasingly – by patients, members of the public and other key stakeholders.

Bate *et al.* (2000) describe a lengthy action research project (which they call 'action ethnography') within an NHS trust in England where they are exploring the complex relationship between culture and structure. In this study they adopt a holistic approach to intervention geared to achieving transformational change by 'interweaving culture and structure through the warp and weft of leadership process' (p.197). In short, they bring together organisational design and organisational development by proposing a culturally sensitive approach to organisational structuring which draws attention to 'the social aspects of organisation and dynamic culturally mediated nature of organisational structure' (p.197).

They outline a four-stage methodology for intervention, which they describe as *culturally sensitive restructuring* or *CSR* (*see* Box 10.3). The approach adopts a 'process as opposed to a variables approach' (Bate *et al.*, 2000, p.198), which comprises four linked and circular subprocesses:

- *manifestation* (linking with assumptions manifested in beliefs and values)
- *realisation* (values manifest in artefacts)

- *symbolisation* (artefacts acquiring surplus meaning and coming to stand for something else)
- *interpretation* (acting back upon and changing the initial assumptions).

Based on this they define culture and cultural change in dynamic terms as 'any ongoing changes in assumptions, values, artefacts or symbols resulting from the interaction of these four processes' (p.198).

Box 10.3: Culturally sensitive restructuring

Cultural framing

- Where are we?
- What are the deeper underlying factors which have made us what we are?
- What collective view of the future can we agree to work towards?

Soft structuring

- Building the capacity to manage change
- Developing temporary spaces
- Constructing new social foundation

Hard wiring

- Turning commitment into new organisational design
- Committing to change

Retrospecting

- What have we made?
- Where is this leading us?
- What can be learnt?

Adapted from Bate *et al.*, 2000.

They conclude that 'by bringing together design and development it is possible to reframe the structure/culture relationship, bringing them together into a single integrated process thereby realising profound and sustainable organisational change' (p.197). As Bate *et al.* (2000) succinctly put it:

> evolution of an organisation's structure is integrally related to the evolution of its culture – and vice versa. Structure and culture co-evolve, each shaping and in turn shaped by the other. The emerging role for organisational design and organisational development specialists and indeed organisational leaders is to attend to the dynamics of simultaneous structural and cultural change (p.197).

Bate and his colleagues' methodology explicitly 'puts people back into design and with them their meanings, aspirations and assumptions' (p.199). They are careful to avoid specifying design choices or offering organisational archetypes and see re-design as highly specific and context driven. The approach, in common with our preferred own style, is aimed at dealing with real-life issues and in doing so acknowledging the metastructure of social roles, relationships, meanings and connections that shape and are shaped by the work community concerned.

In our own work we employ quite an extensive 'tool set' based largely on qualitative and participative inquiry techniques and, although the precise choice and application of the tools is governed by the specific context of the work, an overall frame or flow of work is usually followed (*see* Figure 10.1). These tools are applied in 'face-to-face' project meetings ranging from individual interviews through regular meetings of a couple of hours involving 10 to 12 people, to larger meetings over several days sometimes including as many as 200 people. Importantly, these meetings are always framed as project meetings focused on getting real compelling work tasks achieved. In addition, we have designed a number of Web-based tools for exploring priorities, decision making and systemic project management and review, and in recent years have also begun to use multimedia applications (digital imaging, film and video) to promote inquiry and reflection in the various phases of inquiry, imagination, resolution and review.

How is it done?

INQUIRY	of each other's conditions – rather than 'what's wrong with you?'	✓ enquiry ✗ judgement
IMAGINATION	from different perspectives rather than 'this is what I/we want you to do/be like'	✓ purposes & wants ✗ imperatives
RESOLUTION	through commitment to action steps – rather than discursive consensus or argument	✓ invitation ✗ argument/ consensus
RE-VIEWING	developing a critical stance, noticing what is being made, renewing inquiries	✓ enquiry ✗ judgement

Figure 10.1 Inter-logics as method.

We pay particular attention to forms of talk (Goffman, 1981) and how people become caught up in them (Fairclough, 1989; Brown and Levinson, 1987), as well as the prevailing 'normal' conversational architecture; that is, what people take for granted as 'the way things happen around here'. Both our work and that of Bate *et al.* (2000) appears to enable a significant shift from the traditional view that it is possible to 'design' work, service delivery and organising from a single point of view where 'structure', 'policy' and the sanctity of the 'system' tend to be given priority towards a more pragmatic environment where stakeholders can be more responsive to each other's aspirations, skills and purposes. They also aim to maximise mutual synergy, productivity and commitment, where local action and the quality of actual service made and experienced in the moment are privileged and 'structure', 'policy' and the 'system' become much more adaptable. In the following case study we aim to illustrate this; the similarities between this case and our approach and that of Bate *et al.* (2000) are striking.

A story of practice

We were invited to consult to an NHS trust that was one-year 'post merger'; the second major reorganisation that its members had undergone in the past two years. We were invited to review the 'organisational structure and management processes' and to advise on some of the 'longer-term organisational development issues'. Over the previous six months the chief executive had become increasingly concerned about what he considered to be underperformance in some key areas of the organisation's activity. Some members of the Executive Management Group felt that the problem was structural and that reconfiguration at senior management level was needed. Others felt the problem was rooted in what they described as 'cultural differences' and were calling for a process, which would help to 'realign the values and vision of the top team'. A number of so-called 'confusions' around 'roles and responsibilities' of the different directorates were voiced and, as many tasks were shared and relied upon collaborative working across boundaries, previous attempts to strengthen functional boundaries and redefine responsibilities within them only seemed to have made things worse.

Very quickly we began to identify a number of the real and compelling work tasks around which people urgently need to make progress together. Initially meeting with individuals and then with small groups, we began to gather key stakeholders together to work on these identified tasks. In constructing these task groups, we began to cut through some of the institutional boundaries of departments, divisions, roles and job descriptions that appeared to have been so instrumental in deepening the patterns of interaction that were maintaining the organisation as it was. Using a range of tools and devices to promote inquiry, we invited people to explore episodes of joint working using their own perspectives and experiences to focus on everyday descriptions (neither general opinions nor abstract accounts) in order to share qualitative knowledge about the local meaning of the central themes under exploration. By highlighting specific situations, episodes and action sequences, we were able to explore the functions of particular patterns of action; that is, the specific performative effects and the opportunities and the constraints that these were creating for the various parties.

While we acknowledged problems we avoided highlighting them, instead encouraging a focus on people's purposes; that is to say, eliciting what they were trying to make happen by their talk and actions. We supported joint explorations of particular stakeholder positions and looked at the effects of those positions on others in the system. We experimented with changing the balance between what went on in public and what went on in private, in some cases encouraging more joint participation in meaning making and decision taking, and in others trawling for support and veto for proposals that enabled particular groups to claim temporary ownership of responsibilities that had become unhelpfully distributed across too many interest groups. In effect, we began to engage in the process of restructuring, or what Bate *et al.* (2000) might term the soft structuring, gathering knowledge that people brought from their own local situations rather than privileging knowledge or stories from the top.

By surrendering the apparent convenience of a maxim – 'singing from the same hymn sheet' – we also 'interfered' to some extent with the taken-for-granted power relations in order to create fresh spaces where people could share the important meanings they were seeing in their work. Most importantly, the methods were deployed directly to enable participants at all levels to feel emboldened about declaring their adventurous, sometimes controversial, but very real, aspirations for the future. During the course of the consultation a range of important decisions were taken about changes in structure, in governance and in processes, procedures and practices which would help to 'hard wire' (Bate *et al.*, 2000) some of the commitments made during earlier phases of work. However, rather than being seen as the 'right solutions at the end of a journey', they were treated more as 'temporary and situated'; 'the right thing to do at the time, given what was currently known'.

Of course, all of this work took place over a number of months and involved set backs as well as successes. Some significant renegotiation regarding specific forms of intervention took place, through regular *co-missioning* conversations with a steering group which reflected (rather than represented) a variety of stakeholders within the work system (both inside and outside the organisation itself). By adopting these approaches, however, we think that people began to get a sense of being viewed (by themselves and by others) as knowing, purposeful, interacting participants who were having an effect on each other and their mutual contexts.

Critique

Many early writers warned against treating culture 'scientifically', and also warned of culture being subsumed into the dominant norm of behavioural sciences that emphasises definitions, measurement and quantitative analysis (Deal and Kennedy, 1983). Pettigrew (1979) argued against viewing cultures as static and unified 'objects', preferring to see them as a family of concepts rather than seeking a set of unifying definitions. Peters and Waterman (1982) wrote of the different language that would be needed to appreciate notions of organisational culture (but to what extent one emerged from their work is a matter for some debate). Schein (1985) acknowledged that culture was a complex phenomenon and that a rush to measurement should be avoided until the area was better understood; although one interpretation of his work is that the underlying implication was that in due course, and by the proper application of science, it would be possible to discover and decipher the *real* nature of organisational culture.

Why do these 'scientific' approaches still tend to dominate? What is their instru-mental and/or symbolic value? The following example might suggest some answers. In a consultation interview in the recently merged trust discussed above, the HR director confidently announced that the problems that they were facing with the diversity of views and styles within the senior management team could all have been avoided if a good cultural change programme had been put in place during the merger. Asked if he had ever witnessed lasting changes as a result of such pro-grammes he replied he had not. Nevertheless he told me a programme would have helped to sort out those who were 'with the vision' from those 'who needed to get on board or go overboard'. So, is this approach to organisational culture anything more than just another ideology of control? This totalising image of domination, of management attempting to control employees by acquiring the keys to their hearts and minds (and even their souls) is, at least for us, more than a little disturbing.

As Cummings (2002) observes, even though the 'strong culture hypothesis' has been challenged, the 'myth' of the beneficial implications deriving from unified, homogenous cultures continues. He goes on to point out that the continued use of this type of language indicates that finding the cultural type that leads to efficiency and performance is still the primary goal of management with regard to culture. Moreover, it seems to suggest that a superior (or more evolved) set of cultural traits that best serve all organisations' ends exists and their continued association with positives ('strong' as he points out still sounds better than 'weak') implies that 'good' cultures must aim for unity.

As discussed earlier, many leaders, particularly those who adopt the more instrumental approach to organisational culture, strive for commonality and alignment, whereas our preference is to treat difference as an importance facet of organisational life. In our experience, parties working in complex conditions, such as the NHS, are moved to do things in ways that make sense to them and which meet their own view of their purposes. In situations where people need each other's 'know-how' to get things done, their work is usually impeded or, worse, transformed into suspicion, where one or more parties see it as 'natural' to specify 'how things should be' on behalf of everyone. So instead of trying to restrict groups and individuals into thinking about their worlds in only one way (whether it be the correct culture, structure, values, vision or plan), we need to practise in ways that create the space for a diverse set of perspectives and approaches to be embraced, shared and used. This is, again, for us at least, predominantly a pragmatic rather than an ideological position.

Conclusion

There are, of course, many approaches to developing organisations, each with their strengths and weaknesses, as reflected in the breadth of chapters in this book, and this chapter has set out a number of stories with regard to culture in organisational life. Many of the more traditional approaches, particularly those described in the previous chapter but alluded to in this, tend to focus on structures and rules and have often been found wanting because they tend to ignore the cultural aspects of organising altogether; that is to say, they pay little or no attention to the customs, practices and behaviours of people built up over the years in response to features of the working environment and historical events. Equally, approaches that give attention to issues of culture but largely through training, awareness raising, counselling and learning, most of which are focused on the individual, can also be seen as lacking because they tend to ignore the impact of context and what happens when people interact in their local situations.

Our case example perhaps goes some way towards promoting the idea that changes in structure and culture can come about through movement in patterns of action, of behaviour and of talk. However, we hope it also illustrates that such change is not merely a matter of individual choice or isolated acts of human agency, but is rather a process of actively negotiated and cooperated change between peoples; interaction that can be facilitated by using organisational and management architectures that are designed to more explicitly promote collaborative patterns of exchange.

The relational approach then is offered as an alternative vocabulary for thinking and practice, promoting the idea of redefining and redesigning organisational life. Thus, culture can be tackled by giving attention to *doing things differently with others*, trying new things and developing new lived experiences together around real everyday tasks. It is by no means *the answer* but perhaps it does offer (at least to us as jobbing consultants!) some practical promise for change and difference in these complex times.

Acknowledgements

Thanks must go to our colleagues Tom Boydell and Amynta Cardwell, whose questions and comments have helped to shape the final text. The editor also made some useful comments and contributions.

References

Bate P (1994) *Strategies for Culture Change*. Butterworth-Heinemann, Oxford.

Bate P, Khan R and Pye A (2000) Towards a culturally sensitive approach to organization structuring; where organization design meets organization development. *Organisation Science*. **11**(2): 97–211.

Blantern C and Anderson-Wallace M (1999) Inter-logics as relational practice. *Proceedings of 2nd International Conference on Social Constructionism and Relational Practice*. University of New Hampshire, July.

Brown J (1954) *The Social Psychology of Industry*. Penguin, Harmondsworth.

Brown P and Levinson S (1987) *Politeness: some universals in language usage*. Cambridge University Press, Cambridge.

Chia R (1995) From modern to postmodern organizational analysis. *Organization Studies*. **16**(4): 580–604.

Cummings S (2002) *ReCreating Strategy*. Sage, London.

Deal T and Kennedy A (1983) A new look through old lenses. *Journal of Applied Behavioural Science*. **19**: 498–505.

Department of Health (2002) *Improvement, Expansion and Reform: The Next Three Years: priorities and planning framework 2003–2006*. The Stationery Office, London.

Fairclough N (1989) *Language and Power*. Longman, Harlow.

Field J and Peck E (2003) Mergers and acquisitions in the private sector: what are the lessons for health and social services? *Social Policy and Administration*. **37**(7): 742–55.

Fleck L (1979) *Genesis and Development of a Scientific Fact*. University of Chicago Press, Chicago.

Goffman E (1981) *Forms of Talk*. University of Pennsylvania Press, Philadelphia.

Geertz C (1973) *The Interpretation of Cultures*. Basic Books, New York.

Handy C (1976) *Understanding Organizations*. Penguin, London.

Hosking D (2002) *Constructing Changes: a social constructionist approach to change work (and beetles and witches)*. Brabant Katholieke Universiteit, Brabant.

Hutton J (2000) Interview with Polly Neale. www.community-care.co.uk (accessed 21 November).

Integrated Care Network (2004) *'Culture' in Partnerships: what do we mean by it and what can we do about it?* Department of Health, London.

Jaques E (1951) *The Changing Culture of the Factory*. Tavistock Institute, London.

Meyerson D and Martin J (1987) Cultural change: an integration of three different views. *Journal of Management Studies*. 24(6): 623–43.

Mitroff I and Kilmann R (1976) On organisational stories: an approach to the design and analysis of organisations through myths and stories. In: R Kilmann, L Pondy and D Slevin (eds) *The Management of Organisation Design*. Elsevier, New York.

Parker M (2000) *Organisational Culture and Identity*. Sage, London.

Peters T and Waterman R (1982) *In Search of Excellence*. Warners, New York.

Pettigrew A (1979) On studying organisational cultures. *Administrative Science Quarterly*. 24: 570–80.

Pheysey D (1993) *Organizational Cultures: types and transformations*. Routledge, London.

Schein E (1984) Coming to a new awareness of organizational culture. *Sloan Management Review*. 25: 3–16

Schein E (1985) *Organizational Culture and Leadership*. Jossey-Bass, San Francisco, CA.

Schein E (1990) Organizational culture. *American Psychology*. 45: 109–19.

Schein E (1999) *The Corporate Culture Survival Guide*. Jossey-Bass, San Francisco, CA.

Schneider W (1994) *The Reengineering Alternative: a plan for making your current culture work*. Irwin, New York.

Scott T, Mannion R, Davies H and Marshall M (2003a) *Healthcare Performance and Organisational Culture*. Radcliffe Medical Press, Oxford.

Scott J, Mannion R, Davies H and Marshall M (2003b) The quantitative measurement of organisational culture in health care: a review of the available instruments. *Health Services Research*. 38(3): 923–45.

Selznick P (1957) *Leadership in Administration: a sociological interpretation*. Harper and Row, New York.

Silverman D (1970) *The Theory of Organisations: a sociological framework*. Heinemann, London.

Smircich L (1983) Concepts of culture and organizational analysis. *Administrative Science Quarterly*. **28**: 339–58.

Tetenbaum T (1999) Beating the odds of merger and acquisition failure: seven key practices that improve the chance for expected integration and synergies. *Organizational Dynamics*. **28**(2): 22–36.

Wilkins L and Ouchi W (1983) Efficient cultures: exploring the relationship between culture and organisational performance. *Administrative Science Quarterly*. **28**: 468–81.

Further reading

Burr V (1995) *An Introduction to Social Constructionism*. Routledge, London.

McNamee S and Gergen K (1999) *Relational Responsibility – resources for sustainable dialogue*. Sage, London.

Websites

For further writing on relational and systemic approaches to organisational change:

- www.inter-logics.net
- www.geocities.com/dian_marie_hosking
- www.christineoliver.net

Some useful papers relating to participative and cooperative inquiry:

- www.bath.ac.uk/carpp

CHAPTER 11

Critical appreciative inquiry as intervention in organisational discourse

Christine Oliver

Introduction

This chapter reviews, critiques and develops the claims of *appreciative inquiry* (AI), a prevalent consultancy methodology discourse for working with organisational development (OD) and hailed by some as 'the most important advance in action research in the last decade' (Cooperrider and Whitney, 1999, p.10). It offers a reframing of AI as *critical appreciative inquiry* (CAI), with the intention that this revised approach may construct new meanings and deliver better outputs when the technique is applied. It is argued that traditional AI as a representation of social constructionism in action involves a confusion of theory and a dualism in practice which is ultimately both intellectually and practically unsatisfying. The device of creating a relationship between the critical and the appreciative, however, develops the methodology and constructs greater potential for significant organisational change.

In refining AI as an OD methodology, the chapter also gives consideration to the implications for two connected levels of interest: organisational development and organisational discourse. Discourse is a relevant frame for organisational development in that it offers the opportunity for an exploration of the connections between the patterns lived in an organisation and the stories that get told, which, over time, become embedded in culture, relationship and identity (Pearce, 1994; Grant *et al.*, 1998).

First, this chapter examines discourses embedded in AI methodology and consideration is given to how to extend the methodology so that power and other relational dynamics are made more overt and available for critique. Second, an exploration is offered of the constraining discourses within a piece of consultancy work about management and team development in a health context and an illustration made of the use of the extended AI methodology as CAI. Following from this example, there are some reflections on the development of organisational discourse, which connect theory and practice.

What is appreciative inquiry?

AI could be dismissed as yet another entry in the apparently endless list of con-sultancy fads that bedevil OD, earning consultants lots of money while often creating destructive consequences for organisations (Micklethwaite and Wooldridge, 1996). However, its claims are 'revolutionary' (Cooperrider and Whitney, 1999, p.7), it has gained in popularity in the health context, and it presents itself as acting coherently within a social constructionist discourse appealing (on the face of it) to those of us OD practitioners who are attempting to use a social constructionist framework in a meaningful way in our work (Czarniawska, 2001).

AI has been defined as a 'positive revolution' in organisational change work (Cooperrider and Whitney, 1999, p.7). It is presented as a corrective to problem-solving based approaches, which are argued to lead to negative perspectives where deficit language becomes commonplace, which, in its turn, leads to organisational hopelessness (Hammond, 1998; Cooperrider and Whitney, 1999). A polarisation is deliberately and consciously set up, with AI positioned as an enabling methodology for addressing organisational challenges from the 'other side' or the 'positive change core' which is seen as holding a transformational power to unleash creativity and imagination, predisposing the organisation to create new successful images of the future (Cooperrider and Whitney, 1999, p.8).

The *4D cycle* typically frames an AI change process, creating a particular kind of boundary around the organisation's talk. The frame allows the organisation to explore how it is and could be at its best, using the device of the four phases of *discovery*, *dream*, *design* and *destiny*. The 'appreciative inquirer' explores what works well in an organisation. So-called appreciative questions are asked that encourage story-telling of high-point experiences, core factors that give life, wishes for the health of the organisation and ideas about what is of value.

Thus AI texts speak of the obligation to create positive talk, spirit, energy, and the emotions of joy and pride. With this stress on the construction of the positive principle, AI has presented itself as an expression in action of social constructionist commitments (Cooperrider, 1998; Hammond, 1998; Cooperrider and Whitney, 1999; Elliot, 1999; Barge and Oliver, 2002). In these terms, language is treated not so much as a reflection or transmission of reality but as a making of our social worlds (Gergen, 1999; Shotter, 1993); *see* both the Introduction and below for more discussion of social constructionism.

From a 'constructionist' position, AI critiques problem-solving approaches as typically expressed through confrontation and criticism, thus blaming and labelling people and imbued with deficit language. Within AI, challenge and criticism is positioned essentially as a thing to be won over or overcome: 'The professional malcontents have to be tolerated and given the chance to be committed ... They need to be heard, to be given the chance to speak – if necessary to be critical and even destructive – not least because their negativities may have within them the germ of something that the organization can learn from and work with, especially if it can be subsequently reframed in an appreciative way' (Elliot, 1999, p.26).

It is argued that hierarchy is typically privileged within problem-solving approaches with the consequence of the erosion of power for the individual. AI, on the other hand, is represented as a collaborative participative process where all voices are positioned as equally valid. Hierarchy is explicitly devalued and power distributed, 'when AI is conducted as a whole systems approach ... there is movement toward greater equality and less hierarchy' (Cooperrider and Whitney, 1999, p.23); or as Elliot (1999, p.22) puts it: '... inequalities in power make truthful communication difficult'. This 'post-bureaucratic' model treats power differences as bad; leadership is about letting go. Leaders 'recognise that their greatest job is to get out of the way' (Cooperrider and Whitney, 1999, p.19). The importance of engaging all stakeholders is stressed, thus 'power discrepancies are minimised' (Elliot, 1999, p.23). The link to the ethical aspirations for OD held by writers such as Carnevale (2003), referred to in Chapter 1, are readily apparent in these arguments.

A social constructionist critique of AI

The frame employed here for both the critique and the refinement of the AI discourse is that of social constructionism (Shotter, 1993). This is fitting, given that it is also offered as a theoretical basis for AI (Cooperrider and Whitney, 1999), and it is a frame that has rich potential for consultancy methodology (Oliver, 1996; Oliver and Brittain, 2001; Campbell, 2001; Oliver et al., 2003). From within this frame, the organisation is a relationally and socially constructed phenomenon produced in 'contextually embedded social discourse' (Boje et al., 1996, p.2). Meaning is contextual, negotiated, contested, multiple, partial and unfinished (Alvesson and Deetz, 1996; Barge and Oliver, 2002). Conversation is the site for the development of meaning, holding the power to shape the cultural, social and relational texture of the organisation. For organisational development practitioners, attention is thus drawn to the management of conversation and a significant question becomes: what contexts can be created in the form and content of public conversation that enable it to work most productively?

For AI, the positive principle is the context of significance that gives meaning to dialogue. There is an a priori assumption that the rules for public conversation should, at the level of content, invoke adherence to the 'positive'. For most social constructionists this position would be felt to be problematic because it leads to a decontextualised polarisation, with positive and negative treated as containing intrinsic meaning, whereas a social constructionist perspective says the meaning given to the content of language cannot be prejudged in advance by a third party but is contextual, emergent, partial, multiple and negotiated with and between participants.

It is useful here to evoke the notion of *layers of context*. This is a device that has been elaborated by Co-ordinated Management of Meaning (CMM) Theory (Cronen and Pearce, 1985; Pearce, 1994; Oliver, 1996; Oliver et al., 2003) to create a structure for a social constructionist analysis. The contexts of significance designed here for exploring and developing AI discourse (adapted from CMM) are:

- culture of power
- relationship accountabilities

- subject position
- rules for communication episode
- interpretive act.[1]

The application of these five dimensions to AI is summarised in Box 11.1.

Culture of power

For AI, power is seen as getting in the way of a 'positive' dialogue. Hierarchy is devalued, with the assumption that difference in role with differential access to decision making intrinsically constrains dialogue. A naive approach to power is thus disguised as an equalising of voices, with apparent equality being confused with equity. I would challenge the premise that consciousness about power relations constrains the ability of participants to coordinate a productive conversation. It could be argued that bringing power relations into view can increase the likelihood of democratic modes of managing and organising. If power relations are minimised there is a danger they will be obscured with the potential consequences to the dialogue of:

- ambiguity of entitlements and obligations for participation
- the process of definition of themes and symbols that are of value in a group, organisation or community will be shaped more strongly but less obviously by those who are in formal positions of power
- critique (including self and relational) becomes less possible and the opportunity for expressions of vulnerability, injustice, hurt, protest and fragility minimised
- the cutting off of such contributions could reduce complexity in such a way that important opportunities for organisational development are lost.

Relationship accountabilities

The accountabilities that are characteristically constructed in an AI process are constrained by the injunction to 'be positive', as if 'being positive' will enhance organisational relationships and thus organisational development. However, if it is a participant's view that the theme or topic being discussed is insufficiently meaningful or relevant, the injunction to 'be positive' could undermine both working relationships and the task of the organisation.

Subject position

The available subject positions in AI are those of 'appreciating' and being 'appreciated'. Learning is limited to exploring the conditions for what has, does and will

---

[1] The interpretive act is a reframing of the speech act (Cronen and Pearce, 1985). Here, the interpretive dimension of meaning making is highlighted as a moral choice with moral consequences.

work well. The position of critique is associated with negativity and blame; thus if a participant experiences reservations, differences in view and/or has been impacted by a strategy in an unwanted way there is no place for adopting a learning position to that experience. The subject positions available in those cases could be said to be problem talker, spoilsport or disloyal member.

Rules for communication episode

The frame of the AI process is typically discovery, dream, design and destiny, with the rule and responsibility invoked to engage in affirmative talk not problem talk. Evaluation is seen to be associated with the search for blame or for what is wrong and thus not considered desirable. The injunction is made to 'valuate' not evaluate (Anderson *et al.*, 2001). In AI, it is the person that is affirmed. We could call this *first-order appreciation,* which may be at odds with relational and cultural affirmation. If so, 'person affirmation' could be at the cost of constructive self, relational and organisational evaluation and development.

Interpretive act

What meanings are noticed, interpreted and acted upon in moments of communication will be structured by the appreciation/criticism dualism. Experiences of joy, pride and collaboration will be encouraged and discomfort, challenge, disagreement, evaluation and critique avoided.

Box 11.1: Summary of contextual discourses for AI	
Culture of power	Minimisation of power; critique disallowed
Relational accountabilities	Obligation to positivity; elimination of negativity
Subject position	Appreciative person; problem talk disallowed
Rules for communication episode	First-order affirmation (of person); rule bound at content level not process level
Interpretive act	Mutuality; celebration

Critical appreciative inquiry: a development

The AI claim that language entails creation makes sense, given a social constructionist starting point. However, the link with social constructionism becomes tenuous when it is tied to the 'positive principle'. The injunction to 'act appreciatively' provides an insufficiently complex account of entitlements and obligations for participants in a change process. However, I want to argue that if the words *critical* and *appreciative* are joined, and not separated, in meaning, and are considered as operational at other levels of context than just the content level (e.g. relational, cultural), then a more meaningful OD process is made possible.

For a development process to be relevant, meaningful and effective, participants in that process need to engage in a second-order, reflexive, *critical-appreciative* relationship to their own (and others') communication. Otherwise there is a risk that what is discussed becomes incongruent with how it is discussed, and good intentions will not have the desired outcomes. When *critical-appreciative* are joined, the intention is to invite a critical consciousness about how communication creates powers, opportunities and constraints for action in the dialogue.

The word 'critical' has a Greek etymology and relates to the words 'crisis' (as in turning or tipping point, a theme which recurs many times in this volume) and 'choice'. If human and collective agency are to be encouraged, a blind obedience to 'act appreciatively' might be less life enhancing than an encouragement to appreciate the potential for each utterance to be a turning point and to make choices that anticipate the effects of one's contribution on contexts of significance. Let us return to the five dimensions discussed above and examine CAI through these lenses. Again the examination is summarised (in Box 11.2).

Culture of power

A CAI frame encourages a culture of critical consciousness about the assumptions and positions we ourselves take up and offer to others. This can include a *critical appreciation* of power and interest as a dimension of communication, including mindfulness of how one's formal position shapes speaking and listening in the dialogue. This commitment to inquiry and challenge requires an openness to learn, preparedness to change and a curiosity about the experience of others, positioning self and other as human and vulnerable (Buber, 1970). It requires a kind of humility about one's own position and a sense of obligation to provide accounts to others, where relevant, about our experience and understanding. These commitments would frame the rules for engagement in an inquiry.

In a CAI process, functional hierarchy is respected with people encouraged to speak from within the boundaries and freedoms of their own position as well as from other positions. Agreements are developed in the group about the rules for second-order critique and feedback, with learning framed as the highest context giving meaning to the dialogue. In that sense, all are positioned equally as learners but people's speaking and listening positions are also contextualised by their roles and their associated rights and responsibilities. These roles, rights and responsibilities may or may not be 'backgrounded' for certain purposes.

Relational accountabilities

It is argued here that when openness and curiosity about power is created in this cultural spirit of inquiry and reflection, greater clarity is also achieved about the entitlements and obligations that inform and shape participation with the effect of maximising openings for voices to be heard. The criteria for individuals making judgements about participation in this frame are whether their contributions are expected to be meaningful, purposeful and accountable, given the task and the cultural spirit of agreement invited at the outset. Second-order critique means that:

- 'we' becomes a text for inquiry and reflection
- the discursive structures (of self and group) are questioned including those relating to power
- a recognition is given to the part one plays in the creation of realities, systems, structures and processes so that participants become critical inquirers into their own impact
- contradictions, doubts, dilemmas, vulnerabilities, discomforts and new possibilities are articulated and developed.

Subject position

The subject position imagined is that of conscious reflexive participant, actively contributing in order to develop the dialogue. In the context of offering an experience of doubt, critique, dissent or distress, the participant would be encouraged to do so in a way, given the overall purpose of the dialogue, that was both purposeful and suggested opportunities for development.

Rules for communication episode

Care is taken in the facilitation of episodes of communication to structure the conversation in ways that encourage the reflexive consciousness described. The phases of *crisis*, *choice*, *criteria* and *critique* can be used literally as a substitute for the 4D cycle and as a way of highlighting the centrality of *critical-appreciation*. However, these words can also be treated as metaphors for the process. What is important is that a process is created where it is felt that the relevant people are involved in the dialogue, they are clear about the rules for participation and the process enables a development of pertinent issues from a second-order perspective.

Although care should always be taken with talk, a potentially pernicious consequence of the AI discomfort with evaluation is that the evaluative baby is lost in the valuing bathwater. This can undermine trust. Asch (1952) has defined the conditions for trust as being: the ability to speak with sufficient openness; sufficiently shared perceptions of the present; and sufficiently shared hopes for the future. The injunction for organisational participants to treat each other affirmatively can, in these terms, stifle valid expressions of hurt, vulnerability, injustice and ill treatment. I propose that valuation and evaluation are best treated as if they are in a contextual relationship not in an either/or relationship. Processes of evaluation should occur in the context of an appreciation and curiosity about the values and contributions of the individual in their context. At the same time, valuation should be communicated in the context of a reflexive critical consciousness. In CAI, the question of how organisational and relational priorities are ordered and valued is open to observation and exploration, not assumed. The injunction for accountability in an OD dialogue needs to be less rule bound at the level of content and more rule bound at the level of process, whereby a mindfulness is created about the reflexive effects that are created through one's contribution to the talk.

Interpretive act

Situated judgements are made in relation to the levels of context above for how to notice, interpret and act on and in communication. It can be helpful at this level to treat the communication of others as attempts to contribute to the dialogue and, in the context of apparent ambiguity or incommensurability, intervene to establish the intentions of contributions and/or invite feedback as to how one could invite a response oneself to develop the dialogue from a second-order perspective.

Box 11.2: Contextual discourses for CAI

Culture of power	Critical consciousness; openness to learning; preparedness to change
Relational accountabilities	Obligation for self and group to become text for inquiry
Subject position	Reflexive, vulnerable, learner
Rules for communication episode	Second-order critical appreciation
Interpretive act	Vulnerabilities, doubts, dilemmas, challenges, proposals

---

Developing organisation through discourse: a CAI case study

I was commissioned as an OD consultant to facilitate management development for a multidisciplinary adolescent mental health team. My task was defined as developing management skills at the level of the individual manager and development of management culture for the team. My input was structured in the following way: I conducted a 'needs assessment' evaluation of management practice by interviewing all managers (8) in the senior management team in the first instance, then presented the findings to the management team as a basis for a management development dialogue over two days.

Questions for management interviews were designed to access data at the levels of management culture in the team and in the trust (management relationships, management style and skill, and the detail of episodes of 'performance'). A further aim was to stimulate reflexivity about management practice. On transcribing the data, key phrases were highlighted that were suggestive of strong discourses at different levels of context. The data showed oscillation, polarisation, a lack of stability and a lack of progress. Four themes stood out as significant, and meaningful data was clustered within them:

- strategic coherence
- accountability
- trust and fairness
- appraisal (*see* Box 11.3).

Box 11.3: Management themes and their associated discourses at different contextual levels

Strategic coherence	**Culture**: ambiguity of boundaries of vision **Relationship**: confusion of rights and responsibilities **Identity**: manager unable to act with clarity or confidence
Accountability	**Culture**: accountability disconnected from strategy **Relationship**: us and them **Identity**: accountable to own discipline not team
Trust and fairness	**Culture**: individual prioritised over corporate **Relationship**: inconsistency of staff treatment **Identity**: favoured/unfavoured
Appraisal	**Culture**: instability and insecurity **Relationship**: lack of reflexivity **Identity**: poor competence

---

Developing the OD dialogue

A 4D cycle process was used to structure the dialogue with the management team. I proposed the task of building a picture together, using the data and themes from the interviews as a base from which to explore and identify areas for development.

Discovery: learning from experience

The initial task set was for small groups to take a theme and connect it to their experience, identifying episodes which expressed and contradicted the discourses identified in the interviews. The aim here was to develop a collective understanding (and reflexivity) about management/staff communication.

Dream: developing purpose, role and function of managers

In their groups, people were then asked to take one of three positions (inquirer, listener or speaker). The inquirer was to inquire into the speaker's perceptions about potential effective role and relational responsibilities, expectations, connections and boundaries in the team management context. After 30 minutes, inquirer and listener reflected in front of the speaker on what they had heard, then the interview resumed with the speaker for 5 minutes. Reflections then occurred from each position in the large group. This part of the exercise was designed to encourage a culture of inquiry and learning, facilitated by a layering of reflections. A more convergent exercise followed, involving small groups summarising the learning and working on defining core principles and practices of the management task in the team context.

Design: improving team and individual competencies

In this phase, people worked alone, identifying actions that could be taken to improve management patterns and practices, making concrete proposals which were shared with the team, then negotiated.

Deconstruction: communication, learning and critique

A small group inquiry was conducted about how this OD process showed strength and fragility of management. In particular, people were invited to reflect on the part each individual played in contributing to strength and fragility.

The outcomes – in terms of the discourses that were enabled – of these interventions are summarised in Box 11.4.

Box 11.4: Summary of discourses facilitated by critical appreciative inquiry

Culture of power	Second-order critical appreciation facilitated the development of shared responsibility
Relational accountability	Detailed self- and collective examination facilitated tighter and less-polarised accountability
Subject position	Vulnerable; open; responsible; effective
Rules for communication episode	The context of reflexive learning was set
Interpretive acts	Beginnings of trust; respect; empathy; co-existence allowed

---

Evaluation/research on AI or CAI

Perhaps unsurprisingly, the AI literature has a tendency to be positive about its own impact! It is usually case study based and tightly linked to the 4D cycle methodology. It has a repetitive message based on the premise of working with the 'positive change core'. This is shown in, for instance, the claim of 'vital change like GTE's award-winning union-management negotiations using AI, Hunter Douglas's empowering work leading to breakthroughs in product strategies, or the historic creation of the global charter for a UN-like organisation of all the world's religions, the United Religions Initiative' (Fry *et al.*, 2002, p.ix). Cooperrider, in his foreword to this work, says he sees rigour in the 'compelling cases coupled with soul searching reflection and scholarship in ideas' (p.x). I would suggest, however, that the claims tend to be over-grandiose, littered with words like 'global', 'vital', 'breakthrough' and 'historic'. As yet, AI seems not to have exposed itself to any systematic research initiatives.

Limitations of CAI

CAI has been offered here as a refinement of AI. It is a methodology in its infancy and has not itself been exposed to rigorous evaluation. The feedback given from within and following CAI processes has been generally favourable, in that it is said to allow the complexity of experience to be held by a group while emphasising the importance of reflexive examination of organisational culture, structure and process. However, the word 'critical' often creates an ambivalent effect, particularly in over-critical contexts of mistrust where there is a fear of blame. In introducing an inquiry process I have found myself more and more emphasising the importance of reflexivity as of value in the process. This has led me to develop a methodology that I am now calling 'reflexive inquiry', which draws on five principles, one of which is the critical principle.

Conclusion

This chapter has examined some of the core discursive structures of *appreciative inquiry* as an OD methodology through use of the device of 'layers of context'. It is important that this critique acknowledges the motivation of AI to move beyond the blaming of individuals and processes in organisations. The intention is to enable a more constructive dialogue pattern than characterises much organisational talk. To take a contextual view, an AI process, where the 'life enhancing' is deliberately framed as the contextual purpose giving meaning to the dialogue, could be worthwhile if treated explicitly as a temporary positioning to enable a different pattern and if its connection to other forms of dialogue is clearly made. However, the polarisation of the negative and positive, where the negative is aligned with first-order critique, disallows the potential development that can be offered when second-order critique in the form of *critical appreciative inquiry* frames the OD process.

The argument constructed here is that CAI works as a development of AI in the ways that it proposes a self and relational reflexivity in the frame of second-order critique. The case study shows how this can work in practice where the specific *critical appreciative* context created in the work enabled an invitation to engage in self and team critique within a group context. An exercise was designed which provided fresh insight into management practices for participants and facilitated a moving through the discourse of fragmentation. The 'lived discourse' of the local themes were challenged at different levels of context. Professional coordination became a more meaningful frame than competition through the experience of a co-existence of positions and voices. A reflexive empathetic accountability offered a different experience of relationship and identity, thereby providing the beginnings of a new context for the emerging talk/text.

CAI works at the levels of culture, relationship, identity, episode and interpretive act through positioning power, accountability, subjective experience, and rules and meanings given to communication. It can inform the ways that agreements are handled about what constitutes reflexive talk when contexts and frames are being named and made in an OD process. It can also inform the design of a frame for sequencing the phases of talk in a process, enabling a non-dualistic, complex approach to what is meaningful in OD. It can affect the ways that situated judgements are handled within a process to enable the coordination of meaning and purpose and it can construct learning conversations of (self and relational) critique. Finally, at its most fundamental, it is an approach that focuses on the connection between reflexivity and learning, which constitute the central aims of OD in the definition offered in Chapter 1 of this book.

References

Alvesson M and Deetz S (1996) Critical theory and postmodernist approaches to organisational studies. In: S Clegg, C Hardy and W Nord (eds) *Handbook of Organisational Studies*, pp.191–217. Sage, London.

Anderson H, Cooperrider D, Gergen KJ, Gergen M, McNamee S and Whitney D (2001) *The Appreciative Organisation*. Taos Institute, New Mexico.

Asch S (1952) *Social Psychology*. Prentice Hall, New York.

Barge J and Oliver C (2002) Working with appreciation in managerial practice. *Academy of Management Journal*. **28**(1): 124–42.

Boje D, Gephart R Jr and Thatchenkery T (eds) (1996) *Postmodern Management and Organization Theory*. Sage, Thousand Oaks, CA.

Buber M (1970) *I and Thou*. Simon and Schuster, New York.

Campbell D (2001) *The Socially Constructed Organisation*. Karnac, London.

Carnevale D (2003) *Organizational Development in the Public Sector*. Westview, Cambridge, MA.

Cooperrider D (1998) What is appreciative inquiry? In: S Hammond and C Royal (eds) *Lessons From the Field: applying appreciative inquiry*, p.3. Practical Press, Plano, TX.

Cooperrider D and Whitney D (1999) *Appreciative Inquiry*. Berrett-Koehler, San Francisco, CA.

Cronen V and Pearce W (1985) An introduction to how the Milan method works. In: D Campbell and R Draper (eds) *Applications of Systemic Therapy*. Grune and Stratton, London.

Czarniawska B (2001) Is it possible to be a constructionist consultant? *Management Learning*. **32**(2): 253–66.

Elliot C (1999) *Locating the Energy for Change: an introduction to appreciative inquiry*. International Institute for Sustainable Development, Toronto, Canada.

Fry R, Barrett F, Seiling J and Whitney D (2002) *Appreciative Inquiry and Organisational Transformation: reports from the field*. Quorum, Connecticut.

Gergen K (1999) *An Invitation to Social Constructionism*. London, Sage.

Grant D, Oswick C and Keenoy T (1998) *Discourse and Organisation*. Sage, London.

Hammond S (1998) *The Thin Book of Appreciative Inquiry* (2e). Thin Book, Plano, TX.

Micklethwaite J and Wooldridge A (1996) *The Witch Doctors*. Heinemann, London.

Oliver C (1996) Systemic eloquence. *Human Systems: the journal of systemic consultation and management*. **7**(4): 247–64.

Oliver C and Brittain G (2001) Situated knowledge management. *Career Development International*. **6**(7): 403–13.

Oliver C, Herasymowych M and Senko H (2003) *Complexity, Relationships and Strange Loops: reflexive practice guide*. MHA Institute Inc., Calgary, Canada.

Pearce W (1994) *Interpersonal Communication*. HarperCollins, New York.

Shotter J (1993) *Conversational Realities: constructing life through language*. Sage, London.

Further reading

Rickets M and Willis J (2001) *Experience AI: a practitioners guide to integrating appreciative inquiry and experiential learning*. Taos Institute, New Mexico.

Schiller M, Holland BM and Riley D (2001) *Appreciative Leaders, in the Eye of the Beholder*. Taos Institute, New Mexico.

Srivastva S and Cooperrider D (1990) *Appreciative Management and Leadership: the power of positive thought and action in organisations*. Jossey-Bass, San Francisco, CA.

Websites

- For further papers by the author: www.christineoliver.net
- Taos Institute: www.taosinstitute.org
- Appreciative inquiry listserv: www.ailist@business.utah.edu
- Appreciative inquiry newsletter: www.aradford.co.uk

Reaching the parts: the use of narrative and storytelling in organisational development

Alys Harwood

Introduction

The theoretical physicist F David Peat (1996) wrote in *Blackfoot Physics*: 'Knowledge ... cannot be accumulated like money stored in a bank, rather it is an ongoing process better represented by the activity of coming-to-knowing than by a static noun' (p.55). Stories of one sort or another have always been central to everyday life in organisations, but until relatively recently they have been largely ignored by those who sought to change and develop those organisations. The challenges that now face healthcare managers and clinicians require more effective ways of mobilising staff to adopt and/or adapt new working practices, improve processes and procedures, develop more responsive teams and contribute to more flexible organisations. Storytelling and narrative have grown into the gaps left by more established OD methodologies. In particular, they have begun to be recognised as a means of addressing and reinterpreting some neglected areas, such as the impact of people's emotions, values and beliefs on the workings of the organisation or the ways in which formal and informal systems may work in opposition to one another.

Storytelling alone is not an OD process in itself, but narratives, stories, tales and anecdotes, used consciously and skilfully, are powerful allies to wider development. This chapter examines the place of storytelling in OD in health and social care and primarily explores ways of working with staff (rather than with service users or other stakeholders in the healthcare system). It presents a series of vignettes in boxes in the text to bring the ideas back to the practical human level at regular intervals.

The story so far – theoretical underpinnings

Jungian analyst and storyteller Clarissa Pinkola Estes (1992) uses a potent metaphor to describe the power of story and narrative:

> Ancient dissectionists spoke of the auditory nerve being divided into three or more pathways deep in the brain. They surmised that the ear was meant, therefore, to hear at three different levels. One pathway was said to hear the mundane conversations of the world. A second pathway apprehended learning and art. And the third pathway existed so the soul itself might hear guidance and gain knowledge while here on earth (p.26).

Stories have always been used to instruct, engage, enable, inspire, constrain and contain members of the tribe, and they continue to be employed in this way in the workplace, consciously or otherwise. Stories exemplify personal values or organisational principles, pass cultural information on from one generation to the next, and provide information about both change and continuity. They are immediate, accessible, require no esoteric knowledge, and engage people's values and feelings in a manner few other methods can.

The explicit use of narrative and storytelling in organisations has grown over the past 20 years or so, driven by a range of approaches to individual and organisational change, from psychodynamic theory to complexity science, which are explored in earlier chapters of this volume. No one theoretical approach has developed into a single storytelling OD method; rather, it has combined with and augmented these other OD processes. Much of this interest, in particular from the organisational research community, has been subsumed under the banner of organisational discourse, that is the study of the talk and text used in organisations. Organisational discourse has been described as the 'languages and symbolic media we employ to describe, represent, interpret and theorize what we take to be the facticity of organizational life' (Grant et al., 1998, p.1). In this view, our perceptions of our organisations are the products of the discourses through which we discuss them. In turn, these products constrain the content of future discourse. It is an iterative process, discourse shaping organisation and vice versa; this relationship is connected to and mirrors that between social culture and social structure discussed in Chapters 6 and 10. Scholars and OD practitioners adopting organisational discourse as a research and/or development tool are therefore very much in the tradition of social constructionism outlined in the Introduction to this book (and *see also* Chapter 11).

The power of metaphor – culture, learning and innovation

Metaphor is the central mechanism of the storytelling approach. There is a considerable literature on the nature of metaphor. This chapter adopts the widely accepted interaction theory of metaphor developed by Black (1979). This argues that a metaphorical statement has two distinct subjects, the 'primary' subject and the 'secondary' subject. A metaphor works by 'projecting upon' the primary subject a set of 'associated implications' which are derived from the secondary subject. For Black, the power of a metaphor or simile depends on the degree of resonance created between the primary subject (e.g. the PCT) and the secondary subject (e.g. adolescents) in the not-uncommon assertion in their early years that 'PCTs were adolescent organisations'. Not all metaphorical utterances have power; I am not sure what would be conveyed by describing a PCT as a washing line (and have never heard it being uttered). The concept of resonance recurs in this chapter as a key criterion as to whether stories, symbols, metaphors and similes have the potential power to enable organisational members to re-frame the way in which they view their organisation, its challenges and its opportunities.

Of course, the use of metaphors is not restricted to literature. Much of our everyday discourse is infused with metaphors, although many of these metaphors may have become so commonplace as to be unremarkable; what Black would call 'dead metaphors'. From their research, Pollio and colleagues (1990) found that, 'speakers as varied as politicians engaging in public rhetoric to patients engaging in psychotherapy produce an average of 1.5 novel and 3.4 cliched figures of speech per 100 words spoken' (p.142). Black (1979) contends that metaphors enable us to see aspects of reality that the metaphor's production helps to create and also suggests that the world is thus necessarily always seen from a certain perspective. To describe a PCT as an adolescent organisation directs attention to specific characteristics: that it is still growing and thus immature in its judgements; tends to be stroppy when these judgements are challenged; cannot yet be held entirely responsible for all its actions; may be energetic and yet introverted, etc. In so doing, of course, this metaphor overlooks aspects of PCTs that alternative metaphors may highlight.

In achieving resonance, metaphors in and around organisations can also serve to:

- combine universal and unique interpretations, enabling people to simultaneously associate into the common elements and at the same time draw individual meanings from the material
- condense much information into a rich and multi-layered cluster
- be sensory-rich and textured, and therefore easy to associate with and remember (easier than facts or data)
- enable detachment and repositioning, commonly through a change in perspective on or association with a topic or character.

Morgan's (1986) seminal work on organisational metaphors demonstrates clearly the power of metaphor to condense a huge amount of information into a meaningful whole (*see* Chapter 1 and the Conclusion for much more discussion of Morgan). Talk to any group of NHS middle managers and they will have little difficulty in recognising and describing the characteristics of a 'political system' or an 'organism'. Yet much current planning of the implementation of change ignores that useful experiential knowledge and instead reverts to a 'default' setting based on the metaphor of the organisation as machine. Planning and implementation becomes characterised by top-down, standardised, reproduction of systems and processes (*see* Chapter 9). Benchmarking and other such processes, handled crudely, can reinforce the comforting (but wasteful) illusion of control through the application of mechanistic methods. As Saul (quoted in Cooper and Sawaf, 1997) notes:

> Reason is a narrow system swelled into an ideology. With time and power it has become a dogma, devoid of direction and disguised as disinterested inquiry. Reason presents itself as the solution to the problems it has created (p.258).

The explicit use of narrative and storytelling has been adopted widely by those committed to 'learning organisations'. Stories have been used as a way of understanding different mental models, apprehending the energy flow across and within systems, modelling personal mastery, and for creating and developing shared visions of the future. For example, Senge and his contributors (1996) place great value on seeking what unifies; that is, directing energy into what brings and holds people together, rather than spending time anatomising difference. The use of metaphor in storytelling is a prime way of reminding NHS staff of their most fundamental similarities rather than their more superficial differences. Newer approaches like appreciative inquiry (*see* Chapter 11) also direct attention into generating unity of vision and place much emphasis on discussing what works well. Methods deriving from the performing arts, particularly drama, but also storytelling and music, have been used in the health service on leadership programmes and in team development for some time, and their use is percolating into OD. Symbol, metaphor and story are also intrinsic elements of psychodynamic approaches to OD (*see* Chapter 6).

Regardless of OD 'school', therefore, these approaches have reinforced the use of narrative and storytelling as legitimate material for organisational change processes. Nonetheless, there are differences in the way that 'schools' use them. The most obvious and simplistic difference between psychodynamic and storytelling approaches, for instance, is that the former focuses on understanding 'why' a particular group phenomenon has occurred and the latter puts more attention into the 'what and how' of something happening.

The formal and informal system – using complexity

The application of complexity science to organisations (*see* Chapter 8) has brought about a radical shift in our understanding of how health and social care systems create the conditions for change. Emerging conversations or narratives, instead of being understood as mere records of some underlying reality, are coming to be understood as the very stuff that shapes reality. Recurring workplace stories or anecdotes offer valuable insights into current organisational 'attractors'. Attractors are representations of forces that have a preferential 'pull' in the system, for example, 'it's not what you know, it's who you know that counts around here'. New and co-created stories can then start to explore and shape fresher, more useful, attractors.

Complexity approaches to change in health and social care form a natural alliance with storytelling, particularly emerging narrative, methods in OD. Storytelling activity can be utilised to move an organisation toward the 'tipping point' (that is, the point at which a conversation-based OD intervention is most likely to have a disproportionate effect). Stacey (1996) identifies five key conditions that help take organisations to this point:

- increase in connectivity – multiplying and strengthening the links in the system between people, teams and organisations
- increase in diversity – the amount and volume of different discourses sustained within the system
- increase in information flow – increased connectivity and diversity greatly increase the level and quality of information flowing across the system
- increase in level of contained anxiety – too little anxiety and there is no impetus for change, too much and people become immobilised
- decrease in power differentials – a strong hierarchy will, whether deliberately or not, limit information flow, connectivity and the expression of difference in the system, and thereby stifle change.

Storytelling provides pragmatic ways of addressing all five conditions (within certain limits outlined below) because of its ability to take people to a common level of experience and/or imagination, to articulate dilemmas and to identify the actions that seem to offer the prospect of resolution. The potential importance of proximity to this 'tipping point' to the impact of OD interventions is a recurrent theme in this book which is discussed in more depth in the Conclusion.

Zimmerman *et al.* (2001) pick out the importance of paradox and attention to the shadow system in enabling change in health services. The shadow system is the network of informal relationships, gossip, hallway intelligence and interpretations that take place behind the 'legitimate' system and which inform people's mental models. Few methods embody and legitimise paradox and this shadow system more elegantly than narrative. Parables, fairy tales and folk tales can all help draw out significant paradoxes (what distinguishes a paradox, after all, is that the problem that it encompasses can be recognised but not readily resolved). The OD practitioner can hardly fail to pick up information on the shadow system if he or she simply pays attention to members' stories. Adding skilled storytelling or emergent narrative techniques to this attention can exercise considerable leverage for change.

Currently, knowledge management as a term is less well known in the NHS than in the private sector, and has until recently been more associated with innovation in information technology. The recognition that knowledge is not a 'thing' but a process, contingent and open to multiple interpretations, has recently widened the knowledge management debate in health settings (*see* Chapter 12). Storytelling, and particularly storyboarding (*see* below), have played a major part in developing the non-IT elements of knowledge generation, management and dissemination outside healthcare and deserves even more of a role within it.

Consistent with the argument of Black (1979) concerning metaphors, one of the most fundamental features of storytelling, in all its forms, is the ability to separate what David Bohm (1996), the eminent quantum physicist, called 'presented' and 'represented' reality, and thereby to reframe information to generate new patterns of meaning and understanding. 'Presented' reality is viewed by Bohm as the classical Newtonian physical universe comprised of 'objects' or 'things' that are observable through the five senses, and about which there is common consensus, for example the price of a loaf of bread or how many part-time workers there are in the organisation. In contrast, 'represented reality' then ascribes meanings to presented reality, for example 'that supermarket charges too much for its bread' or 'part-time workers tend to be women'. These realities are not 'in' the data itself, but are interpretations of what the data means, and thus open to alternative readings. This feature of storytelling links the ideas in this chapter closely to those of the death of the meta-narrative in post-modernism (*see* Introduction and Chapter 8).

Problems arise when these two discrete orders of 'reality' – 'presented' and 'represented' – are conflated and packaged as one irreducible whole. One common example is the assertion, familiar to most managers, that any change requires more time/more resources/more staff without which it simply cannot be achieved. The possibility that some changes in practice might contribute to more than one goal, may be simpler, could preclude other costly processes, or whatever, is inadmissable within the terms of this construct. Instead of getting involved in such linguistic wrangles, storytelling activity can take a tangential approach to distinguishing presented and represented 'realities', and reassemble them into more useful constructs.

In his discussion of ways of speeding the diffusion of evidence-based innovation in healthcare, Plsek (2003) proposes three aspects to consider:

- creative generation of ideas
- implementation of the innovation into routine work
- widespread adoption across organisations.

These aspects interact with one another and at any one time all will be in operation in any given organisation in relation to different innovations. Storytelling and narrative approaches can support all three: generating creative thinking; supporting implementation by surfacing values and purpose; and supplying persuasive methods to boost adoption. Relating storytelling to the work of Plsek also serves to connect the arguments of this chapter with those of Chapter 5.

Hearts and minds – emotional intelligence

It is common to hear NHS managers and clinicians talking about engaging hearts and minds in the process of change, but, in practice, understanding of how to do it can be patchy. The burgeoning work on emotional intelligence (EI) has legitimised emotion as being not only central to management and leadership, but also as conducive to better-quality decision making in ambiguous or open-ended situations. Storytelling is a natural EI method and helps bring change alive in organisations.

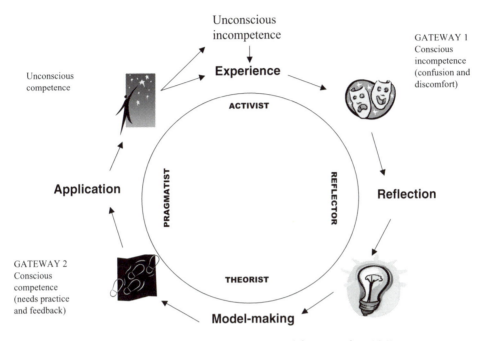

Figure 12.1   Emotional gateways to change (adapted from Birch, 1994).

Figure 12.1 Commentary

This model, from Birch (1994), locates two critical emotional gateways to change on the learning cycle.

It is not uncommon for change initiatives to start with stakeholder meetings at which explanations about the need for change and the direction it should take are made. This approach is made usually at a rational and logical level. At this stage managers have sometimes reported surprise that little discussion was offered and few objections raised. Unless the manager then builds in some experience which involves participants' feelings, this superficial agreement will disintegrate at the first hurdle. The group needs to be moved from their current state of blissful ignorance, or 'unconscious incompetence' into the first emotional gateway to change. This gateway is 'conscious incompetence', which occurs after experience and before internal reflection. It is the point at which an individual suddenly realises that this change is much harder than they thought.

This is a necessary but uncomfortable stage to negotiate, and the manager can expect that all kinds of objections and deflections will be raised at this point, most of which will be unconscious. There are likely to be questions about the need for change, the appropriateness of the methodology proposed, the involvement of particular individuals or groups, and other signs of resistance, covert or overt. It is the role of the manager at this stage to not allow themselves to be distracted but to hold the group and move it toward reflection, after which many of the objections will have dissipated and the others can be addressed more cleanly.

Many methods can be used to move a group into conscious incompetence, and storytelling is one of the most swift and powerful. A story from a patient or service user, the experience of a staff member who has recently received services, an account of what surprised, shocked or heartened a staff member who undertook some research, or an honest account from a senior member of staff about some of the dilemmas they have wrestled with, are all useful.

The second gateway lies between theory and application, at the point where 'conscious competence' is beginning to emerge. At this stage, individuals and groups need practice and feedback to move towards facility in the new capabilities and skills. They can 'do' the change, but not yet do it automatically. Building in practice, determining pilots and establishing feedback loops are the appropriate methodologies at this stage.

Definitions of emotional intelligence (EI) have proliferated over the past few years, but the simplest is probably the most useful in the storytelling context. EI comprises self-awareness and awareness of others in relation to recognising, identifying and acknowledging feelings, and the ability to manage and regulate one's own and others' emotions. Improving the quality of relationships between people will also improve the quality of information feeding decision making, as defensiveness and lack of exploration are replaced with increased openness.

Individuals also carry around numerous clusters of experience that intimately link particular states of thinking, feeling and physiology, and which have profound effects on their resourcefulness in any given situation. For example, think about something that you absolutely hate doing. Notice the thoughts, images, sensations, emotions and especially physiology that are associated with it. Now think about something you love doing, and do the same. We carry these clusters – 'states' – around with us at a less-than-conscious level and, therefore, they are not usually so available for and amenable to change, though they have a considerable impact on what we pay attention to and thus the quality of our decision making. Storytelling is often used to prompt a shift in such states, and to draw attention to that possibility. The ability to consciously change 'state' dramatically extends an individual's emotional and behavioural repertoire, widening the range of options available in any given situation (*see* Chapter 3 for more on repertoire).

Meaning, purpose, values and identity – leadership and spiritual intelligence

As awareness of emotional literacy in organisations increases, some further distinctions are surfacing. Leadership development, particularly for clinicians, is increasingly addressing issues of personal awareness and integrity, authenticity and consistency with espoused values. Putative leaders are being invited to consider their sense of meaning and purpose at work and to engage themselves in 'being' leaders as well as 'doing' leadership. Stories allow access to these more private levels without necessarily requiring open discussion or exposure. Through stories we can have conversations with ourselves and start to attend to our deeper sense of purpose. Why work in health services? What is important about it? What greater whole are we contributing to?

It is in this area of spiritual intelligence or, to take a different perspective on the same subject, what Senge and his colleagues (1996) call 'personal mastery' (pp.226–7) that storytelling has a particular contribution to make. It provides, for example, a process that can articulate the difference between a 'reactive' (things happen to me and I respond) and 'creative' (I can create and influence my future) orientation to the world. Stories provide a built-in facility for reframing. At the simplest level, one can associate with any of the protagonists in the story, or one can perceptually position oneself as the narrator with various degrees of omnipotence over the progression of the narrative.

Some learning disciplines practitioners, as well as other leadership commentators like Covey (1992), also identify a third orientation: 'interdependence' (I am intimately connected with the world, I express my own meanings and am expressive of the meanings of the greater whole). To use the perceptual positions analogy again, a 'creative approach' storyteller would attend to much more than just an individual protagonist, and might even position him/herself as all-seeing. In contrast, an 'inter-dependent approach' storyteller would assume multiple personas with varying degrees of insight. In this latter scenario, the story would be imbued with a sense of the interconnected nature of all the elements in it, but never claim to know the whole story. This ability to refer to something more, ineffable and necessarily approached at a tangent, is one of the unique contributions of storytelling and narrative to deeper OD processes.

Brain power – cognitive approaches

'As hypnosis and brain probes show, it's your subliminal mind that remembers the names of your first-grade classmates; remembers what the surgical team said when you were out cold on the operating table, and knows how many red lights you stopped for en route to the office'(Ostrander and Schroeder, 1994, p.44). There is much physiological and cognitive evidence to demonstrate that we are consciously aware of only a tiny fraction of the processing that is going on second by second in our brains. Change methodologies that engage both right and left brain simultaneously, rather than simply the logical and rational left brain functions, as narrative can, will have far greater impact on the individual.

Neuro-linguistic processing (NLP) is one cognitive approach which is gaining increasing interest in health and social care communities. Put simply, NLP is a study of the structure of communication; both how we communicate with others and, perhaps more importantly, how we communicate with ourselves. It recognises the influence of the images, internal conversations and feelings, both emotional and physiological, that we carry around with us day to day. It provides a way of examining ways of communicating and 'rewriting the software' so as to create, for example, a more resourceful state, a more committed vision or a more confident demeanour (*see* Box 12.1 for an example).

Box 12.1: Planning from the future backward

Time travel

A manager on a leadership programme was confronting his own cynicism about completing what he felt was 'yet another change to patient services'. The change was, overall, something he believed in, and long term he could see many positive results. In the short term, however, he found himself unable to 'see the next steps I need to take'. As he described this myopia, his face became pinched, his voice strangled and harsh, his breathing high in his chest and his neck and shoulders tight. 'Imagine you could lay out the past and future in a line on the desk, with the past to one side and the future to the other,' I suggested, placing myself alongside him and starting to get into rapport by matching his breathing rhythm. His eyes traced the line and he nodded. 'I can see the whole line clearly except the bit just after today – there's a gap and the line comes back fuzzy for a while,' he described. I asked him to go to the point on the line in the future where he had achieved all his aspirations for this project, ensuring that I talked in the past tense, presupposing that he would achieve them. He responded, 'In about a year I will have achieved the outcomes I need; it will take about another year to achieve all I want.' I asked him to go to the two-years-ahead point and in his imagination describe what he could see, hear and feel around him now that his project had really come to fruition. Then I asked him to look back down the timeline toward that day two years ago, and tell me the story of how got from there to here, which he did, with a surprised look and an increasingly relaxed and confident demeanour. He was particularly pleased to have recognised some individual relationships that would prove critical to the project, which he had not anticipated when he tried to plan from the present forward. 'The line is strong now, with just some fuzzy bits at the margins,' he said 'and I think they are becoming clearer too.'

Draws on Hall and Belnap, 1999; Cooper and Sawaf, 1997.

Cognitive approaches, such as NLP, mobilise storytelling and narrative processes to engage both sides of the brain, and also to engage both conscious 'online' resources and the much swifter and more creative unconscious 'offline' resources. Given the vast amount of information that comes in to each of us every moment through our senses, our brains have to prioritise and filter what our conscious mind attends to. An illustration of this is the 'Volkswagen syndrome'. You want to buy a car and you know more or less what kind it will be, but you have not yet made the final decision. Suddenly, you notice that the world is full of that make of car. Narrative and storytelling offer compelling ways to 'change the filter'. In times of organisational change, managers and clinicians will often hear (or indeed utter) the phrase: 'I'll believe it when I see it.' The growing evidence from neurophysiology and allied fields is that the converse is the case: 'I'll see it when I believe it'.

The backward storytelling technique outlined in Box 12.1 derives from NLP and EI and is a graphic way of loosening up individual cognitive clusters of mind–body–feeling in order to reassemble them into a more resourceful state. Linked with the developments in cognition and mind–body–feeling clusters, the field of education has demonstrated some promising results using kinasthesiology. Techniques like Brain Gym, which is a coordinated set of body movements, or 'micro-interventions', designed to stimulate and integrate the brain–body connection, are yielding positive effects on the learning capabilities of children, including those with particular disabilities; 'Brain Gym appears to contribute the minor adjustments necessary to enable the (individual's) system to proceed with the learning process' (Hannaford, 1995, p.110). In the future, it is quite possible that leadership development and OD practitioners will start to capitalise on these innovations.

Reaching the parts – features, types, tools and techniques

Fundamental features and assumptions

Compelling stories and narratives have some common features:

- they engage participants at a personal level
- they involve multiple viewpoints
- they have layers of meaning
- they are inherently anti-hierarchical
- they have a natural momentum that moves through problems towards resolutions.

The use of narrative and storytelling for OD purposes tends to have some underlying assumptions. In my experience, it is difficult for practitioners to use this approach effectively if they do not subscribe, at the level of their beliefs and values, to the following (or similar) assumptions.

- *If perception changes, 'reality' changes.* Much of the power of storytelling derives from reframing current perceptions of 'reality' by bringing in new information, widening perspectives or changing points of view, often through the use of metaphor or simile, as discussed above.
- *Organisations tend to be 'weighted' in favour of overly rational, logical, structured and unemotional discourses and modes of operation.* They have a prejudice towards action, and favour closing down exploration of issues rather than opening them up. Clearly, the pressures on health managers and clinicians make this weighting perfectly understandable, but it does not always serve such management well, particularly when commitment, rather than compliance, to a particular process or course of action is required.
- *It is more practical to focus on 'health' than on 'pathology'.* Impediments to change have meaning beyond their superficial presentation. Blocks which abide in an organisation are more usefully read as inherent in the system, supported by as yet unseen forces, than ascribed to generic or non-specific resistance. The difficulties

of involving doctors in management, for example, was for many years attributed (in managers' private conversations) to professional perversity and recalcitrance rather than being seen as an issue of organisational dynamics. Narrative and storytelling for organisational change puts most impetus into a positive trajectory. This is absolutely not to say that exploration of perceived problems is forbidden, nor does it argue for spin or whitewashing. It simply recognises the point, discussed above, that 'where attention goes, energy flows'.

- *Good quality storytelling is a two-way process.* The storyteller expects to learn as much as the audience. A story has life through the engagement of participants' minds, feelings and spirit. It changes with each group. The story is the medium through which connection is established, not an end in itself.

What is it? – forms of storytelling

There is a huge range of narrative and storytelling activity currently being practised in organisations, whether with a focus on OD or allied work such as leadership development. Storytelling necessarily operates at the level of the individual. A person has to engage with the material that emerges or is presented and each person will filter that material in different ways. How then can it be used with groups to support OD processes?

All storytelling and narrative is a way of accounting for perception and experience. It typically ascribes meaning, often suggests causality and sometimes aspires to prediction. Each account may involve: an interpretation, or reinterpretation, of the past; a description of the here and now; and/or a projection into an imagined future. Different practitioners use terms differently, but most current activity could be broadly divided into three forms, which might be called 'storytelling', 'storyboarding' and 'emergent narrative'. Some typical broad-brush differences are outlined in Table 12.1.

Both storytelling and storyboarding use tales to illuminate a specific issue or argue a particular case. In this form, they are closest to classical rhetoric in that their material is predetermined and largely controlled by the teller and their intention is, to a greater or lesser degree, inclusive and instructive.

Emergent narrative is a much more iterative process, essentially a conversation that pays equal attention to formal and informal and rational and emotional aspects of organisational life. The intention for this type of activity is usually more evolutionary, with perhaps an agreed starting point or topic of discussion, and a statement of the context in which the conversation takes place, from which the group develops a collective viewpoint and sense of the next steps.

The distinction between these three types of activity is, in practice, often less than Table 12.1 might suggest; nor are the different forms mutually exclusive. For example, a structured storytelling session should sow the seeds for further emergent narrative in which the initial themes are revisited and reworked toward deeper understanding and the emergence of direction.

Table 12.1 Storytelling, storyboarding and emergent narrative

	Storytelling	Storyboarding	Emergent narrative
Roots of material	Oral tradition, myth and therapy	Organisational change, specifically knowledge management, and film	Everyday conversation, organisational change and adult learning
Source of material	Pre-existing story, adapted for specific purpose. Adds richness through resonance of its antecedents	Story created specifically for purpose, usually located in workplace. Adds richness through specificity of detail	Conversation in the moment. Adds richness through active co-creation of meaning
Used for	Issues needing more wholehearted involvement, e.g. collaboration with service users	Issues needing action in a particular direction	Issues needing exploration and clarification
Outcome in mind	General outcome in mind, usually related to engaging participants' feelings and values rather than task	General outcome or direction in mind, precise steps typically filled in response to storyboard	No specified outcome – emerges naturally from conversation and dialogue
Style	Inclusive Reflective	Didactic (albeit inclusive) Reflective	Reflective Questioning Challenging
Active role	Designated individual(s)	Designated individual(s)	All present
Practitioner capabilities	Performative	Performative	Authoritative, but less need for performance
Position in OD sequence	• Early, to generate need for change • Intermittently, to create and align vision for future • Late, to promote and disseminate good practice and help generate new local interpretations	• Early, to generate need for change • Intermittently, to create and align vision for future • Late, to promote and disseminate good practice and help generate new local interpretations	• Throughout, combined with more structured storytelling or storyboarding, or alone • Early, to explore organisational constructs and habits

How to do it?

Using storytelling activity, as with any other OD process, requires certain preliminary steps. These can be summarised as follows.

- *Get the executive board actively engaged.* As with any OD process, ownership at a senior level is a crucial prerequisite.
- *Review other OD processes and practices currently in operation.* They may reveal useful information and connection points and guide decision making on the appropriate timing and choice of techniques.
- *Develop a collective point of view on the issue at hand.* Whatever the issue, for example person-centred planning or workforce development, think deeply about what it is that needs to be achieved and the processes that best suit that purpose.
- *Consider all the available alternatives.* Narrative approaches can complement and supplement other OD activities, but are not a substitute for them. Be clear about why this approach is better than alternatives in this particular context.
- *Establish a clear contract.* This should make explicit: the style and approach to be used; what the commissioner of the OD and/or the board can expect to see (and not see); how progress will be assessed (using both qualitative and quantitative measures); and the criteria for involving key individuals. Storytelling activity arguably carries higher risk of perceived lack of impact for its practitioners than some more obviously structured OD approaches as its effects can be less obvious (but more lasting) than other approaches. It is important to make the contract as explicit as possible both to sustain support and to preclude reactive interventions on the part of senior management.

Storytelling

Storytelling uses existing stories, carefully chosen and shaped to match their context. Fairy tales, stories from well-known novels and tales from mythology are all fruitful sources. Storytelling is most useful as a way of engaging resources that people often leave at home, for example their more private feelings and deeper senses of direction, meaning and purpose. Involving service users in the planning and delivery of services is a prime example. It requires a long haul, is emotionally as well as intellectually demanding for all involved and it is counter-cultural; change agents need to be in touch with their values to sustain them through the process.

Mellon (1992) and Lawley and Tompkins (2000) make some further recommendations.

- *Choose a story with resonance.* Storytelling is an ancient art and needs a worthy story with which listeners can engage intellectually, emotionally and even spiritually. Stories about cartoon characters, for example, do not carry the necessary weight.
- *Consider the characteristics of the rich, well-formed story.* Ensure that at least some of these are included:
  - beginning and ending

    – movement and a sense of direction
    – imaginative landscapes within which the story is played out
    – journeying through the elements
    – seasons and moods
    – struggle and transformation
    – paradox
    – characters – good and bad, tricksters and guides, mothers and fathers, companions (animal, human or celestial), mythical creatures, personifications (trees, rocks, etc.)
    – themes of power and of protection.

- *Choose the storyteller with care.* The storyteller may or may not be known to the audience, but either way they need authority, presence and the ability to perform. They need to be able to tell the story in such a way that it continually opens up possibilities of interpretation.
- *Use both familiar and unfamiliar language.* Align with the audience by incorporating familiar language, disrupt habitual thought patterns by using unusual, ambiguous, paradoxical or elliptical language, e.g. 'long, long time ago, quite recently, in a nearby distant land …'.
- *Perform the story.* Make eye contact. Use voice and body as well as words. The larger the audience, the 'bigger' the performance needs to be. Walk about so that people are literally hearing the story from different directions.
- *Be authentic.* If we are asking people to step out of their comfortable habits we must be prepared to reciprocate. Archness, irony or other protective carapaces on the part of the storyteller undermine this. The storyteller must be prepared to risk too.

Box 12.2: Storytelling

The ugly duckling

At one of a series of mental health practice development stakeholder conferences around the UK, one project coordinator eschewed the more usual presentation and chose instead to tell the familiar story of the ugly duckling. The conference was made up of service users, carers, acute ward staff, team leaders, practice development staff, clinicians and senior trust managers. When she had finished the story, the coordinator talked briefly about some of the story's meanings to her in relation to the provision of acute mental health services. There were a small number of raised eyebrows and indulgent smiles, particularly among the senior clinicians and managers, but the majority of the audience reacted positively with much of the anxiety and tension in the air palpably diminishing. The intention was that further stories and anecdotes would emerge in the small group discussions that followed. The job of the ugly duckling story was to set the tone and it did so by enabling the small group conversations to be less defensive and more attentive to one another's views and the emergence of some common themes and some areas of difference. It was a good start to a tricky change process.

At a subsequent stakeholder meeting in another location, I used the same story with some deliberate differences. I wanted to further shape the story so that it caught the imaginations of both users and frontline staff in particular. Our experience on this national project had shown that these two groups often had long and difficult histories. It was a delicate balance because a 'black and white' version of the story could potentially trigger greater defensiveness, with both service users and frontline staff competing over who was the hardest done by.

Estes's interpretation of the classic ugly duckling tale seemed to highlight the themes pertinent to this audience so it was a version of her story that I used. Her tale highlights the mother duck's inability to support her odd offspring against the other mothers. Under their sustained pressure, she finally rejects her child. Prematurely sent out into the world, he continues to search for a place where he can belong. For a while he manages well with some farmyard hens, but he keeps jumping into the pond and this they find very disturbing. The duckling struggles against his nature daily in order to buy acceptance into hen society and each day feels more and more at odds with himself. At last, a wise old fox reframes the problem for him. 'How would they understand? They are chickens – they can't swim …'. The duckling moves on and eventually achieves his transformation into a swan.

Themes of inclusion and exclusion, exile and homecoming, were at play throughout the story that was retold. I offered no explanation or personal interpretation at the end. Once again, the audience reaction was generally positive, and this time as well as a reduction in tension, there was an increase in emotional engagement, evidenced by a few tears, many smiles and nods, and several individual comments as the meeting moved into small discussion groups. There were also, as before, small signs of discomfort, especially among some of the senior staff, though this time eyes were turned downwards and shoulders stiffened. The amused and slightly patronising detachment had gone. It seemed that everyone had an emotional reaction, whether to the story itself or to others' responses to the story.

Draws on Estes, 1992.

Storyboarding

The most typical form of storyboarding is to make up an entirely new story that is rooted in the history, context and everyday life of the particular organisation, and which addresses the challenge of 'what to do' about something. This form of story-telling is currently less practised in the public sector than in the private sector, and less practised in the UK than in the USA. Denning (2001) describes how he crafts tales which embody some of the typical work predicaments of his audience. In describing the origins of this approach, he relates how he had been put in charge of a strategic knowledge management initiative at the World Bank and had exhausted the more usual methods of communicating the need for different responses to changing circumstances. After much thought, he changed tack and took a real incident in which a worker in Zambia had asked for a specific piece of information and had received his answer too late because of the convoluted journey that the request had had to make to reach the right recipient. His created story focused on what might have happened if the organisation's knowledge management processes were swifter, simpler and more efficient, as if it had already happened. He was greatly surprised and heartened by the enthusiastic response the story generated, the direction it indicated and the innovation that sprang from the meeting, which gained swift and positive results.

Denning (2001) and Ready (2002) make several recommendations for those adopting a storyboarding approach to change in organisations.

- *Get the right people to deliver the storyboarding programme.* Storyboarding practitioners need to have respect in the organisation and be recognised as having negotiated some difficult change processes already. Do not assume that every senior manager has these attributes or the necessary enthusiasm and skill to carry the process. One potent variant of this approach is to collaborate with a service user or patient to tell their story. Service user involvement and/or process mapping methodologies (*see* Chapter 5) are well suited to storyboarding. This may take the form of a direct story, a guided interview or a question and answer session, planned in close collaboration with the service user(s) and preferably rehearsed.
- *Devote time and energy to shape the stories.* An effective story will:
  - be rooted in the real life of the organisation, but sufficiently general that everyone can relate to it
  - explore the genuine dilemmas, predicaments and tensions involved in the chosen issue. A story without real tension is only a crude exhortation and may backfire
  - encourage participants to actively identify with the main protagonist and make that person an 'everyman' typical of the part of the organisation concerned
  - embody the change message, but implicitly rather than explicitly. Participants will bring their own uncertainties and scepticism to the story. Keeping the change message implicit requires them to discover their own meaning and thereby increases the likelihood of commitment to any actions that arise
  - with all other considerations being equal, use 'true' material rather than invented. A true story is better than an apocryphal or inspirational one in storyboarding.
- *Perform the story.* As with storytelling, this approach needs a real performance. Unlike the storytelling outlined above, many practitioners use visual aids to illustrate the tale.
- *Rehearse and test.* Shaping a story that achieves its purpose while meeting all the conditions set out above is neither simple nor quick. Rehearsal out loud and testing with different audiences is recommended, particularly where organisational roll-out is planned.

Emergent narrative

Emergent narrative springs from a different source than stories and is in keeping with our developing understanding of change in complex adaptive systems. No pre-created story is used; instead, practitioners elicit information and participate in the co-creation of a narrative or several parallel narratives. A variety of different methodologies are used to generate information during the narrative process, from reflective conversation located very much in the here and now to semi-structured discussion on a particular issue. The emergent narrative approach is deceptively simple and therefore easy to underestimate, both in its power to bring about change and in the skill necessary of the practitioner. As it is so dependent on the individual practitioner, it is also harder to make recommendations about how to do it. However, some basic suggestions might include the following.

- *Describe the context for the conversation.* Orientate people without prescribing how that context is understood.
- *Listen.* In particular listen for information about:
  - the formal and informal systems, the way things are supposed to be done and are really done
  - recurring metaphors, similes and symbols
  - key characters, whether their influence is perceived as useful or otherwise
  - nuances, gaps, trends and patterns.
- *Attend to practitioner's own thoughts, feelings and physiology.* Use them as a tool to help create sense and meaning from the conversation. There are differences in the degree to which practitioners from different narrative 'schools' reveal their own responses. Shaw (2002), for example, is an OD practitioner who works in the context of complexity and uses her own reactions as material for further exploration. She describes her 'sinking feeling' when she is invited to join a group of OD consultants mapping out a major change project in a multinational. Already there is a project plan and formal meetings and roles allocated to key individuals in the hierarchy. She believes this will arrest, not facilitate, the movement the organisation claims it wants. After some reflection, she chooses to share this feeling with the senior managers who invited her in, which eventually results in the whole process being changed to a much more emergent approach. In contrast, practitioners working more in the context of emotional intelligence (*see* Box 12.3) often use their own reactions as information but refrain from imposing them on the group with whom they are working. The difference in approach may also be in part attributable to different stages in the OD process; the former describing the contracting process itself, with the latter occurring in a particular phase of a larger OD initiative.
- *Work to keep options and possibilities open as long as possible.* Resist the organisational bias towards closure and do not accept barriers or limits without scrutiny.
- *Work with whoever turns up.* Do not collude with the notion that some people are more important than others. Change can come from anywhere in the system at any time. Those who turn up are best placed to do the work precisely because they are there and they will self-organise around what needs to happen next. Some

further action may need to be taken if there are glaring gaps, but it is normally preferable for this to be taken by group members rather than by OD practitioners.

- *Improvise.* Try to create the conditions that enable people to shed their normal habits at work and develop something different.
- *Connect.* Focus on connecting ideas, themes, visions, meanings and people. Utilise the informal system. Talk with people in corridors, common spaces, drop in to their workplaces, visit sites, call people who have been mentioned to you, and do so without needing any other reason than to connect.

Emergent narrative is a process that is difficult to describe briefly, partly because it eschews familiar structures and also because it is almost entirely responsive, with each situation requiring and creating a fresh combination of narrative and other techniques.

Box 12.3: Emergent narrative – creating conditions for cultural change

Culture and energy

The Education and Training Corporation (ETC) of a national island government embarked on a plan for radical structural and cultural change as a result of the need to become much more responsive to clients. My colleague was engaged to help with the cultural aspects of the change through a storytelling process – Lifeforce Energy Profiling – that we had researched and developed over some years in which we had postulated a link between perceived cultures and energy levels. It was this aspect that ETC was most interested in, recognising that low energy is a precursor to stress-related sickness and absence.

The process started with an organisation-wide briefing and the completion of an anonymised questionnaire which identified perceptions of both workplace culture and personal energy levels. One important feature of this information-collection stage was that the participants – from directors to cleaners – were all given time and space away from their workstation during their normal hours to complete the questionnaire. This made a significant break from previous practice and sent a powerful message to the whole organisation. Alongside the formal activity, an informal emergent narrative process started and this continued throughout, with much conversation about such subjects as 'how we do things around here', 'what people talk about over lunch', and 'how decisions are really made' being brought forward as legitimate cultural information rather than relegated to office gossip.

The questionnaire results were analysed and the results presented back at several debriefs across different departments. Again, alongside the formal presentation of data, the weaving of represented meanings and interpretations continued. Combining qualitative (conversation) and quantitative (statistical) information was persuasive, as it satisfied both thought and felt experience. In June 2001, the ETC's most significant cultural features were:

- highly 'political' system overall, with cliques seeming to dominate decision making

- in some parts of the organisation, a tendency toward coercing employees rather than developing and motivating them
- in other parts of the organisation, high levels of adaptability to the external environment.

Their energy deficits were:

- lack of reliable information. The 'political' aspects of the organisation were seen to limit and 'contaminate' the flow of information across the system
- similarly, the coercive aspects of the organisation had a negative impact on staff's feelings of control over their own jobs
- low mood among a significant proportion of the organisation was also a serious concern, as our research indicates that this is a predictor of stress-related sickness and absence.

The clear statistical correlations between their dominant cultures and their energy deficits then enabled the organisation to target leverage points for change, or, to put into the language of complexity theory, to identify the attractor patterns that would need disrupting in order to change current culture and energy patterns. For perhaps the first time people in this organisation were able to talk about a tremendously influential part of their working life that had been disavowed and even invisible. It was a huge relief. In addition, because their perceptions were presented in a rigorous statistical framework, the conversation was usefully depersonalised and enabled everyone to be involved in changing things. Further exploration of the differences between departments then started to move the conversation towards the future and how things might be different. Continuing conversations and meetings resulted in a number of action learning groups focusing on developing the business plan for next year as well as tackling the cultural and energy issues. These groups prioritised:

- improving relationships across the organisation, between management and staff and departments, thereby decreasing individual isolation
- improving the free flow of information and its quality, transparency and 'trustworthiness'.

(*See* Box 12.4 for a continuation of the story over the following year.)

Round pegs, square holes – limitations of the approach

As storytelling and narrative most commonly supplement broader OD approaches, the generic limitations apply here. Nonetheless there are some particular points to consider.

Organisational limitations

The timing of these approaches is important. Storytelling typically takes place at the start of a process to help explore and expand on the issue at hand or to get a project that has become too narrow to open up again. Generally, these approaches need to be combined with other methodologies to manage further action.

Storytelling and narrative are subtle and complex processes unsuited to spin or promotion. Real care must be taken to recognise the political context in which all health services operate without succumbing to any temptation to present one particular 'line'. This takes us back to the issue of whose interests OD projects serve that is introduced in Chapter 1.

Personal limitations

The repertoire and skill of the OD practitioner is central to success. Davidson *et al.* (2002) (and *see also* Chapter 3) in their reflections on a two-year leadership development programme involving health and social care managers identify a new model to underpin their work, which they name 'repertoire' leadership. Alongside intellectual and psychological dimensions, they highlight the performative dimension of leadership as emerging during the course of the programme. This dimension is particularly relevant for storytelling practitioners. It involves:

- *use of multiple aspects of the self.* The ability to 'step back' and choose how to behave next is key
- *emotional intelligence.* Recognising and managing one's own and other's feelings
- *physical enactment.* While storytelling is clearly about words, the other two elements of physical enactment, that is voice use and body language, are also critical to the mix. It is suggested that congruence between all three embody the physical characteristics that we read as honesty, integrity and authenticity, and these are crucial to the storytelling practitioner (*see* Figure 12.2 and note).
- *credibility.* The practice of all forms of storytelling in organisations is deceptively simple but profound. In the same way that other OD practitioners need the ability to 'hold' the organisation, so do storytellers. Storytelling and storyboarding, in particular, can be mistaken for 'touchy-feely' soft-mindedness and dismissed as irrelevant to the task at hand. Storytellers need to have considerable personal authority backed by senior management and a comprehensive contracting process, as discussed above.

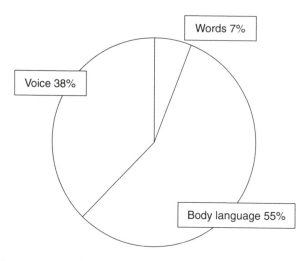

Figure 12.2   Congruence and trust.

This well-known model, used in the NHS Modernisation Agency's *Improvement Leaders' Guide to Managing the Human Dimensions of Change* (2000, p.28), argues that clear interpersonal communication requires congruence at three levels: what a person is saying, the quality of their voice and their body language. Since the human race developed language, we also developed the ability to say otherwise than what we mean or feel. However, we also 'leak' this difference through the elements of our communication over which we have less conscious control; our bodies and our voices. Our brains are hardwired to recognise incongruence, and when we identify it, we are programmed to favour the messages received from body language first (55% of the time), then those from voice (38%) and words last (7%).

Evaluation and research

Storytelling and narrative approaches typically contribute to and augment wider OD initiatives. Box 12.4 presents one example of the changes that this approach, in combination with more formal activity, has made to a public service organisation over one year. Having used storytelling and emergent narrative extensively, I have much anecdotal evidence, but there is little published evaluation evidence for storytelling alone. To paraphrase a PCT chief executive with whom I worked recently, 'The evidence just hasn't been collected yet'. Ironically, however, some of the most recent evaluations of these OD wider initiatives have been undertaken deploying analysis of organisational discourse (*see* the Conclusion of this volume).

Box 12.4: Emergent narrative evaluation measures

Does it work?

ETC, the organisation discussed in Box 12.3, continued to use emergent narrative within the Lifeforce process to develop the organisation from the first energy profile. As things progressed, action learning groups were set up and these reported back to the management committee. After a year in which emergent narrative continued alongside more structured processes and was sustained throughout the organisation, a repeat profile, again involving the whole organisation, was undertaken as one way of assessing the changes that had been achieved. By August 2002, ETC had:

- achieved a genuine consultation process on the business plan for the first time
- significantly changed management style and reduced the coercive features of the organisation's culture
- improved organisational flexibility and responsiveness
- increased the rational and analytical use of information and 'cleaned up' the flow of information across the organisation and beyond
- improved relationships and levels of support
- increased levels of control and autonomy over people's own jobs.

Using emergent narrative to assess what these results meant to the organisation and how they could build on the positive steps made, a number of the action learning group members asked to be trained as action learning advisors and coordinators, and they continue to act as a central resource for support and organisational change.

Conclusion

Complexity science, anthropology, social science, psychology, therapy, linguistics, oral history, theatre, dance, music, literature, organisational life as it is lived; storytelling and narrative are embedded in and integral to them all. The telling of stories is a fundamental and pervasive feature of human interaction whether in small groups or giant organisations. The approaches discussed in this chapter make conscious and considered use of this naturally occurring phenomenon, and thereby enable OD practitioners to tap into a rich mine of information, cultural commentary and motivation for improvement. They really do reach the parts that other methods cannot reach.

References

Birch K (1994) Emotional gateways in change. In: *Proceedings of Facilitation Skills Seminar*, spring, King's Fund, London.

Black M (1979) More about metaphor. In: A Ortony (ed.) *Metaphor and Thought*. Cornell University Press, New York.

Bohm D (1996) *On Dialogue*. Routledge, London.

Cooper R and Sawaf A (1997) *Executive EQ: emotional intelligence in leadership and organisations*. Grossett/Putnam, New York.

Covey S (1992) *Principle-centred Leadership.* Simon and Schuster, London.

Davidson D, Newbigging K and Peck E (2002) Leadership development: reflections and learning on a two-year programme. *The Mental Health Review.* 7(4): 10–14.

Denning S (2001) *The Springboard: how storytelling ignites action in knowledge-era organisations.* Butterworth-Heinemann, Oxford.

Estes C (1992) *Women Who Run With The Wolves.* Rider, London.

Grant D, Oswick C and Keeney T (1998) *Discourse and Organisation.* Sage, London.

Hall M and Belnap B (1999) *The Sourcebook of Magic.* Crown Publishing, Berkeley, CA.

Hannaford C (1995) *Smart Moves: why learning is not all in your head.* Great Ocean Publishers, Alexander, NC.

Lawley J and Tompkins P (2000) *Metaphors in Mind: transformation through symbolic modelling.* The Developing Company Press, London.

Mellon N (1992) *The Art of Storytelling.* Element Books Ltd, Shaftesbury, Dorest.

Morgan G (1986) *Images of Organisation.* Sage Publications, California.

NHS Modernisation Agency (2000) *Improvement Leaders' Guide to Managing the Human Dimensions of Change.* NHS Modernisation Agency, London.

Ostrander S and Schroeder L (1995) *Superlearning 2000.* Souvenir Press, London.

Peat FD (1996) *Blackfoot Physics.* Fourth Estate, London.

Plsek P (2003) Complexity and the adoption of innovation in health care. In: *Proceedings of the National Institute for Health Care Management Foundation and the National Committee for Quality Health Care.* 27–28 January, Washington, DC (available on the NHS Modernisation Agency website www.modernnhs.uk).

Pollio H, Smith M and Pollio M (1990) *Figurative Language and Cognitive Psychology, Language and Cognitive Processes.* 5(2): 141–67.

Ready DA (2002) How storytelling builds next-generation leaders. *MIT Sloan Management Review.* **Summer:** 63–9.

Senge P (ed.) (1996) *The Fifth Discipline Fieldbook: strategies and tools for building a learning organisation.* Nicholas Brealey Publishing, London.

Shaw P (2002) *Changing Conversations in Organisations: a complexity approach to change.* Routledge, London.

Stacey R (1996) *Complexity and Creativity in Organisations.* Berrett-Koehler Publications, San Francisco, CA.

Zimmerman B, Lindburg C and Plsek P (2001) *Edgeware: insights from complexity science for health care leaders.* VHA, Irving, TX.

Further reading

Dilts R (1996) *Visionary Leadership Skills*. Meta Publications, California.

James J (1996) *Thinking in the Future Tense – leadership skills for a new age*. Simon & Schuster, New York.

Kolb DG (2003) Seeking continuity amidst organisational change: a storytelling approach. *Journal of Management Inquiry*. **12**(2): 180–3.

Lucas B (2001) *Power Up Your Mind: learn faster, work smarter*. Nicholas Brealey Publishing, London.

Wilbur K (2001) *A Theory of Everything: an integral vision for business, politics, science and spirituality*. Gateway, Dublin.

Zohar D and Marshall I (2000) *SQ: spiritual intelligence, the ultimate intelligence*. Bloomsbury, London.

Websites

- www.accelerated-learning-uk.co.uk for learning-to-learn information.
- www.anglo-american.co.uk for books and videos on NLP, emotional intelligence and mind-body accelerated learning.
- www.braingym.com for information and resources on Brain Gym.
- www.cleanlanguage.co.uk for information on metaphor and symbolic modelling.
- www.itsnlp for NLP resources, courses and articles.
- www.seal.org.uk Society for Effective Affective Learning site.
- www.sourcelife.co.uk author's website, Source-people energy management.
- www.stevedenning.com for storyboarding and storytelling articles.

Part 3

Organisational Development in Healthcare: reflecting on aspirations

CHAPTER 13

A review of the evidence on organisational development in healthcare˙

Hugh McLeod

Introduction

Organisational development (OD) activity seeks to deliver desired change in performance, where performance is measured in terms of the outcomes of specific interventions, and enhanced capacity to successfully undertake future interventions; in the terms of Chapter 1 of this volume: a 'continually reflexive and learning organisation'. In order to achieve desired change, OD activities must create opportunities for stakeholders to renegotiate working practices and agree new organisational settlements (as argued in Chapter 2). The literature on the topic of change is substantial and many of the challenges associated with achieving change are not specific to healthcare services but are much more widely applicable (Pettigrew et al., 1992; Kotter, 1995; Berwick, 2003). In the context of OD in healthcare settings, several factors stand out from this literature.

First, the role of dominant professionals, and particularly doctors, is of key importance. In Mintzberg's (1979) words, professional bureaucracies, such as those providing healthcare, 'are not integrated entities. They are collections of individuals who join to draw on the common resources and support services but otherwise want to be left alone' (p.372). Professionals are characterised as having a high degree of autonomy and the ability to resist calls for greater integration. In this context, change is the product of 'successive negotiations [which] take place through a process of partisan mutual adjustment and as a plurality of interest groups operate in decision making areas' (Pettigrew et al., 1992, p.14). In developing this nuanced picture of professional collaboration within healthcare organisations, Denis et al. (1999) emphasised three features of collaboration: emergent operating units; differentiated professional influence; and diluted managerial control. Emergent operating units describe the distinctive forms of coordination among professionals that are associated with different categories of patient-group complexity. Whatever the source of complexity, medical control tends to dominate these operating units. In some cases this takes the form of a hierarchical model, while in others a key coordination mechanism is 'mutual adjustment among professionals' (Denis *et al.*, 1999, p.109). Informal ongoing interactions between professionals are influenced by a range of factors, including tacit rules, mutual trust and 'intrinsic power relationships and incentives', and together produce the stable 'negotiated order' of emergent operating units (Denis *et al.*, 1999, p.110). The operating unit 'is the key part of a professional organization because it is here that critical decisions about the content of work are made by professionals' (Denis *et al.*, 1999, p.109). They argue that these semi-autonomous operating units form the *de facto* elementary structures of healthcare organisations, which are dominated by doctors whose knowledge makes them the *de facto* team leaders. This concept has been developed under the 'microsystem' label and has emerged as a focus for clinical quality improvement work (Institute of Medicine, 2001; Nelson *et al.*, 2002). Returning to performance, the traditional autonomy over work practices exercised by senior clinicians has led to wide variations in medical practice; for example, the volume of healthcare provided that cannot be justified in terms of efficacy (Glover, 1938; Wennberg *et al.*, 1987).

Second, while the presence of operating units or microsystems makes this 'level' particularly important for OD activity, Ferlie and Shortell (2001) proposed that whatever type or mode of change is being attempted, it should be considered at four levels in order to maximise the probability of success: the individual; the group, team or microsystem; the overall organisation; and the 'larger system or environment in which the individual organizations are embedded' (p.283). Given the role of physicians as microsystem leaders, the effective engagement of individual physicians in OD activity is critical. Rogers' (1958, 1962) work on the diffusion of innovation among individuals, in which they are categorised in terms of their attitude towards change, has been widely cited in healthcare settings (Action On Orthopaedics and the Orthopaedic Services Collaborative, 2002; Mills *et al.*, 2003; Berwick, 2003). Berwick (2003), for example, suggests that physicians can be characterised in terms of Rogers' typology, in which 'innovators' are the 2.5% of the population who adopt a change more than two standard deviations faster than the mean. These innovators are followed by the 'early adopters' (13.5%), 'early majority' (34%), 'late majority' (34%) and 'laggards' (16%). The model is helpful in highlighting that individuals vary in their adversity to risk, but has been challenged by several commentators who often draw on the application of complexity theory to organisational behaviour (for example, Tsoukas, 1998) with its emphasis on non-linearity (*see* Chapter 8). Van de Ven and his colleagues (1999) argue for a non-linear conceptual framework for analysing the diffusion of innovation, and Mintzberg (1994) has drawn attention to the spread of innovation being distinctive between different organisational forms. In practice, the limited impact of attempts to introduce protocols and guidelines under the auspices of evidence-based medicine, for example, suggests that there is no inevitability about the diffusion of innovation in healthcare settings.

Third, OD activity has to contend with an 'eclectic mixture of instruments' (Ham, 1999, p.169) intended to drive performance, including a mix of central direction and local autonomy, use of both sanctions and incentives, and the deployment of competition and planning. In recent years, the NHS has been subject to relentless efforts on the part of policy makers to develop or refine levers for greater performance and OD activities have gained increasing prominence (as discussed in Chapter 1). Formed in 1998, the National Patients' Access Team (NPAT) adopted a programmatic approach to service development in the first wave of the National Booked Admissions Programme (NBAP) and phase I of the Cancer Services Collaborative (CSC). These first initiatives made 'a sufficiently strong impression on the Government' (Ham *et al.*, 2002, p.12) that 'redesign' was endorsed in *The NHS Plan* (Secretary of State for Health, 2000) and pursued as a priority through the creation of the NHS Modernisation Agency in 2001. By 2002, 'top-down' expectations had reached an unprecedented level; the Modernisation Agency's use of the breakthrough series collaborative model was seen as a key vehicle for introducing best practice via service redesign (NHS Modernisation Board, 2002, 2003). The wider context has also been turbulent. For example, the structural changes associated with the formation of primary care trusts and strategic health authorities were distracting, not least, in the latter case, for the hiatus it has brought to the rapid expansion of the NHS Modernisation Agency (Fillingham, 2004). The expansion in the use of national targets has also led to reflection on how to better manage their impact on frontline staff (Audit Commission, 2003).

Fourth, the available evidence of OD in healthcare is limited and often unsatisfactory (exemplified by the very short discussions of evaluation in many of the chapters in Part 2 of this volume). The literature on efforts to implement approaches to service development based on process-oriented quality improvement is dominated by practitioners' accounts of their own interventions which may overstate impact in the absence of a known denominator (Shortell *et al.*, 1998). The challenges to be overcome in evaluating quality improvement initiatives in healthcare settings are considerable (Øvretveit, 1997). Three issues are emphasised here:

- quantitative data on quality-related process or outcome measures are often not readily available and this often limits the potential for assessing outcomes
- it can be difficult to attribute changes in performance to the intervention in the commonly adopted before-and-after analysis of outcomes
- outcomes are rarely analysed for longer than the short term, which constrains assessment of the sustainability of interventions.

More generally, the use of particular approaches to service development has been fuelled by the potential for desired outcomes rather than by robust evidence of enhanced performance. Furthermore, just as the strength of research evidence in support of change in clinical practice is not a good predictor of its adoption (Fitzgerald *et al.*, 1999; *see also* Chapter 2 for a discussion of this study), the popularity of particular OD activities is not a good predictor of their impact on performance.

These factors seem to highlight the need for OD in healthcare to engage clinicians, and especially doctors, both as individuals and as *de facto* leaders of emergent operating units. Participants must also contend with policy makers' heightened expectations and enthusiasm for changing structures and incentives, which can inhibit OD activity. Moreover, the recent increase in emphasis on OD programmes in the NHS has led to the rapid growth of a support infrastructure which has yet to reach maturity.

This chapter provides a brief review of the evidence on outcomes relating to influential service improvement initiatives in healthcare and focuses on the breakthrough series (BTS) collaborative model which is currently the most widely adopted approach in the NHS. The BTS model is a key element of the NHS strategy to roll out service improvement activity (Secretary of State for Health, 2000). This model is the chosen focus, as other approaches to OD described in this book lack healthcare-related evidence of impact.

Service improvement

The need to achieve fundamental change in traditional working practices in order to secure higher-quality healthcare services is widely recognised (Secretary of State for Health, 2000; Institute of Medicine, 2001). What is less clear, despite considerable experience of piloting a range of models, is how to bring about the required change. The conceptual strength of viewing service (or quality) improvement in terms of processes has long formed the basis of continuous quality improvement (CQI) techniques, which have a considerable track record in industry (Deming, 1986). The relevance of focusing on processes in order to change healthcare services is also readily apparent (Berwick, 1991, 1996). However, the application of this insight to healthcare settings has not been straightforward and the evidence relating to the impact of this approach to quality improvement in healthcare settings is weak.

Since the mid-1980s, CQI techniques have increasingly been applied to healthcare processes. Early efforts were characterised by a desire to control costs and develop a stronger customer perspective through process improvements. There has also been experimentation with organisation-wide attempts to bring about process-oriented fundamental change through corporate-led initiatives based on incremental total quality management (TQM) and its conceptual antithesis, discontinuous business process re-engineering (BPR; *see* Chapter 9). These experiments have informed implementation of the BTS collaborative model. The concepts of CQI, BPR and the BTS collaborative model share a range of common process-oriented service improvement characteristics, which are shown in Box 13.1. These concepts are now summarised in turn, along with an account of the evidence relating to the outcomes of influential initiatives.

Box 13.1: Process-oriented service improvement characteristics common to CQI/TQM, BPR and the BTS collaborative model

- A focus on changing processes (across traditional disciplinary boundaries), rather than individuals' behaviour, as vehicle for improving quality
- Orientation towards the needs of the customers (both patients and internal)
- Recognition of the vital role of clinical and managerial organisational leaders to overcome bureaucratic inertia and provide vision

---

- Use of process mapping (flow chart or walk through) as a key diagnostic tool
- Use of quantitative analysis (of some form) to inform the change process
- Importance of a 'process owner' to manage change

Continuous quality improvement and total quality management

The 'general theses' of TQM described by Berwick *et al.* (1992) were succinctly summarised by Shortell *et al.* (1995) and are shown in Box 13.2. These principles are based on the techniques for improving the quality of industrial mass-production processes developed by Shewhart (1931, 1939) in the 1920s. Shewhart's ideas were exported to Japan by his disciple, Deming, in 1950 (Deming, 1986). Japan's postwar manufacturing strength has been widely attributed to its approach to CQI, as advocated by gurus including Juran (1964, 1988), Deming (1982, 1986), Crosby (1979) and Ishikawa (1985).

Box 13.2: The key principles of CQI/TQM

- The use of cross-functional employee teams
- An explicit focus on both internal and external customers
- A focus on underlying organisational processes and systems as causes of failure rather than blaming individuals
- Employee empowerment to identify problems and opportunities for improved care and to take the necessary action
- The use of structured problem-solving approaches based on statistical analysis

Adapted from Shortell *et al.*, 1995.

Despite limited research evidence (Singhal and Hayes, 1992), CQI/TQM won strong support from commerce (Robinson *et al.*, 1991) during the 1980s (Lawler *et al.*, 1992). The introduction of Griffiths' general management in the NHS in the mid-1980s (NHS Management Inquiry, 1983) 'led to an influx of managerial ideas from areas of industry where the TQM approach had already been adopted, and the pursuit of quality became an increasingly managerial preoccupation' (BRI Inquiry Secretariat, 1999, p.7).

The steps in the CQI process are generic, although the various proponents employ a range of notation (Langley *et al.*, 1996). The key common feature of these approaches is that they advocate the 'scientific method for process improvement ... [that is] state questions, make a plan, formulate hypotheses, gather data to test those hypotheses, draw conclusions, and test those conclusions' (Berwick *et al.*, 1990, p.47).

Blumenthal and Kilo (1998) could not 'identify a health care organization that has fundamentally improved its performance through CQI (or any other means). There simply are no organization-wide success stories out there – no shining castles on the hill to serve as inspirations for a struggling industry' (p.635). This finding underlines that the emphasis on TQM as 'an organization-wide approach and philosophy' (Øvretveit, 2000, p.76) poses a formidable, if not insurmountable, challenge to implementation in healthcare settings. Nevertheless, attempts to implement TQM provide insight into the issues facing many OD projects, as do CQI initiatives focused on single processes without organisation-wide participation. One of the first influential attempts to apply CQI techniques to healthcare processes was hosted by the Harvard Community Plan and is described next.

National Demonstration Project on QI in Health Care (1987–88)

Twenty-one healthcare organisations from across the USA teamed up with an equal number of industrial quality management experts over an eight month period in order to address the question: '*Can the tools of modern quality improvement, with which other industries have achieved breakthroughs in performance, help in health care as well?*' (Berwick *et al.*, 1990, p.xvi). Four projects dropped out and 'at least' 15 of the 21 projects were counted as 'successful' (Berwick *et al.*, 1990, p.144). Berwick *et al.* (1990, p.xix) stated that 'because these are real stories, there are no astounding results to report', but suggested that the 'new ways of thinking, new insights about work processes, new working relationships, and small, permanent breakthroughs in understanding' indicated considerable success. Despite the limitations in terms of the scope of the initiatives, their short duration and the partial reporting of outcomes, Berwick gained key insights into the challenges of applying CQI.

Organisational leadership was viewed as essential, the projects illustrated the use of Shewhart's control charts in aiding remedial action and the benefit of identifying a 'process owner' was highlighted. The emphasis afforded to process mapping (or 'flow charting' or 'walk throughs') by the NHS Modernisation Agency (NHS Modernisation Agency, 2002) is consistent with Berwick *et al.*'s comments on this diagnostic tool:

> discovery of a 'significant difference between how this process was working and how it was designed to work' is ... the almost universal discovery of process improvement teams who sit together to document, perhaps for the first time, how a 'familiar' work process is actually conducted (p.71) ... Having to commit one's understanding of the process to paper enables a group to discover those differing perceptions – often a crucial first step in solving the problem (p.104).

A key lesson for successful implementation of change was to '*provide enough time* ... In general, projects risk more by going too fast than by going too slowly' (Berwick *et al.*, 1990, p.111). This conclusion is noteworthy in the light of Berwick's subsequent emphasis on rapid change in short-term BTS collaboratives. The role of doctors was critical:

> Most projects had some doctors on their teams, but between the lines of their reports we read a slightly different story. It was difficult to involve physicians in quality improvement projects. Anecdotal reports allude to the underlying barriers: The physicians tended to be unavailable for work on teams, too busy to join in, and, perhaps, too sceptical about their possible helpfulness ... *barriers to physician involvement may turn out to be the most important single issue impeding the success of quality improvement in medical care* (Berwick *et al.*, 1990, p.151, emphasis added).

This need to overcome scepticism on the part of physicians about the relevance of CQI/TQM was strongly articulated by Blumenthal (1995), who noted that until a 'verbal bridge was built' between the language of TQM and the language of the physician, and 'until the applicability of TQM to physicians' work could be demonstrated, the possibility remained that physicians would continue to see the tenets of modern quality theory as fundamentally foreign' (p.xiii).

These quotations illustrate a key challenge that remains a decade later: the relevance of process-oriented service improvement activity has to be justified to physicians in order to win engagement. The tools and techniques have to be justified and physicians' recognition of the need for changing current practice cannot be assumed. The Northern New England Cardiovascular Disease Study Group (NNECDSG) illustrates the latter point, while also being one of the most influential examples of process-oriented service improvement initiatives recorded in the literature.

Northern New England Cardiovascular Disease Study Group (1987 to date)

Formed in 1987, the NNECDSG is a voluntary, clinician-led regional consortium which aims to improve the care of patients with cardiovascular disease. Initially, a three-year study of variability in mortality rates across the six participating organisations convinced the members of the study group that the 'observed differences in outcome were real and could not be attributed solely to differences in case mix. ... Juran refers to such a conclusion as a breakthrough in attitude, and notes that such breakthroughs are prerequisite for improvement' (Plsek, 1997, p.87).

In 1990, the NNECDSG set out to improve the hospital mortality rates associated with coronary artery bypass graft (CABG) surgery. All 23 cardiothoracic surgeons in the area participated in an initiative which comprised three elements: sharing analysis of routine data on surgical outcomes and complications at regular meetings; multidisciplinary team visits between the six sites in which each surgical team observed each other team undertaking CABG surgery; and training in CQI techniques followed by promising site-specific changes in processes being tested and implemented. O'Connor *et al.* (1996) record that:

> Surgeons reported numerous changes in surgical care that occurred as a consequence of the interventions. These changes in the provision of care were substantive and

were temporally associated with the reduction in the mortality rate. It was precisely the desired effect of the site visits and process analysis that new technology, new techniques, and new organizational approaches would be rapidly spread among and adopted by the centres (p.844).

Having spent three years studying mortality rates, the CQI activities took a further nine months. Subsequent analysis indicated that hospital mortality rates for CABG surgery fell by 24% (O'Connor *et al.*, 1996). During the 27 months post-intervention, the mortality rate for urgent or emergency patients was 25% lower than expected on the basis of the outcomes experienced during the three pre-intervention years (standardised mortality ratio of 0.75; 95% CIs 0.55 to 0.83; $p < 0.001$) (*see* Figure 13.1). The overall number of observed deaths was 234, 74 fewer than expected, a dramatic improvement. Malenka and O'Connor (1998, p.595) described these interventions as generating 'the "easy" improvement that comes from examining other systems of clinical care and then questioning your own system'. In 1995, the group initiated a further round of quality improvement work to identify the causes and correlates of postoperative mortality through study of the etiology of variability in outcomes.

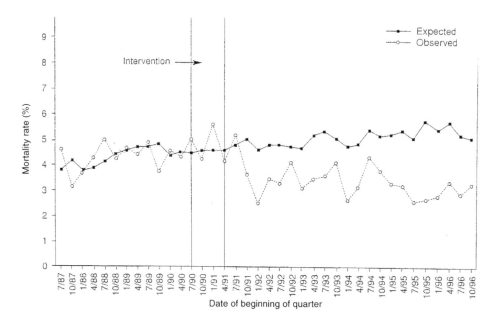

Source: Malenka and O'Connor, 1998, p.596.

Figure 13.1 NNECDSG: mortality for isolated CABG procedures (July 1987 to October 1996).

Total quality management

Many initiatives under the auspices of TQM have been conducted in healthcare settings. One of the most substantial was applied to the NHS in a three-year pilot programme initiated by the Department of Health in 1990 and independently evaluated (Joss, 1994; Joss and Kogan, 1995). The 19 hospitals became hospital trusts during the three-year initiative, 'which means, in effect, 19 different TQM initiatives' (Joss, 1994, p.4). The attempt to introduce TQM was a major undertaking, and it was estimated that 'the cost for an average multiple site acute unit could easily reach £350k–£500k per year for the first two to three years' (Joss, 1994, p.8).

Relying mainly on data drawn from interviews with participants, the evaluation was not able to quantify the extent of change that occurred. The evaluation found that the impact of TQM varied across the pilots and that only two sites made 'considerable progress' (Joss and Kogan, 1995, p.106). The reasons for the limited overall impact included a context in which major organisational change associated with the introduction of the internal market created an unstable environment for work on quality improvement. Having noted this generally unreceptive context, the particular success of one pilot was attributed to its response to a perceived threat from a local teaching hospital. More generally, projects were fragmented, and many relied on 'highly committed and competent' individuals for their design and implementation (Joss and Kogan, 1995, p.88).

Echoing Blumenthal (1995), the researchers noted that the application of TQM to the NHS had to make sense to staff, and they attributed its limited impact in part to the failure to involve doctors fully in its implementation. Two factors appeared to contribute to gaining the support of senior clinicians:

> The first was involvement in the pre-planning phase, including workshop-style strategic planning and training events. The second was the use of survey data from diagnostic and benchmarking results to make clinicians more aware of the expectations and requirements of key internal and external customers ... Our impression was that gathering and disseminating information about process variation increasingly intrigued doctors who were involved in collecting and analysing such data. Involving them in this way was an important precursor to getting them to change working practices (Joss, 1994, p.6).

The use of technical quality 'as a base from which to move forward on the other [systemic and generic] dimensions would have been an important political and pragmatic move' (Joss, 1994, pp.6–7). Instead the researchers noted:

> high quality staff, who were strongly committed to their own notions of quality, being subjected to what they saw, with some justification, as being patronizing and over-simplistic models of quality improvement – an approach which utterly failed to recognize their well-developed research backgrounds and technical competence (Joss, 1994, p.7).

US *studies of the impact of CQI on clinical practice*

Shortell *et al.* (1998) undertook a systematic review of the literature on the clinical application of CQI and identified 55 studies mainly from the USA, spanning a very wide range of initiatives from the NNECDSG to a BTS collaborative. The reviewers noted evidence of 'pockets of improvement' and emphasised the importance of there being a receptive context, sustained leadership, training and support, measurement and data systems, and protection from over burdensome regulation (Shortell *et al.*, 1998, p.609). Shortell *et al.* (1998, p.605) concluded that, for these reasons, 'CQI's major weakness, if you will, is that it is *very demanding* of individuals and organisations along multiple dimensions'. The extent to which the conceptual strengths of CQI are realised 'depends on the ability and willingness of individuals, groups, and organizations to implement them' (Shortell *et al.*, 1998, p.605).

Business process re-engineering in the NHS

Originating in the USA in the early 1990s, business process re-engineering is 'the fundamental rethinking and radical redesign of business processes to achieve dramatic improvements in critical contemporary measures of performance such as cost, quality, service and speed' (Hammer and Champy, 1995, p.32). This high-level generalisation offers little to distinguish BPR from TQM; both focus on processes, the needs of customers and aspire to organisation-wide impact. However, BPR rejected incremental change in favour of a 'top-down', 'all-or-nothing proposition' in which new processes are created from scratch within a short timescale in which discontinuous 'dramatic' change occurs. Furthermore, Hammer and Champy (1995) described implementation via an infrastructure of re-engineering teams and committees and strong leaders who can impose necessary cultural change. In addition to the core characteristics of process-oriented quality improvement noted in Box 13.1, the additional attributes of BPR are shown in Box 13.3.

Box 13.3: The key principles of BPR

- A top-down, all-or-nothing proposition for dramatic change in which new processes are created from scratch
- Organisation-wide transformation
- Implementation via infrastructure of re-engineering teams and committees (including outsiders providing radically disruptive element)
- A short timescale in which discontinuous dramatic change occurs
- Necessary cultural change which can be imposed by strong leaders

Adapted from Hammer and Champy, 1995.

Local interest in BPR led the NHS Executive to fund two acute hospital trusts, King's Healthcare and Leicester Royal Infirmary (LRI), in pilot projects which were subject to evaluation. A mixture of quantitative and qualitative methods was used in both evaluations. In both cases, there was some evidence of change resulting from re-engineering, although it fell short of the ambitious claims made at the outset (Packwood *et al.*, 1998; Bowns and McNulty, 1999; McNulty and Ferlie, 2002).

I want to focus here on the LRI, an organisation perceived to be performing relatively well that would be receptive to the application of re-engineering techniques. In seeking dramatic improvement in organisational performance within two years, the intention was to realise the classic BPR model (Hammer and Champy, 1995). Initial work focused on two core processes: outpatients and diagnostics. Following reported successes, attention turned to the core processes for 'emergency entry' and 'patient stay'. During the two years to July 1996, financial support from the NHS Executive was reported to total approximately £4 million (McNulty and Ferlie, 2002). These funds were reported to have been divided about equally between approximately 30 LRI staff and two firms of management consultants working in BPR 'laboratories'. By August 1995, concerns were increasingly being voiced about the integration and coherence of the plurality of projects underway, and the major differences in rate and pace of change across the different specialties that had become apparent. Slower-than-expected change led to open acknowledgement that implementation was lagging behind the vision. 'Management consultants expressed concern that senior managers within the hospital could not force medical consultants to accept change' (McNulty and Ferlie, 2002, p.127). One of the specialties given particular attention was Accident and Emergency (A&E) services, and this element of the BPR activity illustrates the conflict that emerged between the doctors and re-engineering personnel.

The objective of the A&E initiative was to reduce waiting times for the large majority of the patients attending with minor injuries, known as the 'walking wounded'. The project started in March 1995 and was to be achieved via two interventions. First, clinical triage protocols would allow a transfer of responsibility from doctors to nurses for ordering a limited range of x-rays and providing minor treatment for a proportion of patients. This change was piloted in July 1995. However, efforts to implement the role of triage nurses were hindered by a shortage of staff. It took more than two years from the start of the project to align nursing capacity with the periods of high demand. Second, the BPR project intended to introduce a single queue for all A&E patients. Historically, the walking wounded and trolley patients were managed in separate queues. The complexity of the latter cases varied considerably, and the trolley patients were viewed as being of higher priority than the walking wounded. The re-engineers suggested that staffing arrangements for the two queues were inflexible, and that a single queue would be more efficient. In November 1995, a single queue for all A&E patients was piloted for only a few hours before it was stopped. A doctor reported that 'all hell broke loose and waiting times quadrupled' (McNulty and Ferlie, 2002, p.156). The clinicians viewed the single-queue pilot as a disaster, the re-engineers later referred to it as a mistake, and it was not attempted again.

Quantitative analysis confirmed that the BPR project in the A&E department had no positive impact on waiting times. Several factors contributed to the failure of the A&E project. Critically, the focus on the high-volume walking wounded was contentious. Doctors viewed trolley cases as being more important than the walking wounded in terms of waiting time priority and their perception of the re-engineers' insistence on this being too difficult an issue to start with damaged the project's credibility. Managers and re-engineers characterised doctors' views as believing that the walking wounded 'can wait as long as they like'; this amounted to allowing the majority of patients to be considered as second-class citizens. This situation illustrates the potential for conflict associated with different definitions of quality. The failure to agree on the basic priorities for redesign probably lay at the heart of the ongoing antipathy relating to the perceptions of the doctors' resistance to change.

More tangible is the finding that the re-engineers eventually 'conceded earlier arguments put forward by A&E doctors that nursing resources in A&E were inadequate to fully operate systems of nurses ordering X-rays and administering minor treatments' (McNulty and Ferlie, 2002, p.166). Furthermore, the clinicians' reservations about the single-queue proposal were later borne out by Department of Health guidance promoting streaming of patients into two queues in order to reduce waiting times (Department of Health, 2001). Hence, the BPR's initiative in the A&E department was flawed in that it failed to propose meritorious interventions, secure a consensus for its objectives or assess the capacity requirements for the implemented working practices. If the re-engineers had taken a more astute stance, and built on the importance attached by clinicians to technical views of quality, as suggested by Joss and Kogan (1995), the initial enthusiasm expressed by doctors for process redesign might have been maintained.

National Patients' Access Team

The National Patients' Access Team (NPAT) was formed in 1998 to lead a series of programmes aimed at improving the patient's experience of healthcare services and the use of NHS capacity. In 1999, NPAT took on responsibility for the 'Action On' programme and led work on outpatient services, emergency services, the use of operating theatres, critical care and a number of other high-profile service areas (see Ham et al., 2002). NPAT started with a small team of staff with direct experience of participating in major NHS service improvement initiatives, who occupied a 'hybrid' position midway between NHS staff delivering services to patients and external consultants:

> NPAT made a conscious attempt to ensure that its approach combined evidence as well as experience. The 'reflective practitioners' (Schon, 1983) who made up NPAT's staff were in this sense going beyond previous change management programmes in health care in consciously seeking to make use of research in practice. The ... early work of NPAT in areas such as booked admissions, the cancer services collaborative, and outpatient services made a sufficiently strong impression on the government that the team's staff and resources grew rapidly to enable NPAT to take on the additional responsibilities directed its way (Ham et al., 2002, pp.11–12).

NPAT's first programmes were the National Booked Admissions Programme (NBAP) and the Cancer Services Collaborative (CSC), the first phases of which were subject to evaluation.

National Booked Admissions Programme (NBAP)

The first wave of the NBAP ran from October 1998 to March 2000. Twenty-four pilots were chosen to participate, not because they were representative of experience elsewhere in England, but because they had favourable circumstances which, when provided with considerable additional support and resources, were expected to demonstrate the benefits of booking. The evaluation's proxy measure of booking was the percentage of patients waiting with a booked or 'to come in' date at the quarter end. Between the quarters ending March 1999 and March 2000, this measure of booking increased from 51% to 73%, and then fell to 66% at the end of March 2001. Hence, progress had been made during the life of the programme, even though the objective of 100% booking had not been achieved. However, ground was lost during the year following the end of the first wave. This finding indicated that the sustainability of this major initiative was open to doubt. The key lessons from the evaluation were reported by Ham *et al.* (2003, pp.435–6) and include the following.

- The balance between a top-down and bottom-up approach is precarious. 'Change will continue to be made only in pockets of innovation unless a bottom-up commitment from the staff making the changes is combined with organizational and systemwide leadership.'
- 'Designing quality improvement programs that stimulate change at all four levels [individual, team, organization and the larger system] is much more demanding than change that is directed at clinical teams willing to embrace new practices.'
- 'Establishing long-term responsibility for quality programs at the outset is ... essential' as the time taken to establish new practices is often underestimated and 'the challenges of sustaining improvement were not always understood'.
- 'Staff affected by quality improvement programs must be able to see that they, as well as patients, will benefit from the changes.'
- 'The impact of redesign depends on the local context of the change and the way in which the mechanisms of change are used ... it remains an open question as to whether these challenges can be overcome.'

NPAT's approach to service improvement was strongly endorsed by *The NHS Plan* in July 2000 and resulted in the establishment of the NHS Modernisation Agency in April 2001. This entailed the wide-scale adoption of Berwick's BTS collaborative model. Before reviewing the CSC, and the other early NHS collaborative which was subject to an evaluation – the Orthopaedic Services Collaborative (OSC) – the BTS collaborative model is summarised next.

Breakthrough series (BTS) collaborative model

Berwick formed the Institute for Healthcare Improvement (IHI) in 1991, and in 1995, IHI launched the BTS collaborative model, which 'seeks to achieve unprecedented levels of improved performance in participating organisations in less than 1 year by bringing providers together to understand and drive improvement within a specific topic area' (Kilo, 1998, p.2). In addition to the core characteristics of process-oriented quality improvement (Box 13.1), the BTS collaborative model's key principles are shown in Box 13.4.

Box 13.4: The key principles of the BTS collaborative model

- A bottom-up approach in which activities are changed incrementally in order to create new processes which generate high-quality outcomes
- A focus on a carefully defined topic in which there is a clear gap between current practice and best practice
- Networking across organisations in order to shorten the time required for identifying aims, diagnoses and remedies
- A package of support to facilitate networking, CQI skills acquisition, topic-related evidence-base, and a structured implementation model
- A short timescale in which dramatic change occurs.

Adapted from Kilo, 1998.

Berwick adopted Nolan's 'model for improvement' (Langley *et al.*, 1996) as the key vehicle for implementing fundamental change (*see also* Chapter 5). Berwick (1996) described it as 'a simple and elegant model for achieving changes that are improvements' but acknowledged that its use has not been straightforward: 'These four simple steps – set aims, define measurements, find promising ideas for change, and test those ideas in real work settings – challenge the mettle of the best and push against many deeply held assumptions' (p.620). The BTS collaborative infrastructure is designed to accelerate improvement by supporting the basic CQI approach via:

> directly addressing the common organizational barriers to change ... Collaboration is a key element in the BTS work process. Sharing information shortens the discovery phase of improvement; rapid deployment of new learning accelerates the pace; working with peers is motivating and reduces scepticism; and shared deadlines help to maintain forward momentum even in the press of everyday events (Kilo *et al.*, 1998, p.10).

The number of collaboratives has grown rapidly and their use has spread from the USA to Australia, Canada, England, France, Norway, the Netherlands, Scotland, Sweden and Wales. While the collaboratives' ambition is readily apparent, assessment of their outcomes is less straightforward. There have been several review papers (Øvretveit, 2002; Øvretveit *et al.*, 2002; Wilson *et al.*, 2003), but the published literature on the outcomes of collaboratives is limited.

US collaboratives

At least 47 collaboratives were initiated in the USA between May 1995 and August 2003. Data on the collaborative-wide outcomes for 13 of these collaboratives have been published and are summarised in Table 13.1. The percentage of teams that were reported to have experienced 'breakthrough' change was reported for ten of these collaboratives (Table 13.1). In each case, the basis for defining 'breakthrough' change is noted and this level of performance was interpreted as requiring a desired change in numerical measures of between 20% and 40%. The percentage of teams that were reported to have experienced 'breakthrough' change varied from 14% (4/28) in the first collaborative to 58% (7/12) in a later collaborative. Participants' accounts of US collaboratives are careful to state that the initiatives suggest potential rather than wide-scale achievement (Rainey *et al.*, 1998), but this has not prevented this caveat being ignored by some proponents.

The US collaboratives encountered the typical barriers to engagement by clinicians. For example, in the first Caesareans collaborative, 'failure of intention' to change practice was overcome (in some cases) by 'direct, private, face-to-face meetings between a committed chief of service and each individual staff obstetrician', supported by sharing individual-level analysis of c-section rates (Flamm *et al.*, 1998, p.122). Similarly, in the first Diabetes collaborative, 'many physicians' were reported to feel that they provided high-quality care and saw 'no reason to engage in potentially disruptive system change' (Wagner *et al.*, 2001, p.73). In response, Wagner *et al.* (2001, p.73) noted that 'provider-specific performance data were often critical in convincing reluctant managers and physicians to engage in the process'. In each case, clinicians sought evidence of the need for change, and if they were not prepared to accept the BTS model's contention that 'if the outcome measure is properly selected, adequate baseline data can be collected in a few weeks', they would be branded failures:

> One of the most common causes of failure early in the process was an extended preoccupation with data collection, prompted by the traditional view that 'proof' of the extent of the problem was essential before an attempt could be made to change the process (second Adverse Drug Events collaborative; Leape *et al.*, 2000, p.329).

NHS collaboratives

The first two NHS collaboratives, the Cancer Services Collaborative (CSC) and the Orthopaedic Services Collaborative (OSC), began in the winter of 1999/2000. Both collaboratives were subject to evaluations. Phase I of the CSC included 51 projects across nine programmes and focused on five tumour groups: breast, lung, colorectal, prostate and ovarian (Robert *et al.*, 2003). A key outcome measure was waiting time to the start of the first definitive treatment and the evaluation sought to assess progress against this measure by comparing waiting times between the first quarters of 2000 and 2001. Data covering these periods were made available for only 27% (14/51) of projects. The analysis found that two prostate projects experienced

Table 13.1 US BTS collaborative outcomes summary

Topic	Study	% teams experienced breakthrough change	Definition of breakthrough
Caesarean sections I	Flamm *et al.* (1997)	14% (4/28)	Significant improvement in a major subsystem, e.g. ≥25% reduction in c-section rate or ≥40% increase in vaginal birth after caesarean[†]
Delays and waiting times I	Nolan *et al.* (1996)	48% (13/27)	≥40% reduction in delay for a major subsystem[†]
Asthma	Weiss *et al.* (1997)	58% (7/12)	Significant improvement in a major subsystem, e.g. ≥20% increase in patients receiving follow-up care in the clinic following emergency department treatment[†]
Adverse drug events I	Leape *et al.* (1998)	21% (9/43)	100% of stated goal for a major subsystem, e.g. ≥30% reduction in serious errors in ICU[†]
Adult intensive care	Rainey *et al.* (1998)	24% (9/37)	Significant improvement in a major subsystem, e.g. ≥30% reduction in days on mechanical ventilation[†]
Adult cardiac surgery	Nugent *et al.* (1999)	'most … [of the 41 teams] met or exceeded their goals'	Eight targets representing best practice
End of life care I	Lynn *et al.* (2000)	27% (13/47)	Substantial and measurable improvement
Back pain	Deyo *et al.* (2000)	27% (6/22)	Substantial progress (measurable change in several sites or at system level)[†]
Adverse drug events II	Leape *et al.* (2000)	Teams made 'even greater gains' than in ADEs collaboration I	Not reported
Diabetes	Wagner *et al.* (2001)	Not reported	Significant progress: successful implementation of all chronic care model elements in the target population, evidence of improvement in outcome measures related to the teams' objectives, achievement of at least half of the initial goals and plans to spread changes made
End of life for patients with CHF	Lynn *et al.* (2000)	47% (16/34)	Substantial and measurable improvement
Adverse drug events III	Weeks *et al.* (2001)	52% (14/27)	20% improvement lasting at least 2 months
HIV/AIDS I	DHHS (2002)	31% (14/45)	At, or exceeding, collaborative goal

[†] Definition of experiencing at least rating 4 on IHI's five-point assessment scale.

substantial reductions in mean and median waiting times, while the other projects made comparatively little or no progress against these measures. Although these limited data provided little opportunity to explore the reasons for the range in performance, six general levers for change were identified. The two most important were adoption of a patient perspective (facilitated by process mapping) and the availability of dedicated project management time. The other levers were the provision of 'capacity and demand' training, the facilitation of multidisciplinary team working, the empowerment of staff at all levels, and the opportunities for networking (Robert *et al.*, 2003). The CSC provided useful lessons relating to the coordination and management of future phases; one of the key issues related to quantitative data collection and analysis and the limited reporting regime did not promote confidence on the part of clinicians. For example, a programme clinical lead noted:

> My main concern was always the measurement, that we make proper measurements. My concern is how am I going to stand up and talk about something and say to people it's been a great success, or we've engineered this change, if I can't back it up with some good data that I can use to convince others that it's been a useful change (Robert *et al.*, 2003, p.55).

The Orthopaedic Services Collaborative included 37 trusts. The topic was elective total hip replacement cases and the main objective chosen by 86% (32/37) of the participating teams was to reduce length of stay (Bate *et al.*, 2002). The OSC set a length-of-stay target of five days. The participating teams commonly rejected this target in favour of local targets perceived to be more realistic. Communication between the collaborative leaders and participants relating to targets, data definitions and reporting requirements was problematic. The evaluation's analysis of patient-level data found that the mean postoperative length of stay decreased by one day (12.2%) to 7.2 days between the quarters ending December 1999 and December 2000. This change in performance was less than expected. Readmission rates were not commonly collected and so the efficacy of the change in length of stay is not known. The participating teams that experienced the largest reductions in length of stay made more changes in practice than the other participants, but, in general, the use made of Nolan's model for improvement appeared to be less than that intended by the champions of BTS.

The BTS model has now been implemented across a wide range of services throughout the NHS and the collaborative methodology is central to the NHS Modernisation Agency's efforts to spread best practice. However, the reporting of outcomes is haphazard. Some collaboratives publish nothing, and others tend to limit analysis to changes in mean values rather than presenting project-level results, which inhibits assessment of progress towards best practice by outlier operating units.

Discussion

OD initiatives which attempt to address healthcare performance span a wide range of activities. Berwick's BTS collaborative model provides the basis for the most extensively implemented OD activities involving frontline NHS staff seen to date. For this reason, and the relative lack of evidence relating to other OD efforts, this chapter has focused on the evolution of CQI methods and the BTS model.

The basic concepts of process-oriented change have been used in very different circumstances. At one extreme, the literature includes examples of individual CQI-based initiatives which suggest 'pockets of improvement' (Shortell et al., 1998). At the other extreme, BPR experiments have failed to realise expectations that they would enable senior managers to impose change on clinicians across individual organisations within a short timescale. Along with BPR, TQM efforts also share characteristics of organisation-wide aspirations, equivocal impact on intended outcomes and a lack of ownership on the part of clinicians. Moreover, these highly ambitious initiatives commonly degenerate into more modest topic-specific projects, which suggests that even if they are successful, and a range of advantageous contextual factors are present, a much longer timescale would be required to achieve organisation-wide change.

In between these extremes, the NNECDSG sets a very high standard as a clinician-led, long-term, topic-specific, multi-organisational, voluntary initiative that has facilitated changes in clinical practice resulting in fundamental and sustained improvement in outcomes. If only OD in healthcare could be left to this type of initiative! However, the need to proactively instigate efforts to improve healthcare delivery has gained increasing prominence over the past 20 years and Berwick's BTS collaborative model represents a valiant attempt to build on the NNECDSG experience; in particular, by creating a temporary environment in which multidisciplinary teams from multiple organisations volunteer to share topic-specific experiences and apply CQI tools, the BTS model aims to emulate some of the NNECDSG's key attributes.

Nevertheless, in comparison to the NNECDSG, the BTS model is vulnerable in several key respects. Most important are the consequences of the BTS model's short timescale. The BTS model explicitly aims to promote change more rapidly than the NNECDSG experience by attempting to create the initial 'tension for change' (or 'tipping point') without recourse to potentially time-consuming activity to establish 'proof' of the need for change. A number of issues affect individual clinicians' views on the type and extent of evidence required in order to support changing practice. The one sure thing is that individuals have different views on innovation. The BTS model's approach is to focus on topics for which there is a commonly recognised gap between current and best practice. This is sensible, as an aid to topic selection, but in itself it may not deliver wide-scale buy-in from clinicians because some, like those in the NNECDSG, will first seek evidence that, for example, variation in outcomes is not simply due to differences in case-mix. Moreover, the BTS model maintains an emphasis on rapid change as participants are judged successful if they can report 'breakthrough' improvement for chosen measures within a year. Clinicians who decline to buy into the model's simplistic approach to, for example, quantitative analysis, are labelled as 'resistant to change'. The clinicians of the NNECDSG used statistical analysis of mortality rates as a basis for deciding to seek better clinical practices and assessing the impact of the changes they made. The BTS model's ubiquitous 'run charts' fail to provide similarly robust evidence.

Nonetheless, as many NHS collaboratives have become medium-term interventions via national roll-out supported by considerable resources, clinicians could be offered an opportunity to study their own practice to satisfy themselves that change is desired and to monitor the impact of implemented changes. Service improvement is not a sprint race, and the potential benefit of engaging a larger proportion of clinicians, through greater recognition of their characteristic views on the role of evidence relating to quality and performance, would be enormous. There are welcome signs that the NHS Modernisation Agency has started to wean itself off promoting over-simplistic approaches to collecting and presenting evidence relating to change and it is ideally positioned to provide expertise relating to the use of control charts and other forms of statistical analysis to frontline staff. Closer attention to this element of the OD jigsaw has the potential to promote clinical engagement by providing a credible point of discussion between stakeholders at each level and, at the same time, offers a valid basis for assessing the impact of OD interventions on selected performance measures.

The programmatic approach of most NHS collaboratives provides an important opportunity to develop topic-specific expertise while working with enthusiasts and relatively receptive contexts. However, the short timescale is such that typically only a minority of participating organisations achieve the desired outcomes by the end of the programme. In this situation, insight into the topic-specific issues to be overcome is necessarily limited, and whether participants go on to subsequently achieve the desired outcomes remains an open question. The NBAP first-wave projects experienced difficultly in extending booking during the year following the end of the first wave and, in general, medium-term outcomes are not known. The failure to evaluate the medium-term impact of the early NHS collaboratives, despite the Government's stated aims relating to policy making and evaluation (Prime Minister and Minister for the Cabinet Office, 1999), ranks as a significant omission, equivalent to the Conservatives' failure to evaluate fundholding. In consequence, to a great extent, the Modernisation Agency has been flying blind; developing unrivalled momentum for change fuelled by a mixed and incomplete picture of impact beyond selected self-reported outcomes.

The current phase in the Modernisation Agency's evolution may result in a more productive working relationship with strategic health authorities (SHAs) and frontline staff. In the short term, momentum may be lost. As SHAs assume greater influence over the conduct of OD activities, there is an opportunity to reconsider the use of topic-specific programmes. Their potential to deliver desired change has so far not been tested appropriately. A longer timescale is needed in which clinicians can be encouraged to utilise a wider range of specialist support. Common performance objectives, be they local or national, can be addressed without resorting to a 'one-size-fits-all' faith-driven implementation framework.

The struggle for the hearts and minds of health professionals is formidable. In terms of OD, a key challenge is to better align locally driven priorities for improvement with national imperatives in such a way that specific initiatives can demonstrably deliver on both fronts. Of key importance is the perceived benefit of the proposed change to the clinician, and this issue is repeatedly afforded insufficient attention. For example, booking admissions was afforded political priority in the

NHS as a measure of pseudo-customer choice for patients. The benefit for clinicians was ambiguous, with the natural desire to promote patient benefits offset by a reduction in clinical freedom, a perceived threat to private work and the absence of any robust analysis of how booking would increase efficiency through, for example, reductions in patients failing to attend (Ham *et al.*, 2002). Arguably, this issue provides the greatest challenge for the OD agenda.

It also serves to provide further support for the importance of the definition of OD suggested in Chapter 1. In its emphasis on enabling managers and clinicians to learn how to reflect on their own practice, this definition focuses on those aspects of OD that seem to enhance sustainability. It may be a modest definition – and certainly it does not make the eye-catchingly grand claims of the gurus of TQM and BPR – but, at least on the evidence available to date, it may be none the worse for that.

References

Action On Orthopaedics and the Orthopaedic Services Collaborative (2002) *Improving Orthopaedic Services – a guide for clinicians, managers and service commissioners.* NHS Modernisation Agency, London.

Audit Commission (2003) *Achieving the NHS Plan: assessment of current performance, likely future progress and capacity to improve.* Audit Commission, London.

Bate P, Robert G and McLeod H (2002) *Report on the 'Breakthrough' Collaborative Approach to Quality and Service Improvement Within Four Regions of the NHS.* Health Services Management Centre, University of Birmingham, Birmingham.

Berwick D (1991) Controlling variation in health care: a consultation from Walter Shewhart. *Medical Care.* 29(12): 1212–25.

Berwick D (1996) A primer on leading the improvement of systems. *British Medical Journal.* 312: 619–22.

Berwick D (2003) Disseminating innovations in health care. *Journal of the American Medical Association.* 289(15): 1969–75.

Berwick D, Enthoven A and Bunker J (1992) Quality management in the NHS: the doctor's role – I. *British Medical Journal.* 304: 235–9.

Berwick D, Godfrey A and Roessner J (1990) *Curing Health Care: new strategies for quality improvement.* Jossey-Bass, San Francisco, CA.

Blumenthal D (1995) Preface. In: D Blumenthal and A Scheck (eds) *Improving Clinical Practice: total quality management and the physician.* Jossey-Bass, San Francisco, CA.

Blumenthal D and Kilo C (1998) A report card on continuous quality improvement. *Milbank Quarterly.* 76(4): 625–48.

Bowns I and McNulty T (1999) *Re-engineering Leicester Royal Infirmary: an independent evaluation of implementation and impact.* School of Health and Related Research, University of Sheffield, Sheffield.

BRI Inquiry Secretariat (1999) *BRI inquiry paper on medical and clinical audit in the NHS.* BRI Inquiry Secretariat www.bristol-inquiry.org.uk/final_report/annex_b/images/CH_MedicalClinicalAudit.pdf (accessed July 2003).

Crosby P (1979) *Quality is Free: the art of making quality certain.* McGraw-Hill, New York.

Deming W (1982) *Quality, Productivity, and Competitive Position.* Massachusetts Institute of Technology, Cambridge, MA.

Deming W (1986) *Out of the Crisis.* Massachusetts Institute of Technology, Cambridge, MA.

Denis J-L, Lamonthe L, Langley A and Valett A (1999) The struggle to redefine boundaries in health care systems. In: D Drock, M Powell and C Hinings (eds) *Restructuring the Professional Organization,* pp.105–30. Routledge, London.

Department of Health (2001) *Reforming Emergency Care.* Department of Health, London.

Department of Health and Human Services (2002) *2002 SPNS Report to CARE Act Grantees on Thirteen SPNS Initiatives.* Rockville, Maryland, Health Resources and Services Administration, Department of Health and Human Services, http://hab.hrsa.gov/report_studies.htm (accessed July 2003).

Deyo R, Schall M, Berwick D, Nolan T and Carver P (2000) Continuous quality improvement for patients with back pain. *Journal of General Internal Medicine.* **15**: 647–55.

Ferlie E and Shortell S (2001) Improving the quality of health care in the United Kingdom and the United States: a framework for change. *Milbank Quarterly.* **79**(2): 281–315.

Fillingham D (2004) InforMAtion. NHS Modernisation Agency, Leicester.

Fitzgerald L, Ferlie E, Wood M and Hawkins C (1999) Evidence into practice: an exploratory analysis of the interpretation of evidence. In: A Mark and S Dopson (eds) *Organisational Behaviour in Health Care: the Research Agenda.* Macmillan, Basingstoke.

Flamm B, Kabcenell A, Berwick D and Roessner J (1997) *Reducing Cesarean Section Rates While Maintaining Maternal and Infant Outcomes.* Institute for Healthcare Improvement, Boston, MA.

Flamm B, Berwick D and Kabcenell A (1998) Reducing cesarean section rates safely: lessons from a 'breakthrough series' collaborative. *Birth.* **25**(2): 117–24.

Glover J (1938) The incidence of tonsillectomy in school children. *Proceedings of the Royal Society of Medicine.* **31**: 95–112.

Ham C (1999) The third way in health care reform: does the emperor have any clothes? *Journal of Health Services Research and Policy.* **4**(3): 168–73.

Ham C, Kipping R, McLeod H and Meredith P (2002) *Capacity, Culture and Leadership: lessons from experiences of improving access to hospital services. Final report from the evaluation of the National Booked Admissions Programme first wave pilots.* Health Services Management Centre, University of Birmingham, Birmingham.

Ham C, Kipping R and McLeod H (2003) Redesigning work processes in health care: lessons from the National Health Service. *Milbank Quartery.* 81(3): 415–39.

Hammer M and Champy J (1995) *Reengineering the Corporation: a manifesto for a business revolution.* Nicholas Brealey, London.

Institute of Medicine (2001) *Crossing the Quality Chasm.* National Academy Press, Washington, DC.

Ishikawa K (1985) *What is Total Quality Control?* Prentice Hall, London.

Joss R (1994) What makes for successful TQM in the NHS? *International Journal of Health Care Quality Assurance.* 7(7): 4–9.

Joss R and Kogan M (1995) *Advancing Quality: total quality management in the National Health Service.* Open University Press, Buckingham.

Juran J (1964) *Managerial Breakthrough.* McGraw-Hill, New York.

Juran J (1988) *Juran on Planning for Quality.* Collier Macmillan, New York.

Kilo C (1998) A framework for collaborative improvement: lessons from the Institute for Healthcare Improvement's breakthrough series. *Quality Management in Health Care.* 6(4): 1–13.

Kilo C, Kabcenell A and Berwick D (1998) Beyond survival: toward continuous improvement in medical care. *New Horizons.* 6(1): 3–11.

Kotter J (1995). Leading change: why transformation efforts fail. *Harvard Business Review.* 73(2): 59–67.

Langley G, Nolan K, Nolan T, Norman C and Provost L (1996) *The Improvement Guide: a practical approach to enhancing organizational performance.* Jossey-Bass, San Francisco, CA.

Lawler E, Mohrman S and Ledford G (1992) *Employee Involvement and Total Quality Management.* Jossey-Bass, San Francisco, CA.

Leape L, Kabcenell A, Berwick D and Rossner J (1998) *Reducing Adverse Drug Events.* Institute for Healthcare Improvement, Boston, MA.

Leape L, Kabcenell A, Gandhi T, Carver P, Nolan T and Berwick D (2000) Reducing adverse drug events: lessons from a breakthrough series collaborative. *Joint Commission Journal on Quality Improvement.* 26(6): 321–31.

Lynn J, Schall M, Milne C, Nolan K and Kabcenell A (2000) Quality improvements in end of life care: insights from two collaboratives. *Joint Commission Journal on Quality Improvement.* 26: 254–67.

Malenka D and O'Connor G (1998) The Northern New England Cardiovascular Disease Study Group: a regional collaborative effort for continuous quality improvement in cardiovascular disease. *Joint Commission Journal on Quality Improvement.* 24: 594–600.

McNulty T and Ferlie E (2002) *Reengineering Health Care: the complexities of organizational transformation.* Oxford University Press, Oxford.

Mills P, Weeks W and Surott-Kimberly B (2003) A multihospital safety improvement effort and the dissemination of new knowledge. *Joint Commission Journal on Quality and Safety*. **29**(3): 124–33.

Mintzberg H (1979) *The Structuring of Organisations: a synthesis of the research*. Prentice-Hall, Englewood Cliffs, NJ.

Mintzberg H (1994) *The Rise and Fall of Strategic Planning*. Prentice Hall, Hemel Hempstead.

Nelson E, Batalden P, Huber T, Mohr J, Godfrey M, Headrick L and Wasson J (2002) Microsystems in health care: part 1. Learning from high-performing front-line clinical units. *Joint Commission Journal on Quality Improvement*. **28**(9): 472–93.

NHS Management Inquiry (1983) *Report*. Department of Health and Social Security, London.

NHS Modernisation Agency (2002) *Improvement Leader's Guide to Process Mapping, Analysis and Redesign*. NHS Modernisation Agency, London.

NHS Modernisation Board (2002) *The NHS Plan – a progress report: The NHS Modernisation Board's Annual Report 2000–2001*. Department of Health, London.

NHS Modernisation Board (2003) *The NHS Plan – a progress report: The NHS Modernisation Board's Annual Report 2003*. Department of Health, London.

Nolan T, Schall M, Berwick D and Roessner J (1996) *Reducing Delays and Waiting Times Throughout the Healthcare System*. Institute for Healthcare Improvement, Boston, MA.

Nugent W, Kilo C, Ross C, Marrin C, Berwick D and Roessner J (1999) *Improving Outcomes and Reducing Costs in Adult Cardiac Surgery*. Institute for Healthcare Improvement, Boston, MA.

O'Connor G, Plume S, Olmstead E, Morton J, Maloney C, Nugent W, Hernandez F Jr, Clough R, Leavitt B, Coffin L, Marrion C, Wennberg D, Birkmeyer J, Charlesworth D, Malenka D, Quinton H and Kasper J (1996) A regional intervention to improve the hospital mortality associated with coronary artery bypass graft surgery. *Journal of the American Medical Association*. **275**: 841–6.

Øvretveit J (1997) Assessing evaluations of hospital quality programmes. *Evaluation*. **3**(4): 451–68.

Øvretveit J (2000) Total quality management in European healthcare. *International Journal of Health Care Quality Assurance*. **13**(2): 74–9.

Øvretveit J (2002) How to run an effective improvement collaborative. *International Journal of Health Care Quality Assurance*. **15**(5): 192–6.

Øvretveit J, Bate P, Cleary P, Cretin S, Gustafson D, McInnes K, McLeod H, Molfenter T, Plsek P, Robert G, Shortell S and Wilson T (2002) Quality collaboratives: lessons from research. *Quality and Safety in Health Care*. **11**: 345–51.

Packwood T, Pollitt C and Roberts S (1998) Good medicine? A case study of business process re-engineering in a hospital. *Policy and Politics*. **26**(4): 401–15.

Pettigrew A, Ferlie E and McKee L (1992) *Shaping Strategic Change: making change in large organisations: the case of the National Health Service.* Sage, London.

Plsek P (1997) Collaborating across organizational boundaries to improve the quality of care. *American Journal of Infection Control.* **25**: 85–95.

Prime Minister and the Minister for the Cabinet Office (1999) *Modernising Government.* Cm. 4310. The Stationery Office, London.

Rainey T, Kabcenell A, Berwick D and Roessner J (1998) *Reducing Costs and Improving Outcomes in Adult Intensive Care.* Institute for Healthcare Improvement, Boston, MA.

Robert G, McLeod H and Ham C (2003) *Modernising Cancer Service; an evaluation of phase I of the Cancer Services Collaborative.* Health Services Management Centre, University of Birmingham, Birmingham.

Robinson J, Akers J, Artzt E, Poling H, Galvin R and Allaire P (1991) An open letter: TQM on the campus. *Harvard Business Review.* **69**(6): 94–5.

Rogers E (1958) Categorizing the adopters of agricultural practices. *Rural Sociology.* **23**: 345–54.

Rogers E (1962) *Diffusion of Innovations.* Free Press, New York.

Schon D (1983) *The Reflective Practitioner: how professionals think in action.* Basic Books, New York.

Secretary of State for Health (2000) *The NHS Plan: a plan for investment, a plan for reform.* The Stationery Office, London.

Shewhart W (1931) *Economic Control of Quality of Manufactured Product.* Van Nostrand, New York.

Shewhart W (1939) *Statistical Method from the Viewpoint of Quality Control.* Graduate School of the Department of Agriculture, Washington, DC.

Shortell S, Levin D, O'Brien J and Hughes E (1995) Assessing the evidence on CQI: is the glass half empty or half full? *Journal of Hospital and Health Services Administration.* **40**(1): 4–24.

Shortell S, Bennett C and Byck G (1998) Assessing the impact of continuous quality improvement on clinical practice: what it will take to accelerate progress. *Milbank Quarterly.* **76**(4): 593–624.

Singhal K and Hayes R (1992) An open response to 'TQM on the campus': we need TQM … and more. *Harvard Business Review.* **70**(1): 148.

Tsoukas H (1998) Introduction: chaos, complexity and organization theory. *Organization.* **5**(3): 291–313.

Van de Ven A, Polley D and Venkataraman S (1999) *The Innovation Journey.* OUP, Buckingham.

Wagner E, Glasgow R, Davis C, Bonomi A, Provost L, McCulloch D, Carver P and Sixta C (2001) Quality improvement in chronic illness care: a collaborative approach. *Joint Commission Journal on Quality Improvement.* **27**(2): 63–80.

Weeks W, Mills P, Dittus R, Aron D and Batalden P (2001) Using an improvement model to reduce adverse drug events in VA facilities. *Joint Commission Journal on Quality Improvement.* 27(5): 243–54.

Weiss K, Mendoza G, Schall M, Berwick D and Roessner J (1997) *Improving Asthma Care in Children and Adults.* Institute for Healthcare Improvement, Boston, MA.

Wennberg J, Freeman J and Culp W (1987) Are hospital services rationed in New Haven or over-utilised in Boston? *Lancet.* 23 May. 8543: 1185–9.

Wilson T, Berwick D and Cleary P (2003) What do collaborative improvement projects do? Experience from seven countries. *Joint Commission Journal on Quality Improvement.* 29(2): 85–93.

Conclusion

Edward Peck

Introduction

In the Introduction to this book, I threatened a Conclusion that would seek to challenge some of the ideas and the interventions that fill the pages between there and here. The purpose of this final chapter is, therefore, to explore further the extent to which these ideas and interventions are theoretically robust and to suggest some limitations to the reach and impact of OD. In so doing, I am seeking both to address some of the key conceptual issues that have not yet been tackled, and to model the spirit of reflexivity and learning that I believe should characterise robust theorists and practitioners of OD. After all, it would be profoundly ironic if the OD community was unable to exhibit the very characteristics that Jeanne Hardacre and I suggested in Chapter 1 were the ambitions for effective OD. At the outset, I want to stress that I am acting here as a critical friend to the claims of organisational development; a friend, moreover, who spends much of his time undertaking organisational development in healthcare organisations.

Let us return first to that definition of OD in Chapter 1. There, Jeanne Hardacre and I argue that organisational development is attempting to develop organisations with the ability and willingness to be continually reflexive about their own human processes and social structures. This characterisation of OD might be viewed as rather modest in its aspirations, albeit simple, clear and easy to understand, especially when compared with bolder offerings. In one of the most comprehensive textbooks on OD, Cummings and Worley (2001) construct an overarching definition based on a review of those suggested by other authors: 'organization development is a system-wide application of behavioural science knowledge to the planned development, improvement and reinforcement of the strategies, structures and processes that lead to organiza-tion effectiveness' (p.1). These are bold claims, not dissonant with the definition in Chapter 1, yet much more ambitious, and they serve to remind us why OD is understandably attractive to hard-pressed managers in healthcare.

There are clear connections between the two definitions. Like Jeanne and I, Cummings and Worley (2001) are at pains to distinguish OD from other interventions, such as management training, in five respects. First, they argue, OD addresses an entire system. Second, in focusing on theories derived from behavioural science, OD emphasises the personal and social characteristics of organisational life rather than the technical or the financial. Third, Cummings and Worley (2001) maintain that OD is an adaptive approach to managing planned change, stressing that interventions respond to feedback from the organisation. Fourth, it involves both the creation and subsequent reinforcement of change. Fifth, and finally, OD can improve organisation effectiveness in two ways: 'an effective organization is able to solve its own problems and focus its attention on and resources on achieving key goals ... an effective organization has both high performance, including financial returns ... and a high quality of work life' (p.3). Crucially, they all need to be underpinned by reflexivity and learning in order to have a lasting effect; this is the link back to the definition in Chapter 1.

Despite the emphasis on adaptation and feedback, there is a strong modernist (as opposed to post-modernist) foundation to the definition of Cummings and Worley (2001) with its talk of 'knowledge' and 'planning'. Nonetheless, this chapter will base its examination of some of the thorny issues facing OD on the assumption that it is attempting to make good on the bold claims explicit in this definition, notwithstanding the disappointing evidence, or simple lack of evidence, about the effectiveness of OD presented by Hugh McLeod in Chapter 13.

I begin by going back to look more critically at the two overarching theories sketched out in the Introduction to this book, that is social constructionism and post-modernism. I then turn my attention to Morgan and his metaphors to exemplify the challenges to a particular organisational theorist that this broader critique represents. From there, it moves on to a brief discussion of the impact of OD at 'the tipping point' (an idea first introduced in Chapter 1 and which crops up in several chapters; readers who want an even more detailed discussion of some of the issues raised on this topic should consult 6 and Peck, 2002). Next, it muses again on the current popularity of OD, in particular focusing on the performative and symbolic aspects that have not yet been discussed at length elsewhere. There then follows an extended case study which tries to tie together some of the themes of this chapter and of the book overall before the final conclusion.

The limits of social constructionism ...

Let us start by returning to social constructionism, the suggestion that conversations between members have the power to shape the culture of the organisation and thus the attitudes of its members to change. This belief in the power of talk, albeit talk manipulated by OD practitioners, is central to many OD interventions. Many of the authors in Part 2 reflect this belief to a greater or lesser extent, but they are sensitive to the interplay between talk and text and the social structures that both shape and are shaped by them. It is this sensitivity, for example, that distinguishes Chris Oliver's *critical* approach to appreciative inquiry – with its explicit acknowledgement of the differences of status of participants within such social structures – from the more traditional conceptions of AI. Vega Roberts and Murray Anderson-Wallace and Chris Blantern also address these links between agency and structure in their chapters.

Nonetheless, in being so reliant on discourse (that is, interventions through talk and text), much OD tends to be idealistic in the sense that it assumes a 'power of ideas' model of change that is very optimistic about the impact of human agency. It assumes that the development, improvement and reinforcement of the strategies, structures and processes that lead to organisational effectiveness are to be explained principally by reference to changes in ideas, and that the main restrictions on the menu of ideas that are available to people are limitations of their own intellectual history or cognitive equipment. Hardy *et al.* (2000), for example, refer to discourse as a 'strategic resource', of which most varieties are assumed to be both generally available and to be causally efficacious in bringing about strategic change.

However, this idealism could be argued to privilege human agency over social structure in the explanation of organisational change in ways that are implausible. Indeed, this explanation would simply not be recognised by most traditions of social science that seek to contend that all ideas are not equally available and that many ideas are not causally efficacious in many contexts. Murray Anderson-Wallace, for example, in Chapter 9, has shown that there is clearly something very significant about the impact of social structure on the outcomes of OD, although realigning these structures is not typically within the remit of most OD programmes.

It may be worth recapping a couple of examples from healthcare which illustrate this point. For example, in focusing on the importance of convergence, on how the old shapes the new, McNulty and Ferlie (2002) recognise that their study of business process re-engineering (BPR) within the Leicester Royal Infirmary exemplifies Giddens' (e.g. 1993) 'theory of structuration in an organisational setting … choices and actions of managerial and other agents are mediated by the very same cognitive and relational structures that such choices and actions are designed to modify' (pp.241–2). Giddens (1993) argued strongly that the impact of agency – of the talk and text of individuals – is inevitably constrained by the relationships, predominant styles of sensemaking and established procedures within organisations. It is interesting to note that in their thoroughgoing critique of BPR, Knights and Wilmott (2000) identify tensions between the discourse of the intervention – with its emphasis on employees being 'expected to devote themselves unreservedly to goals that have been determined by others' (p.11) – and the wider institutional context, including the hierarchical and political nature of big organisations, which mean that the impact of BPR is almost always disappointing. Similarly, Bate *et al.* (2000) are clear from their own work in the NHS that OD interventions must address human agency and social structure in one integrated programme (*see* Chapter 10) if they are to deliver on the ambitions of Cummings and Worley.

Of course, no one would deny that how people talk and write matters in organisations. Meetings and documents would not proliferate (and they certainly do proliferate) in healthcare settings if they served no purpose, which is not to say that they always serve the purpose officially claimed for them (*see* Peck *et al.*, 2004). No account of organisational change, and no account of the scope for inducing desirable forms of that change through organisational development interventions, would be adequate that claimed that talk and text were not important. However, there are real problems – both theoretically and practically – with the claims that organisations and the behaviour of their members are all the effects of discourse.

Anthropology (*see* Moore, 1997) is the discipline that has devoted the largest effort to trying to work out where ideas come from, and to what extent ideas are independently causally efficacious and what limits are placed on that efficacy from the social and organisational functions that ideas serve. A central finding of anthropology has been that ideas spring from the settings in social structure in which people find themselves. Writers such as Berger and Luckmann (1966), often seen as the originators of social constructionism, and Goffman (1974) routinely describe the underlying institutions that determine the accountability of individuals and the limitations on ideas and options for discourse that result. In a similar vein, authors such as Douglas (1992) have shown that ideas about what is regarded as 'risks' in any society or organisation, for example, are to be explained by reference to the form of social organisation prevailing. The same arguments, emphasising the institutionalist understanding of organisational ideas and behaviour, have been present in the study of organisations for over five decades, for instance in the work of Selznick (1949), Pugh (1973), Zucker (1988) and Powell and DiMaggio (1991).

In short, whether analysing whole societies or specific organisations, the mainstream of social science has converged on the view that ideas and beliefs are not the unmoved movers of human life, but are also, if not predominantly, to be explained by reference to the social structure in which they occur. Further, changes in institutions and accountabilities are themselves to be explained in terms of institutional and societal dynamics and not simply accounted for by individual human agency. One example of such societal and institutional dynamics that have impacted significantly on healthcare over the past 20 years are the moves from hierarchy through markets to networks – and the changes in the institutions of and the accountabilities within the NHS that have accompanied this trend – as the overarching principle of organising (and which Murray discusses in Chapter 9).

If this argument is accepted, then it represents a significant challenge to much OD practice. Most of the activity of OD consultants consists in producing talk and text and attempts to use such talk and text to persuade organisational leaders and members to change their minds about their attitudes and/or their behaviours. The standard repertoire of interventions – individual role consultation, focus group discussions, action learning sets, stakeholder conferences, open space events – are for the most part processes of using interventions with specially designed talk and text in the hope of influencing the routine talk and text produced within the organisation. If the ambition is modest, such as developing enhanced reflexivity (as in Chapter 1) or refining aspects of the current organisational settlement (*see* Chapter 2), and/or specific, such as containing organisational anxiety (*see* Chapter 6), then interventions based on discourse alone may be efficacious. However, 'the planned development, improvement and reinforcement of the strategies, structures and processes that lead to organization effectiveness' (Cummings and Worley, 2001, p.1) seems both more ambitious and less specific. The institutionalist challenge suggests that there are clear limits to what can be expected of talk-and-text-based interventions deployed on their own in pursuit of these very broad goals.

There is some evidence to support this scepticism emerging from researchers within the organisational discourse tradition. For example, Gordon and Grant (2000) demonstrate that participants in a stakeholder event that they observed 'outwardly appeared to embrace the change initiative under discussion, [but] deeper analysis of the language they employ reveals that they are in fact unable to make the desired leap to a new and unfamiliar discourse' (p.3). Buhanist *et al.* (2000) reveal from their case study that external change agents 'focus change in the project timescale, whereas organisational members see change in a many year context with a much longer history' (p.9). There may be, nonetheless, special circumstances in which using very particular kinds of talk and text might trigger a profound change in an organisation, but these will be ones in which the prevailing institutional settlement permits this (and the potential impact of working at this 'tipping point' is discussed further below).

It is also important to reflect another perspective on this debate. Both Alys Harwood and Vega suggest – albeit in different ways – the potency of the power of feelings in OD (as well as the power of ideas). Furthermore, Deborah Davidson and I, in utilising Schein's (1987) ORJI cycle in Chapter 3, draw attention to the importance of leaders, and OD practitioners, developing emotional intelligence by being aware of and adjusting their psychological responses to situations before choosing an intervention. Of course, it could be argued that the range of emotional responses that is perceived as legitimate to exhibit in organisational life – even during OD sessions – is as limited by the predominant institutional form as is the expression of ideas. Nonetheless, this approach to the debate should not be overlooked in the (perhaps over) intellectual argument in this chapter (which, I guess, some would argue merely reflects my preferred style for, in the terms of Myers-Briggs *et al.*'s (2000) framework, 'thinking' rather than 'feeling').

The limits of post-modernism ...

If there is need for caution with regard to the social constructionist strand in OD theory and practice, what then are the limitations of post-modernism? Applying the characteristics of post-modernism (*see* Bertens, 1995; Harvey, 1990) to organisations, the Introduction broadly suggests that OD practitioners have to recognise the legitimacy of, and work with the influences exhibited by, a number of disparate voices consequent to the death of the so-called 'grand-narrative' of modernism. Hassard (1993), summarising the work of Lyotard, argues that: 'the postmodern epistemology [theory of knowledge] concerns knowledge of localized understandings and acceptance of a plurality of diverse language forms. Thus postmodernism sees the fragmentation of grand narratives and the discrediting of all meta-narratives' (p.9, parentheses added).

Hassard (1993) goes on to apply post-modernism to organisational studies and lists 'the five key elements of a post-modern approach to knowledge' (p.16). Three are particularly relevant here:

- 'representation' – which views any attempt to establish the genuine order of things in the world as naive
- 'reflexivity' – which stresses the importance of being critical of our own intellectual assumptions
- 'writing' – which challenges the notion that language is a sign system which simply represents the objects that exist independently in that world and suggests instead that it indicates the ways in which the author is creating a world through reflection (and there are obvious links here to the process of sensemaking).

Concepts such as representation, reflexivity and writing are rippled through contemporary OD practice (including much of the editor's own) like raspberry sauce through ice-cream and this is no less true of this book; indeed reflexivity is central to definition of OD provided by Jeanne and I.

Post-modernism challenges, therefore, the fundamental assumptions of modernism, although it is interesting to note that a number of authors in Part 2, in common with Hassard (1993), devote considerable time to defining their approach in contrast to modernist models. This suggests, perhaps, a lack of confidence in the widespread acceptance of their position (especially in healthcare organisations populated by clinicians trained in the modernist tradition) or maybe recognition that the influence of the rational and the linear still loom large in most prescriptive or descriptive accounts of organisational behaviour. If some versions of evolutionary psychology are to be believed, the human need to link cause to effect (to have an A for every B) may be too deep-seated for them to remove (Plotkin 1997); it certainly provides one explanation of why the modernist view of organisations remains so powerful and so prevalent (in Murray's words in Chapter 9, 'the organisation in our head is a bureaucracy'). Peeling back another layer of the onion, it has been suggested, by the likes of Jones (2003), that the death of the grand narrative seems like a pretty grand narrative in its own right!

At the very least, therefore, it does seem important to clarify a little the form of post-modernism that still seems plausible in these theoretical circumstances, that is a weak rather than a strong form of organisational post-modernism. A strong form would argue that no mix of public policy and organisational design could be said to achieve better fit with its environment and thus produce better outcomes than any other, and that no approach to the implementation of change could be considered superior to any other. This would result in a sort of 'anything goes' approach to OD practice. This position is, in my view, regularly contradicted by experience. A weak version of organisational post-modernism would be a little more cautious than that. It would suggest that there are combinations of contexts and interventions that will prove more beneficial than others while at the same time rejecting the predominance of the mechanical model of organisations.

This version of post-modernism would also warn us that the institutionalist position contains within it the strong implication of structural determinism, that is that there is no room at all for the power of ideas to shift attitudes and behaviours because these are determined and continued by the grand narrative of the organisation exhibited through its social structure. This is an important warning; in my view, it is human agency that ultimately changes social structure. Typically, though, such changes require developments in societal as well as organisational views of the world (as is illustrated by the examples of changing maternity services provided in Chapter 2 and closing asylums deployed below).

More on Morgan and his metaphors

All of this discussion may be starting to feel a little esoteric. Perhaps it is time to illustrate the implications of the institutionalist challenge to social constructionism and post-modernism by going back to the writings of one of the major influences on OD introduced in Chapter 1: Gareth Morgan and his book on metaphors (1986). Arguably, Morgan's book exemplifies the influence of the 'power of ideas' model on OD thinking. After reviewing a wide range of metaphors through which organis-ations can be understood, he considers the effects of these metaphors. He writes of organisational behaviour as the consequence of people taking metaphors seriously. In the final chapters, Morgan (1986) briefly considers the use of his analysis in bringing about organisational change. His argument is essentially that change is made possible by people within the organisation itself *thinking about* or *talking about* an organisation using a different metaphor from the one currently dominant. He talks of 'switching' between metaphors, as if it were an essentially straightforward matter of changing one's style of speech. His account of organisational change privileges ideas – as represented in particular forms of discourse dominated by what he calls metaphors – as causal agents in themselves. For example, he seems to claim that simply being aware of the range of available metaphors will in and of itself enable people to bring about change in organisations. 'Reading the situation' in terms of multiple metaphors is, for Morgan's quintessentially discourse-based view of organisations, causally the most important thing in generating change. In the light of the institutionalist challenge outlined above, this starts to appear rather an implausible claim.

Nonetheless, there is undoubtedly something important in Morgan's argument that 'our theories and explanations of organisational life are based on metaphors that lead us to see and understand organisations in distinctive yet partial ways ... the use of metaphor implies a way of thinking and a way of seeing' (1986, p.12). Indeed, the book would not still be a standard text in business schools 20 years after its publication if this was not the case. Yet, in this formulation of his position, Morgan (1986) is viewing the reality of organisations as a social construction dependent on the insights generated by the chosen metaphor; indeed, he is moving close to what Hassard (1993) terms a post-modern epistemology where, 'the world is constituted by our shared language and that we can only "know the world" through the particular forms of discourse our language creates' (p.3). The popularity of this text, despite its roots in social constructionism and post-modernism, suggests that the modernists are not having it all their own way.

The problem with Morgan for OD practitioners is the move from the description of the metaphors to their potential use as interventions. Morgan (1986) does not suggest how the analysis based around metaphors provides any basis for action beyond suggesting that the manager must unravel this complexity in the best way s/he can. Further, there is an implication that any one of the eight, or potentially more, metaphors chosen by the organisational analyst is as useful as any other metaphor. Morgan (1986) makes no attempt to attribute relative value to the metaphors that he explores. As each metaphor is only one way of seeing the organisation, then analysts have to acknowledge the limitations of an approach based on the application of that metaphor or deploy more than one metaphor in their analysis. Reed (2000) has drawn attention to the concern that Morgan's failure to attribute relative worth to competing metaphors could transform organisational studies into merely a super-market of metaphors. Alvesson (1993) notes that, of the eight metaphors suggested by Morgan, 'in some of these cases there are hardly any examples of studies in organisation theory informed by the metaphor in question' (p.114). It may be that Alys' notion of metaphorical 'resonance' in Chapter 12 will turn out to be the best guide as to when to use which metaphor.

More fundamentally, Holland (1999) suggests that, in focusing on metaphor, Morgan overlooks any implication that all theories of organisation (and the metaphors through which they are expressed) are tied into clusters of interest groups and their value systems. In this criticism, Holland is taking us back to the challenge of the institutionalists, that is that the metaphors in use and the metaphors available to use will be constrained by the social structures within which the discourse takes place. For OD practitioners in healthcare, it may be dangerous to assume that managers and, in particular, clinicians are capable of shedding their modernist metaphorical commitments as easily as lizards shed their skins.

In place of metaphors, Feyerabend (2000) introduces the useful notion of world-views: 'I shall define a *worldview* as a collection of beliefs, attitudes, and assumptions that involves the whole person, not only the intellect, has some kind of coherence and universality, and imposes itself with a power far greater than the power of facts and fact-related theories' (p.164, italics in original). Different worldviews (such as those represented in Chapters 5 to 12) are capable of dialogue and mutual understanding, but they represent something much more profound to the individuals involved than one more possible way of looking at the world (or their organisation). We shall use this notion of 'worldview' again in what follows.

None of this discussion is meant to discourage readers from taking from Morgan those aspects of his theory that they find useful. Rather, it serves to demonstrate that any theory illuminates one area of the OD field and not others (rather like Morgan's metaphors themselves) and that any theory has its weaknesses. Had space allowed, critiques of the work of Weick, Argyris, etc., could also have been developed.

The 'tipping point'

Many of the current aspirations for OD in healthcare focus on the delivery of 'transformational change'. When defined as, 'a multi-dimensional, multi-level, quali-tative, discontinuous, radical organizational change involving a paradigmatic shift' (Levy and Merry, 1986, p.5), organisational transformation is viewed as revolution-ary and rapid change as opposed to the more evolutionary and gradual change involved in traditional organisational improvement.

Earlier in this chapter, I briefly suggested that talk and text may be able to deliver the ambitions of Cummings and Worley (2001), and indeed Levy and Merry (1986), but only at the so-called 'tipping point'. This is the point at which the existing organisational settlement can be seen to be dysfunctional (in the terms of Chapter 2) or on the brink of chaos (in the terms of Chapter 8); Weick (1995) talks of 'novel moments in organizations [that] capture sustained attention and lead people to persist in trying to make sense of what they notice' (p.86, parentheses added). The challenge for OD practitioners, then, becomes one of developing the capacity of institutional analysis in order to identify just those moments. At that 'tipping point', it may be possible to deliver talk and text that would 'surprise' the system (Thompson, 1992), and so stimulate significant changes in human agency and social structure. It is possible that at or near the 'tipping point' the gathering forces of disorganisation or chaos may be beginning to be clear and in these circumstances it may be possible for many people to see where the organisation might be heading, and so administering a 'surprise' through organisational development interventions based on discourse might be especially effective (although Hugh reminds us of the dangers of OD practitioners or managers in the NHS attempting to contrive a 'tipping point' that is not recognised by clinical colleagues). OD practitioners are looking, therefore, for points where the identification and delivery of information can be used to disrupt organisational worldviews (as in Feyerabend's definition) at the one point at which people might be able to think beyond the confines of their institutional blinkers. It follows that one of the central concerns of effective organisational development work ought to be the design and administration of such 'surprises'. In keeping with the arguments of Alys and Vega, it may that these 'surprises' might be as much (if not more) about the revelation of members' feelings as of their thoughts.

In summary, this 'tipping point' is of absolutely critical interest from the point of view of trying to identify at what point OD interventions based only on talk and text might be effective in bringing about the profound changes envisaged by many writers on OD (and frequently reflected in the claims of many OD practitioners). Thus, OD interventions that work through human agency can achieve such a significant impact (what might be termed in current NHS language 'transformational change') when deployed either in combination with interventions around social structure or alone when an organisation is at the point of crisis.

However, most programmes based on talk and text alone do not have these characteristics, and do not, and indeed cannot, deliver such profound change (again, *see* 6 and Peck (2002) for a more detailed discussion of this point). At most other times, OD practitioners are working on the less spectacular – but scarcely less important work – of enabling organisational members to reflect on and develop their social sensemaking; supporting the capabilities of leaders and the willingness of stakeholders in the negotiation and renegotiation of settlements between interests.

Why is OD so popular?

Given the apparent limitations of OD in routinely delivering profound or transformational change we are still left with the question: why is OD based on talk and text alone so popular? Some answers are offered in Chapter 1, and, of course, there are managers and clinicians in healthcare who will have experienced the major impact of 'surprises' administered by OD practitioners at the 'tipping point'. Yet others will have been involved with OD projects that fulfilled more modest ambitions, such as refining aspects of the current organisational settlement. Perhaps they have seen OD interventions that have enabled their organisations to become more reflexive, which Jeanne and I suggest is the realistic aspiration for much OD. A few will have been participants in OD programmes that worked effectively with human agency and social structure simultaneously. In these circumstances, it is not unreasonable to say that many managers and clinicians will have seen organisational development that has 'worked', and this may well have raised expectations about its potential for the future.

It may be that Alys is also on to something when, in Chapter 12, she discusses the importance of the OD practitioner as performer. Abrahamson (1991) discusses the impact of external agents – in particular management consultants – on the adoption by organisations of what he calls management fashion. Many of these fashions, Abrahamson (1991) argues, relate to process-based OD interventions, such as T-groups and quality circles. He suggests that 'the fashion perspective assumes that organizations in a group imitate other organizations' (p.597), i.e. that fashion demand is based on managers' collective aesthetic tastes. In these circumstances, he suggests that it is easy to see why managers adopt what he terms technically inefficient innovations, such as BPR for example. In the NHS, this adoption is even more understandable when the fashion is accompanied by overt government endorsement (in the form of the Modernisation Agency's enthusiasm for collaboratives).

In a subsequent paper, Abrahamson (1996) qualifies this position. Management fashion must not only appear as beautiful and modern, but also 'rational (efficient means to important ends) and progressive (new as well as improved relative to older management techniques)' (p.255). In making this point, Abrahamson seems to be catching up with an insight that the promoters of process-based interventions, like BPR, have known for years. More importantly, Abrahamson argues that:

> managers do not only adopt management fashions because of sociopsychological forces. They also adopt management fashions in a desire to learn about management techniques that would help them respond to organizational performance gaps opened up by real technical and environmental forces (p.255).

In part, this adoption is, in line with the argument of Meyer and Rowan (1977), aimed at creating the appearance of managerial rationality by using management techniques that important stakeholders – for example, government – believe to be effective. Abrahamson makes reference to the importance of rhetoric in the promotion of fashions, in the manner discussed by Berglund and Werr (2000), and also alludes briefly to the role of the management consultant as guru in this process.

The idea of management consultants as gurus has been familiar in the organisational behaviour literature since the publication of the work of Huczynski (1993), where it was acknowledged that: 'a realistic aim of a guru's persuasive communication is not that his ideas should necessarily and immediately modify the actions of his audience, but that they should alter their beliefs, attitudes and feelings towards his suggestions' (p.86). This strand of thinking again emphasises the symbolic and non-rationalistic aspects of organisational life where the focus is on the sensemaking of managers. Czarniawska-Joerges (1989) argues that her study of public sector reforms in Sweden indicates that 'several possible functions of reforms ... although neglected in conventional perspectives on organizational change are nevertheless important ... these functions are primarily of a symbolic nature' (p.545) and that these functions encompass relegitimising organisational purpose and resocialising organisational members. Again, research based on discourse analysis may illuminate these issues further; for example, the research by Clark and Greatbatch (2000) explored the functions of stories within the adopted styles of five management gurus.

Taking this strand further, Clark and Salaman (1996) argue that 'the work of management gurus resembles the performance of the witchdoctor ... [1] that this type of consultancy activity is essentially a performance and [2] that this resembles a performance of a certain kind – that of a witchdoctor' (p.85). They propose that the analogy between consultant and witchdoctor lies not only in the communication of persuasive ideas identified by Huczynski (1993), but also in the claims of consultants to have special methods for diagnosing and fixing the problems of the organisation and on the importance attached to performance in their repertoire of interventions. This takes us back to the importance of OD practitioner as performer and most of the chapters in Part 2 make explicit or implicit assumptions about the nature of that performance. Once again, though, we seem to be some distance from the modernist ambitions of Cummings and Worley (2001).

Another plausible explanation is that the popularity among managers of talk and text interventions must be based on factors other than their potential to deliver profound change. Perhaps some OD practitioners merely tell managers more or less overtly what they want to hear. On occasions, they may also perform rituals and roles that implicitly validate and reaffirm the prevailing settlements in the organisation; for it may be possible for OD practitioners to construct a plausible argument where talk and text can be used to influence organisational, and in particular to reconcile disparate, worldviews through a series of interventions that enable organisational effectiveness – as defined by managers – to be enhanced. Of course, this again the raises the ethical dimensions of OD and the potential for OD to be, in Carnevale's (2003) words:

> a device to manipulate workers by giving them the illusion that they are empowered when they are caught up in the same old game of let's pretend what you say matters as long as it doesn't really threaten our control in this organization (p.120).

The editor's case study

I required the authors of the chapters in Part 2 to illustrate their arguments with a case study (or studies). It seems only appropriate that I should do the same. This extended case study below attempts to demonstrate that organisational development comprising interventions involving both human agency and social structure can achieve significant change.

Perhaps the most profound transformation in health and social care over the past two decades has been the closure of the vast majority of Victorian psychiatric asylums and their replacement with a network of community mental health services. During much of the 1990s I was an OD practitioner contributing to the closure of these asylums, and this experience provides a revealing insight into the ways in which established organisational settlements can be transformed through a confluence of influences and interventions. In retrospect, three elements of our approach to this transformation seem central:

- the development of a 'social movement for change'
- the adoption of the principles of 'emergence'
- the manipulation of 'sensemaking and meaning'.

The development of a 'social movement for change'

Up until the late 1970s, most asylums were still run according to the priorities and practices of consultant psychiatrists. In many ways, this pre-eminence reflected the established grand narrative of psychiatry, that madness was an illness susceptible to the application of scientific techniques to the individual patient. During the 1980s this grand narrative – and the pre-eminence of psychiatrists in the organisational settlement – started to be challenged by a number of factors. First, the appointment of general managers of hospitals, rarely psychiatrists but frequently nurses or career NHS managers, created an environment where new narratives about mental illness could be articulated in the system. By the early 1990s the introduction of managers from voluntary sector and social services backgrounds brought into the system the so-called anti-psychiatry arguments of commentators such as Goffman (1961). Many of the same ideas were also becoming influential among some key policy makers within the Department of Health.

Second, since the mid-1980s, the voices of service users had become increasingly significant at both a local and national level (*see* Barker and Peck, 1987). These voices contained trenchant critiques of their personal experience of life in asylums, and they were supported and nurtured by national campaigning groups such as MIND.

In this coalition of interests, the policy of asylum closure possessed some of the characteristics of a social movement, similar to the influences that Fitzgerald and colleagues describe as central to the transformation of childbirth (*see* Chapter 2). Of course, the existence of this 'social movement' may have been a necessary condition for change, but it was clearly not sufficient. It needed to be engaged in a formal process for achieving change, which is where we want to turn next.

The adoption of the principles of 'emergence'

Interestingly, one of the key interventions of the implementation process in asylum closure also recalls the research of Fitzgerald and her colleagues. Along with Helen Smith, with whom they were devised, I have written extensively about the central role of stakeholder conferences in the design of service models that would replace the asylums (e.g. Smith *et al.*, 1996). This example is such a good illustration of aspects of emergence in OD that it is also included in greater detail in Chapter 8.

Briefly, these stakeholder conferences were designed and facilitated in order to give particular power to the voices of the service users and less emphasis than normal to those of professionals, especially psychiatrists. These stakeholder conferences took place in a context in which the overall goal – hospital closure – was clear, and where there was a process that ensured regular opportunities for local interest groups to interact. However, there were no pre-determined views about the specific content of any particular local strategy.

However, the production of such a strategy did not in itself overcome one of the major obstacles to change: the prevailing view about the role of money in the closure programme. This leads me on to the third element of transformational change evident in this example: the manipulation of sensemaking and meaning.

The manipulation of 'sensemaking and meaning'

In 1968, the Ministry of Health created a demonstration site to prove that the asylums could be closed. Unfortunately, Powick hospital did not close for over 20 years. Furthermore, a study of the closure (Hall and Brockington, 1991) concluded that the new services cost 20% more than the old ones, and required extensive 'bridging' finance. This became the received wisdom about the financial resources – the meaning of money – necessary to achieve closure. Clearly, this meaning had to be challenged if the closure programme was ever to take off.

In Devon, in the mid-1980s, Exminster hospital had closed using an approach that was based on a five year project plan. The most senior health manager (King, 1991) involved wrote of this process that the inevitability of closure had to be constructed through a scenario fashioned to convince all the actors that nothing else was possible. At the same time he acknowledged that there was no proof at the outset that the closure would be financially viable.

This experience led us to conclude that the construction of a five-year-costed project plan was essential to the creation of confidence in the financial aspects of the change programme; that is, we had to alter fundamentally the prevailing sense that was made of money in the system. These project plans contained detailed projections of the revenue released from ward closures, of capital secured from land sales and of new sources of funding (e.g. benefits to be claimed for discharged patients). Although apparently convincing – and crucial to the attraction of organisational support – the plans were full of assumptions that it was beyond the power of the project team to deliver. For example, the capital receipts were dependent on the outcome of applications for planning consent and the vagaries of the local housing market, and the potential for attracting benefits for discharged patients was at the discretion of local benefit officers. None of the asylums with which I was involved closed either on time or in budget, but they all closed.

These three elements – the development of a 'social movement for change', the adoption of the principles of 'emergence' and the manipulation of 'sensemaking and meaning' – seem, therefore, central to delivering change – or at least 'transformational change' – in healthcare through interventions that seem to promise reforms consonant with some broader societal shift, deploy interventions based in talk and text to initiate a process of change, and then, subsequently, alter the social structure within which services are delivered.

Other perspectives on asylum closure

There are, however, some other interpretations that are possible. First, most senior managers – if not all their clinical colleagues – could see that the asylums were approaching the 'tipping point'. They were devouring increasing amounts of resources to support dwindling numbers of patients in settings that were degrading and prone to abuse; on this account, and in the terms of Chapter 2, the asylum closure could be seen as a reassertion of managerial hierarchy over the final area of professional pre-eminence of the isolate psychiatrists. Furthermore, it is possible to argue that mental health services paid a high price over the next ten years for the marginalisation of psychiatrists during this process of change. This raises again the rather vexed topic of sustainability – and a thorough review of the literature is provided by Greenhalgh *et al.* (2004) – although the importance that Hugh attaches to medical involvement in sustaining service improvement in healthcare cannot be overlooked.

Second, and following the arguments of Abrahamson (1991, 1996), by the time these interventions were taking place asylum closure had become fashionable. It was the preferred contemporary management response to the financial and performance problems apparent in the Victorian asylums; one, moreover, promoted by gurus such as the senior manager from Devon (King, 1991) and, to a much lesser extent, the current author.

Third, it presents a new dimension to the ethical questions raised by authors such as Carnevale (2003). In both the design and delivery of the stakeholder conferences and in the construction of the costed plans, the OD interventions were seeking to manipulate the sensemaking of local interests. In many ways, therefore, the OD practitioners could be accused of the bad faith which he so despises. On the other hand, the empowerment that was being sought, at least in the temporary institutions that these conferences represented, was that of the most powerless in the psychiatric system, that is, the patients. This, it could be argued, justified the manipulation of some members of some staff groups on the basis that you cannot make an omelette without breaking a few eggs.

Conclusion

A number of more general thoughts arise from consideration of the earlier chapters and I want briefly to allude to these as the book moves to a close. First, I want to reiterate the political dimensions of OD, i.e. that it is commonly used by the more powerful to try and change the beliefs and behaviour of the less powerful. In one sense, as when politicians use their democratic mandate to introduce new policies and procedures (*see* Chapter 2), this is a legitimate aspiration (even if they may fail).

However, the attempted manipulation of one group in the interests of another group inevitably raises ethical issues that cannot be simply wished away.

Deborah Davidson's and my chapter draws attention to the current popularity of leadership as an OD intervention, either through the introduction of new leaders or the improvement of existing leaders. That short account of the history of conceptions of leadership is a powerful example of the extent to which the availability of ideas (in this case about the nature of leadership) is constrained by the social structures and accountabilities within which such discussions take place. It would have been inconceivable to have promoted the current list of apparently effective leadership traits (i.e. caring, open, empowering, inclusive, etc.; *see* Hamlin, 2002 for a recent example of what might be termed the 'great woman' theory of leadership) in the 1930s. In many ways it is ironic that New Labour has been promoting better leadership when what it really seems to have wanted to achieve (at least until the replacement of Milburn by Reid as Secretary of State for Health) is better follower-ship (*see* Alimo-Metcalfe *et al.*, 2004).

Nonetheless, I am keen to argue that there is nothing in the theoretical framework that underpins this book that should be taken to suggest that effective national policy adaptation at a local level is not a realistic expectation. Rather, it is arguing that such effective adaptation requires an understanding of existing organisational settlements, and the ways in which they may be transformed, that are more subtle and sophisticated than those commonly in use by politicians and many OD practitioners (in my experience, most managers recognise the limitations of the traditional top-down/bottom-up formulations of policy implementation without necessarily being able to articulate an alternative).

The next issue is the extent to which the organisational theory from which much OD practice is derived is reliant on theory generation in other fields. This is well illustrated by looking at the chapters in Part 2 as a whole. Morgan's (1986) emphasis on the metaphorical aspects of organisational theory highlights this trend; Jones (2003) bemoans it: 'the common complaint these days [is] that theory in organization studies has been done "at a distance" … [and] many of the theorists who have been imported into organization studies in recent years have made their way in through what appear to be cartoon-book introductions' (p.514, parentheses added). We are not suggesting for a moment that Kieran Sweeney or Vega introduce the root theories that inform their OD practice in such a fashion, but they would have to admit they are working at a high level of abstraction from their source material. For instance, the concept of the unconscious is not uncontroversial when imputed to the individual; when applied to an organisation it is obviously a long way from its theoretical origins.

Further, the version of a theory that is most metaphorically useful in OD practice may not be the one that is currently prevalent in its original field; for instance, the systems theory described by Jane Keep seems to rely on a version of the evolution of organisms that is based on the discredited Lamarckian account (that is, if giraffes stretch their necks to eat leaves then their offspring will have longer necks) rather than that of Darwin based on natural selection. Of course, if the purpose of OD is to promote reflexivity and learning then this may not matter if the theories and metaphors have resonance for organisation members; however, if the talk is of the 'system-wide application of behavioural science knowledge', as in Cummings and Worley (2001, p.1) then we may be on more slippery ground.

Which takes me back to the modest, but I think increasingly persuasive, definition of OD offered by Jeanne and I in Chapter 1. Throughout this chapter, I have kept returning to the much more expansive ambitions expressed in the formulation of OD provided by Cummings and Worley (2001) and each time I hope I have further undermined its claims to be a realistic description of most OD projects undertaken in healthcare. Nonetheless, and despite my post-modernist misgivings about its modernist orientation, I am not denying that on some occasions OD programmes with the scope (e.g. intervening simultaneously in human agency and social structure) and thus the impact envisaged by Cummings and Worley (2001) will occur in healthcare agencies (as my case study above seeks to demonstrate); rather, I am merely suggesting that they are too rare to act as the exemplar of OD in this sector. In the language of Chapter 3, transformational change is a potential outcome of OD; however, the impact will more routinely be on organisational transactions. Ultimately, Jeanne and I opted for our definition because it seemed both more reflective of our own typical experience of OD in healthcare and more consonant with the aspirations of the theories and practices of our fellow authors.

It is common for books by academics to end with calls for more research. However, as Hugh has shown, there are so few robust independent evaluations of OD in healthcare (with the exception of some service improvement methods) that it is impossible to judge the impact of most of the interventions described in this book. I want to stress *independent* because all of the authors of the chapters are to a greater or lesser extent 'gurus' in their field. To put it more personally, my case study in this chapter is necessarily self-serving; it lacks any verification by another party who does not share my theoretical predilections and rhetorical intentions. The position outside healthcare is little better; Cummings and Worley (2001) provide extensive anecdotes and case studies but little material that would qualify as 'evidence' of 'a system-wide application of behavioural science knowledge to the planned development, improvement and reinforcement of the strategies, structures and processes that lead to organization effectiveness' (p.1). The generally disappointing results from the evaluations on service improvement techniques – in contrast to some of the claims made for these techniques by both their champions and their clients – should make us wary of the unverified claims made for other interventions. Lynne Maher and Jean Penny describe themselves the journey that is taking the MA into new fields of exploration (such as the Pursuing Perfection programme) which clearly embrace elements of emergence and creativity.

In many respects, therefore, OD remains an underdeveloped field of human endeavour. Most interventions through talk and text may be able to enhance organisational reflexivity and learning and influence organisational settlements, but the impact may depend on the expertise of the performer. On occasions, at the 'tipping point', such interventions may result in significant, indeed transformational, change. Such profound impact will typically, however, only result from simultaneous intervention in human agency and social structure. Currently, though, we know too little about the connection between specific organisational contexts and appropriate OD interventions; that is, about the ways in which existing organisational settlements can be transformed.

Excitingly, though, the continuing growth of interest in OD in healthcare gives clinicians, managers and researchers a great opportunity to collaborate together with OD practitioners in pursuit of changing organisations and enhancing knowledge. I hope that this book has given you both an increased understanding of and renewed enthusiasm for OD, and that it has contributed to your personal development as a reflective and repertoire-rich leader of change.

Acknowledgements

I would like to acknowledge the contribution of Perri 6 to some of the ideas in this chapter and also the comments of Jeanne Hardacre, Alys Harwood, Chris Blantern and Jane Keep on an earlier draft.

References

6 P and Peck E (2002) 'Surprises' with discourse: an argument against the idealism of discourse theories, and towards an alternative theory of effective organisational development practice showing the special cases where changing talk and text might be effective. Paper for the 5th International Conference on Organisational Discourse: organisational discourse: from micro-utterances to macro-inferences. 25–27 July, King's College London.

Abrahamson E (1991) Managerial fads and fashions: the diffusion and rejection of innovations. *Academy of Management Review.* 16(3): 586–612.

Abrahamson E (1996) Management fashion. *Academy of Management Review.* 21(1): 254–85.

Alimo-Metcalfe B, Alban-Metcalfe J and Briggs I (2004) *Leadership: time to debunk the myths and face the real challenges.* Public Management and Policy Association, London.

Alvesson M (1993) The play of metaphors. In: J Hassard and M Parker (eds) *Postmodernism and Organisations.* Sage, London.

Barker I and Peck E (1987) *Power in Strange Places: user empowerment in mental health services.* Good Practices in Mental Health, London.

Bate P, Khan R and Pye A (2000) Towards a culturally sensitive approach to organizational structuring: where organization design meets organization development. *Organization Science.* 11(2): 197–211.

Berger P and Luckmann T (1966) *The Social Construction of Reality: a treatise in the sociology of knowledge.* Penguin, Harmondsworth.

Berglund J and Werr A (2000) The invincible character of management consulting rhetoric: how one blends incommensurables while keeping them apart. *Organization.* 7(4): 633–55.

Bertens H (1995) *The Idea of the Postmodern*. Routledge, London.

Buhanist P, Seppanen L and Virtaharju J (2000) Back to real life: exploring dispersed realities in organisations. Paper given at the 4th International Conference on Organisational Discourse: word views, work views and world views. 26–28 July, King's College London.

Carnevale D (2003) *Organizational Development in the Public Sector*. Westview Press, Cambridge, MA.

Clark T and Greatbatch D (2000) Maintaining audience affiliation through storytelling: the case of management gurus. Paper given at the 4th International Conference on Organisational Discourse: word views, work views and world views, 26–28 July, King's College London.

Clark T and Salaman G (1996) The management guru as organizational witchdoctor. *Organization*. 3(1): 85–107.

Cummings T and Worley C (2001) *Organization Change and Development*. South-Western College Publishing, Cincinnati, OH.

Czarniawska-Joerges B (1989) The wonderland of public administration reforms. *Organization Studies*. 10(4): 531–48.

Douglas M (1992) Cultural bias. In: M Douglas *In the Active Voice*, pp.183–254. Routledge and Kegan Paul, London.

Feyerabend P (2000) *Conquest of Abundance: a tale of abstraction versus the richness of being*. University of Chicago Press, Chicago, IL.

Giddens A (1993) Structuration theory: past, present and future. In: C Bryant and D Jary (eds) *Giddens' Theory of Structuration*. Routledge, London.

Goffman E (1961) *Asylums: essays on the social situation of mental patients and other inmates*. Penguin, Harmondsworth.

Goffman E (1974) *Frame Analysis: an essay on the organisation of experience*. North-eastern University Press, Boston, MA.

Gordon RD and Grant D (2000) Change and the dynamics of power: a critical discursive analysis. Paper given at the 4th International Conference on Organisational Discourse: word views, work views and world views. 26–28 July, King's College London.

Greenhalgh T, Robert G, Bate P, Kyriakidou O, Mafarlane F and Peacock R (2004) *A Systematic Review of the Literature on Diffusion, Dissemination, and Sustainability of Innovations in Health Service Delivery and Organisation*. NHSSDO Programme, London.

Hall P and Brockington I (1991) *The Closure of the Mental Hospitals*. Gaskell, London.

Hamlin R (2002) A study and comparative analysis of managerial effectiveness in the NHS: as empirical factor analytic study within an NHS trust hospital. *Health Services Management Research*. 15(4): 245–63.

Hardy C, Palmer I and Phillips N (2000) Discourse as a strategic resource. *Human Relations*. 53(9): 1227–48.

Harvey D (1990) *The Condition of Postmodernity*. Blackwell, Oxford.

Hassard J (1993) Postmodernism and organisational analysis: an overview. In: J Hassard and M Parker (eds) *Postmodernism and Organisations*. Sage, London.

Holland R (1999) Reflexivity. *Human Relations*. 52(4): 463–83.

Huczynski A (1993) *Management Gurus: what makes them and how to become one*. Routledge, London.

Jones C (2003) Theory after the postmodern condition. *Organization*. 10(3): 503–25.

King D (1991) *Moving On: from mental hospitals to community care*. Nuffield Provincial Hospitals Trust, London.

Knights D and Wilmott H (eds) (2000) *The Reengineering Revolution: critical studies of corporate change*. Sage, London.

Levy A and Merry U (1986) *Organizational Transformation: approaches, strategies, theories*. Praeger, New York.

McNulty T and Ferlie E (2002) *Reengineering Healthcare: the complexities of organizational transformation*. OUP, Oxford.

Meyer J and Rowan B (1977) Institutionalised organisations: formal structure as myth and ceremony. *American Journal of Sociology*. 83(3): 340–63.

Moore J (1997) *Visions of Culture: an introduction to anthropological theories and theorists*. Altamira Press, Walnut Creek, CA.

Morgan G (1986) *Images of Organisations*. Sage, London.

Myers-Briggs I, Kirby L and Myers K (2000) *Introduction to Type* (6e). Oxford Psychological Press, Oxford.

Peck E, 6 P, Gulliver P and Towell D (2004) Why do we keep on meeting like this: the board as ritual in health and social care. *Health Services Management Research*. 17(1): 1–10.

Plotkin H (1997) *Evolution in Mind*. Penguin, London.

Powell W and DiMaggio P (eds) (1991) *The New Institutionalism in Organisational Analysis*. University of Chicago Press, Chicago, IL.

Pugh D (1973) The measurement of organisational structures: does context determine form? *Organisational Dynamics*. 1: 19–34.

Reed M (2000) The limits of discourse analysis in organisational analysis, *Organisation*. 7(3): 524–30.

Schein E (1987) *Process Consultation, Volume II*. Addison-Wesley, Wokingham.

Selznick P (1949) *The TVA and the Grass Roots*. University of California Press, Berkeley, CA.

Smith H, Kingdon D and Peck E (1996) Purchasing mental health strategies: writing a strategy. In: G Thornicroft and G Strathdee (eds) *Commissioning Mental Health Services*, pp.123–32. HMSO, London.

Thompson M (1992) The dynamics of cultural theory. In: S Hargreaves Heap and A Ross (eds) *Understanding the Enterprise Culture: themes in the work of Mary Douglas*, pp.182–202. Edinburgh University Press, Edinburgh.

Weick K (1995) *Sensemaking in Organisations*. Sage, London.

Zucker L (1988) *Institutional Patterns and Organisations: culture and environment*. Ballinger, Cambridge, MA.

Index